MEMORY IN EARLY MODERN EUROPE, 1500–1800

Memory in Early Modern Europe, 1500–1800

JUDITH POLLMANN

OXFORD
UNIVERSITY PRESS

OXFORD
UNIVERSITY PRESS

Great Clarendon Street, Oxford, OX2 6DP,
United Kingdom

Oxford University Press is a department of the University of Oxford.
It furthers the University's objective of excellence in research, scholarship,
and education by publishing worldwide. Oxford is a registered trade mark of
Oxford University Press in the UK and in certain other countries

First Edition published in 2017

Impression: 1

Published in the United States of America by Oxford University Press
198 Madison Avenue, New York, NY 10016, United States of America

British Library Cataloguing in Publication Data
Data available

Library of Congress Control Number: 2017931981

ISBN 978–0–19–879755–5

Printed in Great Britain by
Bell & Bain Ltd., Glasgow

Acknowledgements

Through the generous support of a VICI grant of NWO, the Netherlands Organisation for Scientific Research, I spent much of the years 2008–13 directing a research project entitled 'Tales of the Revolt: Memory, oblivion, and identity in the Low Countries, 1566–1700'. The project had as its objective to study the long-term cultural impact of the Revolt of the Netherlands, a civil war that tore apart the Habsburg Low Countries, and resulted in the formation of two new states: the Dutch Republic that eventually evolved into the current Kingdom of the Netherlands, and the Habsburg Netherlands, which was the predecessor to the current Kingdom of Belgium. Yet as the project progressed, I became ever more interested in resolving a number of questions that, at the start, had seemed a mere side issue, and that revolved around the similarities and differences between modern and early modern memory. Besides offering an overview of what we currently know about memory in early modern Europe, this book is an attempt to answer some of these questions. In researching and writing it, I have not only had to call on all that I have learned in the course of three decades, so much of it from my 'living books', my teachers, colleagues, and students in Amsterdam, London, Oxford, and Leiden, I also needed to move into new interdisciplinary and modern territory. I am very grateful to the guides I found on my way, especially Astrid Erll and Ann Rigney, who organized a memorable conversation at NIAS, Jane Ohlmeyer and Micheál O'Siochrú, who invited us to a groundbreaking conference on the *1641 Depositions* in Dublin, Guy Beiner and David Hopkin, who introduced me to the potential of folklore, and Brecht Deseure, who helped me to make sense of the debate on memory crises and modernity.

More than any of my previous work, this book project has been a collaborative effort. It was a privilege and a pleasure to work with a dream team consisting of postdoc Erika Kuijpers, research students Marianne Eekhout, Johannes Müller, and Jasper van der Steen, and research assistants Lex van Tilborg, Alec Ewing, and Frank de Hoog. David de Boer and Brecht Deseure became honorary members. Together we spent five very intense and memorable years working on the rich memory practices of the Revolt. Many of the ideas in this book first developed in the course of our conversations, during our team trips, and over meals and coffees together; the dissertations, books, and articles have done much to shape its content. In the process, the team was fortunate to be advised by Philip Benedict, Luc Duerloo, Alastair Duke, Willem Frijhoff, Mark Greengrass, Elmer Kolfin, Johan Koppenol, and Henk van Nierop. Audiences in the Netherlands, Belgium, Denmark, Germany, the UK, and the US helped to develop our ideas in their early stages. Erika Kuijpers and I also trialled many of the team's ideas on undergraduate and graduate students in Leiden and beyond; I thank them all for their questions, suggestions, and their criticisms.

For most of the project, we were based in Leiden University's Institute for History, which has been my very happy academic home since 2005. I am very grateful to my fantastic Leiden colleagues for their support in securing the grant and throughout the project. As will become apparent to the readers of this book, my ideas on memory were influenced profoundly by the elaborate memory practices surrounding the sixteenth-century past of the city of Leiden, which also bear out team member Marianne Eekhout's conviction that the study of early modern material culture is essential for studying early modern memory. She and I were fortunate to be involved in an advisory capacity in the exhibition *Vrijheid! Leidens ontzet, 1574–2011* at Leiden's Museum De Lakenhal that was splendidly curated by Jori Zijlmans, and both celebrated and deconstructed the memory culture surrounding Leiden's 3 October tradition. In 2010, we spent four months in Antwerp, where I was supported by a scholarship from the University Centre Saint-Ignatius Antwerp, and we all benefited from the hospitality of the History Department at Antwerp University. I owe a great debt to Guido Marnef and his Antwerp colleagues for all their help and advice there. In 2013 I spent some very productive weeks as a guest in Somerville, my former college in Oxford, benefiting enormously, not only from the resources at the Bodleian Library and hospitality of the Senior Common Room, but also from many inspiring conversations.

I am most grateful to Stephanie Ireland and the Delegates of Oxford University Press for their interest in publishing this book, to the anonymous peer reviewers for their enthusiasm and constructive suggestions, and to Cathryn Steele and her colleagues at Oxford University Press for helping it through the press. I am much indebted to Bart van der Boom, Marianne Eekhout, Erika Kuijpers, and Andrew Spicer for their willingness to read and comment on the penultimate draft of this book, and to Kate Delaney for correcting my English. I am grateful to the Royal Historical Society and Cambridge University Press for permission to reuse, in Chapter 5, the material that I first published in 'Of living legends and authentic tales. How to get remembered in early modern Europe'. *Transactions of the Royal Historical Society*, sixth series 23 (2013), 103–25.

For inspiring conversations, and sharing their ideas, references, comments, and criticism I should also like to thank Antheun Janse, Carolien Boender, Erica Boersma, Marten-Jan Bok, Dennis Bos, Eveline Bouwens, Mario Braakman, Anne Laure Van Bruaene, Liesbeth Corens, Raingard Esser, Raymond Fagel, Dagmar Freist, Andrea Frisch, Silvia Gaiga, Jan Willem Honig, Joanna Innes, Maartje Janse, Geert Janssen, Jelle Haemers, Tom Hamilton, Marijke Meijer-Drees, Ben Kaplan, Marika Keblusek, Anton van der Lem, Carolina Lenarduzzi, David van der Linden, Jan de Lint, Matthijs Lok, Natalia Nowakowska, Thérèse Peeters, Dirk Pfeifer, Cees Reijner, Yolanda Rodríguez-Pérez, Matthias Schnettger, Robert Stein, Anita Traninger, Henk te Velde, Ramon Voges, Alexandra Walsham, Peter Wilson, and Jori Zijlmans. Koen Evelo and Simone Nieuwenbroek offered valuable practical assistance.

Finally, and most importantly, I want to thank my wife, Florence Gaillard, not only for her interest and support throughout the writing process, but, above all, for making me a much, much happier woman at the end of this project than I was at its inception.

Leiden
15 December 2016

Contents

List of Figures

Introduction

In early modern Europe the past served as a main frame of moral, political, legal, religious, and social reference. It determined who you were; social status was inherited, and for princes and bishops as much as for burghers and serfs, rights and obligations were based on tradition. The past determined right and wrong; law courts often ruled by precedent, social relations were shaped by custom, and churches competed by claiming to be closest to the practices of the early Christians. Yet this respect for the past did not lead to stagnation. When early modern people wanted to do something new, they usually found a way of making it look older than it was; when people wanted to challenge a ruling, they argued that it clashed with traditions. And precisely because the past mattered so much, it was also hotly contested, subject to constant manipulation, reappropriation, and reinvention, and reused in new contexts. This was not the work just of politicians. Since memories of the past could also bring shame and confer prestige, individuals, families, and communities took care to manage their reputations and those of their ancestors.

Because it was so important, knowledge about the past was not just stored in chests with old charters or in history books. Although most Europeans were illiterate, there were many practices through which memories of the past could become 'public knowledge'—through rituals, storytelling and singing, through images and street-signs, through annual processions, and sermons and prints, and the performance of plays and the eating of commemorative dishes. Village communities had strategies to pass on to new generations knowledge of the past by reiterating it in public meetings. Elements in the landscape, rocks, fields, and trees were used as markers of the past, and people kept material relics of past events. Only some of this activity can be described as 'history' in the modern sense of the word, but all of it can be classified as a type of 'memory', a form of individual or collective engagement with the past that meaningfully connects the past to the present.[1]

Most memories are personal and private, and inaccessible to the historian. Yet memory is also something that people practise. Memories of a real or imagined past are shared through storytelling, performing, parading, decorating, singing, cooking, and eating, as much as through the writing of memoirs, histories, and the collecting and archiving of 'memorable' texts and memorabilia, objects that help us remember. Such practices take on a social significance and can very well be

---

[1] Very helpful on definition issues are Astrid Erll, *Memory in culture*, trans. Sara B. Young (Basingstoke, 2011), which first appeared as Astrid Erll, *Kollektives Gedächtnis und Erinnerungskulturen. Eine Einführung* (Stuttgart, 2005), 6–9 and Geoffrey Cubitt, *History and memory* (Manchester, 2007), 9–25.

studied.[2] This book is an introduction to the way in which Europeans practised memory in the three centuries between 1500 and 1800. Since the 1960s many scholars have argued that the age of revolutions at the end of the eighteenth century transformed the way in which Europeans experienced the past and came to think about the future. This book contends that while some memory practices had indeed profoundly changed by 1800, they changed for other reasons and in other ways than most students of modern memory have argued. New ways of thinking about the past were the outcome not only of the age of revolutions. Neither did these revolutions lead to a sea change in ways of doing memory. A key contention of this study is that the emergence of new ways of engaging with the past was a more gradual process and did not put an end to traditional ways of thinking about it; rather, old and new ways came to exist side by side, and, to a surprising extent, continue to do so to our own day.

WHY STUDY MEMORY?

Sometime in the late 1580s, a law student in the Dutch city of Utrecht began to chronicle the events of his own time, starting with the years just before his birth in 1565. One of his earliest memories related to a one-eyed Spanish soldier, who had been quartered in his family home in 1571–2. Quartering was a common practice because there were as yet no barracks, but it was also a practice dreaded by contemporaries. Soldiers tended to demand food and services from their hosts without having the money to pay for them, sexually harass the women in the house, and be violent when anyone objected. The soldiers who had come to the Netherlands to suppress the rebellion we know of as the Dutch Revolt were exceptionally badly paid and notorious for their nuisance value. The soldier in the house of young Arnoud van Buchel was no exception. Not only did he terrify the six-year-old by popping his glass eye out of its socket, he also threatened to take the boy away with him to serve as his armour-bearer when he next went on campaign. His mother and stepfather protested loudly, but Van Buchel remembered that their pleas cut no ice with the soldier

> for he used to say that all the Netherlands had been found guilty of lèse majesty and had been granted as booty to the Spanish soldiers. He wanted the best of everything to be given to him and proclaimed that we ought to obey him . . . as slaves do their masters.[3]

When I first encountered this entry, in the early 1990s, I found it puzzling. While young Arnoud's fear of the soldier with his scary eye had a definite air of veracity, what he said about the soldier's claim of entitlement did not; I recognized it as

  [2] Peter Burke, *What is cultural history?* (Cambridge, 2004), 59–64. The role of practice was first theoretically explored by Pierre Bourdieu, *Esquisse d'une théorie de la pratique, précédé de trois études d'ethnologie kabyle* (Geneva, 1972), translated as *Outline of a theory of practice* (1977) .

  [3] Judith Pollmann, *Religious choice in the Dutch Republic. The Reformation of Arnoldus Buchelius, 1565–1641* (Manchester, 1999), 36.

coming straight out of the anti-Spanish propaganda that had been spread by the supporters of Dutch rebel leader William of Orange.[4] So what was going on here? Was Arnoud van Buchel making up one part of the story, while telling the truth about the other? Had the soldier come to believe enemy propaganda, and was he now living up to rebel expectations? Was it Arnoud's parents who got mixed up when they passed the story on to him? Did he himself perhaps not remember it properly?

It took several years before I found an explanation, in a 1992 book titled *Social memory*, by the anthropologist James Fentress and medieval historian Chris Wickham. Fentress and Wickham recounted an insight that scholars had only recently rediscovered: our memories, however personal and individual they feel, are shaped to large extent by the memories of the people around us and the culture in which they are being remembered.[5] This meant it was perfectly conceivable for the memories of young Arnoud van Buchel to have been reconfigured under the influence of stories circulating in war propaganda. Such reconfigurations happen all the time. Memory is not fixed, and it is not just something between our brains and our 'selves'; memory is a form of cognition that interacts with social processes. It follows that memory also has a history; if different societies today practise memory in different ways and for different purposes, they also do this in ways that differ from how societies did so in the past.

This approach to memory was pioneered by three scholars who worked in the 1920s and 1930s. The French philosopher and sociologist Maurice Halbwachs was, in his *Les Cadres sociaux de la mémoire* of 1925, the first to argue that individual memory develops in interaction with that of people's social networks and the larger community. He showed that as the product of social change, moreover, memories were not stable, but ever-changing representations of the past. Using very different methods, the psychologist Frederick Bartlett showed in 1932 that in the process of remembering, humans rely on existing summaries or 'schemes' of the past—when a person 'recollects' what happened in the past, he or she will reconstruct a memory from these schemes, often adding or changing details. The anti-Spanish stereotypes reiterated by Arnoud van Buchel can be considered such a 'scheme', for instance. The schemes that people use for this purpose are usually very much influenced by the schemes that circulate in their environment or in their broader culture. Studying this circulation, finally, the German scholar Aby Warburg developed the notion of *Bildergedächtnis* ('iconic memory') to describe the long-term reception and influence of visual imagery.[6]

---

[4] See for this e.g. *Artyckelen ende besluiten der Inquisitie van Spaegnien om die van de Nederlanden te overvallen of verhinderen* (n.p., [1568]); K.W. Swart, 'The Black Legend during the Eighty Years War', in *Britain and the Netherlands V. Some political mythologies. Papers delivered to the fifth Anglo-Dutch historical conference*, ed. J.S. Bromley and E.H. Kossmann (The Hague, 1975), 36–57.

[5] James Fentress and Chris Wickham, *Social memory* (Oxford and Cambridge MA, 1992).

[6] Maurice Halbwachs, *Les Cadres sociaux de la mémoire* (Paris, 1925); Frederic C. Bartlett, *Remembering. A study in experimental and social psychology* (Cambridge, 1932); Aby Warburg's work was much less theoretical and more associative, see e.g. Aby Warburg, *Der Bildatlas Mnemosyne*, ed. Martin Warnke and Claudia Brink, Aby Warburg Gesammelte Schriften vol. II.1 (Berlin, 2003). For a discussion of these three roots see also Erll, *Kollektives Gedächtnis*.

Although these ideas had been around for the better part of the twentieth century, little was done with them until the late 1980s, and even in the mid-1990s they seemed brand new to me. Like all historians of my generation, I had been taught as an undergraduate that our discipline had evolved and altered over time. In the early 1980s, we were taught the history of historiography as a linear tale of progress, in which Europeans since the Middle Ages had gradually learned to distinguish between past and present, to use primary sources, to analyse these with critical rigour, and to arrive at causal explanations for historical developments. Alternative forms of engagement with the past were regarded by our tutors with a rather condescending and definitely Eurocentric air—as primitive, the stuff of legends and myths, or as the tools of self-serving politicians. We were therefore not encouraged to ask ourselves why these alternatives were nevertheless so attractive, effective, and powerful, both in our own societies and in the past.

David Lowenthal's famous and influential *The past is a foreign country* of 1985, which laid a theoretical cornerstone for the field we now know of as 'heritage studies' or 'public history', was perhaps the first major study to thematize and analyse the many different ways in which the past is present in our own age.[7] The book signalled a new wave of interest in the theory and practice of 'memory' that began in the late 1980s and led to the emergence of an interdisciplinary scholarly field that is often referred to as 'memory studies'. That field now has its own journals, book series, courses, and conferences—according to some critics, it has developed into a 'memory industry'.[8] It has taught us to think about memory as a powerful phenomenon that emerges in a constant dynamic between individuals and societies, that retains its power in unexpected places, and that is subject to interventions by a wide range of stakeholders.

EARLY MODERN MEMORY

Fentress and Wickham's book made such an impression on me not only because it helped solve the riddle of young Arnoud's war memories, but also because it invited me to take a fresh look at existing work on the role of the past in early modern culture. Fentress and Wickham themselves had little to say about this period, but as an early modernist, I could think of quite a few phenomena that we might explore further by using the concepts and ideas that their book had introduced me to. Early modernists before me had been well aware that the past mattered to

 [7] David Lowenthal, *The past is a foreign country* (Cambridge, 1985).
 [8] For overviews and analyses of developments in the field see e.g. Fentress and Wickham, *Social memory*; Jeffrey K. Olick and Joyce Robbins, 'Social memory studies. From "collective memory" to the historical sociology of mnemonic practices', *Annual Review of Sociology* 24 (1998): 105–40; Erll, *Kollektives Gedächtnis*; Karen E. Till, 'Memory studies', *History Workshop Journal* 62 (2006): 325–41; Jay Winter, *Remembering war. The Great War between memory and history in the twentieth century* (New Haven, 2006), 17–51; Cubitt, *History and memory*; Astrid Erll and Ansgar Nünning, eds, *Cultural memory studies. An international and interdisciplinary handbook* (Berlin, 2008). A very critical view of the 'memory industry' in Kerwin Lee Klein, 'On the emergence of "memory" in historical discourse', *Representations* 69 (2000): 127–50.

Europeans in this period. Renaissance scholars had shown how Italian cities built their Renaissance reputations on their claims to antique fame.[9] There were seminal books and essays on the 'sense of the past' in the Renaissance and in early modern England, where the Reformation left a landscape scarred with the ruins of monastic houses that reminded everyone of the pre-Reformation past.[10] Historians had long realized the political importance of the past and knew that both princes and republics built their reputations on the feats of their ancestors, real or imagined, and used new feasts and changes in the calendar to propagate the commemoration of days of collective importance.[11] Students of revolts and revolutions were well aware that rebels in early modern Europe often supported their claims with references to the past, claiming to be restoring a right order as it had allegedly existed in a past untouched by innovation and corruption.[12] Others had shown that propagandists in north-western Europe from around 1500 mobilized the Germanic past in order to fight 'Roman' domination, while French lawyers rejected Roman law in favour of the *mos gallicus*, allegedly ancient, local legal traditions.[13] In religious conflict, too, historians had shown that the past played a major role. Historians of the Reformations highlighted how central the past was to Reformation debates, with Protestants devoting much energy to proving continuity with the practices of the early church and earlier religious dissenters, while Catholics sought to use excavations and historical research to prove papal Rome's pre-eminent and ancient role as the centre of the Christian tradition. All churches cherished memories of martyrs of recent religious conflicts to keep the fires of confessional strife burning.[14] Memories

[9] Roberto Weiss, *The Renaissance discovery of classical antiquity* (London, 1969); Patricia Brown, *Venice and antiquity. The Venetian sense of the past* (New Haven, 1996).

[10] The phrase originated with Henry James, *The sense of the past* (London and Glasgow, 1917) but was popularized among early modernists by Peter Burke, *The Renaissance sense of the past* (London, 1969); Margaret Aston, 'English ruins and English history. The Dissolution and the sense of the past', *Journal of the Warburg and Courtauld Institutes* 36 (1973): 231–55; Arthur B. Ferguson, *Clio unbound. Perception of the social and cultural past in Renaissance England* (Durham NC, 1979); Keith Thomas, *The perception of the past in early modern England*, The Creighton Trust Lecture 1983 (London, 1983).

[11] For examples see e.g. Jan Dirk Müller, *Gedechtnus. Literatur und Hofgesellschaft um Maximilian I* (Munich, 1982), 207–10; Robert Stein, 'Brabant en de Karolingische dynastie. Over het ontstaan van een historiografische traditie', *Bijdragen en Mededelingen betreffende de Geschiedenis der Nederlanden* 110 (1995): 329–51; Stuart Piggott, *Ancient Britons and the antiquarian imagination. Ideas from the Renaissance to the Regency* (London, 1989); Simon Schama, *The embarrassment of riches. An interpretation of Dutch culture in the Golden Age* (London, 1987); David Cressy, *Bonfires and bells. National memory and the Protestant calendar in Elizabethan and Stuart England* (London, 1989).

[12] J.H. Elliott, 'Revolution and continuity in early modern Europe', *Past & Present* 42 (1969): 35–56, at 41–2; Robert Forster and Jack P. Greene eds, *Preconditions of revolution in early modern Europe* (Baltimore and London, 1970), 15–16.

[13] Most famously by Ulrich von Hutten, whose *Arminius Dialogus Huttenicus* first appeared in print in 1529; Frank L. Borchardt, *German antiquity in Renaissance myth* (Baltimore and London, 1971). For similar sentiments in France, see Quentin Skinner, *The foundations of modern political thought*, 2 vols (Cambridge, 1978), vol. II, 268–72; and Miriam Yardeni, *La Conscience nationale en France pendant les guerres de religion (1559–1598)* (Louvain, 1971); and in the Netherlands, Ivo Schöffer, 'The Batavian myth during the sixteenth and seventeenth centuries', in *Britain and the Netherlands V. Some political mythologies. Papers delivered to the fifth Anglo-Dutch historical conference*, ed. J.S. Bromley and E.H. Kossmann (The Hague, 1975), 78–101.

[14] Bruce Gordon, ed., *Protestant history and identity in sixteenth-century Europe*, 2 vols (Aldershot, 1996); David Loades, ed., *John Foxe and the English Reformation* (Aldershot, 1997); Brad S. Gregory, *Salvation at stake. Christian martyrdom in early modern Europe* (Cambridge MA, 1999).

of recent events might take on the shape of older ones. In a fascinating study, Philippe Joutard demonstrated in the 1970s how resistance tales of World War II in the Cevennes echoed memories from the eighteenth-century Protestant Revolt of the Camisards of 1702, which were in their turn modelled on Old Testament tales.[15]

It took time before we came to realize that early modern memory might be an interesting phenomenon in its own right. While leading early modernist Peter Burke had suggested as early as 1989 how his colleagues could make use of the new ideas on memory, there was a lingering tendency among early modern scholars to see the use of legends, spurious historical evidence, and objects of dodgy historical provenance in early modern societies either as the last remnants of an oral world of 'popular culture' that was slowly being destroyed by the world of letters, new media, and print, or as a dubious leftover from the Middle Ages. Yet, when early modernists like myself at last became interested in engagement with the past as a form of 'memory', there was thus already plenty of early modern evidence to think with.[16]

This evidence has become ever more abundant once historians of early modern Europe grew accustomed to doing what ancient historians and medievalists had been doing for decades: using the full range of media at their disposal and working together with other disciplines. For a long time, early modern historians had left visual evidence to art historians, material culture to the archaeologists, and ballads and poems to students of literature. This began to change only in the 1980s.[17] Moreover, they had been accustomed to treating the worlds of print, script, and oral communication as quite distinct; it was tacitly assumed that once print had appeared, scribal and oral communication had become much less relevant.[18] Once we dropped these assumptions, around 2000, and broadened our range of evidence, we could, much helped by digitization projects and the Internet, truly come to appreciate the omnipresence of memory-related media in early modern culture, and so come to think more about their function. When historian Adam Fox, for instance, showed how closely interrelated the worlds of oral and literate culture remained in England throughout the early modern period, he also highlighted that historical events popped up in legends, ballads, folktales, and through features in the landscape, as much as they did in historical studies.[19] When studying the 'social circulation of the past', Daniel Woolf found that material memories were as

---

[15] Philippe Joutard, *La Légende des Camisards. Une sensibilité au passé* (Paris, 1977).

[16] Peter Burke, 'History as social memory', in *Memory. History, culture and the mind*, ed. Thomas I. Butler (Oxford, 1989), 97–113.

[17] And had immediately led to an early interest in memory, see e.g. R.W. Scribner, 'Incombustible Luther. The image of the Reformer in early modern Germany', *Past & Present* 110 (1986): 38–68; Schama, *The embarrassment of riches*.

[18] See on this issue e.g. Julia Crick and Alexandra Walsham, eds, *The uses of script and print, 1300–1700* (Cambridge, 2004).

[19] Adam Fox, *Oral and literate culture in England, 1500–1700* (Oxford, 2000). See also Andy Wood, 'Custom and the social organisation of writing in early modern England', *Transactions of the Royal Historical Society* 6th series 9 (1999): 257–69. Groundbreaking on material memory culture in the Netherlands was Wim Vroom, *Het wonderlid van Jan de Wit en andere vaderlandse relieken* (Amsterdam, 1997).

important as texts in early modern England.[20] Alexandra Walsham uncovered how elements in the religious landscape had structured memories of England's religious past, while Andy Wood demonstrated how popular memory had been used by illiterate miners and peasants in England to defend their rights.[21] For Ireland, where memory has been both deep and politically explosive, early modernists began to use folktales and toponyms to show how early modern memory cultures could function in communities with very low literacy levels.[22] In Germany, a team in Giessen explored early modern noble and urban memory, and new work on the rich urban chronicling tradition began to approach this as a form of memory.[23] Memory practices surrounding sacred space and relics received new attention.[24] How ritual, music, religion, and art could intertwine to create a local memory landscape was beautifully demonstrated by Iain Fenlon in his study of the memorialization of plague and the 1571 battle of Lepanto in the Venetian Republic.[25]

At the same time, our own cultures' experience with the 'long shadow' of the past, to use the phrase of Aleida Assmann, inspired early modernists to ask how early modern memories of (civil) war and persecution affected future generations.[26] Among students of the great Wars of Religion in early modern France, England, Germany, and the Low Countries, there has been a growing interest in memories of violence, in texts, rituals, images, and public space.[27] Rachel Greenblatt wrote a

---

[20] Daniel Woolf, *The social circulation of the past. English historical culture 1500–1730* (Oxford, 2003).

[21] Alexandra Walsham, *The Reformation of the landscape. Religion, identity and memory in early modern Britain and Ireland* (Oxford, 2011); Andy Wood, *The memory of the people. Custom and popular senses of the past in early modern England* (Cambridge, 2013).

[22] Guy Beiner, *Remembering the year of the French. Irish folk history and social memory* (Madison, 2007); Sarah Covington '"The odious demon from across the sea". Oliver Cromwell, memory and the dislocations of Ireland', in *Memory before modernity. Practices of memory in early modern Europe*, ed. Erika Kuijpers et al. (Leiden and Boston, 2013), 149–64.

[23] See *Erinnerungskulturen*, Gießener Sonderforschungsbereich 434, Justus-Liebig-Universität Gießen, accessed 2 May 2016, http://www1.uni-giessen.de/erinnerungskulturen/home/sfb-konzept. html. Early modern work emerging from this project e.g. Werner Rösener, *Adelige und bürgerliche Erinnerungskulturen des Spätmittelalters und der Frühen Neuzeit*, Formen der Erinnerung 8 (Göttingen, 2000); Susanne Rau, *Geschichte und Konfession. Städtische Geschichtsschreibung und Erinnerungskultur im Zeitalter von Reformation und Konfessionalisierung in Bremen, Breslau, Hamburg und Köln* (Hamburg and Munich, 2002).

[24] E.g. Joachim Eibach and Marcus Sandl, eds, *Protestantische Identität und Erinnerung. Von der Reformation bis zur Bürgerrechtsbewegung in der DDR*, Formen der Erinnerung 16 (Göttingen, 2003); Andrew Spicer, '(Re)building the sacred landscape. Orleans, 1560–1610', *French History* 21/3 (2007): 247–68; Alexandra Walsham, ed., *Relics and remains, Past & Present* supplement 5 (2010); Arne Bugge Amundsen, 'Churches and the culture of memory. A study of Lutheran church interiors in Østfold, 1537–1700', in *Arv. Nordic Yearbook of Folklore 2010* (Uppsala, 2010), 117–42.

[25] Iain Fenlon, *The ceremonial city. History, memory and myth in Renaissance Venice* (New Haven, 2007).

[26] Aleida Assmann, *Der lange Schatten der Vergangenheit. Erinnerungskultur und Geschichtspolitik* (Munich, 2006).

[27] Starting with Benigna Krusenstjern and Hans Medick, eds, *Zwischen Alltag und Katastrophe. Der Dreissigjährige Krieg aus der Nähe* (Göttingen, 1999); Hans Medick's contribution to this collection was translated as 'Historical event and contemporary experience. The capture and destruction of Magdeburg in 1631', trans. Pamela Selwyn, *History Workshop Journal* 52 (2001): 23–48; Heinz Duchhardt, 'Münster und der Westfälische Friede. Kollektives gedächtnis und Erinnerungskultur im Wandel der Zeiten', Supplement of *Historische Zeitschrift*, new series 26 (1998): 853–63. On Britain Blair Worden, *Roundhead reputations. The English Civil Wars and the*

compelling book on the way in which members of the Jewish community in Prague both commemorated persecution and celebrated survival.[28] The picture is varied, and in many ways patchy, but enough work has now been done to see the contours of patterns and trends that transcend the local, the regional, and the national, and to survey what we do, and do not, know about early modern memory.[29] The first aim of this book is to do just that.

MEMORY STUDIES

A second aim of this book is to initiate a much needed conversation between students of memory before and after 1800. As an early modernist who began to work on memory, I found that existing theories of memory had very little to say on memory before 1800. Most students of modern memory, I discovered, proceed from the assumption that public memory as we know it today is a modern phenomenon that emerged in the wake of the age of revolutions of the late eighteenth century, when mass media began to appear, nation states became more interested in defining national identities and in educating and indoctrinating their subjects, and history was at its most politicized. As we will see below, students of nationalism have argued that mass communication, revolutions, and state formation around 1800 were the catalysts for profound changes in collective memory practices. Many scholars have also seen a heightened interest in personal memory as a by-product of rapid changes brought about by revolutions, industrialization, new technologies, and globalization, arguing that such changes gave people a stronger sense that their lives differed from those lived by preceding generations. Such a

<hr>

passions of posterity (London, 2001); Jacques Berchtold and Marie-Madeleine Fragonard, eds, *La Mémoire des guerres de religion. La Concurrence des genres historiques (XVIe–XVIIIe siècles)* (Geneva, 2007); Philip Benedict, 'Divided memories? Historical calendars, commemorative processions and the recollection of the Wars of Religion during the Ancien Régime', *French History* 22/4 (2008): 381–405; Susan Broomhall, 'Reasons and identities to remember. Composing personal accounts of religious violence in sixteenth-century France', *French History* 27/1 (2013): 1–20; Philip Benedict, Hugues Faussy, and Pierre-Olivie Léchot, eds, *L'Identité huguenote. Faire mémoire et écrire l'histoire (XVIe–XXIe siècle)* (Geneva, 2014); Mark Stoyle, 'Remembering the English Civil Wars', in *The memory of catastrophe*, ed. Peter Gray and Kendrick Oliver (Manchester, 2004), 19–30; Matthew Neufeld, *The Civil Wars after 1660. Public remembering in late Stuart England* (Woodbridge, 2013). Our Leiden project has resulted e.g. in Judith Pollmann, *Het oorlogsverleden van de Gouden eeuw* (Leiden, 2008); Jasper van der Steen, *Memory wars in the Low Countries, 1566–1700* (Leiden, 2015); Johannes Müller, *Exile memories and the Dutch Revolt. The narrated diaspora, 1550–1750* (Leiden, 2016); Marianne Eekhout, 'Material memories of the Dutch Revolt. The urban memory landscape in the Low Countries, 1566–1700', doctoral thesis, Leiden University (2014); and Erika Kuijpers et al. eds, *Memory before modernity. Practices of memory in early modern Europe* (Leiden and Boston, 2013).

[28] Rachel L Greenblatt, *To tell their children. Jewish communal memory in early modern Prague* (Stanford, 2015).

[29] See also Judith Pollmann and Erika Kuijpers, 'Introduction. On the early modernity of modern memory', in *Memory before modernity. Practices of memory in early modern Europe*, ed. Kuijpers et al. (Leiden and Boston, 2013), 1–23.

'sense of change' is often considered to be the key defining characteristic of what it means to be 'modern'.[30] Once people are aware that their lives differ from those of their ancestors, some scholars have argued, memories take on new significance in their lives. Only people with such a sense of change, it is claimed, can feel nostalgia or think of things as 'old fashioned'.[31] We will return to this topic in Chapter 2 and in the conclusion of this book.

But how did people engage with the past before they thought of themselves as 'modern'? Theorists of memory have so far given rather sketchy answers to this question. Some have argued that before 1800 memory was primarily an 'art'.[32] Indeed, there existed an *ars memoriae*, or 'art of memory', in early modern Europe. Building on classical examples, this was a technique for memorizing complex information by associating it with places and objects in an imaginary space. We will never know how many people in early modern Europe put this technique into practice, but it was certainly taught and practised by the highly educated. Yet this tells us only some of what we need to know to understand how early modern Europeans practised memory in the other sense of the word, to make the past relevant to the present.[33]

Pierre Nora, one of the founding fathers of memory studies in the 1980s, distinguished between a primordial world in which people lived in *milieux de mémoire*, memory communities in which the past constituted a shared identity, and a modern world of historical remembrance in which only *lieux de mémoire*, sites of memory, were left to constitute a sense of a shared past to people who were otherwise living as individuals more than in a community.[34] Others, by contrast, believed that in pre-modern societies, memory was relevant only to elites. When outlining a history of national memory in 1994, historian John Gillis argued that in the pre-modern period only the elites had need of institutionalized memories; what there was by way of national consciousness in a place like late Tudor England, he believed, 'scarcely penetrated the consciousness of more than a small part of the population. Institutionalized forms of memory were too precious to be wasted on ordinary

---

[30] E.g. Jacques le Goff, *Histoire et mémoire* (1st edn, 1977; Paris, 1988), 74–5, 155–60, 252–3; Marshall Berman, *All that is solid melts into air* (New York, 1982), 17; Paul Connerton, *How societies remember* (Cambridge, 1989), 6–7; Richard Terdiman, *Present past. Modernity and the memory crisis* (Ithaca NY and London, 1993), 3–32; John E. Gillis, 'Memory and identity. The history of a relationship', in *Commemorations. The politics of national identity*, ed. Gillis (Princeton 1994), 3–24, at 7; Anthony D. Smith, *Nationalism* (Cambridge, 2001), 49–53; Frank Ankersmit, *Sublime historical experience* (Stanford, 2005).

[31] Peter Fritzsche, *Stranded in the present. Modern time and the melancholy of history* (Cambridge MA, 2004).

[32] Aleida Assmann, *Erinnerungsräume. Formen und Wandlungen des kulturellen Gedächtnisses* (Munich, 1999); Jens Brockmeier, *Beyond the archive. Memory, narrative and the autobiographical process* (Oxford, 2015). An early and influential study on this topic was Frances A. Yates, *The art of memory* (Chicago, 1966).

[33] See Woolf, *The social circulation*, 259–63; Andrew Hiscock, *Reading memory in early modern literature* (Cambridge, 2011), for a useful study that brings the two together.

[34] Usefully summarized in Pierre Nora, 'Between memory and history. *Les lieux de mémoire*', special issue on Memory and Counter-Memory of *Representations* 26/1 (1989): 7–24. Nora's notion of *milieux de mémoire* relied on ideas about village communities that were about to be abandoned by social scientists, see Connerton, *How societies remember*, 107, note 20.

people.' These, in any case, 'felt the past to be so much a part of the present that they perceived no urgent need to record, objectify and preserve it'.[35] Yet neither Nora nor Gillis referred to actual pre-modern communities to check these broad assumptions.

There are many students of memory who, like Gillis, have assumed that in so far as early modern people were interested in the past at all, they thought about it in a non-historical manner, that is to say that they did not really see a difference between past and present, and thought that history would either just repeat itself in cycles, or was moving only in the sense that human history was no more than an interlude before the end of time. This idea owes much to the seminal work of Reinhart Koselleck on early modern historical consciousness. Koselleck's classic essay *Vergangene Zukunft*, first published in German in 1968 and translated into English in 1985 as *Futures past*, argued that pre-modern historical consciousness could best be understood by considering how it related to the future.[36] In his view, pre-modern historical consciousness had two strands. First, there was the eschatological tradition, which expected a second coming of Christ and the end of time, and for which secular history was in many ways irrelevant. This way of thinking had gradually lost traction in the course of the seventeenth century. Secondly, there was the classical notion of history as *magistra vitae* (a teacher for life), examples from the past that could be reapplied one-to-one in new historical conditions. We will come back to this idea in Chapter 2. Modern historical con-sciousness, on the other hand, is believed to hinge on the perceived difference and *distance* between past and present, and this also had implications for expect-ations for the future; unlike early modern culture, modern cultures expect novelty as a matter of course. Koselleck thought this form of consciousness was funda-mentally new and had mostly emerged in what he called a *Sattelzeit*, a period of transition, lasting from *c.*1750 to 1850. Koselleck's work has been tremendously influential among students of modernity, as much as among students of memory.[37] Yet his essay was originally a contribution to the history of the philosophy of history, and readers in the social sciences and cultural studies have been rather too quick to assume that his findings can be extrapolated to characterize all of early modern memory culture.[38] This book aims to show not only that there is much more to early modern memory, but also that some knowledge of early modern memory practices is helpful in thinking about, and accounting for, many phenomena in modern memory that are currently ascribed to the coming of 'modernity'.

---

[35] Gillis, 'Memory and identity', 6–7.

[36] It was republished in his collected essays, Reinhart Koselleck, *Vergangene Zukunft. Zur Semantik geschichtlicher Zeiten* (1979; Frankfurt am Main, 1989), which were translated as *Futures past. On the semantics of historical times*, trans. Keith Tribe (Cambridge MA, 1985).

[37] As is evident, for instance, from the excellent review article by Olick and Robbins, 'Social memory studies'; Berman, *All that is solid*; Connerton, *How societies remember*, 6–7.

[38] Interestingly, many of the subtleties laid out in Eric Hobsbawm's impressive article, 'The social function of the past. Some questions', *Past & Present* 55 (1972): 3–17, were lost in subsequent discussions on memory.

ROOTS

Before we set out, I think it is useful to reflect for a moment on the reason why the memory studies field, and especially the theorizing about memory, has been so dominated by those interested in the world after 1800. This has much to do with the roots of memory studies. Around 1990, scholars from three directions in the humanities and social science community became highly attuned to Halbwachs's and Bartlett's suggestions that there is a relationship between changing social discourses, practices, and expectations, and the way in which individuals will remember the past.[39] First, among historians and social scientists in the 1980s, there had developed awareness that the relationship between nations and their past was different from what students of nationalism had traditionally assumed. National identities do not grow organically out of a common past. The opposite is true: the past, as it is recalled in schoolbooks, drama, rituals, and monuments, has been widely used to create and sustain national identities. As such, these scholars argued, memory, tradition, and history had become deeply political instruments that state builders in the nineteenth and twentieth centuries used to shape nations and forge national identities, as well as to place groups 'outside' the national past.[40] In this approach, the focus was thus primarily on memories as they were imposed and inculcated by *nation-building elites*. Since 'nation states', that is, states that identify a polity with a people, had emerged only around 1800, nationalism before 1800 was irrelevant. This position has since been hotly contested, but it meant that, to start with, students of national memory did not believe they had any business thinking about the world before 1750.

Secondly, the growing awareness that twentieth-century war memories cast a much longer shadow than anyone believed likely and seemed to be getting more powerful rather than receding into oblivion, raised an interest in, and appreciation for, the afterlives of wars and genocide. From the awareness of the long-term impact of the Holocaust on survivors and their descendants, there emerged a growing interest in the Freudian concept of trauma and the condition we now call post-traumatic stress disorder (PTSD).[41] The idea that traumatic memories could be 'repressed' drew the attention not only of psychologists, but was also added to the theoretical repertoire of students of literature and culture.[42] At the same time,

---

[39] E.g. Elizabeth Tonkin, *Narrating our pasts. The social construction of oral history*, Cambridge studies in oral and literate culture 22 (Cambridge, 1992); Connerton, *How societies remember*; Pierre Nora et al., *Les Lieux de mémoire*, 3 vols (Paris 1984–92); Nora, 'Between memory and history: *Les Lieux de mémoire*'; Jan Assmann, *Das kulturelle Gedächtnis. Schrift, Erinnerung und politische Identität in frühen Hochkulturen* (Munich, 1992), is the one founder of the field whose interests lay in the very distant, Egyptian, past.

[40] E.g. Benedict Anderson, *Imagined communities. Reflections on the origin and spread of nationalism* (1983; 2nd rev. edn London, 1991); Eric Hobsbawm and Terence Ranger, eds, *The invention of tradition* (Cambridge, 1983); Ernest Gellner, *Nations and nationalism* (Ithaca NY, 1983); Nora et al., *Les Lieux de mémoire*.

[41] Dominick LaCapra, *Representing the Holocaust. History, theory, trauma* (Ithaca NY, 1994). Winter, *Remembering war*; Ido de Haan, *Na de ondergang. De herinnering aan de Jodenvervolging in Nederland, 1945–1995* (The Hague, 1997).

[42] For a very critical assessment of this development, Wulf Kansteiner, 'Genealogy of a category mistake. A critical intellectual history of the cultural trauma metaphor', *Rethinking History* 8 (2004): 193–221.

the work of psychologists was demonstrating the extent to which memory is subject to change over time and (self-)manipulation, issues that became politically controversial from the late 1980s through the 'recovered' memories of alleged victims of sexual abuse and the trial of war criminal John Demjanjuk, where one of the issues at stake was the reliability of the memories of his victims.[43] Because this second line of enquiry focused primarily on painful memories and their effect on *individuals*, this made the period before 1800 difficult terrain. As we will see in Chapter 7, it is a complex business to find evidence for early modern people's handling of painful memories. Moreover, since it is also accepted wisdom in many circles that 'the individual' is itself a modern phenomenon, the conceptual framework in which to thematize individual painful memories before 1800 was not at all obvious.[44]

Finally, there was the interest among anthropologists and historians for the 'people without history', a phrase used to indicate groups that left little written evidence about their past—peasants, workers, women, and groups that in postcolonial studies are known as 'subaltern'. It was argued that their stories about the past were passed on orally, often using traditional story formats, which were associated with features in the landscape and material objects, so producing 'counter-memories' that could subvert the versions of the past as propounded by the state or other dominant groups. Students of oral history who struggled with the criticism that the evidence they collected from storytellers was historically 'unreliable' began to realize that, at the very least, such stories are valuable evidence of what people make of the past in the here and now. They show which memories matter and are used to structure thinking about the present.[45] This line of enquiry focused especially on *groups outside the dominant classes*, but of necessity relied on living informants. Nevertheless, there were important links here for students of those societies in the past where memories were transmitted orally. This is, for instance, how Fentress and Wickham came to the subject, and this is also an obvious link to historians of early modern Europe.

That scholars approached the subject of memory from different directions was reflected in a discussion about terminology. This, too, deserves some attention, so as to clarify how this book will talk about memory. Halbwachs's use of the term 'collective memory' was rejected by some on the grounds that memory is an individual matter, and so can never be said to be collective.[46] Many students of literature and some philosophers have come to prefer the term 'cultural memory', while historians

[43] See on the acrimonious recovered memory controversy, e.g. R.J. McNally and E. Geraerts, 'A new solution to the recovered memory debate', *Perspectives on Psychological Science* 4/2 (2009): 126–34. On Demjanjuk, Willem A. Wagenaar, *Identifying Ivan. A case study in legal psychology* (Cambridge MA, 1988); Willem A. Wagenaar, *The popular policeman and other cases. Psychological perspectives on legal evidence* (Amsterdam, 2005).

[44] Most influentially Charles Taylor, *Sources of the self. The making of the modern identity* (Cambridge MA, 1989). See also *Rewriting the self. Histories from the Renaissance to the present*, ed. Roy Porter (London, 1997).

[45] Eric R. Wolf, *Europe and the people without history* (Berkeley, 1982); Tonkin, *Narrating our pasts*. A good overview in Fentress and Wickham, *Social memory*.

[46] See e.g. Fentress and Wickham, *Social memory*, introduction.

and social scientists more often use the term 'social memory'. In practice these differences in terminology point less to diverging definitions of communal memory than to different approaches to studying it. Halbwachs had developed an approach based on sociological categories of analysis—family, class, religion. Many students of 'cultural memory' initially came to the subject with a strong interest in recollection, repression, and the subconscious, sometimes informed by psychoanalytical thought, and often also tracing these in literary and visual sources, as well as new media. They subsequently rediscovered the work of Aby Warburg, whose *Mnemosyne* project had tried to uncover the unconscious connections between visual forms that had been produced in many different times and places and can be seen to constitute a form of memory. Students of cultural memory have shown how this can also be extended to other media.[47]

Experts on 'social memory' tend to focus more on the social environment of memory and ask how individual stories about the past interact with existing narratives and other forms of commemoration.[48] Some scholars explicitly presented this 'social memory' as a realm of resistance against the public, dominant version of memory that is known as 'history'. If traditional history was a 'hegemonic' discourse about the past that was produced by the victors and that privileged those who had generated written evidence, memory, by contrast, might be seen as the repository of knowledge of people without history or traumatized communities who might remember as an 'act of faith'.[49] Others have argued that while social memory can be used very effectively as an alternative for dominant and state-supported views of the past, it may not be helpful to construct our understanding of social memory around its a priori opposition to dominant, literate or state-associated memory.[50] This is also the view taken in this book.

As we will see, more often than not early modern social memory was the result of a blend between *public* and *personal* forms of memorization. Public memory, memories that are shared among a larger audience and are considered to be of communal significance, can well be produced and promoted by individual stakeholders, people who have a personal interest in the continued significance and commemoration of a past event. Conversely, memories that people think of as personal are often affected by public memories, as we have seen happen to Arnoud van Buchel. Memories are, above all, dynamic and change in new generations. The German scholar Jan Assmann has emphasized that the social memory of an event will change once there is no one alive to tell the tale from his or her own experience or to have heard it told by those who experienced it themselves. Assmann argues that at this stage 'communicative' memory (*kommunikatives Gedächtnis*) will transform itself into 'cultural' memory (*kulturelles Gedächtnis*), a more abstract

---

[47] Erll, *Kollektives Gedächtnis*, esp. 19–22, 45–8.

[48] On these different terms and approaches see e.g. Erll, *Kollektives Gedächtnis*; Till, 'Memory studies'.

[49] See e.g. Luisa Passerini, 'Memory', *History Workshop* 15/1 (1983): 195–6; Tonkin, *Narrating our pasts*; Winter, *Remembering war*, 34–6; Y.H. Yerushalmi, *Zakhor. Jewish history and Jewish memory* (Seattle, 1982); Klein, 'On the emergence of "memory"'.

[50] Good examples of dissenting memory in Fentress and Wickham, *Social memory*.

form of memory.[51] My own research group found that this was a helpful way of thinking about the transitions that we saw in memories of the Revolt of the Netherlands.[52]

METHOD

As indicated above, early modern personal memories mostly remain hidden from view. Although we sometimes get glimpses of them in legal evidence, for instance, or in stories reported by others, for personal memories we mainly depend on the memoirs written by the literate, a small and mostly male minority in the early modern European population. These will be discussed in Chapter 1. Sometimes there are also traces of personal memories in material objects. One of the delights of working on public memory, on the other hand, is to discover that it is everywhere. In many European towns and even villages, one can start by looking at the names of early modern streets, houses, fields, and waterways; toponyms relate not only to trades and crafts, but very often refer to events, battles, or miracles. By walking around, looking at gable-stones and church windows, inscriptions on houses, public buildings and fountains, plague columns and city gates, in churches and public buildings, one can usually bring in another harvest, while a visit to local museums offers access to objects, of lesser or greater authenticity, that relate to local memories. Descriptions and histories of cities and regions, travel journals, local memoirs, local plays, collections of songs, all add to the picture. Researching early modern memory is thus often very much a multimedia affair, in which one object, text, ritual, or work of art refers to another.[53] By working backwards in time, it is possible to reconstruct and explain how public memories have morphed and changed meaning over time, often under the influence of one stakeholder or another, who sees an interest in passing on a tale, or new versions of it. By comparing evidence in different media, and analysing its context, we can find out why new meanings emerge and old ones get discarded, why some memories are contested, and others seem to be passed on or forgotten without further ado. This happens not for reasons of politics, religion, or personal interest alone; issues of genre and changing tastes also play a role.

It is harder to establish whose memories we are studying, and how long these matter; after all, we all have walked by monuments without asking ourselves what they were for. To find out, we need to cast our net even wider and look at indicators of what actual people did with the past, what stories they were ready to pass on,

---

[51] Assmann, *Das Kulturelle Gedächtnis*; Jan Assmann, 'Communicative and cultural memory', in *Cultural memory studies. An international and interdisciplinary handbook*, ed. Astrid Erll and Ansgar Nünning (Berlin and New York, 2008), 109–18.

[52] See e.g. Müller, *Exile memories*, 64–83, 201–11; Erika Kuijpers, 'Between storytelling and patriotic scripture. The memory brokers of the Dutch Revolt', in *Memory before modernity. Practices of memory in early modern Europe*, ed. Erika Kuijpers et al. (Leiden and Boston, 2013), 183–202.

[53] See for an excellent example of how this works Alexandra Walsham, 'Domesticating the Reformation. Material culture, memory, and confessional identity in early modern England', *Renaissance Quarterly* 69/2 (2016): 566–616.

what memorialization they were willing to pay for, and who had access to media of memory. As so often in early modern cultural history, this means we need to work with a great diversity of examples transmitted in different media and contexts, rather than large consistent datasets which can be treated as 'representative'. That the poor innkeeper Cornelis Joppensz asked the town council of the Dutch city of Leiden to be considered for a post as skipper in 1588, on the basis that he in 1574, aged thirteen, had been the first to venture into the sconce which a besieging army had abandoned, is not the sort of information one usefully goes to look for by reading all incoming correspondence of an early modern town. We know of it because of Cornelis's subsequent, apocryphal, reputation as an 'orphan' who took a 'cooking pot' containing the symbolic commemorative dish of *hutspot* into the hungry town, which in the twentieth century prompted a focused search in the records.[54] In similar ways, by working backwards, and following the 'memory career' of objects like medals, Marianne Eekhout found much other evidence to show that, in the Dutch Republic, both contemporaries and their descendants had a stake in keeping memories of war alive.[55] Inevitably, the very poor rarely emerge in such records. Yet even these sometimes leave their traces. When visiting the museum of the Thomas Coram foundling hospital in London, and looking at the heart-breaking tokens that mothers and fathers had handed in with their children so as to be able to identify them later, I discovered that several destitute parents had handed in medals that had been struck in memory of victories. James Amison, who was later apprenticed as an enameller in Clerkenwell, had been handed in with a medal marking a naval victory in Panama in 1736. Several other foundlings came in with medals from the Seven Years War (1756–63). When Jane Strudnall of Lombard Street tried to reclaim her daughter in 1762, she reminded the hospital that she had left 'a medal of brass' as a token for her baby, only to be told that her daughter Priscilla had died.[56] Although it is perhaps telling that Jane Strudnall did not name the event that her medal had commemorated, the reach of commemorative medals was clearly much greater than we had imagined.

By necessity, only some of what follows is based on my own research in primary evidence. My timeframe is broad, covering the period from 1500 to 1800, and there is more evidence to consider than any one historian can handle. Most of what I have to say is therefore based on work done by others or on published sources. Some of the cases I discuss can be considered 'representative', but others are much more exceptional and the geographical coverage of the book cannot be comprehensive. I have benefited enormously from the insights of a team of scholars who, between 2008 and 2013, worked with me on memories of the Dutch Revolt in the early modern Low Countries, which explains why the Low Countries are playing

---

[54] H.J. de Graaf, 'De Leidsche hutspot', *Leids jaarboekje* 21 (1927–8): 65–75; Ingrid L. Moerman and R.C.J. van Maanen, *Leiden, eeuwig feest* (Leiden, 1986), 23–6.

[55] Eekhout in 'Material memories', 78–105, traced a considerable number of examples, both by following the ownership and subsequent display of war medals, and by searching for affidavits mentioning contributions to the war effort in the Dutch Revolt.

[56] Janette Bright and Gillian Clark, *An introduction to the tokens at the Foundling Museum* (London, 2011), 11–12.

a more central role in this book than their size warrants. England is the only country for which general books on early modern memory already exist. This means that I have had to work with a host of smaller case studies and the (published) evidence in languages that I am familiar with. As a consequence I can say very little, for instance, on Scandinavia or Eastern Europe (although Central Europe will be quite frequently discussed), on which less work also seems to have been done, and less than I would have liked to about Italy and the Iberian peninsula.

The starting date of our discussion, around the year 1500, is there for practical reasons more than because I believe this to be a turning point. As I will highlight from time to time, many memory practices in early modern Europe were a continuation or variation of ways in which earlier generations had engaged with the past—even though the printing press added a new medium to the range that was already available, new ways of framing the past emerged as a result of Europeans' growing awareness of cultures overseas, and religious changes led to the development of new ways of doing memory. For the same practical reason, too, my comparative ambitions are mostly focused on comparisons in time. There are some chapters in which geographical comparisons are possible, such as in the chapter on 'acts of oblivion', where I compare French, English, and Netherlandish use of oblivion clauses. In others, I will be comparing and contrasting Catholic and Protestant memory practices. But I do not think that we can as yet make robust comparisons about 'general' traits that are typical for 'memory' in one area rather than another in this period—such a comparison would reflect the gaps in very patchy national historiographies as well as those in my knowledge rather than be based on a good and evenly balanced body of evidence. What I hope the book will do is to suggest directions that early modernists working on various parts of Europe may want to explore, whether with a view to showing that everything was different there or to highlight similarities; in the current state of the field, either will be helpful.

I have selected my examples mainly because they seem to me to shed interesting light on the themes that structure this book. These themes have been chosen to highlight, first, what was pre-modern about early modern memory practices; second, to show how and why they changed; and third, to facilitate comparisons with the modern world, so as to encourage a conversation with students of modern memory. There are seven of them: personal identity, historical consciousness, the changing status of custom and tradition, local and national memory, the relationship between myth and history, the politics of memory and oblivion, and finally memories of trauma and atrocity. I will not myself be examining modern cases or evidence in any detail. Ideas on modern memory play a role in this book rather as a point of departure and as a perspective for comparison.

Chapter 1, on personal memory, discusses how important it was for early modern people to have knowledge of their past or that of their families, analyses why early modern people memorialized their own past in ways other than people do today, and explains why this began to change in the eighteenth century. Chapter 2 discusses one of the most important reasons offered by early modern people for studying the past: to learn from historical examples. It analyses the attractions of this *anachronistic* way of thinking to early modern Europeans, but also demonstrates that this mindset coexisted with ways of thinking about the past that look much more modern, that focused on change, and on differences between past and present. Chapter 3 moves to the status and authority of custom, first to show how 'custom' could be used both to affirm and to challenge authority. In the course of the early modern period the status of custom changed, and the second aim of this chapter is to explore why it did so. Chapter 4 focuses on community memory, discussing the relationship between local and national memories. Chapter 5 asks what it took for memories to last, and analyses the relationship between legends, history, and memory. The final two chapters focus on memories of conflict. Chapter 6 discusses the 'acts of oblivion', agreements to 'forget' about civil wars and conflict, which were a major peacemaking tool for early modern Europeans, and asks if and how early modern Europeans thought such oblivion on command could work. Chapter 7 explores how we might study the existence of war trauma in early modern societies, and shows how memories of atrocity and victimhood were used in transnational contexts. In the Conclusion we will turn to the theme of change as a catalyst for the emergence of new forms of memory.

1

Scripting the Self

In 1507, after twenty years in the city of Venice, Frederik Jacobs van der Moelen returned to his native town of Haarlem in Holland to discover that virtually all his relatives were dead. He had neither 'father nor mother, neither sister nor brother, neither uncle nor great uncle, nor any children thereof'. The only kinspeople he could find were 'poor relatives from his mother's side'.[1] Like so many boys in early modern Europe, Frederik had left home early. He was eleven years old when he moved to Venice to start working for the Italian branch of the family's mercantile business. Now that he found himself back in the Netherlands, and without any relatives, he realized that he knew virtually nothing about his family's past. This was inconvenient because he believed that a better knowledge of this past might be important to him and could support his claims to noble status. As a child, Frederik's father had told him about coats of arms he had seen on the dilapidated shields that *his* father had taken into battle on seventeen occasions during the endless civil wars that had torn apart the province throughout the fifteenth century; his father had also told him about one other heirloom, a chest of drawers that had been in the possession of his father's mother and which had been decorated with her coat of arms. Yet both the shields and the chest were now long gone, with only the memory of them remaining to support the claims to nobility that Frederik was interested in pursuing.

That these claims were not self-evident had to do with the outcome of the civil wars, or so Frederik believed. Having fought on the losing side of the civil conflict, Frederik's grandfather was reported to have lost most of his possessions; he had bequeathed to his son no more than a golden ring and two fourteenth- and early fifteenth-century manuscripts, in which earlier Van der Moelens had made some notes.[2] From such snippets and by talking to distant relatives and old acquaintances Frederik now pieced together the rest of his fragmented family history. In 1531 he found the Count of Anguillar prepared to lobby the Emperor Charles V to grant Frederik the right to bear a coat of arms similar to the one his father was alleged to have seen on the family heirlooms.[3] Once having achieved this, Frederik took care to pass on what little family knowledge he possessed to his son Pieter, who in 1545 decided to write it down and added to it from his own observations

---

[1] O. Schutte, 'De familiekroniek van der Moelen', in *Uit diverse bronnen gelicht. Opstellen aangeboden aan Hans Smit ter gelegenheid van zijn vijfenzestigste verjaardag*, ed. E. Dijkhof and M. van Gent (The Hague, 2007), 293–307, at 297.

[2] Schutte, 'De familiekroniek', 294–6.   [3] Schutte, 'De familiekroniek', 297.

and conversations before passing it on to his own descendants. By the seventeenth century there were several copies of the text in the family; clearly no one wanted to risk another bout of family amnesia.

Most of us do not have claims to nobility to pursue, but, like Frederik, we need memories to know who we are. Cognitive psychology teaches us that humans are wired to forget most things that they experience within a very short space of time; if we did not do so, we would soon suffer from information overload. Yet people need to retain memories of some of their experiences and not only for practical purposes. Our memories shape what is known as our 'identity'—we need memory to know who we are, where we belong, and what our position is in relation to others. Memories provide us with essential social knowledge; they help us to take decisions about whom to trust and whom to fear—they underpin networks of friendship and mutual obligation. And although scholars have shown that our memories change over time, under the influence of both subsequent experiences and of people around us, we tend to experience them as a stable anchor and a source of knowledge about ourselves.[4] Yet what people choose to remember, what they value in personal memories, and how and why they will transmit them also changes from culture to culture. In this first chapter, we will explore why personal memory mattered to early modern people and what they thought was memorable about themselves.

Some aspects of personal memory are subject to historical change. This is partly because the brain is affected by changes in cultural practices; thus, people who cannot read memorize things in ways that differ from those employed by people who can. Research suggests that activities like prayer and meditation or frequent multitasking actually change the brain and may thus affect our memories. Cultural neuroscientists are trying to research such forms of interaction between culture and cognition.[5] Unfortunately, there is no way we can compare early modern brains to those of modern people. Yet whatever the physical process, personal remembering is also very much a social and cultural phenomenon; as we have seen, both the process of remembering itself and the transmission of such memories are shaped by social and cultural expectations and conventions, and because these differ from culture to culture and from time to time, we can assume that there is a history of personal memory to be written.

Students of memory have argued that modernity has changed what people do with their own memories, and on some levels this is indeed self-evident. For twenty-first-century Europeans, Frederik's predicament is highly unlikely. In societies of near-complete literacy like our own, we do not have to rely just on the memory of living relatives to know who we are; many people now own some documentation relating to the lives of their ancestors; there are public archives where we can find basic information about their dates of birth and death, siblings, marriages, addresses,

---

[4] Modern insights on this issue are summarized e.g. in U. Neisser and Lisa K. Libby, 'Remembering life experiences', in *The Oxford handbook of memory*, ed. Endel Tulving and Fergus I.M. Craik (Oxford, 2005), 315–32.

[5] See e.g. 'Cultural neuroscience', ed. Joan Y. Chiao, special issue of *Social Cognition and Affective Neuroscience* 5/2–3 (2010): 109–10.

and occupations. In a world of digital photography, we can retain and share thousands of images of moments, people, and events that we find important and select from these to tell tales about our personal past. A century ago, photographs were taken only at special occasions; even my father, born in 1939, and my mother, born in 1940, have only a few photographs of themselves as children. Yet scholars have also argued for differences at a much more structural level. Paul Connerton thinks that in the sort of village communities in which early modern people lived there was 'little if any space for the presentation of self' because in such communities 'to a large degree individuals remember in common'.[6] John Gillis believes that modern people, by contrast, 'cannot rely on the support of collective memory in the same way people in early periods could' and that 'an increasing burden' to remember 'is placed on the individual'.[7] Underpinning such conclusions are two influential ideas. First, Connerton and Gillis imply that people practise memory *either* as individuals and 'selves' *or* collectively, but not both at the same time. Secondly, they suggest that, in the West, the coming of modernity has also involved a transition from a world in which most people lived and thought as 'communal' beings, to a world in which they live and think as individuals—a world in which, as Pierre Nora argued, 'memory' is virtually lost because there are no longer any 'milieux' to sustain it. This chimes well with the widely accepted idea that a 'sense of the self' had to be 'discovered', much like a 'sense of the past' had to be, and that this happened sometime towards the end of the early modern period.[8] Yet it also means that we define early modern people by their lack of modernity and that definition does little for making sense of them in their own right.

The assumption that pre-modern Europeans did not have a sense of self and thus no personal memory is mostly based on what they wrote, and did not write, when they recalled their lives in autobiographical texts. Quite a number of such texts were written in early modern Europe, mostly by men from middling and higher ranks, and as we will see, these are indeed quite different in form and substance from modern memoirs and autobiographies. Yet these differences had other, and more interesting, reasons than their 'lack' of a sense of self. This chapter will first explore the importance of family memory for early modern people before moving to the question of how people structured their memories and why they did so. Departing from the observation that early modern personal memories were more often associated with bodies than with emotions, we then seek to explore how memoirists selected memories for their exemplary potential. I will argue that memoirs were often used to show how someone had 'performed' his life in accordance with cultural 'scripts' that were used to give meaning to personal experiences and made them easier and more useful to share. I will then show how this helps explain the memorialization of two particular types of personal religious experience—martyrdom and conversion. Finally, this chapter will explore how, in the eighteenth century, memoirs were first put to a new use, to construct

---

[6] Connerton, *How societies remember*, 17.
[7] Gillis, 'Memory and identity', 14–15.   [8] Taylor, *Sources of the self*.

a history of one's own emotional and moral development, so adding an important new cultural script to the existing repertoire that is more in line with modern expectations.

FAMILY MEMORY

In late-medieval and early modern Europe the predicament of Frederik van der Moelen was not unusual. It was only in the course of the sixteenth century that Western European parishes began to systematically record baptisms, marriages, and funerals—in other parts of Europe this record-keeping came even later. Many people lost their parents young, and epidemics could wipe out siblings at a stroke, while cities and villages might also be depopulated by wars. Wars also separated families. Reformed minister Willem Baudartius, who lived in the seventeenth-century Dutch Republic, complained that he knew almost nothing about his relatives who lived in the nearby enemy territory of Flanders, 'as if they lived in the East and we in the West Indies'.[9] But in any case, pre-modern people were often mobile and might not see their families for long spells of time; boys left home for years of apprenticeship, to serve in armies far away, or to study. Fishing or overseas trade, migrant seasonal labour, and service jobs also took both male and female Europeans away from home for months or even years on end. All this could make it very difficult to piece together family histories. Yet such family histories were important, and not just for those people who, like Frederik, wanted to stake a claim to noble descent.

While modern European societies tend to treat adults as individuals first and foremost, there continue to be certain legal rights that are transmitted to us by our parents, like the right to reside somewhere, for instance. Although there are fewer degrees of kinship today that prohibit people from marrying than there were in early modern Europe, family relations also continue to determine who we can and cannot marry. In many cases knowledge of the family past is also necessary to determine who will and who will not inherit. For pre-modern Europeans there were many more rights and obligations that were determined by birth. The most elementary of these was whether one was born free. Not only were there slaves living in many parts of early modern Europe, imported from Africa or the Americas, and also captured and traded across the Mediterranean where they manned the galleys of both Christian and Muslim states, many more people were tied to the land or had inherited obligations. In some parts of Central and Eastern Europe landowners had responded to the loss of workers after the Black Death of the fourteenth century by tightening their hold on the remaining peasants, who owed services to their lords and might not be able to move house or marry without their landlord's saying so. Serfdom was usually transmitted in the female line, and some obligations might continue even after someone had moved into another territory, while people might

[9] Willem Baudartius, 'Autobiographie van Wilhelmus Baudartius', in O.C.B.R. Roelofs, *Wilhelmus Baudartius*, (Kampen, 1947), 201–23, at 203.

also lose their freedom by living on, or farming, certain lands for too long.[10] People who wanted to challenge or limit seigneurial claims thus had better be sure about their family histories.

Too much awareness of family history might prove lethal; to prevent blood feuds, in some Sardinian communities genealogical knowledge was kept secret and remained the province of a select number of older women until the later twentieth century.[11] Other people's lives were stained by the dishonour incurred by their ancestors.[12] Yet in most cases pre-modern people wanted to guarantee that genealogical knowledge was retained and passed on, and they had good reason to do so.[13] Although serfdom had been abolished in most of Western Europe after the Black Death, there were usually still services and moneys due to the seigneurs; what one was obliged to pay was also partly determined by the legal rights and status that one's ancestors had enjoyed. In cities, too, it could be necessary to prove that one's parents or grandparents had been recognized as burghers, for instance when trying to acquire citizenship, or when applying to enter a guild, or in gaining permission to buy a property. New officials sometimes had to prove local ancestry. Legitimacy could also be extremely important; men born illegitimate, for instance, did not get their father's status. Thus, they could not inherit their noble titles or become Catholic priests, and because illegitimate children did not, automatically, inherit, they enjoyed far fewer opportunities on the marriage market. In Spain, only 'old Christians', people without Jewish or Muslim ancestors, could fulfil certain offices, while 'new Christians' were more prone to investigation by the Inquisition. It was thus no wonder that people there would take care to note that they were of old Christian stock, and that old Christians could go to considerable lengths to prove their ancestry.[14]

There were also spiritual reasons to keep the bonds between the living and the dead alive. Not everyone had a personalized grave, so there was not always a sign to remember the departed. Yet one of the key concerns for traditional Christians in the later Middle Ages was that people would pray for their souls after they died. If they could afford it, they would have one or more masses said for their souls and have these repeated every year, while *memoria* was also supported by paintings and poems, epitaphs, and stained glass. For Catholics such practices continued throughout the early modern period and beyond. Jewish communities also followed religious precepts when remembering the dead, while some Jewish families also kept an annual day of remembrance, for instance in honour of the safe deliverance

---

[10] Paul H. Freedman and Monique Bourin, eds, *Forms of servitude in Northern and Central Europe*, Medieval texts and cultures of Northern Europe, 9 (Louvain, 2005).

[11] Marinella Carrosso, 'La Généalogie muette. Un cheminement de recherche sarde', *Annales. Économies, Sociétés, Civilisations* 46 (1991): 761–9.

[12] See for an example of the impact this could have e.g. Joel F. Harrington, *The faithful executioner. Life and death, honor and shame in the turbulent sixteenth century* (New York, 2013).

[13] Giovanni Ciappelli, 'Family memory. Functions, evolutions, recurrences', in *Art, memory and family in Renaissance Florence*, ed. Giovanni Ciappelli and Patricia Lee Rubin (Cambridge, 2000), 26–38.

[14] María Elena Martínez, *Genealogical fictions. Limpieza de sangre, religion and gender in colonial Mexico* (Stanford, 2008), 61–87.

of ancestors during particularly dangerous incidents.[15] Although Protestants believed that the living could do nothing for the deceased and rejected prayers for the dead as superstitious, they proved equally committed to preserving and honouring the memories of the dead. In Germany, the dead were commemorated in funerary sermons, which were often kept and printed. More extensively than most people do today, testators themselves stipulated in wills how they wanted to be commemorated. Family Bibles were widely used to record genealogies and were transmitted across generations.[16]

All in all, there were thus plenty of reasons for early modern Europeans to be interested in, and pass on, a certain amount of family history down the generations. Such family details were, and are, first and foremost passed on by word of mouth. Unlike Europeans today, however, pre-modern people could not check and verify such tales in state records. To guarantee continuity, some pre-modern people rehearsed lineages in public ceremonies. Pedigrees might be painted and ancestral portraits put on display. Most often, however, such stories were told within the confines of the family, often by women. It was his grandmother who first instructed wine merchant Hermann von Weinsberg in Cologne about his ancestry, and most of the informants he consulted about the family in later life were also women.[17] Daniel Woolf noted that English gentlemen in the seventeenth century often seemed to rely on their wives for the details of family relationships.[18] Women exerted themselves to instil a sense of lineage in their children, sometimes linking it to places that were important to family memory.[19] This should perhaps not surprise us, since in the West, at any rate, women continue to act as the expert keepers of family history; research on modern memory shows that it is usually women who keep family photographs in order, for instance.[20]

Yet family history was never just a female monopoly, and it is no wonder that when pre-modern lay European males had the ability to write, many of them began to keep some form of family record. Sometimes no more than a list of names inscribed on the flyleaf of a family Bible, or a page or two in an account book, such texts were often also combined with other information, for instance about family possessions and dowries, or to store experiences that might be of interest or of use to one's descendants. In some regions such records developed into a distinctive

---

[15] Greenblatt, *To tell their children*.

[16] Peter Sherlock, *Monuments and memory in early modern England* (Aldershot, 2008), 71–95; Bruce Gordon and Peter Marshall, 'Introduction', in *The place of the dead. Death and remembrance in late medieval and early modern Europe*, ed. Bruce Gordon and Peter Marshall (Cambridge, 2000), 1–16.

[17] Hermann Weinsberg, 'Liber senectutis', 10v–11r. Only the titles of his manuscripts are in Latin; the texts are in German. The diplomatic edition of Weinsberg's writings can be consulted online at http://www.weinsberg.uni-bonn.de/Edition/Liber_Senectutis/Liber_Senectutis.htm, accessed 23 June 2016.

[18] Woolf, *The social circulation*, 116–17.

[19] Katharine Hodgkin, 'Women, memory and family history in seventeenth-century England', in *Memory before modernity*, ed. Kuijpers et al., 297–313; Ciappelli, 'Family memory', 34; Elizabeth V. Chew, '"Repaired by me to my exceeding great cost and charges": Anne Clifford and the uses of architecture' in *Architecture and the politics of gender in early modern Europe*, ed. Helen Hills (Aldershot, 2003), 99–114.

[20] Fritzsche, *Stranded in the present*, 198.

genre that acquired a name of its own: that of *livre de raison* in France, *Hausbuch* in Germany, and *ricordanze* in Italy. In other instances such texts developed into memoirs or urban chronicles. Unpublished, but frequently passed down to and continued by descendants, such texts are an important source of evidence for pre-modern personal and family memory practices—albeit unfortunately almost exclusively those of literate men only. Most women lacked the writing skills to undertake such a task.[21] Yet taken together, they do give us a good insight into what these men, at least, wanted to remember and be remembered for.

BODIES

In the twenty-first century, people who want to know how to tell the story of their lives can have recourse to websites, courses, and coaches that explain to them how to write it. These encourage would-be authors to create a developmental narrative that explains how the narrator has become who he or she is:

> Be bold, write the story of your life. Write who you were, what you did and how you became the person you are now. Recalling your own history can offer remarkable vistas.

> If you know who you are only through your memories, your sense of self will be as tangled as an old storage closet. By creating a written narrative, your past takes shape, offering a clearer vision of who you are today.[22]

Such a narrative is usually not limited to describing 'what happened to me' but will also routinely ask 'how did that affect me?' In this way, memoirs can become coherent narratives that create a causal connection between experiences and personality in past and present and that may even have a plot. This can and is, of course, done frequently in conversation. But the process of writing, it is often claimed, is itself useful because some of these connections may not be immediately obvious to us and will become apparent only through the process of recall. By recovering and recording memories, we are discovering 'who we are'.

Before the mid-eighteenth century authors rarely wrote about their lives in terms of personal development.[23] When people deployed an overall frame to describe their experiences, they tended to compare life with a journey or a pilgrimage. The destination of that pilgrimage did not lie in life, but beyond it, in salvation and

---

[21] Eric Ketelaar, 'The genealogical gaze. Family identities and family archives in the fourteenth to seventeenth centuries', *Libraries & the Cultural Record* 44 (2008): 9–28; Jean Tricard, 'Les Livres de raison français au miroir des livres de famille italiens. Pour relancer une enquête', *Revue Historique* 304 (2002): 993–1011; Woolf, *The social circulation*; Ciappelli, 'Family memory', rightly emphasizes the continuities with medieval genealogical practices. A BBC television show that reconstructs the genealogies and family histories of well-known Britons is significantly called 'Who do you think you are?'

[22] Marry Rietveld, 'Hoe schrijf je je levensverhaal', accessed 14 January 2016, http://www.coachy.nl/zelfcoaching/hoe-schrijf-je-je-levensverhaal/; Jerry Waxler, 'Ten reasons why anyone should write a memoir', accessed 14 January 2016, http://memorywritersnetwork.com/blog/ten-reasons-boomers-should-write-their-memoir/.

[23] Yuval Harari, *Renaissance military memoirs. War, history, and identity, 1450–1600* (Woodbridge, 2004), 130–2.

life after death. In the course of his or her life's journey, the pilgrim would experience different environments, travel in changing company, and occasionally lose his or her way; if all went well a pilgrim would learn what dangers to avoid and become ever more aware of the true aim and value of the journey. Previous experiences thus mattered to the pilgrim because they were a source of knowledge. He would be keen to remember them, just as he might learn from the experiences of others, and he might want to pass this knowledge on. But he was usually less interested in explaining how he had become who he was now than in considering how this prepared him for the future. His memories did not have to cohere into a story with an overall plot, although many episodes in that life might be read as morality tales in their own right.

One consequence of this attitude is that to modern readers the memoirs and autobiographies of pre-modern people can be a disappointing read. Even a specialist like James Amelang has complained about their 'relentless focus on externalities'.[24] Early modern authors do little to build up a picture of themselves that we would deem 'personal'. They record experiences as events, but do little to reflect on them; they do not present themselves as the unique product of their own life's trajectory or personalize their emotions in the way many modern Europeans do. The notion of emotion itself was yet to be discovered; early modern people thought in terms of 'affects', 'passions', or feelings, but even these are rarely thematized.[25] Authors' priorities can seem puzzling anyway: soldier Blaise de Monluc recorded more sorrow about the death of his Turkish horse than when mentioning the death of his spouse.[26] Memoirists make references to the deaths of infants, children, siblings, and partners in what to us seems a very non-emotive manner. That is not to say they did not feel or recognize such pain. Nobleman Hans von Schweinichen noted that his father was devastated when his mother died.[27] Merchant Lucas Rem recorded that the fatal illness of his twenty-week-old son Bechtold was 'the most pitiful that I ever saw'.[28] Young Arnoud van Buchel did not explain the motives for his attempted suicide in his memoirs, but he did do so in a letter to a friend.[29] In telling the story of their lives, pre-modern people had agendas that differed from those we might expect them to have.

To be sure, much of what cognitive psychology teaches us about the ways in which modern humans remember also applies to pre-modern people. Then as now it was not so easy to distinguish one's earliest memories from family tales.[30] Memories of the earliest experiences that early modern memoirists recorded were

---

[24] James S. Amelang, *The flight of Icarus. Artisan autobiography in early modern Europe* (Stanford, 1998), 123.

[25] Ute Frevert et al., eds, *Emotional lexicons. Continuity and change in the vocabulary of feeling, 1700–2000* (Oxford, 2014).

[26] As noted by Harari, *Renaissance military memoirs*, 136.

[27] Hans von Schweinichen, *Denkwürdigkeiten*, ed. Herman Oesterley (Breslau, 1878), 30–1.

[28] Lucas Rem, *Tagebuch des Lucas Rem aus den Jahren 1494–1541. Ein Beitrag der Handelsgeschichte der Stadt Augsburg*, ed. B. Greiff (Augsburg, 1861), 66.

[29] Pollmann, *Religious choice*, 22–3, 57.

[30] Jean Piaget, *La Formation du symbole chez l'enfant. Imitation, jeu et rêve. Image et représentation* (Neuchatel, 1945) has offered the most famous example of this effect.

passed down to them by their parents, as part of family lore. The Augsburg book-keeper Matthäus Schwarz was told how, after a bout of illness at age two, he had been believed dead. Having been sewn into a piece of linen, his body was taken into church to be buried, only for him to start moving his foot; in 1520 he had the scene depicted in an autobiographical costume book, about which we will say more in Chapter 2.[31] Stralsund burgomaster Bartholomeus Sastrow had heard how, as a toddler, he had once embarrassed his mother by relieving himself on every one of the three altars in the parish church where she, 'according to the custom of the papists', went every day in Lent to say a Pater Noster and an Ave Maria, 'and always took her little Bartholomäi with her'.[32] This tale must have been considered particularly amusing once the family shed its papist links and became Lutheran, but the Sastrow family was, in any case, fond of relating family tales; Sastrow also recalled how his little sister Gertrud, when told at age five that Imperial Diets existed to make laws, expressed the hope that the Diets 'could forbid spinning for little girls'.[33] Some authors identified what they thought of as their earliest memory. Matthäus Schwarz said that he 'started to remember' from age five—he recalled his mother's death and learning how to read, but these early memories were 'like a dream'.[34] The Basel physician Felix Platter also distinguished between stories he had heard from others, and those that had happened after 'the first time of my memory'. One of his earliest recollections was of imagining that he had fallen out of a window while sitting at a table in the house of his father's patron.[35]

That such memories stayed with memoirists was no surprise. Just as today, older people in early modern Europe tended to have more vivid memories of the first decades of their lives than they had of life in middle age.[36] And then as now, old people took pleasure in talking about the past. Many memoirists recalled hearing elderly people talk about their memories.[37] In 1630, the octogenarian Dutch merchant Jacques Manteau said that he felt positively rejuvenated by writing down his fifty-five-year-old memories of the siege of Zierikzee.[38] Older people's memory for other things, of course, declined. At age sixty, Cologne diarist Hermann von Weinsberg noted that he was best at recalling things that happened in the distant past, but complained that his memory got steadily worse; keeping a diary helped him to remember things.[39] This effect is familiar to older people in the twenty-first century; on this level, nothing has changed.

---

[31] August Fink, *Die Schwarzschen Trachtenbücher* (Berlin, 1963), 100.

[32] Bartholomäus Sastrow, *Social Germany in Luther's time. Being the memoirs of Bartholomew Sastrow*, ed. H.A.L. Fisher, trans. Albert D. Vandam (Westminster, 1902), 29.

[33] Sastrow, *Social Germany*, 6–9.   [34] Fink, *Trachtenbücher*, 102.

[35] Felix Platter, *Tagebuch (Lebensbeschreibung), 1536–1567*, ed. Valentin Lötscher (Basel and Stuttgart, 1976), 58.

[36] Douwe Draaisma, *De heimweefabriek. Geheugen, tijd en ouderdom* (Groningen, 2008).

[37] Fox, *Oral and literate culture*, 178–88; Fink, *Trachtenbücher*, 98.

[38] Jacques Manteau, 'Memorie', in *Tweehonderd-jarig jubelfeest ter gedagtenisse der verlossinge van de stad Zierikzee uit de Spaensche dwingelandij plegtig geviert op den zevenden november 1776 in eene kerkelijke leerreden over psalm LXVI vs. 12*, ed. Joannes van de Velde (Zierikzee, 1777).

[39] Weinsberg, 'Liber senectutis', 33r.

Yet on other levels, early modern memoirists are very different from us. While they often have little to say about their feelings, they devoted considerable attention to their bodies. When commissioning his autobiographical costume book in 1520, Matthäus Schwarz included two views of his naked body, one from the front and one from the back.[40] Fifty years later, Hermann von Weinsberg saved spending money on a painted portrait of himself by giving a page-long description of his physique at age sixty,[41] and when he began the next volume of his journal ten years later, he gave the reader a quick update on the condition of his body and faculties, as well as of his mind.[42] This interest in the state of their bodies was not just an indication that for early modern people their health was a source of constant care and worry. Early modern people treated the state of their bodies as an index of more than physical health alone. Memoirist Thomas Platter, for instance, had almost no relationship with his peasant mother, who, toiling to feed many children by successive husbands, was very 'rough' and showed very little interest in him. According to Platter, it was his mother's inability to breastfeed him herself that 'had been the start of my misery'. Without mother or wet nurse, Thomas had survived on cow's milk that had been fed to him through a small horn; he believed that, from the start, this had marked him out for an extremely tough childhood.[43] The French memoirist Pierre Prion noted that he had been born in 1667 without a caul and without a placenta; a clear indication that he would never make any 'pecuniary progress' and was destined for a life of misery.[44]

People were quick to make such connections because in early modern medical theory, too, there was a close relationship between the condition of the body and that of the mind; both were believed to be determined by the balance within the body of the four fluids known as 'humours', blood, phlegm, black bile, and yellow bile, as well as the body's temperature and degree of moisture. Those who had a bit more black bile were of a melancholic disposition, while those with more yellow bile might have a choleric temper. The balance between the humours was affected by a range of factors, such as diet and climate, as well as by age and the zodiac sign under which one had been born.[45] This made it sensible for sixty-year-old Hermann von Weinsberg, for instance, to describe himself as follows in his 'Liber senectutis':

> I think I am of a sanguine complexion, because I am warm and moist by nature,
> I liked being cheerful and jolly, and no depression has stayed with me for long. In the
> course of time, I have changed a bit, and become melancholic, but not much so: cholerics

---

[40] Fink, *Trachtenbücher*, 145–6.   [41] Weinsberg, 'Liber senectutis', 30–9r.

[42] Hermann Weinsberg, 'Liber decrepitudinis', 5v–6r, accessed 23 June 2016, http://www.weinsberg. uni-bonn.de/Edition/Liber_Decrepitudinis/Liber_Decrepitudinis.htm.

[43] Thomas Platter and Felix Platter, *Thomas und Felix Platter, zur Sittengeschichte des XVI. Jahrhunderts*, ed. Heinrich Boos (Leipzig, 1878), 4.

[44] Pierre Prion, *Pierre Prion, scribe*, ed. Emmanuel le Roy Ladurie and Orest Ranum (Paris, 1985), 40.

[45] Vivian Nutton, 'Humoralism', in *Companion encyclopedia of the history of medicine*, ed. W.F. Bynum and Roy Porter, 2 vols (1993; repr. paperback edn, London, 1997), I, 281–91; on the impact of humoral thought on the conception of childhood, see Hannah Newton, *The sick child in early modern England, 1580–1720* (Oxford, 2012).

and phlegm have never gained much with me. In my young days I used to bleed a lot, I am quite bashful and would go red in the face easily. I like to see and hear joy, to tell juicy tales when in company, in inns I have been talkative and jolly, I never refuse a bite, and have always liked singing, dancing and hopping around, and music pleases me very much.[46]

A change in humoral balance was believed to have mental as well as physical effects. Bartholomeus Sastrow from Stralsund ended the first section of his memoirs with a note that 'the continuation of this tale will show how from being sanguine, my temperament became melancholy, and how my gaiety and recklessness vanished'.[47] He conceptualized this change in temperament first and foremost as a physical process and did not connect it to external factors. To a modern reader such factors rather jump to the fore because the next section of his story tells how at age eight Bartholomeus, his siblings, and his mother moved from Greifswald to Stralsund to join his father who had been in exile there for the previous five years. Once he started living with his father, corporal punishment became a much more regular feature of Bartholomeus's life than it had been when he was living with his mother 'who was gentleness and tenderness itself'.[48] While we might consider there to be a link between this change in family circumstances and Bartholomeus's change in 'temperament', he himself framed it purely in terms of his humoral complexion.

This may be because he did not disapprove of his father's use of violence against him; Sastrow revered his father's memory and warned his children to correct the young 'temperately, without compromising either their health or their intelligence, but at the same time not to imitate the apes who from excess tenderness smother their young'.[49] Yet Sastrow was by no means the only early modern memoirist to connect the states of body and mind. Authors frequently recalled details about illnesses and health problems, not only when these had had a lasting effect, but also when these had been overcome. Weinsberg was perhaps unique in recalling all of his childhood afflictions, including his suffering from lice and worms, but less prolific authors also found many diseases and accidents worthy of commemoration.[50] Virtually the only personal details recorded by merchant Lucas Rem concerned his health, dangerous fevers, attacks of gout, and the stroke from which he recovered relatively well. He noted proudly that

God has protected us! I have had plague in the house eleven times, and many salesmen, maids etc. etc. died on me. Through the intercession of Mary His venerable mother, Saint Sebastian and all God's Saints, God has protected me most miraculously.[51]

---

[46] Weinsberg, 'Liber senectutis', 32r.   [47] Sastrow, *Social Germany*, 32.
[48] Sastrow, *Social Germany*, 31.   [49] Sastrow, *Social Germany*, 31.
[50] Weinsberg, 'Liber senectutis', summarized them all. Robert Jütte, 'Krankheit under Gesundheit im Spiegel von Hermann Weinsbergs Aufzeichnungen', in *Hermann Weinsberg, 1518–1597, Kölner Burger und Ratsherr. Studien zu Leben und Werk*, ed. Manfred Groten (Cologne, 2005), 231–51.
[51] Rem, *Tagebuch des Lucas Rem*, 10.

That illnesses were worth remembering was thus not only because for early modern people any illness could be potentially lethal, but also because to overcome them could be interpreted as a sign of divine favour and evidence of God's caring hand in one's life. Illnesses were also frequently remembered as moments of spiritual awakening and triggers for conversion experiences; both the founder of the Jesuit order, Ignatius Loyola, and the Reformed theologian Theodore de Bèze recalled a period of illness as a catalyst of spiritual renewal.[52]

Sixteenth-century authors also recalled ways in which physical pain could bring more direct emotional gain. Matthäus Schwarz commissioned a picture of his three-year-old self in bed with chicken pox, playing with his toy soldiers and being looked after by his sister Barbel, who was keeping the flies away from him—clearly this memory was not all bad (Figure 1.1). Felix Platter recalled getting nice sweet pears to eat when he was ill as a child and thinking 'you'd better be ill for long, so that you can eat good things for a long time'.[53] Quite a few sixteenth-century memoirists noted how a period of separation from their parents ended in illness, but also resulted in special care. Fifteen-year-old Weinsberg fell sick while at school in Emmerich and recalled that this had gained him a very loving letter from his father, who also sent him a blessing—it was a rare thing for his father to take such trouble over his letters or to express his approval of his son.[54] Illness secured young Arnoud van Buchel the right to live at home with his mother and stepfather rather than at the Utrecht school he hated.[55] St Teresa of Ávila found that God had shown her special mercy by sending 'a serious illness, which compelled me to return to my father's house, and when I was better they took me to stay with my sister, who lived in a country village'. It was because of this circumstance that she came to meet the uncle who was to point her to her destiny, as the founder of a religious order.[56] In a culture that thought of emotional change as a physical process, the decision to structure memories around the state of one's body was an obvious choice.

EXEMPLARY TALES

Yet why record personal memories at all? Like Frederik van der Moelen, Basel theologian Konrad Pellikan had grown up with virtually no knowledge about his

---

[52] Judith Pollmann, ' "A different road to God". The Protestant experience of conversion in the sixteenth century', in *Conversion to modernities. The globalization of Christianity*, ed. Peter van der Veer (Routledge, New York, and London, 1996), 47–64, at 49–50; Ignatius of Loyola, *The autobiography of St. Ignatius of Loyola. With related documents*, ed. John C. Olin and trans. Joseph F. O'Callaghan (New York, 1974).

[53] Fink, *Trachtenbücher*, 101; a recent edition in English was published as *The first book of fashion. The book of clothes of Matthaeus and Veit Konrad Schwarz of Augsburg*, ed. Ulinka Rublack, Maria Hayward, and Jenny Tiramani (London and New York, 2015); Platter, *Tagebuch*, 64.

[54] Weinsberg, 'Liber senectutis', 19r.   [55] Pollmann, *Religious choice*, 37.

[56] Teresa of Ávila, *The life of Saint Teresa of Ávila by herself*, ed. and trans. J.M. Cohen (Hardmondsworth, 1957), 31.

Figure 1.1. Matthäus Schwarz, aged three years and six months, sick with chicken pox. Note the ball and toy soldiers; his sister Barbel is keeping the flies away. Schwarz had this scene depicted by artist Narziss Renner in his *Klaiderbuchlein*, or costume book, the manuscript of which is now in the Herzog Anton Ulrich Museum, Braunschweig, 1.3r. More on this project can be found in Chapter 2.

parents. It was this circumstance that in the 1540s prompted him to write an autobiography for his relatives:

> What I did not know, you should know: the history of your ancestors, their stock, their occupations, residences and fate, as information, as a warning and as an example of good for you yourself and your descendants.[57]

Pellikan made it clear that he was not going to limit himself to genealogical information, but that his memories could also serve as a source of knowledge about life itself.[58] The exemplary potential of their personal experience was central to many other authors' declared intentions in their work. In 1508, Francesco Guicciardini's *Memorie di famiglia* stated:

> To have knowledge of one's ancestors, and particularly when these have been worthy, good and honoured citizens, cannot but be useful to their descendants, since this is a continuing stimulus to behave oneself in such a way that their glory cannot turn into shame.

He had set down the family memoirs, Guicciardini added, so that they could be useful. That is why he would note all he had found out about his ancestors, including

> their defects and errors, so that anyone who reads it will not only be stirred to imitate the virtue they possessed, but will also be able to flee their vices.

In writing his own *ricordanze*, he in turn provided the building stones for his descendants to continue the family memory and to learn from his experiences as well as from those of his ancestors.[59]

It is not surprising to see a humanist historian like Guicciardini stress the exemplary value of past experience, but autobiographical writers of all walks of life echoed the very same consideration. The value of one's own memories was not limited to oneself but could be transmitted to others, since a record of such memories invited authors and readers alike to chart and to recognize patterns in human behaviour and its consequences, just as many of such texts tried to chart these for the link between natural, human, and divine phenomena: the coincidence of a wet spring and high food prices, the relationship between a burning sky and political disaster, or between sinfulness and divine punishment.[60]

That texts like these were destined for a readership of descendants, of course, affected what the authors thought they could include in them, but because many authors thought that children could learn from bad as well as good experiences of the writer, they could be surprisingly candid. Thus authors might deem it useful to

---

[57] Cited in Hans Rudolf Velten, *Das selbst geschriebene Leben. Eine Studie zur deutschen Autobiographie im 16. Jahrhundert* (Heidelberg, 1995), 91.

[58] I discussed some of the material in this and the following paragraphs earlier in Pollmann, *Religious choice*, 16–24.

[59] Francesco Guicciardini, *Ricordi. Diari. Memorie*, ed. Mario Spinella (Rome, 1981), 33.

[60] Judith Pollmann, 'Archiving the present and chronicling for the future in early modern Europe', in *The social history of the archive. Record keeping in early modern Europe*, ed. Liesbeth Corens, Kate Peters, and Alexandra Walsham, *Past & Present* 230 (2016) Supplement 11, 231–52.

tell readers about marital squabbles, as did Hermann Weinsberg, or about gambling, as did Girolamo Cardano and Leon of Modena, about begging, theft, and poverty, as did Thomas Platter and Johannes Butzbach, about their first encounter with female nudity, as did Thomas's son Felix and nobleman Hans von Schweinichen, or about laziness at school, an attempted suicide, and love affairs, as did Utrecht humanist Arnoud van Buchel.[61] Some things and people were not deemed worth commemorating. Noble soldiers might not think it worth recalling the names of heroic commoners. Conquistador Bernal Díaz recorded the characteristics of all the horses that Hernán Cortés and his men took with them to Mexico, but did not give a name to the many local women whom the Castilians were gifted with, swapped, and married.[62]

According to these authors, what made events worth recording, and memories necessary or useful, was the fact that they taught people not only about the consequences of particular human decisions and forms of behaviour, but also about the ways in which divine providence intervened in their lives. Thus, the Silesian nobleman Hans von Schweinichen decided to describe 'the course of my life' so as to document how God had taught him to recognize his sins and 'to better my life'.[63] The French Catholic nobleman Henri de Mesmes included the remembrance of the gifts and deliverances God had bestowed on him as one of the reasons for setting down his text:

> And furthermore, that after me, you, my son, by reading of my life, will have a domestic example to fear God, follow virtue and despise fortune.[64]

Henri's invitation to his son to relive, as it were, the life of his father is unusual. Authors of all types echoed the warning of Guicciardini to learn from the bad as well as from the good experiences of the writer, and so avoid repeating their mistakes The French noble soldier Jean de Saulx offered his kinsmen 'examples and precepts...as if they were a compass intended to direct you along your destined path and to avoid the many misfortunes that I have suffered'.[65] Even the simple autobiography of Adriaen Doedenszoon, a pharmacist from Alkmaar in Holland, stated that his memoirs served as 'an exhortation to the young to spend their time better than he had done'.[66]

---

[61] Matthew Lundin, *Paper memory, A sixteenth-century townsman writes his world* (Cambridge MA, 2012), 87–8; Girolamo Cardano, *The book of my life (De vita propria liber)*, trans. Jean Stoner (Londen, 1931), 54, 73–4; see for Leon of Modena, Natalie Zemon Davis, 'Fame and secrecy. Leon of Modena's *Life* as an early modern autobiography', *History and Theory* 27, supplement 27 (1988): 103–18; Platter and Platter, *Thomas und Felix Platter*; Johannes Butzbach, *Des Johannes Butzbach Wanderbüchlein. Chronika eines fahrenden Schülers*, ed. and trans. D.J. Becker (Leipzig, 1906); Platter, *Tagebuch*, 108; Von Schweinichen, *Denkwürdigkeiten*, 16; Pollmann, *Religious choice*, 37–8, 61, 66–74.

[62] Harari, *Renaissance military memoirs*, 177; Bernal Diaz, *The conquest of New Spain*, trans. J.M. Cohen (Harmondsworth, 1963), 55.

[63] Von Schweinichen, *Denkwürdigkeiten*, 6–8.

[64] Henri de Mesmes, *Mémoires inédits de Henri de Mesmes, seigneur de Roissy et de Malassise*, ed. Édouard Fremy (Paris, 1886; repr. Geneva, 1970), 127–8.

[65] Quoted in Robert J. Knecht, 'Military autobiographies in sixteenth-century France', in *War, literature, and the arts in sixteenth-century Europe*, ed. J.R. Mulryne and Margaret Shewring (London, 1989), 3–21, at 14.

[66] GAA, Collectie Handschriften, Eikelenberg, Volume E A 20, 1409. I am much indebted for this reference to Alastair Duke, who generously made his notes on this MS available to me.

There were many other genres of writing to teach such lessons, yet authors stressed that there was an added value to knowledge that derived from personal experience. Behind this stress on the exemplary value of one's own experience lay the assumption that knowledge was most reliable when it was derived from direct observation. The personally experienced consequences of one's own folly, laziness, or lust, or conversely the personally experienced benefits of study, obedience, and so on, lent extra weight to the truth of precepts. In our eyes, this creates a paradox. On the one hand, authors stressed that knowledge was reliable only when it was based on first-hand observation, but, on the other hand, they suggested that one could learn from the experiences of others.

Yet what they did made sense when we consider experience not only as a personal thing but also as something that belonged to the family collectively. Hermann Weinsberg stressed that he and the nephew who would succeed him as *Hausvater*, head of the family, would in that respect be as 'one person', and his nephew therefore needed to know all 'my circumstances, mine and those of the *Haus* and understand its secrets'.[67] He and others also urged descendants to make sure that knowledge that might bring shame to the family would not be disclosed any further.[68] Hans von Schweinichen also reminded his descendants to be discreet in passing on information derived from his memoirs.

When they talked about their childhood, memoirists did therefore not hesitate to recall the early fears, beliefs, and convictions which in modern times, too, play a central role in early childhood memories.[69] Thomas Platter recalled believing that the little wooden horse that his older brother had brought him as a souvenir from the wars might actually run away. He also remembered being rather worried after his adult brother stepped over him and told him that Thomas would therefore not grow any more.[70] Thomas's son Felix grew up in much more comfortable circumstances, but he recalled some major frights nevertheless: of the hospital cow that was stabled opposite his home and that he believed might eat him, of the ghosts that old women told him about and that made him afraid of sleeping alone, and of a very scary neighbour, who came after him with an axe.[71] Hans von Schweinichen remembered how much he had been frightened by a thunderstorm.[72]

There was no embarrassment in such memories. Early modern Christians recognized that humans would go through various stages of development. As the Epistles of St Paul indicated, it was natural for a little child to act childlike, 'but when I became a man, I put away childish things' (I Corinthians 13). Young people might well have some fun, as Ecclesiastes 11 conceded: 'rejoice, o young man, in thy youth; and let thy heart cheer thee in the days of thy youth, and walk in the ways of thine heart, and in the sight of thine eyes'. Yet the text continued with a warning: 'but know

---

[67] Hermann Weinsberg, 'Liber iuventutis', 6v, accessed 23 June 2016, http://www.weinsberg. uni-bonn.de/Edition/Liber_Iuventutis/Liber_Iuventutis.htm.
[68] Von Schweinichen, *Denkwürdigkeiten*, 6–8.
[69] Douwe Draaisma, *Vergeetboek* (Groningen, 2010), 17–36.
[70] Platter and Platter, *Thomas und Felix Platter*, 6.
[71] Platter, *Tagebuch*.   [72] Von Schweinichen, *Denkwürdigkeiten*, 26.

thou, that for all these things God will bring thee into judgement'. Both classical authors and pre-modern preachers suggested ways in which one could define different stages in life, either by age or by condition and status. In a famous speech which starts

> All the world's a stage, and all the men and women merely players;
> They have their exits and their entrances,
> And one man in his time plays many parts,
> His acts being seven ages,

William Shakespeare took his audience through the stages man would go through: as a child, a boy, young man, soldier, 'justice', and old age, before he would reach the last stage of all, 'that ends this strange eventful history, is second childishness and mere oblivion, sans teeth, sans eyes, sans taste, sans everything'.[73] Though most memoirists did not reflect on this explicitly, their memories were often framed by such notions about stages and transitions.[74] Musician Thomas Whytehorne, for instance, echoed such scripts when he announced his memoirs would treat 'of the childs life, togyther with a young mans life, and entring into the old mans lyfe'.[75]

For boys, the moment when they began to wear breeches clearly marked an important rite de passage. Arnoud van Buchel could date the moment when he no longer had to wear toddler's dress to the time around his fourth birthday in July 1569.[76] Felix Platter could not name the year, but recalled it had happened on a Sunday and that it had ended in disappointment; he got so sick after eating too many cherries that he had to take off the new red trousers that he had so proudly started to wear earlier that day.[77] Soldiers' memoirs might omit childhood details, but begin the narrative at the moment when the author was 'old enough to mount a small horse' or to handle a weapon.[78] To be given his first sword, at age fifteen, was a memorable moment in the life of nobleman Hans von Steinichen, but he also marked other new possessions such as new clothes he had been given, as also did Hermann von Weinsberg and Matthäus Schwarz.[79] Growing a beard, too, was a moment worth marking as a transition between boyhood and manhood.[80]

Another fixture in memoirists' accounts of themselves was how they had been trained and had become accepted in the trade of their choice. They often detailed who taught them how to read—tailor Ambrosius Müller recalled being taught by his father from age three. One-time goatherd Thomas Platter, by contrast, took eighteen years before he achieved his aim of becoming properly literate. Almost everyone who had been to school recorded the names of their tutors, just as people who had been apprenticed recalled the names of their masters. Many men expressed sorrow about wasting precious time at school, but they also recalled the often very

---

[73] William Shakespeare, *As You Like It*, Act II Scene VII.
[74] Although some did, see e.g. Weinsberg, 'Liber senectutis', 2v–5v.
[75] Thomas Whytehorne, *The autobiography of Thomas Whytehorne*, ed. James M. Osborn (Oxford, 1961), 3.
[76] Pollmann, *Religious choice*, 36; see for a similar example also Weinsberg, 'Liber senectutis', 17r.
[77] Platter, *Tagebuch*, 59.   [78] Harari, *Renaissance military memoirs*, 141–2.
[79] Von Schweinichen, *Denkwürdigkeiten*, 22.
[80] Weinsberg, 'Liber senectutis', 21v; Pollmann, *Religious choice*, 15.

violent treatment they had received at the hand of teachers or masters. Pierre Prion recalled that he had been beaten almost every day by his master. Matthäus Schwarz, aged nine, ran away from school because the priest who taught him 'hit him too hard' and had almost drowned him. He spent some time begging for his bread before returning to his teacher's household (Figure 1.2).[81] Sexual experiences before marriage could also be related fairly freely, even if these were surrounded by misgivings. Hans von Schweinichen related in detail how keen he had been to gain some sexual experience and how he had first fallen in love. Weinsberg noted how angry he had made his mother by getting one of her maidservants pregnant, while Van Buchel noted experiences with 'loose women' in inns and on barges.[82]

Even if authors were more often than not completely silent about the levels of companionship in their marriages, marriage as such was marked as an important personal rite of passage. Hans von Schweinichen decided at the end of 1580:

> to arrange my life differently and so as to follow God's word and guidance, I have called on God and prayed, so that it would be a blessing and good for my body and soul, to shed light in my heart, and [let me know] what course to take, whether I should remain in my current state, or perhaps should get married.[83]

Soon, he felt sure of God's advice: he should marry. In the 1590s Arnoud van Buchel also wanted to remember his marriage as the means by which he had ended his 'wandering life', an opportunity to turn over a new leaf, and an occasion to record a vow of fidelity in his journal.[84] According to the English tinker and preacher John Bunyan, his marriage in 1650 had brought spiritual improvement, not least because his wife owned some books that influenced him for the better. For some authors, marriage was itself the trigger to start keeping a record of events in their life.[85]

Having achieved the necessary skills and knowledge, and having established themselves as husbands, the professions, trades, and networks in which men worked determined much of their social identity. This was not only a society of 'orders', in which people were given their rank by birth, and in accordance with God's providential order, which was to be accepted by all. It was also a society of corporate culture, especially in the cities. Artisans in early modern London might give tools and samples to their guilds as a memorial of their craftsmanship.[86] Family relations, neighbourhood, profession, guild membership, membership of a religious community, confraternity, or conventicle often overlapped, and reinforced one another. This was as much the case, for instance, for the prolific seventeenth-century Barcelona tanner Michael Perets as it was for textile worker Pierre-Ignace

---

[81] Prion, *Pierre Prion*, 122

[82] Von Schweinichen, *Denkwürdigkeiten*, 32, 35–8, 47–9; Weinsberg, 'Liber senectutis', 21v; Pollmann, *Religious choice*, 68–9.

[83] Von Schweinichen, *Denkwürdigkeiten*, 246–7.

[84] Pollmann, *Religious choice*, 72–3.   [85] Amelang, *Flight of Icarus*, 187.

[86] Jasmine Kilburn-Toppin, 'Material memories of the guildsmen. Crafting identities in early modern London', in *Memory before modernity*, ed. Kuijpers et al., 165–81.

Figure 1.2. Having run away from the priest who was his tutor, Matthäus Schwarz spent some time 'singing for bread' and herding cows before returning home, a scene he also asked Narziss Renner to depict in his *Klaiderbuchlein*, Herzog Anton Ulrich Museum, Braunschweig, 1.7r.

Chavatte from Lille, whose journals have been analysed by James Amelang and Alain Lottin respectively.[87] For Perets and Chavatte, professional, personal, and urban identities were closely intertwined; in their journals they devote more attention to the fortunes of their cities, neighbourhoods, parishes, guilds, and fraternities than to events that we would deem 'private'. They identified with their community, just as Connerton argued people in village societies do; yet at the same time, they felt they, personally, had to take charge of recording what was memorable about their lifetimes.[88]

SCRIPTS

For most memoirists the point at which they were married and established is when their personal development was complete; of the subsequent course of their lives they recorded instances in which they had experienced the workings of providence, perhaps some spiritual observations or the occasional vow or prayer, professional achievements, setbacks, and observations on public life. They rarely recorded memories of personal change; in other words they recorded how they performed in their particular adult role, as men and as husbands, but their identity was now fixed. How do we explain this?

In a seminal article medievalist Caroline Walker Bynum in 1980 pointed to the importance of role models and group identities for the development of a sense of self. She argued that the development of group identities and role models in the twelfth century, the emergence of ideal types of the knight, the monk, the widow, and so on, had played a key role in that twelfth-century innovation 'the discovery of the individual' and the concomitant emergence of the 'self' in written texts. Such life-writing, she emphasized, was not an end in itself, but above all a way of demonstrating how one could, in one's specific, and even lay, role, also follow Christ.[89] Although Bynum was happy to concede that this link between self and role models might have disappeared in the fifteenth-century Renaissance, recent research actually suggests otherwise. As the emphasis on the stages of life in pre-modern memoirs shows, private writers from the early modern period remained very much concerned with archetypes and role models. These could differ considerably between social groups. Yuval Harari has found, for instance, that the only memories early modern noble soldiers were inclined to record about themselves were *gestes*, deeds, because these defined their honour, and so their identity; these men *were* their deeds.[90]

---

[87] Amelang, *Flight of Icarus*, 80–114; Pierre-Ignace Chavatte, *Chronique mémorial des choses mémorables par moy Pierre-Ignace Chavatte 1657–1693. Le mémorial d'un humble tisserand lillois au Grand Siècle*, ed. Alain Lottin (Brussels, 2010).

[88] Pollmann, 'Archiving the present'.

[89] Caroline Walker Bynum, 'Did the twelfth century discover the individual?', *Journal of Ecclesiastical History* 31 (1980): 1–17.

[90] Harari, *Renaissance military memoirs*.

For pre-modern memoirists personal identity was thus about performing the identities for which one was born or trained; there existed social and cultural scripts for being a child, a man, a father, an artisan, soldier or intellectual, an identity as a citizen of a particular city, or as the servant of a noble house. Yet they followed such scripts as individuals, with their own humoral make-up, their own life trajectory, and their own moments of insight and evidence of divine providence—that is why personal experiences mattered, and why it was through a combination of these roles that people distinguished themselves from others.

Families, moreover, could have scripts of their own; thus, in quite a few medieval aristocratic families, crusading was considered a family tradition, memories of which were kept alive through a range of media, by storytelling and written texts, memorabilia and epitaphs.[91] Jewish, Protestant, and Catholic families all cherished family memories of exile, as evidence of a religious commitment, steadfastness, and election with which their ancestors had relived the biblical script set by the people of Israel.[92] Thus, after his death in 1655, London alderman John la Motte was reported to have taken pride in the decision of his Protestant parents to leave Ypres in the 1560s to flee persecution. He gathered friends and family every year 'to eat bread with him before the Lord (as Jethro and Moses did) in remembrance of such and such signal Mercies and Deliverances whereof his memory was a living chronicle'.[93] Around the same time Amsterdam poet Joost van den Vondel recalled how his Mennonite parents had been forced to leave Cologne, like Joseph and Mary on the flight to Egypt, so repeating the experience of their own ancestors, who had had to leave Antwerp to escape persecution.[94] Other families passed on traditions of political resistance. It was no accident that it was during an uprising of the Ghent guildsmen in 1539 that weaver Jan de Rouc copied his father's account of the great Revolt of 1477.[95] A 1747 Orangist rioter in the Dutch town of Zierikzee also claimed to follow family role models: her grandmother had taken to the streets to support the House of Orange during the turbulent year 1672.[96]

The insight that people's memories were shaped by existing cultural scripts helps us better to understand two influential genres of early modern memorialization that sometimes made it into print: martyrs' accounts and conversion tales. Personal accounts of the many martyrs who died for their religious convictions in the course of the sixteenth century were collected in martyrs' books—Calvinists, Mennonites, and Catholics throughout Europe were avid readers of such martyrologies throughout

---

[91] Paul Nicholas, *To follow in their footsteps. The Crusades and family memory in the high Middle Ages* (Ithaca NY, 1999).

[92] Greenblatt, *To tell their children*; Judith Pollmann, *Catholic identity and the Revolt of the Netherlands, 1520–1635* (Oxford, 2011), 131–42; Müller, *Exile memories*.

[93] Cited in Müller, *Exile memories*, 124–5.

[94] Judith Pollmann, 'Vondel's religion' in *Joost van den Vondel (1587–1679). Dutch playwright in the Golden Age*, ed. Jan Bloemendal and Frans-Willem Korsten (Leiden and Boston, 2012), 85–100.

[95] Jelle Haemers, 'Social memory and rebellion in fifteenth-century Ghent', *Social History* 36 (2011): 443–63.

[96] Rudolf Dekker, *Holland in beroering. Oproeren in de 17de en 18de eeuw* (Baarn, 1982), 60.

the early modern period and beyond. Published conversion narratives gained growing popularity throughout the seventeenth and eighteenth centuries; Teresa of Ávila's *Life* (first published in 1588) and John Bunyan's *Grace abounding to the chief of sinners* (1666) became classics; many more are known to have been published both in print and in manuscript.

Modern scholars reading such texts, however, have been faced with the problem that while these offer some of the most personal and emotive recollections that we possess for the early modern period, they are also incredibly similar to one another, sometimes virtually interchangeable. In the case of martyrs' accounts this has led some scholars to suspect that narratives that were presented as martyrs' own recollections of their ordeal had in fact been written by editors who sought to produce 'conduct books' for believers.[97] Yet further research has shown that editorial interventions usually did not go so far at all; in most instances we hear the testimonies of the martyrs' themselves.[98] And once we take into account the importance of role models for early modern personal memory practices, we perhaps need not be so surprised that the martyrs' accounts were so similar to one another. The whole point of the fateful decision to become a martyr was to follow that greatest role model of all, Christ, as the martyrs of the early church had done, and there was a clear script for the stages that were to lead up to the moment of execution. This script, first of all, involved 'witnessing' to the truths for which the martyr was to die, but also resisting pressure from others, like the relatives who were recruited by inquisitors to talk sense into their kin who were preparing to die for the faith. Since sixteenth-century people believed that it is 'not the punishment but the cause that makes a martyr', and since one could not be certain of being able to demonstrate appropriate behaviour during an execution, it made sense to validate one's experience by recording it. Moreover, rumours about recantations were common (sometimes even appearing in print), and writing served to reassure one's family and community that one had remained steadfast.[99] Taken together, this meant that both the experience of becoming a martyr and the decision to write about it could be simultaneously highly personal and very much scripted.

This is also true for pre-modern conversion narratives. The Christian tradition of the conversion narrative goes back to the times of the early church. The New Testament tells how divine intervention on the road to Damascus turned Saul, the persecutor of Christians, into Paul, the zealous defender of Christ and his gospel. A different and even more influential model for conversion experiences were St Augustine of Hippo's *Confessions*, in which he told of his long struggle to attain faith. Paul and Augustine provided archetypes for the tales, and perhaps

---

[97] John King, 'Fiction and fact in Foxe's Book of Martyrs', in *John Foxe and the English Reformation*, ed. John Loades (Aldershot, 1997), 12–35; Andrew Pettegree, 'Haemstede and Foxe', in *John Foxe and the English Reformation*, ed. John Loades (Aldershot, 1997), 278–94; David Watson, 'Jean Crespin and the writing of history in the French Reformation', in *Protestant history and identity in sixteenth-century Europe* II. *The later Reformation* (Aldershot, 1996), 39–58, at 55–6.

[98] See on this issue Gregory's introduction to *The forgotten writings of the Mennonite martyrs*, ed. Brad S. Gregory, Documenta Anabaptistica Neerlandica VIII (Leiden and Boston, 2002), xiii–xlii.

[99] Gregory, *Salvation at stake*.

for the experiences, of later converts.[100] In Martin Luther's accounts of his so-called 'Tower Experience', the Reformer followed the Pauline path of a sudden enlightenment:

> I meditated night and day on those words until at last, by the mercy of God, I paid attention to their context: 'The justice of God is revealed in it, as it is written: "The just person lives by faith".' I began to understand that in this verse the justice of God is that by which the just person lives by a gift of God, that is by faith…All at once I felt that I had been born again and entered into paradise itself through open gates. Immediately I saw the whole of Scripture in a different light.[101]

It was rare for converts to record such experiences. The few sixteenth-century accounts of conversions to Protestantism that we possess, like those of Luther, the Calvinist theologian Theodore de Bèze, or the Anabaptist leader Menno Simons, tended to be produced in very specific contexts, in which the authors were trying to account for a gap between their past and present views. Luther, for instance, wanted to explain why his earlier works were not as anti-Catholic as a new generation of Lutheran readers had come to expect and used the tale of his conversion in the introduction to his *Opera omnia* as a device to explain the difference between his earlier and his later texts. Theodore de Bèze, Calvin's successor as leader of the Reformed in Geneva, had to show how he had become a different man from the one who, a few years earlier, had written frivolous love poems. Menno Simons wanted to stress that it was divine inspiration, not the preaching of the unruly Anabaptists who had proclaimed the New Jerusalem in Münster, that first made him reject infant baptism. In Catholic circles it became customary to publish the narratives of those who abandoned Protestantism and returned to the mother church—at times Protestant churches responded in kind.[102] But otherwise even those first-generation converts to Protestantism who wrote autobiographical texts of some sort tended to be silent on the subject of denominational change. They were keener to present their choice for Protestantism as a form of learning than as a rejection of their former selves (and by implication also their ancestors). They had not broken with the past, but had acquired new knowledge, such as a child does when growing up.[103]

It was much more common for people to write an account of how they had found faith *within* their religious tradition than to describe how they came to abandon the Church in which they had been brought up. St Teresa of Ávila's conversion, for instance, was not about accepting Catholicism but about her progress towards a

[100] Paula Fredriksen, 'Paul and Augustine. Conversion narratives, orthodox traditions and the retrospective self', *Journal of Theological Studies* new series 37 (1986): 3–34.

[101] Martin Luther, 'Vorrede zu Band I der Opera Latina der Wittenberger Ausgabe. 1545', in *Luthers Werke in Auswahl*, ed. Otto Clemen, 6th edn (Berlin, 1967), vol. IV, 421–8, I am citing the translation of Andrew Thornton, http://www.iclnet.org/pub/resources/text/wittenberg/luther/preflat-eng.txt, accessed 22 June 2016.

[102] Keith Luria, 'The politics of Protestant conversion to Protestantism in seventeenth-century France', in *Conversion to modernities. The globalization of Christianity*, ed. Peter van der Veer (New York and London, 1996), 23–66; Alastair Duke, 'The search for religious identity in a confessional age. The conversions of Jean Haren', in Alastair Duke, *Dissident identities in the early modern Low Countries*, ed. Judith Pollmann and Andrew Spicer (Farnham, 2009), 223–50.

[103] I first discussed this in Pollmann, 'A different road to God'.

real religious life. Her journey to that end was gradual, like that of St Augustine, whose *Confessions* actually played a great role in Teresa's spiritual breakthrough. In memories of conversion like Teresa's, converts tend to draw a sharp contrast between their sinful past and enlightened present. Teresa famously recalled how she and her brother as children

> discussed ways and means of becoming martyrs, and we agreed to go together to the Land of the Moors, begging our way for the love of God, so that we might be beheaded there. I believe that our Lord had given us courage enough even at that tender age, if only we could have seen a way. But our having parents seemed to us a very great hindrance.[104]

Yet she also added that her motives for wanting to die for the faith had been wrong because she had wanted this 'not out of conscious love for Him, but in order to attain as quickly as [the martyrs] had those joys which, as I read, are laid up in Heaven'. Whereas most memoirists were indulgent of children's foibles, converts rejected the notion that they had ever been innocent. At the Protestant end of the spectrum, convert John Bunyan and his godly contemporaries were as tough on their unconverted selves as was Teresa of Ávila.[105] Bunyan's thoughts of hell

> when I was but a child, but nine or ten years old, did so distress my soul, that then in the midst of my many sports and childish vanities, amidst my vain companions, I was often much cast down, and afflicted in my mind therewith, yet could I not let go my sins: yea, I was also then so overcome with despair of life and heaven, that I should often wish, either that there had been no hell, or that I had been a devil; supposing they were only tormentors; that if it must needs be, that I went thither, I might be rather a tormentor, than be tormented myself.

Yet he was quick to reject the notion that such thoughts pointed to early religiousness. He said he had soon forgotten the dreams:

> wherefore with more greediness, according to the strength of nature, I did still let loose the reins of my lust, and delighted in all transgressions against the law of God: so that until I came to the state of marriage, I was the very ringleader of all the youth that kept me company, in all manner of vice and ungodliness.[106]

Martyrs' tales and tales of conversion were much more emotive than those of memoirists, but they were thus strictly scripted, so as to meet the expectations of what the martyr and converts should experience. This involved emotions, but the point of describing these was not to show they were unique. The aim of recording them was to testify and authenticate the state of the believer, but not to individualize him or her.

---

[104] Teresa of Ávila, *The life of Saint Teresa of Ávila*, 24.
[105] See on the genre e.g. Paul Seaver, *Wallington's world. A puritan artisan in seventeenth-century London* (London, 1985) and F.A. van Lieburg, *Levens van vromen. Gereformeerd piëtisme in de achttiende eeuw* (Kampen, 1991).
[106] John Bunyan, *Grace abounding to the chief of sinners* (London, 1904), 7–8, accessed 12 April 2013, http://www.gutenberg.org/files/654/654-h/654-h.htm.

A SCRIPT WITHOUT PRECEDENT?

The first person to write a memoir that had as its main aim to show what distinguished the writer from his fellow man was probably the French *philosophe* Jean-Jacques Rousseau, whose autobiographical *Confessions* of 1767 open as follows:

> I have entered upon an undertaking which is without precedent, and which will find no imitators. I mean to present my peers with a man in all the starkness of nature; and this man, he shall be me.
>
> Me alone. I know my heart, and I know mankind. I am made like none of those I have known; I have reason to believe that I am different from everyone else in existence. I may not have been better, at least I am different.[107]

If this stated aim was unique, Rousseau's text also had a purpose that was quite familiar: he wanted to clear his reputation from the many 'calumnies' that his enemies had spread about him. His candour was meant to build trust in the truth of his account, while its title, moreover, echoed a very familiar script, that of St Augustine's *Confessions*, who had not been afraid to expose his struggle to come to faith. With all its candour, Rousseau's prime aim was to assert that he was telling the truth and nothing but the truth and so to exonerate himself—he said that on Judgement Day he would be able to present his book to God. In the meantime, he clearly hoped that his contemporaries would show equal faith in him. By inviting his readers to come so close to him, he more or less forced them to take him and his sentiments seriously.[108] In doing so he created what scholar Philippe Lejeune has famously called the 'autobiographical pact' between autobiographers and their readers.[109]

But Rousseau was wrong that his *Confessions* would find no imitators. To the contrary, his autobiographical undertaking was to be so avidly read and so frequently emulated that it created new conventions for writing memoirs that continue to influence us today. The text did not owe its popularity to its main aim, to exonerate Rousseau; it was his strategy for doing so that captured the imagination. While Rousseau claimed his undertaking was unique, and thus unscripted, because he himself was so 'different from everyone else in existence', he paradoxically inspired others to do the same. Following Rousseau, many other authors, too, now wanted to show how unique and different they were, and they came to do so in a format that quickly developed into a new script.[110]

That the text could become so popular and so easy to emulate was, arguably, not only because Rousseau himself was such a compelling role model or because his *Confessions* were such a good read, but also because his project both reflected and

---

[107] Jean-Jacques Rousseau, *Les Confessions* 1782 (livres I–VI) and 1789 (livres VII–XII) (Paris, 1889), I, accessed 22 January 2016, http://athena.unige.ch/athena/rousseau/confessions/rousseau_confessions.html.

[108] Jean Starobinski, *Jean-Jacques Rousseau. La Transparence et l'obstacle, suivi de Sept essais sur Rousseau* (Paris, 1971), 216–39.

[109] Philippe Lejeune, *Le Pacte autobiographique* (Paris, 1975).

[110] Jean-Marie Goulemot, 'Temps et autobiographie dans les *Confessions*. Une tentative de reinscription culturelle', in *Lectures de Jean-Jacques Rousseau. Les Confessions I–IV*, ed. Jacques Berchtold, Elisabeth Lavezzi, and Christophe Martin (Rennes, 2012), 27–47.

gave a new twist to a cultural phenomenon that was already becoming very widespread, that of the novel. Rousseau himself tells us that after his mother died, he and his father took pleasure in reading all the *romans* she had left. The consequence of this, he believed, was that long before 'I had conceived of things, I had felt them'. He became an expert in sentiment:

> The confused emotions which I experienced one after the other did not affect the reason which I did not yet possess, but they helped to me to forge reason of another type, and gave me bizarre and romanesque ideas about human life, of which experience and reflection have fully been able to cure me.[111]

Ever since the Middle Ages, European audiences had enjoyed 'romances', texts describing great love stories and heroic quests, some of them fictional, like the novels surrounding the English King Arthur and his Knights, others based on historical fact, like the adventures of the knight Roland in his fight against the Saracens. Romances were read as life scripts, and some readers scripted memories of their experiences, and perhaps even the experiences themselves, in accordance with their reading of romances. The sixteenth-century memoirs of Hernán Cortés, Bernal Díaz, and other conquistadors of Mexico, for instance, resounded with imagery and metaphors derived from romances.[112] By the late sixteenth century, the Spanish novelist Miguel de Cervantes created his character Don Quixote, a poor man so deranged by the reading of romances that he sets out on an unlikely quest of his own, imagining himself to be a noble hero, fighting windmills and hoping to be worthy of the hand of a peasant girl whom he imagines to be a princess. The premise was that romances created a script that, when acted out for real, or by the wrong person, could create ridiculous results.

From the seventeenth century, there emerged a trend towards a more realist, new literary genre that we know as the novel. Novels used the 'histories' of fictional characters not only to recount exciting romantic endeavours and adventures on the battlefield, but to bring to life and illustrate the moral impact of events and decisions in the course of human lives. In this way, they habituated readers to imagining trajectories of personal development that were determined by a combination of character, the exercise of virtue, and external circumstances. Just as had happened with the romances, readers were soon said to identify themselves with the characters in the novels to such an extent that they began to imagine themselves following in their footsteps and to remediate fiction in their own lives. This had happened, for instance, with Rousseau's own novel, *Julie ou la nouvelle Heloïse* of 1761. The identification became all the easier since the heroines and heroes of the new novels were much more middle class, and the settings in which they operated much more familiar and contemporary, than had been those of the heroes and heroines of the romance tradition.[113]

---

[111] Rousseau, *Confessions*, I.

[112] J.H. Elliott, 'The mental world of Hernan Cortes', in *Spain and its world, 1500–1700. Selected essays*, ed. J.H. Elliott (New Haven and London, 1989), 27–41, at 30.

[113] Taylor, *Sources of the self*, 267–89; Ian Watt, *The rise of the novel. Studies in Defoe, Richardson and Fielding* (Berkeley CA, 1957); Lynn Hunt, *Inventing human rights. A history* (New York and London 2007), 35–69.

When Valentin Jamerey-Duval, historian and antiquary, sat down in the 1740s to write his memoirs, he therefore had models at his disposal unavailable two centuries earlier. Born in 1695 as the son of a French wheelwright who died when Valentin was eight, he had received no education at all in his home village. He recorded that he was 'brought up in the same way in which one grows plants, that is to say in a vegetative manner'. Having run away from a cruel stepfather, and roaming around the roads of France, picking up work where he could, Valentin was taught to read by fellow shepherds in his mid-teens and learned how to write as a servant in a religious house two years later. Discovered as something of a prodigy by the Duke of Lorraine, he was offered the chance to learn Latin and became the duke's librarian before moving on to a glittering career as a historian and antiquary. Jamerey-Duval's memoirs are extraordinary because they are so reflective, especially on the subject of learning, but they are also written with a plot in mind. Thirteen years after Jamerey-Duval left his home, and now a highly educated and wealthy man, he paid a visit to his native village and his mother and stepfather. They did not recognize him, but when he at last disclosed who he was, his stepfather fell on his knees and begged his forgiveness. Magnanimously, Jamerey-Duval told him that this was unnecessary. His stepfather had done him a favour; had it not been for his cruelty, he would never have made such a stellar career.

Jamerey-Duval constantly highlights the contrast between his past and his present situations, and between France and Lorraine, by evoking the total ignorance in which he had been brought up, noting that he had never seen silver money or heard a church organ and had imagined that Paris 'might be four or five times as large as our village'. He had originally wanted to learn how to read so that he could read romances, but once he encountered other books, he emphasizes, he also became a critical reader, just as he was a critical and enlightened observer of his native France, suffering from war, excessive taxation, and heartless officials. He contrasts the dismal rural poverty of France with idyllic Lorraine, the place where his talents were discovered, and which differed from France in every possible way, as much as his new life differed from his old.[114] Their reflectiveness and their novel-like plot mark Valentin Jamerey-Duval's memoirs as those of a new generation of readers. But because he was willing to share his manuscript memoirs only with some others, notably with Jean-Jacques Rousseau, the book was not, initially, published, and it was left to Rousseau to revolutionize the genre.

Himself a novelist and a reader of novels from his early youth, it was perhaps no surprise that Jean-Jacques Rousseau was also inspired by the novel when he came to present his *Confessions* and turned his memoirs into a new type of autobiographical novel, which applied the moralizing strategies of the novel to the writing of one's own life. It was this aspect that caught the imagination of his readers. From now on, more and more memoirists aspired to present their life as a novel, with themselves as the unique heroine or hero; the memories such authors selected for inclusion became therefore much more personal, more focused on moral dilemmas,

[114] Valentin Jamerey-Duval, *Mémoires. Enfance et éducation d'un paysan au XVIIIe siècle*, ed. Jean Marie Goulemot (Paris, 1981), 112.

and more focused on a developmental narrative than had been common before. Even so, many other memoirs continued to be written in a vein that was much more traditional—many of the nineteenth-century workers' memoirs analysed by Emma Griffin, for instance, retained features that had characterized early modern memoirs. Some of these British workers' tales strongly resembled classic tales of conversion, while others were like so many early modern memoirs, silent on wives and children, but eloquent about the community in which the author lived.[115]

CONCLUSION

This chapter has argued that it was important for all early modern people to preserve personal and family memories, and not only because the past determined much of their social status. Early modern ideas on the relationship between people's physical and psychological make-up were reflected in the way in which memoirists recalled their personal development. When recalling the story of their lives, male memoirists often echoed cultural scripts that suited their social status and that defined stages of human experience, privileging information and episodes that they believed could be useful or that had exemplary potential. Experiences like martyrdom and conversion, too, were memorialized in compliance with existing cultural expectations. Influenced by the new genre of the novel, eighteenth-century memoirists began to develop new ways of thinking about the self, which have come to shape Western ideas about the purpose of personal life-writing. The script of modern lives in the West is for each person to be unique, and that is reflected in what we tend to value in our personal memories.

Modern memoirists do not tend to think of their lives, or their memories, as being scripted. Even so, when modern people write their memoirs, they too often follow culturally and socially existing scripts. Yuval Harari has shown that modern war memoirs privilege completely different tales about battle experiences than did early modern ones; modern memories are about the revelations brought by battle and about the life-changing experiences and emotions that accompany war.[116] Between them, these modern war memoirs are just as similar as were soldiers' memories of the sixteenth century. Even the imagery they invoke is familiar. Students of memory have noted how many soldiers in World War I described their experiences in the language and imagery they borrowed from John Bunyan's description of the valley of the shadow of death in his *Pilgrim's progress*, a text that had been incredibly popular in the Protestant world ever since the seventeenth century. This is not to suggest that the survivors of the Great War plagiarized; rather, the way they remembered, and perhaps even experienced, their plight was

---

[115] Emma Griffin, *Liberty's dawn. A people's history of the Industrial Revolution* (New Haven and London, 2013), 1–10. See also Cubitt, *History and memory*, 148–9.

[116] Yuval Harari, *The ultimate experience. Battlefield revelations and the making of modern war culture, 1450–2000* (Basingstoke, 2008).

'premediated' by their reading of Bunyan's description of the valley of death.[117] Examining their farewell letters to their families, historian Jolanda Withuis found that individual Dutch communists who were about to be executed by the Nazis all used a very similar script of dying a 'good death', having committed their lives to the working class and giving their lives for a socialist future. It was a narrative that they had internalized to such an extent that they felt they were living it.[118]

What people remember, and certainly how they will record memories, thus remains to a large extent premediated by the 'scripts' that their culture offers them. These scripts not only determine by and large what we consider to be memorable about our lives, but perhaps even how we experience life itself. By the time we write memoirs, we often remediate such scripts.[119] It is the same mechanism that we also see at work in pre-modern memoirists describing the 'stages' of their lives, their choice for martyrdom or their experience of conversions. What has changed since the early modern period is first and foremost that the number of possible scripts has been extended to include ones that focus on, and privilege, personal development, and our self-definition as individuals.

---

[117] Paul Fussell, *The Great War and modern memory* (New York, 1975), 138–9; Paul Stevens, 'Bunyan, the Great War, and the political ways of grace', *Review of English Studies* 59 (2008): 701–21.

[118] Jolanda Withuis, *Erkenning. Van oorlogstrauma naar klaagcultuur* (Amsterdam, 2002), 177–211. I thank Bart van der Boom for alerting me to this study.

[119] Erll, *Memory in culture*, 139–43; David J. Bolter and Richard Grusin, *Remediation. Understanding new media* (Cambridge MA, 1999); Astrid Erll and Ann Rigney, eds, *Mediation, remediation and the dynamics of cultural memory* (Berlin and New York, 2009).

2

Past and Present: The Virtues of Anachronism

For some years now, my students and I have been enjoying a clip from the Norwegian TV show *Øystein og jeg*, which shows an exchange between a medieval monk called Ansgar, who has just moved from using scrolls to using books, and an equally medieval helpdesk worker, who is patiently taking him through the steps required to use the complex new technology of the bound book. The clip is so funny because it simultaneously plays on our *sense of distance* to a past situation in which people do not know how to open a book and on our *sense of analogy* between past and present; we can identify with the monk's exasperation about a new system and recognize in the medieval helpdesk worker the professionally patient tone that we know from our own IT helpdesks.[1]

In the context of this study the clip is interesting because it both appeals to, and undermines, what scholars call our 'sense of anachronism', our sense that the past is fundamentally different from the present. Many believe that such a sense of anachronism is a hallmark, perhaps even 'the' hallmark, of what we call modernity. Over the last decades, the idea of modernity has become tightly bound to the study of historical consciousness. This is partly because social scientists have found it difficult to agree on other 'objective' criteria for modernity, such as urbanization, literacy, industrialization, the rise of the nation state, or a sense of the individual. To use such criteria, after all, seemed to suggest that the trajectory followed by a handful of nation states in the West was the only path towards modernity. One solution for that problem is to acknowledge the existence of a variety of 'modernities'.[2] Yet having abandoned the notion that there is only one path to modernity, more and more scholars have also come to define modernity primarily as a cultural habitus. Modernity is not about doing objectively modern things, but a form of self-awareness that makes people think of themselves or others as modern and as different from the people in the past. In this definition, modernity implies above all an awareness of diachronic change and a sense that the past is non-repeatable, in short a 'modern' form of historical consciousness.[3] This solution creates problems of its own, of course, because it can seem to suggest that societies that prefer other, and

---

[1] Knut Nærum, 'Medieval helpdesk', *Øystein og jeg*, Norwegian Broadcasting (NRK) (2001), accessed 12 May 2016, http://www.youtube.com/watch?v=pQHX-SjgQvQ.

[2] See e.g. the theme issues 'Early modernities', *Daedalus* 127 (1998) and 'Multiple modernities', *Daedalus* 129 (2000).

[3] Berman, *All that is solid*; Stuart Hall, 'Introduction', in *Formations of modernity*, ed. Stuart Hall and Bram Gieben (Cambridge, 1992), 1–16, esp. 15; Christopher Bayly, *The birth of the modern world, 1780–1914* (Malden and Oxford, 2004), 9–10.

especially non-Western, ways of engaging with the past are not modern.[4] Nevertheless, both in the field of memory studies and among many historians of the modern world it is the advance of a new form of historical consciousness that is now generally considered to have signalled a huge shift to modernity and thus also to have enabled the emergence of 'modern memory'. According to this line of thought, modernity, and modern memory, became possible only once people in the West gave up on a much older and pre-modern way of thinking about the past, which has been called *synchronic* or *analogical* because it privileges the similarities rather than the differences between past and present, which it treats as one and the same thing.[5]

This analogical or synchronic way of thinking about the past was very common in medieval and early modern Europe. It enabled Europeans, for instance, to appeal to political, philosophical, and moral precedents and precepts that they knew from classical Roman texts without worrying too much about the rather different historical, and pagan, contexts from which these originated and to ignore the historically specific circumstances in which these had taken place. It was, therefore, nothing unusual to suggest to a fifteenth-century noble warrior that he should take a leaf out of the book of an ancient hero like Alexander the Great or to tell a ruler in Renaissance Europe that he should rule by imitating Julius Caesar or King Solomon. We have already seen how memoirists thought their descendants could learn from their experiences; in the same way, 'history' in medieval and early modern Europe was deemed a *magistra vitae*, a way of learning about life. Analogical thinking was, moreover, also deeply embedded in Christian theological traditions. In the Gospels, the life of Christ was presented as the 'fulfilment' of the promises made in the Old Testament. Christians read the Old Testament because they believed that events in the history of the people of Israel 'prefigured' those in the life of Christ. In this line of reasoning, there was a clear and sacred analogy between Abraham's willingness to sacrifice his son Isaac in the Old Testament and God's sacrifice of His only son, Jesus Christ, in the New, for instance. Such a sense of the past could be combined with some form of linear thought—in which mankind was on its way to the second coming of Christ and the end of time. It could also be conceived of as cyclical—as a never-ending cycle of rising and falling kingdoms, for instance. Yet what it did not do was to 'historicize' the past as different from the present.

THE TREE OF KNOWLEDGE OF PAST AND PRESENT

The word anachronism itself was first used in the seventeenth century to denote a mistake in chronology. New knowledge about the methods by which past societies had computed time made it possible to compare chronologies; this famously enabled

---

    [4] See e.g. the objections of Dipesh Chakrabarty, *Provincializing Europe. Postcolonial thought and historical difference* (Princeton, 2000).

    [5] See e.g. Burke, *Renaissance sense of the past*. See on the notion of analogical thinking and the idea of sharp transitions from one system to another also Mary Douglas, *Leviticus as literature* (Oxford, 1999), 13–40.

scholars to show, for instance, that the ill-starred lovers Dido and Aeneas in Virgil's *Aeneid*, one of the most famous texts from Roman antiquity, had actually lived three centuries apart. Yet its meaning was gradually extended not just to indicate chronological mistakes themselves, but also to describe a habit of thought that ignored the incongruence of such mistakes.[6] Scholars disagree on the moment when a new emphasis on the differences between past and present, and thus a 'sense of anachronism', began to appear in European culture. Most students of memory opt for the period around 1800 as the major watershed. In so doing they follow a tradition common among social scientists and historians of the modern world, who think that the age of revolutions forged changes so radical that they more or less shocked people into modernity.[7] We will revisit this idea in the conclusion to this study.

Historians of historiography, art history, and humanism, on the other hand, have traditionally focused on the Italian Renaissance or the German Reformation as the moment when the 'discovery' of the difference between past and present was made. In an influential scheme, historian Peter Burke suggested in 1969 that for a 'sense of history' to develop, Europeans first needed to develop not only a sense of anachronism, which they did in the Renaissance, but also a sense of evidence and a sense of explanation, which came in the seventeenth and eighteenth centuries. The latter two would not have been possible without the first.[8] Scholars in this tradition do not see a sudden conversion but a gradual evolution, a 'rise' of modern historical consciousness during the early modern period, which they have tended to chart by presenting a sequence of great books and thinkers who set their cultures on the high road to modernity. Only Daniel Woolf has recently devoted systematic thought to the question of how these intellectual developments might have interacted with changes in the rest of society. Building on older ideas by Eric Hobsbawm and Keith Thomas, he thinks that in England, in any case, they were enabled by and coalesced with a growing sense of change in society more broadly.[9]

Because scholars have generally thought of the emergence of a sense of history as a mark of scholarly and cultural progress, they have often been rather disdainful when talking about anachronism. They talk of the 'sin' of anachronism and describe

---

[6] Margreta de Grazia's essay, 'Anachronism', in *Cultural reformations. Medieval and Renaissance in literary history*, ed. Brian Cummings and James Simpson (Oxford, 2010), 13–32, offers both an overview of the history of the concept and a very astute critique of existing approaches to it. See also Margreta de Grazia, 'The modern divide. From either side', *Journal of Medieval and Early Modern Studies* 37 (2007): 453–68.

[7] E.g. Berman, *All that is solid*, 17; Terdiman, *Present past*, 3–32; Björn Wittrock, 'Early modernities. Varieties and transitions', *Daedalus* 127/3 (1998): 19–40; Gillis, 'Memory and identity', 7; Ankersmit, *Sublime historical experience*, 321–4.

[8] While certainly different in their selection of texts and authors, the linear approach to the subject of Anthony Kemp, *The estrangement of the past. A study in the origins of modern historical consciousness* (New York, 1991) and Zachary Sayre Schiffman, *The birth of the past* (Baltimore, 2011) remains strikingly similar to that of Burke, *Renaissance sense of the past* or Koselleck, *Vergangene Zukunft*.

[9] He nevertheless remains focused on charting this as a process of linear change; Woolf, *The social circulation*. See also Hobsbawm, 'The social function of the past'; Thomas, *The perception of the past*.

it as the result of ignorance, naivety or even of 'innocence'.[10] They have therefore also been rather too ready to assume that once people in the West had eaten from the tree of knowledge of past and present, they would no longer want to reason by historical analogy. But whereas today's historical researchers do indeed take care to avoid anachronisms (even if many historians will invoke analogies between past and present when they teach), others who engage with the past, for instance when practising memory, are not usually so shy in pointing to parallels between past and present. Side by side with the professional 'sense of the past' of the historical disciplines, there exists a wide range of discourses about the past in which analogies between past and present continue to reign supreme. This is not only the case outside the Western societies with which this study (and the history of historiography) is mainly concerned.[11] It has also continued to be true in modern Europe and North America.

People in nineteenth-century Lorraine, for instance, were well aware of the differences between past and present. They routinely referred to the bad old days of the forced labour services or *corvées* that had ruled their lives before the French Revolution. Yet when deciding on courses of action in the present, they would also rely on historical analogies, so as to predict possible scenarios for the future. People in Lorraine routinely modelled expectations of new invaders on local experiences with Swedes and Croats in the Thirty Years War two centuries earlier. David Hopkin has suggested that by seeing new invaders through that lens they were 'pre-remembering' new events before they even happened.[12] A recent anthropological study of historical consciousness of a Greek mining community on Naxos in the nineteenth and twentieth centuries draws attention to the prophetic analogies these modern Greeks see between the times of 'ancient Egyptians', the Turks, and modern Greece.[13] Yet this is not just some atavistic folk habit. In the early twenty-first century foreign-policy makers and military leaders still routinely look for historical analogies when making their decisions,[14] and reasoning by historical analogy also remains a powerful form of aesthetic and cultural engagement with the past. In an influential 2009 book, Michael Rothberg coined the term 'multidirectional memory' to describe the way in which memories of slavery and the Holocaust affected one another in the second half of the twentieth century. While many have insisted on the uniqueness of the experiences of slavery, the Shoah, and colonialism, he shows that philosophers, film makers, and novelists have also frequently and creatively used anachronistic ways of thinking to create a dynamic traffic between readings of past and present. As Rothberg notes, 'memory's anachronistic quality—its

[10] De Grazia, 'Anachronism', 13. See e.g. Burke, *Renaissance sense of the past*, 13 and Thomas M. Greene, *The light in Troy. Imitation and discovery in Renaissance poetry* (New Haven CT, 1982), 30.

[11] Dipesh Chakrabarty, 'Minority histories, subaltern pasts', *Postcolonial Studies* 1 (1998): 15–29.

[12] David Hopkin, 'Legends of the allied invasions and occupations of eastern France, 1792–1815', in *The bee and the eagle. Napoleonic France and the end of the Holy Roman Empire, 1806*, ed. Alan Forrest and Peter Wilson (Basingstoke, 2009), 214–33.

[13] Charles Stewart, *Dreaming and historical consciousness in island Greece* (Cambridge MA, 2012), 1–20.

[14] Scot Macdonald, *Rolling the iron dice. Historical analogies, regional contingencies, and Anglo-American decisions to use military force* (Westport CT, 2000).

bringing together of now and then, here and there—is actually the source of its powerful creativity, its ability to build new worlds out of the material of old ones'.[15]

Whereas scholars have usually thought of synchronic and diachronic approaches to the past as successive *stages* in a linear history of historical consciousness, other evidence suggests that in the modern world they actually *coexist*.[16] Whether we use the one or the other will depend on who we are, but also on the context, on the mode in which we are talking or thinking, and on what we want to achieve. This observation has two benefits for the study of early modern memory. First, it can free us from the idea that people have to give up on old notions of the past before accepting new ones. When people use anachronistic modes of thought or representation, this does not imply that they *cannot* conceive of a 'cognitive distance' between past and present. Rather, they may choose not to deploy a diachronic mode, but instead opt for a synchronic one; tomorrow they may do differently. Secondly, it opens up the possibility that early modern anachronism, too, may have been a matter of choice, rather than the result of inability or unwillingness to perceive change.

A SENSE OF CHANGE

In a famous essay entitled *Vergangene Zukunft* or *Futures past* of 1968, the German historian Reinhart Koselleck began his analysis of the differences between analogical and modern approaches to the past by describing a painting that Bavarian artist Albrecht Altdorfer made in 1528–9 of a classical scene: Alexander the Great's defeat of the armies of the Persian king Darius in the battle of Issus in 333 BC (Figure 2.1) Koselleck observed that Altdorfer had put a great deal of effort into getting the details about the military situation right. Yet at the same time, he had done nothing to try and make the armies look ancient; the Greek soldiers were dressed in contemporary sixteenth-century German clothes, and the Persians were depicted much like the Turks who were about to besiege Vienna. Koselleck argued that Altdorfer's lack of interest in the difference between past and present epitomized the anachronistic, analogical way that pre-modern people thought about history.[17] Three hundred years after it had been painted, Koselleck argued, Europeans had come to think about the past quite differently. When the Romantic critic Friedrich Schlegel saw Altdorfer's image of the *Alexanderschlacht* in the early nineteenth century, it prompted him to reflect not on the analogies but on the differences between his own time and the time in which it was painted, and on the distance that separated him from that moment. Schlegel's historical consciousness, in short, was modern.

[15] Michael Rothberg, *Multidirectional memory. Remembering the Holocaust in the age of decolonization* (Stanford, 2009), 5.
[16] A similar point is made by Robin Fox, *The tribal imagination. Civilization and the savage mind* (Cambridge MA, 2011), and Douglas, *Leviticus as literature*, 28.
[17] Republished with related essays in Koselleck, *Vergangene Zukunft*.

Figure 2.1. Albrecht Altdorfer (1482–1538), *Der Alexanderschlacht, 1528–29*, also known as the *Battle at Issos*, now at the Alte Pinakothek in Munich. The painter took care to set the scene in its historical location, and also offered supporting detail on the event in the caption on the banner, but notably dressed the armies in contemporary outfits. The armies of the Persian king Darius therefore wear turbans, so evoking the Ottoman armies who were at that time threatening the Holy Roman Empire. When Schlegel saw the painting in 1803, it was at the Louvre in Paris, where it had been taken as war booty by the armies of Napoleon.

Figure 2.2. Narziss Renner, *Der Augsburger Geschlechtertanz*, 1522, Maximiliansmuseum, Augsburg. Image Kupferstichkabinett Staatliche Museen zu Berlin/Bpk. The arrow indicates the tree trunk.

Yet five years before Altdorfer completed the *Alexanderschlacht*, and only fifty kilometres from Munich, the Augsburg bookkeeper Matthäus Schwarz, whom we have already met in Chapter 1, had commissioned a painting that suggested an outlook much like Friedrich Schlegel's. Instructed by Schwarz, Augsburg artist Narziss Renner made a painting on parchment depicting a so-called *Geschlechtertanz*, 'a dance of lineages' (Figure 2.2). The painting shows thirty patrician couples engaged in a stately dance, the dancers wearing styles dating from the thirteenth century to that of the time the painting was made. Six of the pairs are dressed in fourteenth-century clothes, twelve in the fashions of the early fifteenth century; these are followed by later-fifteenth-century couples, and the procession closes with seven couples dressed in the fashions of 1522. Ahead of the dancers Renner included a tree trunk bearing the inscription: 'the difference between the old and the new world, 1200–1522'.[18] Similar images were made for other Augsburg patrons. Thus an image of a *Geschlechtertanz* dating from 1550 has a caption that explains that the figures are wearing the dress that was customary 'around 1500'.[19] Such

---

[18] Fink, *Trachtenbücher*, 31–40.

[19] For this and other examples of *Geschlechtertanze*, see Fink, *Trachtenbücher*, 31–40; Ulinka Rublack, *Dressing up. Cultural identity in Renaissance Europe* (Oxford, 2010), 50.

images show not only that it was *possible* for early sixteenth-century Bavarians to conceptualize such differences, but also that in some circumstances they chose to highlight rather than to ignore the differences between the old and the new.

This was definitely the case when they disapproved of them. By and large early modern people were resistant to the idea that changes in the religious, social, or political order could be a good thing. In their view, such things should be 'unchanging' because they had been decreed by divine or natural law. If and when moral, religious, and political change occurred, as it did all the time, this was usually seen as something that had to be resisted. Early modern people who favoured changes therefore tended to dress them up as a correction to the changes that had been imposed by others. For that reason, it was important for the Protestant Reformers of the sixteenth century to present themselves as people who came to remove the 'corruptions' that the Catholic hierarchy had introduced and to 'return' to the days of the early Christian church.[20] English parliamentarians in the seventeenth century who rebelled against the policies of King Charles I hastened to deny that they wanted change; instead, they were in the business of protecting the 'ancient constitution'.[21]

Even so, when European societies experienced a major transformation, such as happened during the Reformation, the sense of rupture was palpable. In England, for instance, there was widespread nostalgia for the pre-Reformation past, when England had been 'merry', life had been simpler, and charity and hospitality abounded. Many lamented the lost abbeys and other sacred spaces of the Catholic world, and antiquarians set out to document their existence before the last traces had vanished, and this sense of loss resulted in a rush to salvage what remained.[22] English Catholics experienced the break with the religious past in a very nostalgic manner.[23]

> The tyme hath been wee had one faith
> And strode aright one ancient path
> The thym is now that each man may
> See new religions coynd each day
> The tyme hath been the prelate's dore
> Was seldome shotte against the pore
> The tyme is now, so wives goe fine
> They take not thought the kyne.[24]

The break with the past caused deep anger. A Catholic antiquarian in England took action against the Protestant perpetrators of iconoclasm by refusing to include their names in his *Survey of London* because they were: 'worthy to be deprived of that memory of which they have injuriously robbed others'.[25] But there was also melancholy: 'Nothing in the world remains certain. Nature does not persist in its

---

[20] Gordon, *Protestant history*.

[21] J.G.A. Pocock, *The ancient constitution and the feudal law. A study of English historical thought in the seventeenth century* (1957; rev. edn Cambridge, 1987).

[22] Aston, 'English ruins and English history'.

[23] Adam Fox, 'Remembering the past in early modern England. Oral and written tradition', *Transactions of the Royal Historical Society* 6th series 9 (1999): 233–56; Alison Shell, *Oral culture and Catholicism in early modern England* (Cambridge, 2007); Walsham, *Reformation of the landscape*.

[24] Woolf, *The social circulation*, 340.

[25] Quoted in Walsham, *Reformation of the landscape*, 275.

own laws, and all laws lie in confusion,' wrote Arnoud van Buchel. As a consequence of the Revolt and the ensuing Reformation in the Netherlands, he also documented a strong sense of rupture and loss:

> I suppose nothing at all has been done outside the usual and just order, when the ancient laws have been powerless…in the town of Utrecht, so that, with the council brought down, cobblers may rule…While the common people live according to their own wishes…the feeble decrees of the inert council are changed with every hour. Hence right and wrong are put to similar uses and the widest door is open to every possible crime.

Van Buchel had a large stake in the existence of the old order; as the illegitimate son of a Utrecht canon, he saw the Revolt destroy both the church in which his father had made his career and his own prospects for a career in the city's elite. The social order had been turned upside down, and he thought the consequences were dire. He reported that 'today, one may safely defame another man's reputation, thefts, too, go unpunished, deceit and perjury are profitable'.[26] In religion, everything had changed:

> Our ancestors had one way to [the] true goal, those who live now have another. Now the altars of the saints have been overturned, the images and ornaments variously destroyed, many monasteries and churches lie torn down to their foundations. This is the eagerness of mortals for novelty.

The loss of the past moved him to start documenting the material remains that were under threat; he copied epitaphs, drew stained-glass windows, and described buildings, because:

> [Protestants] neglect the monuments of the ancients and do not attend to the memorial masses of our ancestors, saying that their names have already been written in heaven, so that some of them seem more barbaric than the Goths themselves.[27]

He spent the rest of his life as an antiquarian scholar, documenting the past.[28] The experience of rupture in the Reformation could thus result not only in a sense of loss but also in an acute awareness of the risks of oblivion and an agenda for action to counteract these threats.

Van Buchel became a historian with a keen sense for the 'mutations' in history, but it was not only scholars who reflected on the past. Many Dutch Catholics in the early seventeenth century engaged with the past in a nostalgic fashion. People recorded memories of church interiors and procession routes. Catholic lay sister Greetje Quispel in seventeenth-century Haarlem paid 'mind visits' to the past while sewing, mentally visiting the lost interiors of the seven churches and chapels in the city that, before the Reformation, had been dedicated to the Virgin.[29] Other Catholics in the Dutch Republic ordered painted images of the church interiors that were no longer theirs, in a virtual repossession of church space.[30]

---

[26] Quoted in Pollmann, *Religious choice*, 52.   [27] Pollmann, *Religious choice*, 86.
[28] Pollmann, *Religious choice*, 191.
[29] Joke Spaans, *De levens der Maechden. Het verhaal van een religieuze vrouwengemeenschap in de eerste helft van de zeventiende eeuw* (Hilversum, 2012), 106–7.
[30] Almut Pollmer, 'Kirchenbilder. Der Kirchenraum in der holländischen Malerei um 1650', doctoral dissertation, Leiden University (2011), 357–84.

In the early modern period we also find less emotional references to differences between past and present. This has been well studied for seventeenth-century and eighteenth-century England, where it became a commonplace to talk about 'constant change'.[31] The late-seventeenth-century writings of the antiquarian John Aubrey, for instance, are littered with references to the differences between past and present—varying from the first introduction of new industries in Wiltshire to the traditions of storytelling in the days 'before women were readers' and his observation that in his youth 'fathers were not acquainted with their children'.[32] But to refer to such changes was hardly new. A century earlier, the memoirist Hermann von Weinsberg from Cologne, for instance, had reflected frequently on the changes in his society. Weinsberg developed an eye for change early on in his life. He had commenced writing a history of the family when he was in his early thirties, with a clear view to handing on this important information to his successor as *Hausvater*, or head of the family. He was just over forty when he began his *Book of my youth* in 1558 with the remark that at the family party that had been held to celebrate the occasion of his baptism, on Epiphany 1518, men and women had been seated separately, 'as was customary at that time, and that has changed since'.[33] In 1584 he noted, referring to one of the most famous authors of antiquity, that 'a new Ovid should emerge to write a new book of *Metamorphoses* about the changes of my time'.[34] And when he began the fourth volume of his life-writings in 1588, aged seventy, he remarked

> It goes with me like with the deceased when they rise from the dead and from the grave start to go into the world again…I see throughout Cologne great changes in all streets and alleys, on all markets and squares, other buildings than fifty years ago, new lords in the council, in convents, new citizens in parishes, and few of my age, new manners, customs, laws and statutes, other clothes, other manners of speech and words, other scripts and letters, and other ways of preaching and of learning, other taxes, other currencies and many more changes. Is that not as if one is rising from the grave and seeing a new world.[35]

Weinsberg agonized about some of these changes. Like so many others, he deplored the Reformation and its impact, and frequently affirmed that he would stick with his old beliefs. There were other things he disapproved of; thus, he thought that the adoption of a new type of writing by clerks was likely to cause problems in the future because there would be no one left to read the older texts. Yet he was very positive about other innovations, for instance when thinking about new buildings, and agnostic about yet others, such as when it came to changes in fashion, and he did not think that change was necessarily to be resisted.

---

[31] Paul Langford, *A polite and commercial people. England 1727–1783* (Oxford and New York, 1989), 7; Woolf, *The social circulation*, 19–43.

[32] John Aubrey, *Aubrey's natural history of Wiltshire. A reprint of The natural history of Wiltshire* (Newton-Abbot, 1969), e.g. 102–3, 105, 109; John Aubrey, *Three prose works*, ed. John Buchanan-Brown (Carbondale IL, 1972), 289–90; John Aubrey, *Brief lives*, ed. Richard W. Barber (Woodbridge, 1982), 9.

[33] Lundin, *Paper memory*, 231–5; Weinsberg, 'Liber iuventutis', 6r.

[34] Weinsberg, 'Liber senectutis', 447r.   [35] Weinsberg, 'Liber decrepitudinis', 3r–v.

It is significant that Weinsberg saw evidence for positive change especially in the material world—buildings, clothes, new inventions. We can also see such a material way of thinking about change among other sixteenth-century Europeans. In 1590 Florence, the Bruges artist Jan van der Straet, also known as Johannes Stradanus, began to produce a series of prints entitled the *Nova reperta* to celebrate 'new discoveries', starting with the 'discovery' of the Americas, but focusing especially on the invention of new technologies: the compass, printing press, gunpowder, mechanical clocks, and so on (Figure 2.3).[36] In the Dutch city of Leiden, the clothiers' guild in 1594 commissioned a set of paintings that showed all stages of cloth production. Celebrating the arrival of the 'new draperies' that produced a lighter, superior form of cloth, the transition was represented by a painting in which an allegorical figure of the city of Leiden, accompanied by an old woman representing the 'old trade', welcomes a young woman who allegorizes the 'new trade' (Figure 2.4).

Ulinka Rublack has drawn our attention to the extraordinary costume book left by the Nuremberg bookkeeper Matthäus Schwarz, the same man who had ordered the *Geschlechtertanz* in Augsburg. Schwarz was one generation older than Weinsberg. He was twenty-three when in 1520 he decided to document the tale of his life by having himself drawn in different sets of clothes at frequent intervals. He began by commissioning twenty-eight images that recorded his life so far, starting with drawings of his parents—showing his mother pregnant with him—before progressing through the different stages of his childhood and youth, which we encountered in the Chapter 1. Once having commissioned the first series, Schwarz continued having new images made from time to time, with a longer gap before finally completing it in 1560. A caption on one of the images explains that he had first got the idea for this collection because he took pleasure in hearing older people talk about the ways in which dress had changed and continued to change 'every day'. Reflecting that this would probably continue to happen throughout his life, he imagined that it would be worthwhile to document these changes. And change interested him in other ways, too. The costume book was originally the counterpart to a chronicle in which he described the *Weltlauf*, the course of the world.[37] Although the latter is lost, it is clear from his references to it in the costume book that Schwarz recorded changes in himself and his world side by side.[38] Men dressed differently at different stages of their lives, while fashions themselves changed throughout their lifetimes and marked the progression of time itself. This idea, of course, was also behind his commissioning of the *Geschlechtertanz* in 1522.

People were thus well aware of change, and especially when change was material they might be quite proud of it. That it was the material that embodied positive change for people like Schwarz and Weinsberg need not surprise us, and neither does it necessarily need to be explained as a symptom of the growing consumerism

---

[36] See on this project e.g. E.H. Gombrich, 'Eastern inventions and Western response', in *Science in culture*, ed. Peter L. Galison, Stephen R. Graubard, and Everett Mendelsohn (New Brunswick and London, 2001), 193–206.

[37] Rublack, *Dressing up*, 39–50; Schwarz and Schwarz, *The first book of fashion*.

[38] E.g. Fink, *Trachtenbücher*, 103.

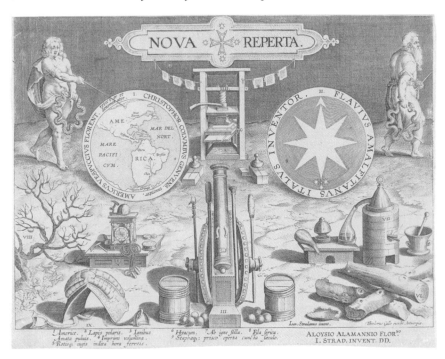

Figure 2.3. Jan Collaert after Johannes Stradanus, title page of *Nova reperta* (Florence, *c.*1590). Rijksmuseum, Amsterdam. On the left a young woman, perhaps representing the new times, points to a map of the newly discovered Americas. On the right, an older man, possibly representing the past, walks away. Both hold the snake Ouroboros, who bites his own tail and is often used to represent the cycle of time. On the right also the rose of a compass, a new instrument. In the middle, taking pride of place, a printing press. At the front a range of other sixteenth-century novelties are on display: a tree with silk worms, a saddle and spurs, a mechanical clock, a cannon and gunpowder, and instruments for distilling.

and materialism of bourgeois city-dwellers in the German cities of the sixteenth century. It is more useful to think about it along the lines set out by the anthropologist Daniel Miller, who has written about the way in which Londoners today express themselves and tell their own life-stories and tales about their relations with others through engagement with their material possessions: their clothes and postcards, music collections and Christmas decorations. In a recent study he emphasizes how important possessions are as a vehicle for shaping social relations.[39] Historians are becoming more and more aware that, in all societies, material things play a crucial role in shaping cultural meaning, and thus also in structuring and transmitting memories.[40] Even, or perhaps especially, in a world in which there are fewer possessions, or fewer changes, a little bit of either may be experienced as very significant.

---

[39] Daniel Miller, *The comfort of things* (Cambridge, 2008).
[40] Leora Auslander, 'Beyond words', *The American Historical Review* 110 (2005): 1015–45; Chew, 'Repaired by me'.

Figure 2.4. Isaak van Swanenburgh, *Allegory of Leiden with the old and new trade 1594,* Museum De Lakenhal, Leiden. The allegorical figure in the middle can be recognized by the keys on her livery to represent the city of Leiden, which is also visible in the background. She is holding the hand of the 'old trade', who is carrying an hour glass—perhaps suggesting her time is up—and welcoming the young figure of 'new trade', who is presented by the allegory of Time. The painting celebrates the introduction of 'new drapery' techniques for the production of lighter and cheaper cloth by Flemish and Brabantine immigrants, who were invited into the city to help revive its economy after the siege, and who were themselves fleeing war and persecution in the Southern Habsburg Netherlands. Tools of the trade lie scattered about. Leiden is treading on a shield with the Andrew's cross, signifying its resistance to its Spanish Habsburg overlord.

THE VIRTUES OF ANACHRONISM

If early modern people were so well aware of change and saw evidence of it all around them, why did they so often prefer analogical and anachronistic ways of thinking about the past? There was certainly more to this than naivety, ignorance, or innocence. Niccolò Machiavelli, known as one of the most innovative thinkers of the sixteenth century, was simultaneously very much aware of historical change and given to analogical history. In the *Discourses* that he wrote in the 1510s, for instance, he explained what lessons a modern ruler might obtain from reading the ancient historian Livy's *History of Rome*:

> Let him who has become a prince in a republic consider, after Rome became an Empire, how much more praise is due to emperors who acted like good princes in accordance with the laws, than to those who acted otherwise. If the history of these emperors be pondered well, it should serve as a striking lesson to any prince and should teach him to distinguish between the ways of renown and of infamy, the ways of security and of fear . . . Let a prince put before himself the period from Nerva to Marcus, and let him compare it with the preceding period and with what came after, and then let him decide in which he would rather have been born, and during which he would have

chosen to be emperor. What we will find when good princes were ruling, is a prince securely reigning among subjects no less secure, a world replete with peace and justice…If he then looks attentively at the times of the other emperors, he will find them distraught with wars, torn by seditions, brutal alike in peace and in war.[41]

While Machiavelli acknowledged that one period might differ from another, he was thus simultaneously using his knowledge to try and deduce maxims that would hold true in any period, especially in his own city of Florence. To him, that was the whole point of history. In the introduction to his *Discourses* he blamed the 'weak state' to which the world of his own day had come to on the 'lack of a proper appreciation of history':

> the great bulk of those who read it take pleasure in hearing of the various incidents which are contained in it, but never think of imitating them, since they hold them to be not merely difficult but impossible of imitation, as if the heaven, the sun, the elements and man had in their motion, their order and their potency become different from what they used to be.[42]

Interestingly, Machiavelli here denounces his contemporaries' misguided distance from the past. What his analogical, anachronistic approach enabled him to do, by contrast, was to give an astute analysis of the recent political history and current predicaments of his native Florence, by reading them through the lens of ancient Rome. That was especially relevant since, just as the Roman Republic had become an empire, the Florentine Republic was increasingly under the control of the Medici family and seemed on its way to becoming a monarchy. For Machiavelli, the virtues of offering such an analysis through the route of historical analogy were several. First, a comparison with Rome, which had ended up as an empire, offered not only insights about the past, but also about the possible consequences of the various political scenarios that to the Florentines were as yet open and a matter for the future. Secondly, Livy's history offered a fixed, authoritative and non-partisan point of reference for Machiavelli's analysis that no Florentine critic could quarrel with, yet that nevertheless did not inhibit him from giving it his own spin. Quite the opposite. He could both benefit from its authority and superimpose his own agenda on his analysis. Anachronism, in short, enabled Machiavelli to do the things that he wanted to do in and for the present, and to do so to maximum effect. History was a means to that end: a source of authority and a stock of ideas, as well as a rhetorical tool.[43]

Although the Roman past was especially authoritative to early modern Europeans, that past did not have to be Roman to be useful; from the sixteenth century onwards, Northern Europeans, especially, began to forge new historical role models for themselves that suited their needs in the present. Using the Roman historian Tacitus's description of the Romans' Germanic foes, Scandinavians, Germans, and the Dutch invented an ancestry for themselves of Germanic heroes—when fighting Holy Roman Emperor Charles V, for instance, sixteenth-century Germans

---

[41] Niccolò Machiavelli, *Discourses*, ed. Bernard Crick, trans. Leslie J. Walker and Brian Richardson (London, 1970), 136–7.

[42] Machiavelli, *Discourses*, 98–9.

[43] Felix Gilbert, *Machiavelli and Guicciardini. Politics and history in sixteenth-century Florence* (Princeton, 1973).

invoked the precedent of the tribal leader Hermann, or Arminius, who had led the Germanic tribes in their victory over the Roman legions.[44] Comparisons with Germanic times could also be used to draw attention to change. Thus, the German play *Julius redivivus* of 1585 recounts how Julius Caesar and Cicero return to earth in the sixteenth century to find everything and everyone much changed, mostly for the worse. Italians no longer speak Latin, the French are decadent. Only the German leader Hermann, a descendant of Arminius, has mainly positive changes to report.[45]

The reason why anachronism remained a very popular way of thinking about the past throughout the early modern period was thus above all that it enabled a lively traffic between past and present. How this worked can be seen especially well in visual imagery. In their *Anachronic Renaissance*, Alexander Nagel and Christopher Wood have argued that the anachronic 'quality' of Renaissance art is the 'ability to hold incompatible models in suspension without deciding'. Anachronisms allow the artists to draw on different sets of associations simultaneously, and as such it is highly useful. They therefore argue that from the Renaissance onwards 'any painting that stages past events in modern garb and surroundings has to be suspected of sophistication, that is knowing exactly what it is doing before it is accused of negligence or indifference'.[46] By introducing anachronic elements, Renaissance painters were making clear and powerful points about the relationships between past and present. And although Nagel and Wood suggest that the hybridity of the images that they study was no more than a temporary phenomenon in the development of Western art, we can nevertheless see in visual and material culture how early modern Europeans continued to call upon anachronisms for specific and useful purposes, and to bounce images and ideas back and forth in time.

PLAYING WITH ANACHRONISM IN THE SEVENTEENTH-CENTURY LOW COUNTRIES

In 1661 Amsterdam publisher Jan Jacobsz Bouman produced a new edition of the *Geusenliedboek*, or Beggar's song book, a classic collection of songs about the Dutch rebellion against the Habsburgs that had first appeared in the 1570s.[47] Bouman was a good and modern publisher, who was perfectly capable of producing sophisticated and up-to-date book designs. Yet for this particular work he did not do so. On the title page he used old gothic typeface, as well as a very primitive woodcut that depicted the symbols of the Beggar movement, a begging bag and cups, with the portrait of its leader, while the two joined hands over the bag symbolized fidelity (Figure 2.5). In this way he produced a title page that was the spitting image of the one that had been used in dozens of earlier editions ever

---

[44] Caspar Hirschi, *The origins of nationalism. An alternative history from ancient Rome to early modern Germany* (Cambridge, 2012), esp. 167–95.

[45] Nicodemus Frischlin, *Julius redivivus* (1585), discussed in Rublack, *Dressing up*, 164.

[46] Alexander Nagel and Christopher S. Wood, *Anachronic Renaissance* (New York, 2010), 18, 35.

[47] *Geuse liet-boeck, waer in begrepen is den oorsprongh vande troubelen der Nederlandsche oorlogen* (Amsterdam, 1661). See on the genre Louis Grijp, 'Van geuzenlied tot Gedenck-clanck. Eerste deel: het geuzenliedboek in de Gouden Eeuw', *De Zeventiende Eeuw* 10 (1994): 118–32.

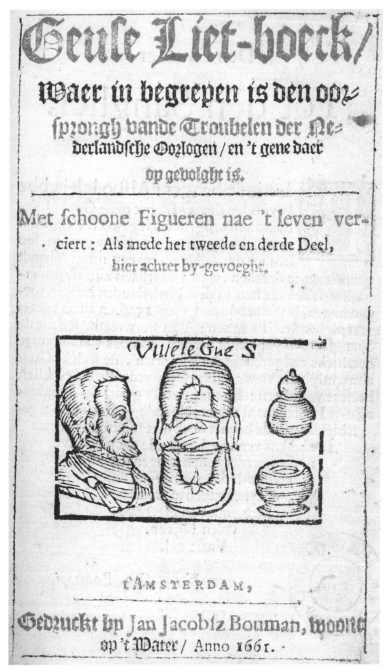

Figure 2.5. Title page of a 1661 reprint of the *Geusenliedboek*, University Library, Vrije Universiteit, Amsterdam. This collection of 'Beggar songs' presented songs and ballads relating to themes and episodes from the Dutch Revolt in chronological order, so creating a basic historical account. First published in the 1570s, the book became immensely popular, and was constantly expanded, reworked, and reprinted into the eighteenth century. The woodcut shows the profile of Hendrik van Brederode, leader of the 'gueux', or 'Beggars', the rebels who in 1566 had joined forces to oppose the Habsburg heresy legislation, and who had adopted the begging bowl, represented on the right, as their symbol.

since the late sixteenth century. Apparently the otherwise so fashion-conscious customers of the biggest city in the Dutch Republic wanted this book to look exactly like its predecessors. There were a few other books for which that was also the case. In 1645, the Leiden pastry cook Reinier Bontius had published a new play on the siege of Leiden in 1574 that became an instant hit.[48] It was performed every year, not just in Leiden but also in Amsterdam, and travelling troupes toured with it throughout the province of Holland. We know of a hundred printed editions before 1800. But as we saw with the *Geusenliedboek*, many publishers opted to keep the look of this book always more or less the same, referring the reader back to an original woodcut that showed the Leiden coat of arms, flanked by two famous Leiden literary characters holding the iconic herring and white bread that the city's liberators had brought to the starving citizens (Figure 2.6).[49] Such printers consciously chose a primitive 'ancient' vernacular look for these books, undoubtedly because this helped convey to the readers that these were 'authentic' books about a specific period in the past, the era of the Revolt that created the Dutch Republic. Chapbooks published in Germany, France, and England, also retained their 'old-fashioned' looks.[50] An awareness of difference between past and present, and a sense of anachronism, did thus not automatically result in a decision to avoid anachronistic imagery.[51]

Playing with anachronism could serve useful political purposes. In 1643 Clara van Assendelft commissioned a picture of the finest hour of her father, Leiden's heroic burgomaster Adriaan Van der Werf (Figure 2.7). When faced with demands by hungry citizens that Leiden surrender itself to the Spanish enemy during the siege of 1574, Van der Werf had allegedly offered them his own body to eat and so impressed the population with this gesture that they decided to fight on. In the painting that Clara commissioned from painter Joris van Schooten, Van der Werf is seated behind a table that may be there to evoke the Christological nature of his offer. His hat and his open collar suggest a seventeenth-century look, and this is certainly also the case for the female figure seated on the other side of the table, who may be modelled on Clara herself. The figure is richly clad, in seventeenth-century fashion. The other figures in this image, however, are clearly dressed in a sixteenth-century manner, so that the woman in the black garment and the soldiers on the right evoke the past rather than the present. They are not prospering; they are suffering: starving and burying the many dead of the siege. The image thus combined, and so also made a connection between, the splendour of the modern figure, representing the prosperity of seventeenth-century Leiden, and the suffering of the century before, heroically linking the past to the present

---

[48] Reynerius Bontius, *Belegering ende het ontset der Stadt Leyden*, ed. A.J.E. Harmsen (Leiden, 1645), accessed 28 April 2016, http://www.let.leidenuniv.nl/Dutch/Ceneton/Bontius/Bontius1645.html.

[49] As in the edition published in 1736 by the heirs of the widow G. de Groot in Amsterdam, Reynerius Bontius *Belegering en ontsetting der stadt Leyden ... Treur-bly-eynde-spel*. They had published an edition with a much more modern frontispiece in 1716. See for the various frontispieces the Short Title Catalogue Netherlands.

[50] See e.g. Lisa Andries, *La Bibliothèque bleue au dix-huitième siècle. Une tradition éditoriale* (Oxford, 1989).

[51] A nice example from seventeenth-century England, for instance, is discussed in Chew, 'Repaired by me'.

BELEGERING en ONTSETTING
DER STADT

LEYDEN,

Geschiet in den Jare 1574. Beginnende
den 27. May, en Eyndigende den 3. October
daer aen volgende.

Seer levendig afgebeelt door

REYNERIUS BONTIUS.

TREUR-BLY-EYNDE-SPEL.

Verciert met schoone Figuren/ en al de Vertooniu-
gen/ soo voo2/ in/ als na het Spel.

PIERO   TROM
                                             PET

t' AMSTERDAM,

By d' Erbe van de Wed: G: de Groot , Boekverkooper op de
Nieuwen-dijk/ het derde Huys van de Arm-steeg/ 1736.

Figure 2.6. Title page of Reynier Bontius, *Belegering en ontsetting der stadt Leyden*, 1736.

Figure 2.7. Joris van Schooten, *The sacrifice of burgomaster Van der Werf*, 1643, Museum De Lakenhal, Leiden.

through the anachronistic figure of Van der Werf and his descendants. Here, the anachronistic use of seventeenth-century clothes for Van der Werf enhanced the contrast between the miserable past, and a prosperous and happy present, the present in which Van der Werf's descendants were bidding for a return to power. The painting was part of a successful campaign by Clara and her husband to recoup political power for the family, which had been in disgrace since 1618.[52]

A similar example of such subtle play on the links between past and present is a 1630 painting by Cornelis de Vos, which portrays members of the Antwerp Snoeck family, as well as a number of other prominent Antwerpers in contemporary dress, while in the process of presenting a bishop with a monstrance and sacred vessels, some of which contain hosts (Figure 2.8). The image would have struck any seventeenth-century Catholic as unusual. The laypeople in the picture are here handling objects that should normally be touched only by priests and others who are ordained to do so. Yet there was one episode in Antwerp's history

---

[52] See on Leiden's memories of the siege and the myth surrounding Van der Werf: Jori Zijlmans, 'Pieter Adriaensz van der Werf. Held van Leiden' in *Heiligen of helden. Opstellen voor Willem Frijhoff*, ed. Joris van Eijnatten, Fred van Lieburg, and Hans de Waardt (Amsterdam, 2007), 130–43; Judith Pollmann, 'Herdenken, herinneren, vergeten. Het beleg en ontzet van Leiden in de Gouden Eeuw', 3 Oktoberlezing (Leiden, 2008), accessed 3 May 2016, https://openaccess.leidenuniv.nl/handle/1887/16331; and Judith Pollmann 'Een "blij-eindend" treurspel. Herinneringen aan het beleg van Leiden, 1574-2011', in *Belaagd en belegerd*, ed. H. van Amersfoort et al. (Amsterdam, 2011), 118–45.

Figure 2.8. Cornelis de Vos, *Antwerp citizens present St Norbert with the monstrance and sacred vessels which they had hidden from Tanchelm*, 1630, Museum voor Schone Kunsten, Antwerp.

in which this had happened, an episode closely related to the history of St Michael's abbey and the Nortbertine order, which one of the Snoeck children had entered. In a recent vernacular book, the abbot of the Antwerp Norbertines had recalled how in the twelfth century many in the city had fallen under the sway of the heretic Tanchelm. At that time, a number of orthodox laypeople had protected sacred liturgical vessels from the clutches of the heretics by hiding them at home. When St Norbert and his disciples arrived in the city, Tanchelm's spell could at last be broken, and subsequently Antwerp's laypeople had presented Norbert with sacred vessels that they had hidden during Tanchelm's regime.[53] It was this scene that was evoked here.

Yet the scene had an interesting twist. While having themselves painted into this medieval tale, the Snoecks cheerfully ignored the abbot's claim that the Antwerpers had felt 'remorse' over their possession of the sacred vessels. Instead they proudly presented themselves as the seventeenth-century equivalent of those same Antwerp laypeople who had salvaged the faith in the days of medieval heresy. By doing so, they were primarily making a point about the present. In the very recent past, between 1579 and 1585, Antwerp had once again been ruled by heretics. For six years during the Revolt of the Netherlands against the Habsburgs, the city had become a Calvinist Republic. A Catholic restoration had commenced only after the city's fall to the armies of the Habsburg commander Alessandro Farnese in 1585.

[53] Annemieke Bartholomeus, 'De iconografie van Cornelis de Vos. De burgers van Antwerpen brengen de monstrans en gewijde vaten terug naar de heilige Norbertus', *Rubensbulletin* 2 (2008): 131–5; Johannes Chrysostomus van der Sterre, *Het leven vanden H. Norbertus, sticht-vader der ordre van Praemonstreyt ende apostel van Antwerpen* (Antwerp, 1623), 202–23.

At the time of the city's surrender it was agreed that the past would be forgotten—an early modern practice to which we will come back in Chapter 6. This collective amnesia, of course, suited the many people in Antwerp who had a rebel or even a Protestant past to live down. Yet to those who could boast about their commitment to the Catholic Church in the days of rebellion such an official act of oblivion was, of course, a bit disappointing. The Snoeck family found an ideal alternative solution. By presenting themselves, in contemporary gear, as the stalwart supporters of the Church in the days of Tanchelm, they circumvented the acts of oblivion and simultaneously asserted their unwavering commitment to the Catholic religion during the more recent heretical past. There was thus certainly nothing innocent or ignorant about the way they appropriated the story. They knew full well the difference between past and present but chose to ignore it for a better purpose.[54]

The extent to which anachronism was a matter of choice and purpose can finally also be demonstrated by a closer look at Jan Lievens's painting *Brinio lifted onto a shield* of 1661, one of a series of paintings that concerns the revolt of the Germanic tribe of the Batavians against Roman overlordship in AD 69–70 (Figure 2.9). The series was commissioned in 1659 to decorate Amsterdam's newly built town hall on Dam square and was meant to support the civic and political ideals of the booming city.[55] In the Dutch Republic, the Batavians were often cited as the ancestors of the Hollanders, and their rebellion was believed to have prefigured the Dutch Revolt against 'Spanish tyranny' in the sixteenth century.[56] Amsterdam poet Joost van den Vondel, who wrote the quatrain that served as a caption to this image, made this very explicit:

> The valiant Brinio is raised onto a shield, a mark of honour among the men of Kennemerland [a coastal area of Holland], who swear an oath of allegiance. Just so did Nassau [rebel leader William of Orange] gain the command, in defiance of the Spanish host, and from the duny sands arose the state's edifice.[57]

No wonder, then, that the Amsterdam city fathers had favoured an image that showed the great Batavian leader Brinio in contemporary garb and surrounded by late sixteenth-century followers. The leader himself wears an antique-looking tunic and sandals, but his cape, plumed hat, and hairstyle mark him as an early modern European. He is surrounded by soldiers who wear a hybrid mix of sixteenth- and seventeenth-century military dress and armour.

In painting this scene Lievens followed a pictorial tradition in which the Batavians were dressed as 'landsknechte', German and Swiss mercenaries. Because this military fashion was believed to be many centuries old, it was considered very suitable for depicting scenes from antiquity.[58] When the Italian engraver Antonio

---

[54] Pollmann, *Catholic identity*, 175–8.

[55] Elmer Kolfin, 'Past imperfect. Political ideals in the unfinished Batavian series for the town hall of Amsterdam', in *Opstand als opdracht. Flinck, Ovens, Lievens, Jordaens, De Groot, Bol, Rembrandt/ The Batavian commissions*, ed. Renske Cohen Tervaert (Amsterdam, 2011), 10–19.

[56] Schöffer, 'The Batavian myth'.

[57] Cited in Kolfin, 'Past imperfect', 17. I have amended the English translation.

[58] Peter van der Coelen, 'De Bataven in de beeldende kunst', in *De Bataven. Verhalen van een verdwenen volk*, ed. L.J.F. Swinkels (Amsterdam and Nijmegen, 2004), 144–87.

Figure 2.9. Batavians in early modern dress. Jan Lievens, *Brinio lifted onto a shield by the Caninefates*, 1661, Koninklijk Paleis op de Dam, Amsterdam.

Figure 2.10. Batavians depicted as *Landsknechte* in Antonio Tempesta after Otto van Veen, *Batavorum cum Romanis bellum / à Corn. Tacito lib. IV & V.: Hist. olim descriptum, figuris nunc aeneis expressum, auctore Othone Vaenio Lugdunobatava* (Antwerp, 1612), Rijksmuseum, Amsterdam.

Tempesta, in close collaboration with Otto van Veen, published a series of Batavian scenes in 1612, this was also the look he chose to represent (Figure 2.10).[59] When painting a similar series for the meeting hall of the Dutch States General in 1614, Otto van Veen himself had toned down the *landsknechte* aspect. His Brinio was much more rustic and had a 'simple peasant' look, which suited an intellectual tradition that had described Batavians as virtuous because of their simplicity. This was, for instance, how they had been described by the famous humanist scholar Desiderius Erasmus (Figure 2.11).[60]

While Tempesta and Van Veen had thus followed an iconographic tradition based on Tacitus's *History*, there was another tradition of depicting Batavians

[59] Antonio Tempesta after Otto van Veen, *Batavorum cum Romanis bellum* (1612); H. Van de Waal *Drie eeuwen vaderlandsche geschied-uitbeelding 1500–1800. Een iconologische studie*, 2 vols (The Hague, 1952), I, 213.

[60] Van de Waal, *Drie eeuwen*, vol. I, 214–15. On this Erasmian tradition see M.E.H.N. Mout, 'Het Bataafse oor'. *De lotgevallen van Erasmus' adagium 'Auris Batava' in de Nederlandse geschiedschrijving*, Mededelingen der Koninklijke Nederlandsche Akademie van Wetenschappen Afdeeling Letterkunde, new series 56 (1994).

Figure 2.11. Batavians represented as simple rustics by Otto van Veen, *Brinio's elevation*, 1600–13, Rijksmuseum, Amsterdam.

that based itself on Tacitus's ethnographic description of the Germanic tribes in his *Germania*. This Germania tradition, dating to the early sixteenth century and revived in the illustrations of Philip Cluverius's antiquarian book *De Germania antiqua* of 1616, emphasized the difference between past and present. In Cluverius's book the Batavians had a tribal look, wearing skins and sporting the distinctive Suebian knots that the Germanic tribes wore in their hair to look taller and more fearsome (Figure 2.12).[61] The different iconographies reflected thus not only different sources, but also different modes in which one might think about the Batavians—whereas the tribal style suggested a significant temporal gap, the *landsknecht* style was suitable for analogical thinking and suggests a synchronic notion of time. Lievens and his Amsterdam patrons were well aware of both iconographies, but they, quite understandably, did not consider the tribal look appropriate for the political message that this painting, in this location, was supposed to send.

---

[61] Van der Waal, *Drie eeuwen*, I, 56, 164–6 shows that the Germanic knot had first been depicted in 1543; Philip Cluverius, *De Germania antiqua* (1616) had recently revived this tradition. See also Van der Coelen, 'De Bataven'.

Figure 2.12. Batavians with a tribal look: Simon Frisius, *Brinio's elevation*, in Philippus Cluverius, *De Germania antiqua libri tres* (Leiden, 1616), Rijksmuseum, Amsterdam.

CONCLUSION

Early modern Europeans thought that one of the main purposes of remembering the past was to teach them something about the present and believed that learning from the past was best done by looking for analogies. This made it both relevant and useful to mix references to things past and things present, and to appreciate and encourage the 'dynamic traffic' between them. To use historical analogies was thus useful less because of what it allowed people to say about the past than because it made it possible to structure and manipulate representations of the present in a way that suited one's own objectives. This use of the past flies straight in the face of what professional historians today believe is of value in their work. They have therefore tended to dismiss it as an antiquated and ignorant practice that rightfully died when modern historical consciousness came into being. Yet that is wishful thinking. The fact of the matter is that it never died, but continues to exist throughout the modern world. Those who argue today that non-modern ways of engaging with the past do retain some value in the modern world have to look no further than the West to see this confirmed. As historian Lewis Namier observed in the 1940s:

> One would expect people to remember the past and to imagine the future. But in fact, when discoursing or writing about history, they imagine it in terms of their own experience, and when trying to gauge the future they cite supposed analogies from the past; till by a double process of repetition, they imagine the past and remember the future.[62]

Even if historians no longer believe that we can learn 'lessons from the past' in an analogical way, it is clear that historical analogies are widely used today for many purposes, and by the very same people who, in other circumstances, may well emphasize the distances and difference between past and present. This chapter has shown that in early modern Europe the case was no different. First, people were both well aware of, and interested in, the existence of change. The widespread use of historical analogies, and the anachronistic thinking that enabled this, was therefore not the result of ignorance or innocence. Rather it was a matter of choice and one, very effective, rhetorical technique for structuring a spin on the present. It could be used to persuade with, to play with, to do politics with, to give status, and to pre-empt criticism. But those who did so knew full well that there were differences as well as similarities between past and present. This continues to be the case today.

Yet, there is a second conclusion to be drawn. Rather than thinking of the history of memory as a linear process in which the rise of new forms of engagement with the past implies the fall of all that came before, it is much more useful to conceive of it as a cumulative process. New ways of engaging with the past have emerged side by side with older ones and coexist, or even interact, with them. The modernity of modern memory does not consist in its replacing older ways of engaging with the past, but in adding to them.

---

[62] L.B. Namier, 'Symmetry and repetition' in L.B. Namier, *Conflicts. Studies in contemporary history* (London, 1942), 69–70 (originally published in *Manchester Guardian*, 1 January 1941), cited in Beiner, *Remembering*, 318.

3

Customizing the Past

In the summer of 2012 a number of property owners in the Dutch village of Kamerik received an unexpected notice that they owed an 11 per cent land charge, or 'thirteenth penny', on land they had bought in the previous decades. The claim came from a charitable foundation whose statutory aim is to maintain the medieval castle of Renswoude; in order to pay for the restoration of the castle, and in anticipation of the impending abolition of thirteenth-penny charges by the Dutch government, the foundation had decided to exercise its customary right to levy this charge, a right that dated back to the Middle Ages and that had somehow survived all law reforms of the last two centuries. Local landowners should perhaps have known that this was a possibility because on an earlier occasion, in 1991, the foundation had already revived the levy and won the legal battle that ensued. On that occasion, the outcome had not been so obvious; lawyers made a case that a customary charge that had fallen out of use could not suddenly be revived, even if it had never formally been abolished. Nevertheless, the courts ruled that the charges had been levied recently enough for these to be considered 'in usage'.[1] Legally, the angry landowners of Kamerik thus did not have much of a leg to stand on. Yet the reason why their predicament made it into the national media and gave rise to questions in Parliament was not only that it emerged in the thick of the silly season. What attracted attention and genuine surprise was that it was possible in the twenty-first-century Netherlands to base a valid legal claim on 'unwritten', fifteenth-century customs.

Although early modern European landowners might also have contested such a charge, no one would have batted an eyelid at its existence. In early modern private law most rights and duties were defined in terms of custom, tradition, and existing usage. Standing the 'test of time' was considered good evidence for the quality and validity of any practice. The past was thus not only a prime source of legal authority, but also a standard for morality and social legitimacy, the status of which was rivalled by the sacred alone. As we have seen in Chapter 2, to say that an idea, law, or tradition was ancient implied that it was better than a 'new' equivalent; in morality, politics, and religion to call something 'new' or an 'innovation' was to render it suspect. Yet while the value of the ancient was undisputed, that is not to say that there was consensus

[1] I.W. Opstelten, *Antwoorden kamervragen over heffing dertiende penning Kamerik* (The Hague, 2012), accessed 2 August 2013, http://www.rijksoverheid.nl/documenten-en-publicaties/kamerstukken/2012/09/22/antwoorden-kamervragen-over-heffing-dertiende-penning-kamerik.html; T. van Es, 'Dertiende penning nieuw leven ingeblazen in Kamerik', *Heemtijdinghen. Orgaan van de Stichts-Hollandse Historische Vereniging* 30 (1994): 12–26.

about the past or about its implications for the present. Quite the opposite; far too much depended on it for it to remain uncontested.[2]

To determine what exactly anyone's customary communal or indeed individual rights were, reference had to be made to past practice, and the existence of such practice had to be confirmed by evidence. As we have seen in Chapter 2, when talking about the past in an analogical manner, early modern people were often not terribly interested or precise about what historical evidence might support their statements about the past. Yet side by side with the analogical approach to the past, there existed a quite different way of handling knowledge about the past, which focused on establishing the authority of evidence. Memory played a key role in this. Evidence could take the shape not only of a written document, signed and sealed by someone whose commitments were considered binding to coming generations. It could also be 'unwritten', by which contemporaries meant that it was not the result of some act of lawgiving, but the result of a living practice, a matter of custom, that was deemed to have existed 'from time immemorial'. Evidence for its legitimacy would have to come from the recollections of local people. Even when such practices were eventually recorded in writing, in a legal sense they remained 'unwritten' because they derived from the 'memory of the people'.[3]

The first aim of this chapter is to show how such custom could be used both to affirm and to challenge authority. Custom has long had a bad press, both among supporters of strong states, who believed it stood in the way of proper state development, and among their critics, who have seen custom essentially as a force for conservatism.[4] Yet we will see that the status of custom as such did not preclude change, as has sometimes been believed. Quite the opposite—it was quite well suited to accommodating it. Although the revolutions of the late eighteenth century pointed to custom as the source of oppression and inequality that had to be destroyed if there ever was to be systemic change, we will see for much of the early modern period that custom was valued by those lower on the social ladder just as much as it was by the elites. Custom was certainly the source of much inequality, but historian Andy Wood has highlighted how it was also the best defence people had against encroachments on it. People of all social ranks were well aware that an appeal to custom was their best bet if they wanted to fend off challenges to existing rights.[5] Even the indigenous peoples of the New World discovered quickly that under Castilian colonial rule, an appeal to local custom was the most efficient way of challenging decisions of settlers or colonial officials.[6]

---

[2] A useful discussion of the status of the past e.g. in Gerald Strauss, *Law, resistance and the state. The opposition to Roman law in Reformation Germany* (Princeton, 1986), esp. 96–135. See on the importance of 'debatability' for custom Arjun Appudarai, 'The past as a scarce resource', *Man*, new series 16 (1981): 201–19.

[3] Fox, *Oral and literate culture*, 262.

[4] Richard Kagan, *Lawsuits and litigants in Castile, 1500–1700* (Chapel Hill NC, 1981), 29; Andy Wood, 'The place of custom in plebeian political culture. England, 1550–1800', *Social History* 22 (1997): 46–60, at 48.

[5] See e.g. Wood, 'The place of custom'.

[6] Jeremy Ravi Mumford, 'Litigation as ethnography in sixteenth-century Peru. Polo de Ondegardo and the Mitimaes', *Hispanic American Historical Review* 88 (2008): 5–40.

Nevertheless, in the course of the early modern period the status of custom changed, and the second aim of this chapter is to explore why it did so. I will argue that three factors played a role in this development. First, princes sought ways of exercising more control over customary law by writing it down, but this codification of custom rendered it less flexible than it had once been. Secondly, the emergence of new ways of testing historical truth claims after 1400 eventually led to more scepticism about the past as a stable source of authority. Finally, and most importantly, as a consequence of European contacts with non-Europeans, there emerged new ideas on the development of human culture, in which the abandoning of custom came to be seen as a hallmark of civility.

CUSTOMS AND PRIVILEGES

One of the most obvious differences between the legal cultures of early modern Europe and those in the modern West is what has been called 'legal pluralism'.[7] Most states were 'composites' of many different polities and jurisdictions, such as duchies and counties that each retained their own legal traditions, and within these, towns and villages, parishes and seigneuries might all have their own local rules for the dispensing of property, the common use of land, the rights to graze and to glean, for charging local dues, taxes and tithes, using roads, waterways, and bridges. Scholars do not agree on how long this had been the case, but at the start of our period, the rights and duties of masters and journeymen, tenants and landlords, husbands and wives, parents and children were largely defined by customary rules.[8] Scholars estimate that in sixteenth-century Western and Central Europe there were about 2,000–3,000 different 'custom areas'; France had 600 of them, the much smaller Low Countries about the same number, Castile about 100.[9]

The German jurist Justin Gobler argued in 1550 that:

> It is a necessary part of a custom that it be properly approved and accepted; and this happens either when a prince or magistrate issues a written declaration that such a custom has been accepted and confirmed, or when such a custom is substantiated from charters, records of litigation, or other public instruments, or from the testimony of a distinguished man of learning.[10]

---

[7] Lauren Benton, *Law and colonial cultures. Legal regimes in world history, 1400–1900* (Cambridge, 2002), 7–12.

[8] A very interesting challenge to the idea that customary law preceded the emergence of written law is in Simon Teuscher, *Lords' rights and peasant stories. Writing and the formation of tradition in the later Middle Ages* (Philadelphia, 2012), first published as Simon Teuscher, *Erzähltes Recht. Lokale Herrschaft, Verschriftlichung und Traditionsbildung im Spätmittelalter* (Frankfurt am Main and New York, 2007). On the basis of evidence from Savoy, Teuscher argues that the notion of custom as something that was transmitted by 'old men' across the ages was in fact a fifteenth-century invention. I am grateful to Peter Hoppenbrouwers for alerting me to this book.

[9] J. Gilissen, *Historische inleiding tot het recht*, vol. 1, *Ontstaan en evolutie van de belangrijkste rechtsstelsels*, ed. F. Gorlé, 3rd rev. edn (Antwerp, 1991), 191–2; William F. Church, *Constitutional thought in sixteenth-century France. A study in the evolution of ideas* (Cambridge MA, 1941), 105–20; Kagan, *Lawsuits*, 22–8.

[10] Justin Gobler, *Der Rechten Spiegel* (Frankfurt am Main, 1550), cited in Strauss, *Law, resistance and the state*, 100–1.

Indeed, between 1400 and 1800 many European rulers took the initiative to have customs 'codified'—written down—with a view not only to try and create some form of cohesion between them, but sometimes also to treat them as 'laws', which the prince could therefore also change. Yet that did not eradicate their importance or their diversity. At the end of the Ancien Régime, France still counted sixty-five general and three hundred local sets of customary law. Different legal notions continued to operate side by side in the British Isles.[11] Codification thus did not put an end to many situations in which customs and privileges could be used as a legal tool; laws coexisted even where they contradicted each other, and rulers might also award people the privilege of being tried under a form of law different from their own.[12] In any case, rights and duties were determined not just by the juris-diction in which people lived; the rights of individuals in the same custom area were not the same: nobles had rights beyond those of non-nobles, citizens had more rights than residents, men than women, free than unfree, while membership of a guild, clerical or student status might also bring with it sets of particular privileges, rights, and duties. Such rights and duties could be overridden, yet there were many judicial ways to resist attempts to do so.[13]

So what was custom? The sixteenth-century Flemish jurist Philip Wielant defined it as:

> unwritten law, that originates in usage and continuous acts of successors and practi-tioners, used publicly without being challenged by the greatest majority of people, for such a long time that it can be considered a custom.[14]

How long it took for a habit to turn into a recognized 'custom' differed from place to place, but the consequences for anyone wanting to assert a customary right were obviously more or less the same. One had to show that the usage had existed publicly and continually 'for a long time' and had not been challenged by 'most' people. Courts tended to interpret 'a long time' as the living memory of the current generation or what these had heard from their ancestors. A recent study on Switzerland has suggested that the emphasis on age and tradition to confer legitimacy may have been a late-medieval innovation, but by the sixteenth century this had become an essential element.[15] Not all customs were deemed acceptable; customs had to be rational, not in conflict with other legal principles, especially 'natural law', and could also be declared invalid because they were considered superstitious, as happened in many places after the Reformation. There were also times when people recalled the dictum of St Augustine: 'The Lord said in the Gospel "I am the truth"'; he did not say 'I am custom'.[16] Yet on balance,

---

[11] René Filhol, 'La Rédaction des coutumes en France', in *La Rédaction des coutumes dans le passé et dans le present. Colloque organisé les 16 et 17 mai 1960 par le Centre d'histoire et d'ethnologie juridiques*, ed. John Gilissen (Brussels, 1962), 63–85, esp. 77; R.A. Houston, 'People, space, and law in late medieval and early modern Britain and Ireland', *Past & Present* 230 (2016), 47–89.

[12] Gilissen, *Historische inleiding*; Kagan, *Lawsuits*, 2.

[13] Kagan, *Lawsuits*, 29; Strauss, *Law, resistance and the state*.

[14] Cited in Gilissen, *Historische inleiding*, 186.   [15] Teuscher, *Lords' rights and peasant stories*.

[16] Augustine of Hippo, *De baptismo libri VII*, introd. and notes by G. Bavaud, trans. Guy Finaert, ed. Y. Congar, Traités anti-donatistes 2 (Bruges, 1964), book 3, ch. 6.

in early modern Europe to say that something was customary, traditional, and ancient was the best way to legitimize it.

There were many different ways to establish what was and what was not customary. Some of these relied primarily on oral testimony. In many German villages, for instance, this was done in a ritual question-and-answer session during community assemblies that were held three times a year. On these occasions peasant jurors gave binding answers, so-called *Weisungen*, to the questions put to them by the lord or his representative; all men in the community were in attendance and could at times challenge the jurors' views. As Gadi Algazi has emphasized, this can be seen as a repressive ritual because one of its main functions was for peasants to publicly accept and reaffirm all the duties and obligations that they had to their lords. Yet there was room for manoeuvre and contestation, too. Algazi himself gives the example of a group of unfree villagers from Klotten, who by custom were permitted to marry the folk from a neighbouring lordship, who were known as the 'people of St Peter', without paying the customary penalty for such a marriage to their overlord, the monastery of Brauweil. When around 1500 they began to claim that this custom also permitted them to marry subjects of the archbishop of Trier because these also had St Peter as their patron, the monks of Brauweil forced them at a *Weisung* to retract this interpretation of the phrase 'man of St Peter' and had the 'original' meaning set down in writing. Nevertheless, a century and a half later the Brauweil peasants in Klotten were actually marrying such people without penalty. As Algazi puts it: 'legal competence was ascribed to peasants by the very same gesture that sought to install lords' archives in their "memory"'. In Klotten they clearly did avail themselves of this possibility.[17]

There is also other evidence that the public rehearsal of local rights was seen as beneficial by subjects. Sixteenth-century subjects of the Count of Katzenellenbogen in the village of Menzingen, for instance, complained that the count had ordered that village freedoms were no longer to be pronounced in open court 'which proves unbearable to us poor people'.[18] In an anonymous German dialogue between two noblemen from 1670, the hot-headed young aristocrat Rodericus complains to his cousin Fredericus that the courts are not

> letting me treat my subjects as I want, but send me one princely order after another. I am supposed to let them stay at their places of birth, I am not to burden them with more tasks and loads than they had in the time of my ancestors.

Outrageously, his subjects had even demanded to see the *Urbarbuch*, the book in which fifty years earlier his father had recorded 'in an orderly manner, what, how much and from what every peasant is to give'. It takes cousin Fredericus many pages to persuade Rodericus that fairness, imperial law, and religion really required him to abide by such customs.[19]

---

[17] Gadi Algazi, 'Lords ask, peasants answer. Making traditions in late medieval German village assemblies', in *Between history and histories. The making of silences and commemorations*, ed. Gerald Sider and Gavin Smith (Toronto, 1997), 199–229, esp. 207.

[18] Peter Blickle, *From the communal reformation to the revolution of the common man*, trans. Beat Kümin (Leiden, 1998), 170.

[19] 'Discurs zweyer vom Adel auss der freyen Reichs-Ritterschafft. Wie man die Unterthane tractiren und recht nützlich gebrauchen solle' (1670), in *Bäuerlicher Widerstand und feudale Herrschaft in*

In England, the rehearsal of custom was not enforced by overlords, but it happened in many places nevertheless. In the Derbyshire Peak district, the 'Barmote' court of the mining communities studied by Andy Wood frequently rehearsed the customs that ruled the life of the free lead miners there until the late eighteenth century. Twenty-four Barmote jurors elected from among the males in this mining community met frequently to resolve disputed issues among themselves, using customary law to do so. Collectively Derbyshire's free miners also regularly invoked custom in the courts of the Duchy of Lancaster in Westminster and the Court of the Exchequer where they battled with lords and investors who sought to encroach on the community's rights with reference to local custom. Wood traced thousands of legal depositions made by miners between the sixteenth and late eighteenth centuries, some of which invoked memories going back a century and a half to support their claims. The transmission of such memories was done with care and not just collectively. Within mining families, fathers made sure to instruct their sons in their customary rights, by walking and pointing out boundaries, for instance.[20] The miners of the Derbyshire Peak were exceptionally well organized, but other English village communities and individuals in them also guarded their customs. Parishes made a collective annual perambulation around the boundaries of the parish to remind themselves and others of the customary bounds of their jurisdiction. When necessary, such communities, too, would submit witness statements made by the 'ancient men' of the village to equity courts, whose task it was to resolve conflicts between customary law of their localities and the common law of the land. Especially when it came to defending themselves from the enclosure of common land and forests, such testimony was crucial.[21]

In France and parts of the Low Countries courts could avail themselves of a special procedure for establishing the truth about customs: when the local court was unsure about a point of custom, it would call around ten local men for a *turbe* (*turba* means gathering in Latin), who would be asked to affirm unanimously whether they agreed that something was or was not customary.[22] In late-medieval cities like the Flemish town of Kortrijk this procedure was to some extent professionalized. When talking about issues of inheritance law and the like, for instance, the court there tended to call a *turbe* that consisted of people with legal experience, often also former magistrates, to tell them whether they were familiar with a custom or not. Yet when there were issues relating to particular crafts, they would bring in guildsmen, while innkeepers were consulted over issues relating to the settlement of collective tabs.[23] On 236 occasions in the century after 1485, so just over twice

---

der frühen Neuzeit, ed. Winfried Schulze (Stuttgart, 1980), 233–47, esp. 234. See on the use of custom in resistance also Strauss, *Law, resistance and the state* and Teuscher, *Lords' rights and peasant stories*.

[20] Andy Wood, *The politics of social conflict. The Peak Country, 1520–1770* (Cambridge and New York, 1999), 127–43. Wood, *The memory of the people*.

[21] E.P. Thompson, *Customs in common* (New York, 1991), 97–100.

[22] Gilissen, *Historische inleiding*; J. Monballyu, ed., *Costumen van de stad en van de kasselrij Kortrijk*, vol. 2, *Turben afgenomen door de Kortrijkse schepenbank, 1485–1581. Costumen van het graafschap Vlaanderen, kwartier Gent XII* (Brussels, 1989).

[23] Monballyu, ed., *Costumen*, xii–xiii, 38.

a year, *turbes* were called in Kortrijk to talk about a wide range of topics. The most frequent subjects of discussion were issues of inheritance and property. A *turbe* might be asked to confirm that the goods of a bastard child should always revert to the family of its mother or that a servant who left before the harvest forfeited part of his wages. The jurors in Kortrijk were also well aware that customs might change. When asked to confirm in May 1553 that husbands of tradeswomen did not formally have to register the activities of their spouse to the magistrates, a *turbe* agreed that such a custom had existed, but that this had lapsed about thirty years earlier.[24] Once custom was codified, *turbes* were considered to be no longer necessary, although in practice they might still be called. In the Netherlands they were eventually banned; in France the *turbes* were replaced with jurists who were asked to draw up *attestations des coutumes*, a sign of the formalization of legal procedures, which may have guaranteed more consistency but which also removed legal practice one more step from the people who had to live with it.

IN DEFENCE OF CUSTOM

Even so, the respect for customary law did not diminish quickly. The best evidence for its widespread acceptance as a legal and moral principle is the frequent appeal to it in rebellions and revolts; throughout the early modern period, rebels rallied to defend customary rights and privileges. Some of these were real enough and could be attested with reference to documents, existing practice, or living memory. Thus, propagandists for the Dutch Revolt in the 1560s and 1570s frequently referred to the 'privileges' that the medieval subjects of the Dukes of Brabant had wrested from their overlords in times of crisis, and especially the so-called 'Joyous Entry' of the Dukes of Brabant, which gave Brabanters the right to depose their lord if he defaulted on his oath to them. This Brabantine tradition was expanded into a right to resist their Habsburg king Philip II of Spain and became the legal foundation for the abjuration of the king in 1581.[25] In England, references to the antiquity of common law underpinned the conviction that England had an 'ancient constitution' which had to be defended from innovations. It was with reference to such arguments that English parliamentarians legitimized their war against King Charles I in the 1640s.[26] Yet much lower down the social ladder, too, protestors referred to the past to support their resistance.[27] Thus the seventeenth- and eighteenth-century subjects from the territories of the city of Basel vehemently resisted new taxes imposed on them by the city with reference to the past, arguing that both customary law and ancient charters, and the oath by which Basel had joined the

---

[24] Monballyu, ed., *Costumen*, 53, 95.

[25] Guido Marnef, 'Resistance and the celebration of privileges in sixteenth-century Brabant', in *Public opinion and changing identities in the early modern Netherlands. Essays in honour of Alastair Duke*, ed. Judith Pollmann and Andrew Spicer (Leiden, 2007), 125–39.

[26] Pocock, *The ancient constitution*.

[27] Wood, 'The place of custom' draws attention to the similarities between the elite uses of the past and those in plebeian culture.

other Swiss cantons, forbade the city from infringing on the existing rights and privileges of the people in the *Landschaft*.²⁸ It is true that resistance often proved unsuccessful. The inhabitants of five villages in Ajoie went to court in 1730 to defend the common rights to their forest against the encroachments of the prince-bishop of Basel. They had a charter from 1517 in which these rights had been set down on paper and which served as their best argument during ten years of petitioning and litigation in a range of courts. In the end, though, the case was not decided in court. Troops were sent to Ajoie to arrest the villagers' representatives, who were eventually executed.²⁹

Yet as long as many ordinary people's sense of justice remained closely tied to what was customary, the past played a central role in the bitter contests over the use of common land in the Holy Roman Empire, England, Scotland, and France. When landlords 'enclosed' fields that had previously been in common use, first with reference to old feudal rights and later in the name of reform, villagers defended such rights with reference to customary law. In Richmond near London, a brewer, a shoemaker, and a stonemason took the king's daughter to court to challenge her blocking of customary rights of way through Richmond Park, and in 1758 actually won their case.³⁰ The womenfolk of the village of Hénin Liétard in Artois assembled on 23 October 1784 to chase away the labourers who had come to dig ditches that would prevent their beasts from gaining access to the common land in the village. The labourers returned with soldiers in tow, but the women were undeterred, refilled the ditches, and made so much noise that 'they were no longer women but one would have believed them to be she-devils'.³¹

Sometimes rebels were convinced that older customs had been obscured. Gadi Algazi argues that what German landlords called 'wild' claims by peasants about the past really referred to *vor zeiten*, literally the time 'before time', that is to say a time before the age of lordship and *Weisungen*.³² In cities, such ideas could also lead to major conflicts. In 1612–14 Frankfurt a group of citizens under the leadership of pastry-cook Vincenz Fettmilch campaigned to see the city's historical charters, so as to establish whether the city council had deprived them of privileges that they believed they had at one time possessed. He and his supporters met with point-blank refusals by the council, but called upon higher powers to help them get access to their rights. Imperial intervention indeed resulted in a compromise, but since access to the charters continued to be denied, Fettmilch and his supporters staged a coup and took over power in the city. Fettmilch's regime was to be short-lived, not only because the emperor disapproved, but also because it presided over a pogrom that led to the loss of lives as well as the plundering of the Frankfurt ghetto and the expulsion of the Jews from the city. After intervention by

---

²⁸ Niklaus Landolt, *Untertanenrevolten und Widerstand auf der Basler Landschaft im 16. und 17. Jahrhundert* (Basel, 1996), 386–94, 575–82.

²⁹ Yves-Marie Bercé, *Révoltes et revolutions dans l'Europe moderne, XVIe–XVIIIe siècles* (Paris, 1980), 13–14.

³⁰ Thompson, *Customs in common*, 97–184, esp. 112–13.

³¹ Yves-Marie Bercé, *Croquants et nu-pieds. Les Soulèvements paysans en France du XVIe au XIXe siècle* (Paris, 1974), 93.

³² Algazi, 'Lords ask, peasants answer'. See also Teuscher, *Lords' rights and peasant stories*.

the emperor, Fettmilch and his supporters were executed, his house was razed to the ground, and a commemorative column placed in front of it to warn off any other potential rebels.[33]

Rebels in the Netherlands sometimes also claimed that they were defending 'the old privileges, liberties and customs' without necessarily knowing exactly which ones they meant.[34] In the Dutch city of Dordrecht, rumours about the existence of a *Houtboek* that contained a list of all existing burgher privileges became so persistent that in 1649 a delegation of angry guildsmen had to be given access to the strongroom in the city hall to search for it—that they found no trace of it did nothing to abate their suspicions. The main proponent of the book's existence (so-called because its flyleaf reputedly encouraged the reader to *hout* or 'hold' all the customs contained in it) was a local lawyer called Johan Walen, who campaigned for years against the way in which Dordrecht's patrician elite ignored the customary rights of the citizens when appointing people to office. He was banned for life for writing pamphlets in which he condemned the 'perjury' of Dordrecht's council and had called on burghers to fight for the restoration of their privileges.[35] Elsewhere, too, rebels agitated to be shown non-existent evidence. In Naples, the followers of rebel leader Masaniello claimed in 1647 that Emperor Charles V had given them a perpetual exemption from taxes a century earlier and demanded to be shown the document that proved it. Mythical exemptions from taxation by rebels are also known from France.[36]

Such rebel calls to see the documents reflect that, as time went on, legal memory was increasingly believed to reside in written records. Some scholars have argued that the growing codification of customary laws and the increased use of written evidence in courts automatically put illiterate people at a legal disadvantage. Yet as Andy Wood and Adam Fox have shown, many communities in England handled this challenge actually quite well. Collectively, they were well able to adjust to a written legal culture.[37] In Germany, villagers realized that a lack of written evidence might also be in their favour. Gerald Strauss cites the serfs of the monastery of Sonnenfeld who complained in 1525:

> We have requested several times that we be shown the letters in which it is recorded
> how our forefathers came to be transferred from the Bishopric of Bamberg to the

---

[33] Christopher E. Friedrichs, 'Politics or pogrom? The Fettmilch uprising in German and Jewish history', *Central European History* 19 (1986): 188–228; Robert Jütte, 'Die Frankfurter Fettmilch-Aufstand und die Judenverfolgung von 1614 in der kommunalen Erinneringskultur', in *Memoria. Wege jüdischen Erinnerns. Festschrift für Michael Brocke zum 65. Geburtstag*, ed. Birgit E. Klein and Christiane E. Müller (Berlin, 2005), 163–76. I am grateful to Prof. Matthias Schnettger of the Johannes Gutenberg Universität in Mainz for pointing me to this article.

[34] Juliaan Woltjer, 'Dutch privileges, real and imaginary', in *Britain and the Netherlands V, Some political mythologies. Papers delivered to the fifth Anglo-Dutch historical conference*, ed. J.S. Bromley and E.H. Kossmann (The Hague, 1975), 19–35.

[35] Willem Frijhoff, 'Johan (van) Waalen', in *Dordts biografisch woordenboek*, ed. Willem Frijhoff et al., accessed 12 August 2013, http://www.regionaalarchiefdordrecht.nl/biografisch-woordenboek; J. Wille, 'Het houten boek. Democratische woelingen te Dordrecht, 1647–1651', *Stemmen des tijds. Maandschrift voor Christendom en cultuur* 1/2 (1912): 1154–79, 1263–84.

[36] Peter Burke, 'The virgin of the Carmine and the Revolt of Masaniello', *Past & Present* 99 (1983): 3–21, esp. 16.

[37] Wood, 'Custom and the social organisation'.

monastery of Sonnenfeld. If such a letter exists, and if it is read to us, we will do and keep all that we owe to the said monastery, in accordance with the charter.[38]

Simon Teuscher, moreover, has suggested that the legal status of oral memory had itself been formulated in tandem with the emergence of written laws and the adoption of Roman law in the late Middle Ages.[39]

Nevertheless, the use of codification had other important consequences. The benefit of a customary law system is that it can both use the past as a benchmark and retain considerable flexibility. The legal fiction behind it was that it was 'unchanging', and this gave it its authority, yet in practice it accommodated change all the time. New practices would take some time to be accepted as customary, but obsolete ones were gradually and conveniently forgotten so that the system did, in practice, move on. That this became much more problematic when customary law was codified, was not because it required literacy, but because codification of custom had the effect of freezing it in time. By the eighteenth century, legislation that had been codified a century earlier could seem obsolete and was fodder for clever lawyers at best, but often no longer a reflection of actual practice.[40] This probably contributed to a loss of credibility, and a growing willingness to consider alternatives.

THE DESTABILIZATION OF TEXTUAL AUTHORITY

Yet it was not the codification of custom alone that made reliance on the authority of the past gradually less self-evident. There was also a change in the status of ancient texts. Side by side with custom, European culture in the later Middle Ages had relied heavily on readings of a small number of ancient texts that were seen as highly authoritative. The most important of these was obviously the Bible, which in the West was read in the so-called 'vulgate' Latin translation made by St Jerome, and the work of the Church Fathers, the early commentators on the Christian tradition. In the twelfth century, Western scholars rediscovered the *Codex Iustinianus*, the sixth-century codification of Roman law, which offered a highly attractive way of thinking of law codes as a system rather than as a set of idiosyncratic rules. At the same time, the jurist Gratian also produced an influential codification of canon law, the law of the Church, which is known as the *Decretum Gratiani*. Yet it was not just Judaeo-Christian texts that were considered authoritative. In accordance with the biblical dictum that Israel should 'spoil the Egyptians', that is, take advantage of gentile achievements when they could, texts by non-Christian Roman and Greek authors retained a great deal of popularity and prestige, even if they were often read in rather fragmented form.[41] From the twelfth century,

---

[38] Cited in Strauss, *Law, resistance and the state*, 107.
[39] Teuscher, *Lords' rights and peasant stories*.
[40] Fox, *Oral and literate culture*, 293; Gilissen, *Historische inleiding*, 200.
[41] As was argued by the church father Origen in a letter to Gregory in the late second century, basing himself on Exodus 3. For the letter, see *The Philocalia of Origen*, ed. J Armitage Robinson

Greek texts like those by the philosopher Aristotle were read in Latin translations of Arabic versions of the texts. But texts in the original Greek were a closed book for almost all people in the West, until Italian scholars made real progress in reading ancient Greek in the fifteenth century.[42]

That there were Italians who wanted to do so was no accident, since it was there that lawyers had taken the lead in the readoption of 'Roman law', the legal principles that had been in use in the Roman empire. The use of this body of law, of course, raised questions about terms and customs in antiquity, and from the early fourteenth century the Italian scholars whom we call 'humanists' started to develop new techniques to read other ancient texts, too, which soon spread to the rest of Europe. Reading ancient texts was not so easy, first, because endless copying by scholars whose own Latin had evolved over the centuries meant that many extant copies of texts were 'corrupt'. Original wordings had to be recovered by comparison of different manuscripts of the same text, by trying to find confirmation of the meaning of words in other texts, and by working out whether wordings fitted the metre of poems, for instance. Yet more was needed: over time, Latin and Greek had changed, and so had the meaning of words. Texts and terms had to be placed in chronological and geographical context to understand what exactly they might be referring to. Authors had to be differentiated from other authors with the same name (it took scholars quite some time, for instance, to discover that there were two classical authors called Pliny), places distinguished, ranks made known, references recognized, concepts understood, for scholars to really be able to read and understand classical texts in the context in which they had been written.

To account for this huge investment in the restoration of texts by the best brains of Europe, we need to realize that they were moved not just by a love of ancient poetry and culture alone. The ability to say authoritative things about authoritative ancient texts potentially gave humanist scholars a great deal of power. One of the best and most famous examples of that power was the ability of scholar Lorenzo Valla to challenge the authenticity of the 'Donation of Constantine', a document that the papacy cited as evidence that the first Christian emperor Constantine had transferred his power to the popes. The idea was that because the papacy had 'reinvested' Constantine with his imperial power, any subsequent emperor also required papal approval. The political importance of this document was thus evident, and it had in fact been challenged before. Yet by an analysis of the linguistic characteristics of the Latin that was being used in the document, as well as exposing inconsistencies in its dates, in 1440 Lorenzo Valla could prove definitively that the document could not possibly have been written during Constantine's reign. It was a forgery probably dating from the eighth century.

(Edinburgh, 1911), ch. XIII, accessed 23 June 2016, http://www.tertullian.org/fathers/origen_philocalia_02_text.htm#C13.

[42] On Renaissance humanism and textual criticism, see e.g. Jill Kraye, ed., *The Cambridge companion to Renaissance humanism* (Cambridge, 1996); Charles Nauert, *Humanism and the culture of Renaissance Europe* (Cambridge, 1995); Anthony Grafton, *New worlds, ancient texts. The power of tradition and the shock of discovery* (Cambridge MA, 1992).

Valla's achievement was mirrored in many greater and smaller philological discoveries that had the power to challenge authority and that raised hopes and expectations. Philologists and theologians expected, for instance, that better editions and translations of original Bible texts might make it possible to establish their true meaning; this was one of the reasons why the German Reformer Martin Luther was so confident that the Bible could be interpreted *sola scriptura* 'by scripture alone'. In the course of the fifteenth and sixteenth centuries, many young men encountered the new philological ideas, at school or at the ever growing number of universities, and while very few humanists made discoveries with such wide-ranging impact as did Valla, many well-educated Europeans put philological skills to legal and political use.

Because many legal cases revolved around the scrutiny of old deeds, charters and registers, as well as custom, lawyers who could distinguish true from false documents had a definite edge over the competition. It was no accident that many of the people who became collectors and experts of the past and its material remains and who were known and respected as 'antiquaries' had originally trained in the law. Through the study of legal evidence, there also emerged systematic attempts to do for the medieval past what earlier generations of humanists had done for Roman antiquity. It was legally and politically useful to have lists of bishops, catalogues of seals, genealogies of important dynasties, information on past boundaries, coinage, place names, epitaphs, coats of arms, feudal landholding, tolls, and privileges. Once the opposition had access to such information, it was essential to do the same if one were to stand a chance in court. Thus it was by consulting his large collection of genealogical evidence that the Utrecht lawyer Arnoud van Buchel, whom we encountered in the Introduction of this book, in 1637 could prove that a medieval charter had to be a forgery; among its signatories were two people who had simply not been alive at the time the document had allegedly been written. The property claims of the charter's owners were therefore invalid.[43] Dull as the collection and production of lists, catalogues, and genealogies may seem to us, in a world without public archives, Wikipedia, or its printed encyclopedic predecessors, they were extremely useful, and to work on them was at the cutting edge of new scholarship.

The importance of philological and antiquarian skills had also become very evident in religious affairs. In response to the Church's claims that it was the guardian of an unbroken tradition of Christian worship, Martin Luther argued that the Catholic Church had gradually been corrupted and was in need of a 'Reformation', that is to say a return to the days of the early Christian church. New histories, like the so-called *Magdeburg centuries*, were used to offer learned support for this idea. In England, Reformers began to collect evidence for an unbroken English tradition of ecclesiastical independence from Rome to justify Henry VIII's break with the papacy. The English crown ordered every parish to buy a copy of the work of John Foxe, who expounded this idea in his *Acts and monuments*.[44]

---

[43] Utrecht University Library, MS 1053 160v–163v, 'Arnoldus Buchelius (Arnoud van Buchel) to Matthaeus Vossius, 10 June 1637'. See also Pollmann, *Religious choice*, 119.

[44] Loades, *John Foxe and the English Reformation*.

Catholic apologists responded by detailed investigations of the evidence for the antiquity and early evidence for the continuity of Catholic practices. This led to huge antiquarian projects like that of Cesare Baronio in Rome, who documented the practices of the early church, taking advantage of the recent exploration of the Roman catacombs for evidence of the early Christian history of the city. Throughout Europe, Catholic antiquarians began to record evidence for local Christian traditions. Philology and antiquarian knowledge was also brought to bear on the evidence for miracles and the lives of the saints, both of which had been derided by Protestant theologians; in the Catholic *Acta sanctorum* project, which was started in the seventeenth century and continues to this day, all written evidence for the lives and miracles of saints was brought together and subjected to critical philological scrutiny. The accusation that the Reformers were preaching novelties thus became a stimulus for the collecting of evidence about early religious practices; in confessional debates, a customized version of the past proved to be a powerful weapon.[45]

Yet as there were more humanists and antiquaries about, the scholarly stakes did, of course, get ever higher—by recovering so much detailed evidence, it also became clear that this collection of 'data' rarely produced what lawyers, theologians, and politicians claimed one might find there, that is, unequivocal clarity about the past. As new editions and the printing press enabled scholars to have a greater range of texts at their disposal, it was also clearer that ancient texts frequently contradicted each other and that they also contained things that conflicted with contemporary experience. New experimental scientists used ancient texts as their point of departure, but often ended up concluding that there were improvements to be made. By the seventeenth century, the confidence in the authority of ancient texts was thus beginning to pale considerably. In the so called 'Battle between the ancients and the moderns', some poets and scholars controversially argued that modern authors might in fact be superior to older ones.[46] Others began to abandon Latin in favour of vernacular languages. Significantly, the seventeenth-century French philosopher René Descartes did so, expressing the belief that 'my ideas may get a more favourable reception from those who use their natural reason than from those who only believe what it says in ancient books'.[47]

Perhaps most importantly, critical research into Bible texts uncovered that these could not be the stable product of one moment of revelation, but had come into existence gradually, and were the work of many authors who had written at different times. New ways of reading scripture had to be pioneered if the Bible was to retain its authority. One of the ways in which this was done was by 'historicizing' the Bible, for instance by arguing that the earlier parts of the Old Testament had

---

[45] Katherine van Liere, Simon Ditchfield, and Howard Louthan, eds, *Sacred history. Uses of the Christian past in the Renaissance world* (Oxford, 2012). See on the intellectual importance of this field also Dmitri Levitin, 'From sacred history to the history of religion. Paganism, Judaism, and Christianity in European historiography from Reformation to Enlightenment', *The Historical Journal* 55 (2012): 1117–60.

[46] Although Dan Edelstein, *The Enlightenment. A genealogy* (Chicago, 2010) emphasizes that respect for the ancients was to remain great among the 'moderns', and many Enlightenment thinkers sought to emulate rather than replace thinkers from the past.

[47] Jean Robert Armogathe, 'Postface', in *La Querelle des anciens et des modernes*, ed. Anne-Marie Lecoq (Paris, 2001), 801–49, the quotation on 833–4.

been created for a people who were still 'primitive', so that it had been necessary to accommodate the text to their 'superstitions', until a moment in the future when these would have become redundant.[48] Considering the widespread identification of early modern Christians with the people of Israel, this was an extraordinary and radical departure from existing tradition, and its great influence is therefore quite remarkable. Yet its rapid acceptance was arguably facilitated by the growing popularity of two other strands of thought in early modern Europe: first, the notion that cultures 'developed' and, secondly, the notion that there was a hierarchy among cultures.

FROM CUSTOM TO CIVILIZATION

In the course of the sixteenth century, Europe saw a revival of scholarly and social interest in what the ancient Greeks used to call 'barbarians': speakers of unintelligible 'barbar', who were supposed to be less 'developed' than the city-dwelling Greeks themselves. Not all assessments of 'barbari' were negative. Classical authors like Thucydides had already surmised that the Greeks themselves had initially lived like their barbaric neighbours, and as we saw in Chapter 2, people in Western and Northern Europe had enthusiastically adopted the idea that they were the descendants of 'simple' but virtuous Germanic tribes. What the renewed interest in barbarians implied, above all, was an interest in the notion of 'cultural development'.[49] A collection of New World images around 1600 included a picture of the Celts, for instance, in order to show 'how the inhabitants of the great Brettanie have been in times past as sauvage as those of Virginia'.[50]

   One of the most outspoken and sophisticated early proponents of such a notion of cultural development was Louis Le Roy, a jurist working as a professor of Greek in Paris, when he published his fascinating *De la vicissitude ou variété des choses en l'univers* (On the vicissitude and variety of things in the universe) in 1575. In this book Le Roy described and compared all known societies 'from the time when civility and human memory began, to the present'.[51] As Werner Gundersheimer has pointed out, Le Roy presented an interesting combination of cyclical and linear notions of change.[52] Partly, he relied on very traditional ideas about the unchanging universe and on the rise and fall of empires, yet he combined these concepts with a linear view of how progress happened by a succession of cyclical fits and starts, which had enabled mankind to move from a rough and primitive brutality in the past to its current and unprecedented levels of sophistication. Of course, there was much to worry about in his own society: not least the tragedy

---

[48] Levitin, 'From sacred history', 1131.

[49] Robert Nisbet, *History of the idea of progress* (London, 1980), 147.

[50] Cited in Malcolm Gaskill, *Between two worlds. How the English became Americans* (Oxford, 2014), xxii.

[51] Louis Le Roy, *De la vicissitude ou variété des choses en l'univers* (1575), ed. Philippe Desan (Paris, 1988). There were five French reprints as well as an Italian and an English edition before the end of the sixteenth century.

[52] Werner L. Gundersheimer, *The life and works of Louis le Roy* (Geneva, 1966).

of religious strife since the Reformation. Like so many of his contemporaries Le Roy affirmed that

> for a long time there has not been more malice in the world, more impiety and disloy-
> alty. Devotion is extinct, simplicity and innocence are mocked, there remains only the
> shadow of justice. All is pell-mell, confounded. Nothing goes as it should.[53]

Similarly, he pointed to the contemporary evils of rising prices and the emergence of syphilis, which Europeans had brought back with them from the New World. But, characteristically, he also noted that it seemed that cures were being discovered for the latter, while the constellation of the stars that had favoured its spread was also about to change. Le Roy not only believed in progress, like the *Nova reperta* we discussed in Chapter 2, he also emphasized the importance of new inventions in making that possible. He argued that the printing press, the compass, and firearms had made the world a better and more sophisticated place—much better, too, than the world of antiquity. Le Roy thus not only appreciated change but also believed it was likely to continue—with fits and starts, and rises and falls in between. Despite all its shortcomings he lived in a society of greater 'excellence' than any seen before:

> We can truly affirm that all of the world is today entirely manifest, all of mankind
> known, all mortals now able to communicate their goods among themselves and help
> each other in their mutual indigence, as inhabitants of one community and world
> commonwealth ('comme habitans en une mesme cite en republique mondaine').[54]

All that now was needed was for humans to try and maintain this level of civility; one way of doing so was through greater piety, but spending generously on arts and letters would also be a great help—obviously, Le Roy liked to see the status of professors of Greek maintained.

This emphasis on the potential for greater excellence famously was to be reiterated in seventeenth-century England, where it came to be connected to the idea that economic change could also create 'improvements' in society. But it was not limited to England alone. The English were building on ideas and examples developed on the continent, especially in Bohemia, Germany, and the Dutch Republic, from which many people had come to England as refugees or to engage in trade, bringing new ideas and networks with them.[55] In the eighteenth century, many parts of Europe were replete with clubs, societies, and publications that promoted economic progress through innovation and civility.[56]

---

[53] Le Roy, *De la vicissitude*, 381.

[54] Le Roy, *De la vicissitude*, 418, cited in the translation of Gundersheimer, 116.

[55] Paul Slack, *From Reformation to improvement. Public welfare in early modern England* (Oxford, 1999). Pointing to the lack of similar terminology in continental Europe, Paul Slack, *The invention of improvement. Information and material progress in seventeenth-century England* (Oxford, 2015), 4–8 believes that this was primarily an English phenomenon, but Hugh Dunthorne, *Britain and the Dutch Revolt* (Cambridge, 2013), 198–233, suggests that the Dutch Republic was a major inspiration for English ideas on improvement, while many of the ideas, ambitions, and contacts of the Hartlib circle derived from and resembled those in Calvinist circles on the European continent. See Mark Greengrass, Michael Leslie, and Timothy Raylor, eds, *Samuel Hartlib and universal reformation. Studies in intellectual communication* (Oxford, 2002).

[56] See e.g. Koen Stapelbroek and Jari Marjanen, eds, *The rise of economic societies in the eighteenth century. Patriotic reform in Europe and North America* (Basingstoke, 2012).

Yet this positive spin on the virtues of civility and progress had a flipside. While congratulating themselves on how far they had come, simultaneously Europeans began to identify people who had yet to go through that process. This happened especially in the context of debates about the rights of the people in the Americas, where some argued that people who did not live in cities or who practised human sacrifice were so 'barbarian' that they qualified as 'natural slaves'.[57] Others saw them, in a more benevolent but patronizing way, as 'children', who had to be guided by the missionaries and the Castilian crown until they came of age. 'The incapacity of their minds, the ferocity of their customs, does not derive from natural inclination or from the effect of climate', concluded the influential Jesuit historian José de Acosta in 1588, 'so much as from a prolonged education and customs like those of beasts.'[58] While Acosta argued that 'Indians' were reasonable beings and thus might be taught the error of their ways, he also wanted to show that 'barbarians' were not all the same. He argued that they should be divided into three types. There were barbarians with laws, cities, and rulers, who also used writing. These included the Chinese and Japanese, to whose rational capacities one might appeal in order to make them change their mind and accept Christianity. Next came peoples who lacked a system of writing but who formed empires, had a social organization, and some form of organized religion, like the Mexica and the Inca; the best way to transform these was to translate their pagan customs into Christian ones.[59] Finally, there were people like the Carib hunter-gatherers who, because they lived like 'brute beasts', would have to give up all their habits but might still learn reason in the end.[60] Such ideas were not confined to learned books, but in Catholic Europe also spread through images, theatrical displays, and processions.[61]

In this way Acosta developed an influential notion of a cultural hierarchy which was to become refined and redefined many times in the centuries to come but was inevitably structured around a number of benchmarks for 'civility' that were predicated on those of Christian Europe. Many of these benchmarks related to religion and social customs, and to what people from around 1670 began to call 'society'.[62] New knowledge about the customs of people in Africa and Asia was making Europeans very aware of the vast range of religious and cultural practices in existence. This could, and occasionally did, lead people to conclude that religion

[57] Anthony Pagden, 'Dispossessing the barbarian. The language of Spanish Thomism and the debate over the property rights of the American Indians', in *The languages of political theory in early-modern Europe*, ed. Anthony Pagden (Cambridge, 1987), 79–98.

[58] José de Acosta, *De procuranda Indorum salute* (Seville, 1588), cited in Anthony Pagden, *The fall of natural man. The American Indian and the origins of comparative ethnology* (Cambridge, 1982), 160.

[59] Pagden, *The fall of natural man*, 162–8.   [60] Pagden, *The fall of natural man*, 162–92.

[61] Johan Verberckmoes, 'The imaginative recreation of overseas cultures in Western European pageants in the sixteenth to seventeenth centuries', in *Forging European identities, 1400–1700*, ed. Herman Roodenburg, Cultural exchange in early modern Europe IV (Cambridge, 2007), 361–80.

[62] Pagden, *The fall of natural man*, 168–71. See on the emerging notion of society Keith M. Baker, 'Enlightenment and the institution of society. Notes for a conceptual history', in *Main trends in cultural history. Ten essays*, ed. Willem Melching and Wyger Velema (Amsterdam and Atlanta, 1994), 95–120. On p. 99 he cites one of the first dictionaries to discuss the term in its new meaning, Antoine Furetière's, *Dictionnaire universel* (1690), characteristically noting that 'Les sauvages vivent avec peu de *société*.'

and culture, too, were a matter of custom, and that many or all truth claims in such matters might be relative. Yet a much more common result was to use alien religious and social customs as benchmarks for the level of 'development' a people had attained; evidence of practices that were deemed 'idolatrous' or 'superstitious' by European authors relegated a people to a lower cultural level.[63] And while Acosta still believed that the attainment of culture might be reversible, in the course of the seventeenth and eighteenth centuries this idea became less common. Instead, by plotting the notion of cultural hierarchy onto a development over time, it became common to think of human cultures as being at different 'stages' of a developmental, linear trajectory that came to be called the 'progress' of 'civilization'. Different peoples went through this process at a different pace, depending on the circumstances in which they were living.[64]

In this hierarchy, race and ethnicity initially played less of a role than they were to do in the eighteenth and nineteenth centuries. There was also plenty of condescension, for instance, for fellow Europeans who were deemed 'backward' because they were 'superstitious' or 'uneducated'. Both the Irish and the Russians were dismissed as 'wilde', and all country dwellers, too, were considered primitive. There were classical precedents for this kind of thought—the Roman historian Tacitus had described how his father-in-law had tamed the original inhabitants of Britain and introduced them to 'the pleasures of tranquil and stable existence'.[65] In England, Thomas Starkey noted in 1530 that men had been 'brought by lytel and lytel from the rude lyfe in feldys and wodys' into the 'cuvyltye' of town life, and worried that gentlemen might revert to such 'rudeness' if they spent too much time in the countryside.[66] Acosta argued that it was no wonder that Indians were unwilling to abandon their customs because

> we may see, even in our own Spain, that men born in villages, if they remain among their own kind, persevere in their inept and gross customs; but if they are taken to schools, or to the court, or to famous cities, they are remarkable for their ingenuity and ability, and are overtaken by no-one.[67]

An important concomitant of the notion of a cultural hierarchy was thus a change in the appreciation of custom and by extension also of customary law. In the eyes of intellectuals the abandoning of certain customs and cultural habits came to be a mark of greater 'civility'. Custom and tradition, which for so long had been the measure of the legitimate, could come to be seen as its opposite, a hindrance to 'development' and progress of 'society'. The existence of common lands, Quaker

---

[63] Lynn Hunt, Margaret C. Jacob, and Wijnand Mijnhardt, *The book that changed Europe. Picart and Bernard's 'Religious ceremonies of the world'* (Cambridge MA, 2010); John Hale, *The civilization of Europe in the Renaissance* (London, 1993), 356–72.

[64] Brett Bowden, *The empires of civilization. The evolution of an imperial idea* (Chicago, 2009), 47–75; Karen O'Brien, *Narratives of Enlightenment. Cosmopolitan history from Voltaire to Gibbon* (Cambridge, 1997), 122–66.

[65] Hale, *The civilization of Europe*, 358.

[66] Hale, *The civilization of Europe*, 362–3. He cites Starkey on 363.

[67] Cited in Pagden, *The fall of natural man*, 161.

Reformer John Bellers argued in England, 'make the poor that are upon them too much like Indians', doing nothing to develop and improve their lands, so that commons were 'a hindrance to Industry' and 'nurseries of idleness'.[68] By the mid-eighteenth century the French *philosophes* Diderot and Alembert noted in their *Encyclopédie* that it was nonsense to stick with the continuing prestige of customs:

> We should not consider the preference of peoples for their ancient customs, but the common good. By making all customs uniform for the future, it would not change what was done in the past; and this would not cause any problem.[69]

Introducing one general custom, they thought, would be no harder than it was to standardize weights and measures.

In the long run this new view of custom had profound consequences for the way in which people began to think about the moral relationship between past and present. Rather than to draw attention to historical parallels, history could become a tale of progress. The so-called 'conjectural historians' of the Enlightenment dismissed the philological nitpicking of earlier generations of philologists and antiquarian historians in order to speculate instead about human nature and historical evolution, using a virtual past with which to reason about the course of human development. Whereas in earlier times, enthusiasm about the present had often been toned down with warnings that rising empires would one day be falling, superlatives about living in a Golden Age came to be heard much more often. But discourses of cultural development could also be used to argue its opposite; in a radical reversal of developmental direction, Rousseau's *Discourse on inequality* (1755) came to define the emergence of polities as inimical to the liberty that man had enjoyed when he was a 'noble savage' and had lived in a time before custom.[70]

There always had been alternatives to custom. Divine law had been invoked to trump custom, for instance, by the English priest John Ball during the peasant revolt of 1381, when he famously asked 'when Adam delved and Eve span, who was then the gentleman?' German peasants who resisted their overlords in 1525 called upon the lessons of the gospel to counter claims that 'custom' demanded that they perform labour services for their lords.[71] The Reformation had wiped out many customary rights and rituals by claiming that these contravened divine law. Since antiquity people had also recognized the existence of 'natural law' as a type of virtual benchmark for the legality of others' legislation, regardless of the polity or religious environment in which people lived. Natural law had subcategories, like the 'law of nations', which was used to define rules of conduct between subjects of different princes. Thus, the Castilian lawyer Francisco de Vitoria, for instance, used the law of nations to argue that the original inhabitants of the New World

---

[68] John Bellers, *John Bellers, 1654–1725. Quaker, economist and social reformer. A memoir*, ed. A. Ruth Fry (London, 1935), cited in Thompson, *Customs in common*, 165.

[69] Edme-François Mallet, 'Coutume', in *Encyclopédie ou dictionnaire raisonné des sciences, des arts et des métiers*, ed. Denis Diderot and Jean Baptiste le Rond d'Alembert (1751–2), accessed 2 June 2016, http://xn--encyclopdie-ibb.eu/index.php/non-classifie/712614146-COUTUME.

[70] R.V. Sampson, *Progress in the age of reason. The seventeenth century to the present day* (London, 1956), 67–94. Earlier examples of the idealization of 'savage' life in Hale, *The civilization of Europe*, 171.

[71] Blickle, *Communal reformation*, 149–77; Strauss, *Law, resistance and the state*, 118–19.

could reasonably be expected to allow Castilians to trade in their territories. Their 'refusal' to do so had given the Castilians the right to use force.[72] In the early seventeenth century, the Dutch jurist Hugo Grotius used natural law to argue that no sovereign anywhere could claim sole control over the seas, so invalidating the 1494 papal bull that had divided the world into two zones of influence between the Spanish and the Portuguese by drawing an imaginary line through the Atlantic Ocean.[73] Yet while such natural law benchmarks could be used universally to declare some things legitimate or illegitimate, natural law was also meant to be unchanging. Any assertion that a law or a custom or a religion was 'natural' might be met by much evidence that human practice had, in fact, been different and continued to be so.

This stalemate was broken by the introduction of the notion of cultural development. This turned law, custom, and religion into something that might be natural in essence, but that could change according to context and thus be something that could be left behind, and perhaps *had* to be left behind if 'societies' were ever to make any 'progress'. This, at least, was the conclusion, first of English entrepreneurs and then of Enlightenment philosophers. It was French revolutionaries who were to make an attempt to put it into practice, by famously identifying privilege and custom as the greatest enemies to social change and symbolically starting history from scratch by introducing a new calendar by which to measure post-Revolutionary time.[74] Their experiment was not to last for very long. By the early nineteenth century the past was back with a vengeance, not now, however, as a source of custom, but as evidence of a historical 'process'. In the meantime, however, the legal weight and prestige of custom had been seriously dented and seemed on its way to extinction.

CONCLUSION

One of the most common and important forms of memory in early modern Europe related to the knowledge and use of what was 'customary'. It is no accident that in European history, the term 'custom' is used to describe both cultural, local usages, and usages that have acquired legal power. The two were tied very closely together. Both the legal and the moral status of custom derived from its being ancient and its being common knowledge; in early modern Europe this made it hard to contest a well-attested customary right or due. As such, custom was not only used as an elite tool to keep the poor in place, it was simultaneously the best strategy poor people had to defend themselves against unwanted changes. The guarding of custom required the existence of communal memory practices, which could be oral but were increasingly also attested in writing.

[72] Pagden, 'Dispossessing the barbarian'.
[73] W.E. Butler, 'Grotius and the law of the sea', in *Hugo Grotius and international relations*, ed. Adam Roberts, Benedict Kingsbury, and Hedley Bull (Oxford, 1990), 209–20.
[74] Mona Ozouf, 'Le Calendrier', in *Dictionnaire critique de la Révolution française*, ed. François Furet and Mona Ozouf (Paris, 1988), 482–91.

The growing use of writing was not, as such, a threat to the customary rights of communities in which few people could read or write themselves; what was more problematic were codifications of custom that meant that practices did not continue to evolve as they had done before. This may be one reason why custom began to lose some of its prestige. Another is the appearance of critical intellectual tools that, while initially devised to establish and make better-attested claims about past practices, ultimately exposed that even 'common' knowledge about the past was easy to contest.

Simultaneously, the contact with unfamiliar peoples who maintained customs that were very different and the desire to find arguments for the superiority of European customs led to the emergence of ideas about historical and cultural progress. Europeans were willing to admit that the customs of their ancestors had at one time been as peculiar as those of non-Europeans, but now stressed that they themselves had acquired civilization by the *abandoning* of customs. In the long run this enabled people to start imagining a world in which customs carried less prestige and might give way to 'rational' systems of social organization in which the special rights and privileges associated with custom no longer existed. If, in the long term, this is what enabled the end of the 'society of orders', in the short term it was not always good news for those at the bottom of the social ladder. For poor communities, custom also meant protection from arbitrary changes that they did not perceive to be in their interest. That social reformers in the nineteenth and twentieth centuries, therefore, often had to do battle with custom before they could get people to accept changes was therefore less a sign of 'backwardness' than of sound common sense among people whose social memory told them that custom kept them safe.

4

Imagining Communities

In 1625 a German mercenary who had fought in Italy travelled across Switzerland on his way to the battlefields of the Holy Roman Empire, where there was renewed action to be expected. Peter Hagendorf had enjoyed being in Italy, even though his paymasters' money had run out and he was now begging his way home. Having lost a comrade in the Gotthard Pass, he descended towards Altdorf, where he took a boat across Lake Vierwaltstätter, which took him back into German-speaking territory. Begging there was so good that he was able to buy himself a pair of shoes, but that was not all that was memorable about this journey. On his way across the lake, he noted in his journal, he had seen 'the chapel where Wilhelm Tell, to whom the Swiss owe their liberty, had jumped [ship]'.[1]

When Peter Hagendorf recorded this entry, the history of William Tell was about 150 years old. It had probably come into being in the 1470s during the so-called Burgundian wars, when some of the Swiss cantons had united to fight the might of the Dukes of Burgundy. In support of the Swiss cause, it appears, some writers near Lucerne invented a prehistory for the union between the Swiss regions and dated it to the early fourteenth century, when a local hero by name of Wilhelm Tell had allegedly refused to defer to a ducal 'bailiff'. First, this tyrant punished Tell by ordering him to place an apple on the head of his son and shoot it off. Having famously achieved this remarkable feat, Tell once again offended the bailiff, and he was arrested. While he was being transported by boat to prison, however, a storm forced his guards to loosen his bonds, and he took the opportunity to jump ship and proceeded to ambush the evil bailiff and kill him. After this tale had been printed in the early sixteenth century and had been popularized further in the 1570s, it became associated with a chapel near the spot where Tell was said to have jumped; it was this chapel that the boatmen or fellow-passengers must have pointed out to our soldier as he crossed the lake.[2]

To students of modern memory, one of the most significant differences between modern and early modern periods is the energy that both nation states and aspiring nations since the age of revolutions have devoted to the invention, circulation, and

[1] [Peter Hagendorf], *Ein Söldnerleben im Dreissigjährigen Krieg. Eine Quelle zur Sozialgeschichte*, ed. Jan Peters (Berlin, 1993), 41. The soldier was later identified as Peter Hagendorf.

[2] Jean-François Bergier, *Guillaume Tell. Légende et réalité dans les Alpes au Moyen Age* (Paris, 1984); Marc H. Lerner, 'Cultural memories of a Swiss revolt. The prism of the William Tell legend', in *Rhythms of revolt. European traditions and memories of social conflict in oral culture*, ed. Éva Guillorel, David Hopkin, and Will Pooley (Abingdon, forthcoming). I am grateful to Mark Lerner for sharing his manuscript with me in advance of publication.

manipulation of 'national' memories.[3] By 1900 no European nation state was deemed complete without national archives, historical museums, days of com-memoration, monuments, centenaries, school books, and history paintings. Operas, plays, songs, poems, novels, and children's books were used to encourage citizens to identify with figures from their national past. (Pseudo-)historical figures like William Tell, the English seafarer Sir Francis Drake, peasant visionary Jeanne d'Arc, or the singing shoemaker Hans Sachs from Nuremberg were presented as embodiments of national qualities. Similar practices were replicated in the new nation states that were forged in the twentieth century. As the new media of film, radio, and television arrived, it became ever easier to present such 'national' memories to large audiences. National histories have proven to be a powerful instrument for inclusion and exclusion, for identifying who is part of 'us' and who belongs to 'them'. People with the same nationality have been encouraged to think of themselves as the joint heirs of one 'national' past, usually the past of the dominant constituents in the nation state of the present. Those who wanted to free themselves of the rule of colonial powers have often done so under the banner of 'national' sovereignty—legitimizing their bid for independence with reference to a shared past as well as a shared language, ethnicity, or religion.

Since the 1980s many scholars have argued that such forms of national con-sciousness should not be seen as the organically grown outcome of centuries of shared traditions, political affinity, or linguistic convergence, as used to be believed, but should be considered as 'invented traditions', 'cultural artefacts', forged by and for 'imagined communities'.[4] The tale of William Tell is an excellent example of how such an invented tradition, first imagined to give prestige to a political union in a specific context, was spread and popularized to become a national tale of origin. Not only did our German soldier seem to know what 'Swiss liberty' signified, but Tell's renown as its founder was apparently great enough for it to be passed on by the local boatmen. Yet in the view of many students of national consciousness, the seventeenth century is too early to speak of 'national' memory cultures. One influ-ential school of thought argues that the invention of national consciousness, and certainly the ideological expression of it that we call 'nationalism', required other forces of modernization, like secularization and the emergence of new notions of time and historical consciousness, the rise of print capitalism and mass media, and the growth of bureaucracies and state power.[5]

Many medievalists and early modernists, on the other hand, have argued that even if 'nationalism' was a post-1800 phenomenon, a form of 'national consciousness' had emerged in many European regions much earlier and for reasons other than those that most theorists of nationalism have alleged. Colette Beaune related the spread of national imagery in France to the Hundred Years War between the kings

---

[3] E.g. Gillis, 'Memory and identity', 11–17.

[4] Gellner, *Nations and nationalism*; Anderson, *Imagined communities*; Hobsbawm and Ranger, *The invention of tradition*. Excellent summaries of the debates since in Smith, *Nationalism*, and Anthony D. Smith, *Nationalism and modernism* (New York, 1998).

[5] Gillis, 'Memory and identity', 6–7.

of France and England.[6] Adrian Hastings associates it with the rise of written vernaculars and especially the spread of Bible translations in Protestant Europe. Alain Tallon has shown how it was mobilized during the French Wars of Religion and propped up by memories of sacred kingship in medieval France, while Colin Kidd, Philip Schwyzer and Krishan Kumar have shown how English, Welsh, and Scottish identities were defined, frequently through theological as well as ethnic and literary lineages that stretched deep into the past of the British Isles.[7] Howard Louthan has shown how, after 1620, a national, Bohemian past was reinvented to suit the Catholic restoration agenda of the Habsburg rulers.[8] In the German context, Caspar Hirschi has highlighted how both the church councils of the late Middle Ages and the disdain of Italian humanists for the 'barbarians' elsewhere turned issues of nationhood into a matter of cultural and political honour for their Northern neighbours. In these readings, nationhood was thus a matter of memory politics and imagined communities right from the start.[9]

So far, modernists have not been particularly impressed by these arguments, not least because they believe that any national consciousness before 1800 must have been the province of small elites, who neither wanted nor had to worry about engaging subjects in a national project. In any case, they find it hard to imagine how this could have been achieved before the days of cheap print and mass literacy.[10] In recent decades, however, much has changed in our understanding of early modern media. Rather than postulating a division between the culture of the literate and the oral cultures of the illiterate peasant majorities of early modern Europe, scholars have discovered the intensive, dynamic traffic between the oral media of speech and song and the world of the written text. They have looked at the interplay between images and texts, and script and print, and have highlighted how both material objects and features of the early modern landscape could be used as mnemonic markers.[11] Our soldier's observation seems to confirm that we should not underestimate the reach of early modern media; the tale of William Tell may have

---

[6] See e.g. Colette Beaune, *Naissance de la nation France* (Paris, 1985).

[7] Adrian Hastings, *The construction of nationhood. Ethnicity, religion, and nationalism* (Cambridge, 1996). For a summary of the debate on English national history, see Krishan Kumar, *The making of English national identity* (Cambridge MA, 2003), and for a balanced discussion of the broader issues at stake see Hirschi, *The origins of nationalism*, and Peter Hoppenbrouwers, 'The dynamics of national identity in the later Middle Ages', in *Networks, regions and nations. Shaping identities in the Low Countries, 1300–1650*, ed. Robert Stein and Judith Pollmann (Leiden, 2010), 19–41. Alain Tallon, *Conscience nationale et sentiment religieux en France au XVIe siècle* (Paris, 2002); Colin Kidd, *British identities before nationalism. Ethnicity and nationhood in the Atlantic world* (Cambridge, 1999); Philip Schwyzer, *Literature, nationalism and memory in early modern England and Wales* (Cambridge, 2004). See also Alain Tallon, ed., *Le Sentiment national dans l'Europe méridionale aux XVIe et XVIIe siècles (France, Espagne, Italie)* (Madrid, 2007).

[8] Howard Louthan, *Converting Bohemia. Force and persuasion in the Catholic Reformation* (Cambridge, 2009).

[9] Hirschi, *The origins of nationalism*, and Caspar Hirschi, *Wettkampf der Nationen. Konstruktionen einer deutschen Ehrgemeinschaft an der Wende vom Mittelalter zur Neuzeit* (Göttingen, 2005).

[10] See e.g. Steven Grosby, Joep Leerssen, and Caspar Hirschi, 'Continuities and shifting paradigms. A debate on Caspar Hirschi's *The origins of nationalism*', *Studies on National Movements* 2 (2014): 1–48.

[11] See e.g. Beaune, *Naissance de la nation*, 346–9; Fox, 'Remembering the past'; Adam Fox and Daniel Woolf, eds, *The spoken word. Oral culture in Britain, 1500–1850* (Manchester, 2002); Walsham, *Reformation of the landscape*.

spread first through print, and we are fortunate that Peter Hagendorf was literate enough to keep a journal, yet the tale probably actually reached him through oral transmission—there existed many songs commemorating Tell, for instance—and was supported with reference to a feature in the landscape. One of the aims of this chapter is to show that once we take other media into account and realize that early modern memory was a multimedia affair, we can understand how memory cultures could reach many more people than the book-buying elites alone.

Yet this immediately raises the issue of scale and relevance. Even if we want to accept that early modern media also reached below the ranks of the elite, why should we assume that early modern people saw any purpose in imagining communities, national or otherwise? Was the nation not far too remote a reality for people to feel any connection to it or to its memories? The local community seems a more likely and obvious candidate for identification processes in the pre-modern world, but some scholars have argued that an interest in local memory is an even more recent phenomenon than national memory. In this chapter we will see that, precisely because local memory practices were very vibrant, they were an important vehicle also for the proliferation of national memory practices. Local memories were used both to distinguish that community from other communities and the world at large and to forge virtual relationships to it. They could also be used to assert one's importance to the larger world of region, state, kingdom, and nation, and conversely, rulers might forge a relationship with a community by becoming a stakeholder in a local memory culture. In this way, local memories could play a key role in mediating the nation.

SACRED MEMORIES AND BLESSED COMMUNITIES

Local memory cultures in the pre-modern period were often closely bound to religion. Of course, Europeans knew that Christ had died not just for the people in their own town or village. Moreover, Latin Christians shared with each other, and to some extent also with their Orthodox co-religionists in Eastern Europe, not only their faith, but also their liturgical calendar, their feast days, and many of their memories. Still, for all its transcendence and universality, sacred power was neverthe-less also believed to manifest itself in some communities more, or at least differently, than in others. The Virgin Mary was available as intercessor to all, yet there were specific emanations of the Virgin—'black madonnas', virgins 'of the rock', 'of the garden' for instance, that were known to be particularly efficacious when invoked by people of a particular community, or at particular localities. Saints were also known to have special relationships with specific communities, because they had historical links with them, because the people there showed exceptional devotion or trust in him or her, or because their relics, their bones, or other objects associated with them were kept and revered in this or that locality.

Most local memory cultures in the Middle Ages originated in the desire to remind both locals and outsiders of these special relationships and to commemorate the instances in which these had manifested themselves. As a consequence, public commemorations were part and parcel of European urban culture of the later Middle Ages; sometimes in conjunction with the feast day of a saint, cities held annual processions to commemorate and celebrate the role of saints or the Virgin in their liberation from epidemics, the end of sieges, the signing of peace agreements, and so on, thus both keeping memories of the events themselves alive and celebrating their special relationship with the sacred. Such processions were accompanied by sermons, sometimes preached in the open air, which would recall the events of the past and remind audiences of the significance of the occasion. In such 'general' processions, not only the city's clergy and elites usually participated, but also all the corporate bodies in the cities, like militia companies, religious confraternities, and craft guilds. Streets had to be swept and decorated when a procession was about to pass. In this way, processions not only reflected the hierarchy in the city, and also the divine order, but also demanded the participation of a large part of the population.

Many of these ceremonies were associated with 'patron saints' of cities, their special protectors and intercessors. A city was especially lucky if it could boast having had a saint in its midst. Thus the city of Maastricht prided itself on the decision of the fourth-century saint Servatius to make his domicile in godly Maastricht after the Huns had destroyed his original seat of Tongeren, allegedly because the sinful population of this town had forfeited divine protection. The tale of Servatius's transfer was told and retold in the later Middle Ages with many additional details, both in Latin and in the vernacular, and was used to bolster a variety of political objectives. The saint was depicted on medals and pilgrimage insignia, and became the subject of early woodcuts. From the eleventh century, the Maastrichters began to associate St Servatius with an ancient key that was kept in the cathedral's treasury, an object actually made around the year 800. The key was believed to have been a gift from St Peter to St Servatius, and was credited with special virtues: when dipped into water it acquired healing powers, and could also be used to exterminate the mice that overran the fields. Every day, at a fixed hour, the key was put on display in the cathedral, and it was also used to bless believers on feast days. In this way the rituals around the key became an important medium for the transmission of memories of the saint, as well as those of the city's old rivalry with Tongeren and the bishopric of Liège.[12]

Cities that could not boast a native saint had to make do with relics and tales of a special relationship with patrons whose intercession had been particularly effective, usually on more than one occasion. Thus a whole series of late-medieval Flemish cities sent an annual procession to an image of the Virgin Mary in Tournai to commemorate her intercession during a terrible epidemic of ergotism, or 'St Anthony's fire', at the end of the eleventh century.[13] On the eve of Candlemas, the feast of the purification of the Virgin, the Venetian Republic every year celebrated the Festival

---

[12] A.M. Koldeweij, *Der gude Sente Servas* (Assen and Maastricht, 1985).

[13] Robert Stein, 'An urban network in the medieval Low Countries. A cultural approach', in *Networks, regions and nations. Shaping identities in the Low Countries, 1300–1650*, ed. Robert Stein and Judith Pollmann (Leiden and Boston, 2010), 43–71, at 48–52.

of the Twelve Maries to commemorate the defeat of a group of pirates, who, in the tenth century, had raided San Marco to steal the dowries that had been presented to twelve poor virgins and had kidnapped the girls themselves.[14] In the Burgundian city of Dijon, between 1513 and 1640, the citizens held an annual procession for the Virgin, whose intercession had brought a besieging Swiss army to the negotiating table in 1513. The episode was celebrated in an enormous tapestry; the place where the Swiss had camped is still known as the 'fontaine' of the Swiss.[15]

Miracles conferred special and lasting prestige on localities. For centuries, the people of Brussels revered a number of sacred hosts that had allegedly started to bleed after they had been 'stolen by Jews' in 1370. A repentant convert to Judaism handed in the hosts to the parish priest of the Church of Our Lady of the Chapel; six Jews were executed for this alleged crime on the orders of the court of the Duke of Brabant. Possession of the hosts immediately became a bone of contention between the parishioners of the Chapel church and the chapter of the much more important Church of St Gudula in Brussels, but once the latter prevailed, it made the hosts the focus of an annual procession and attempted to obtain indulgences, that is to say a reduction of time to be spent in purgatory, for anyone who prayed in the chapel where they were kept. When a rival focus for the devotion emerged in a chapel erected on the location of the former synagogue, the chapter of St Gudula again saw off the competition and made sure that the rival chapel, unlike their own, was not open to the public.[16]

In the course of the fifteenth century, and certainly partly to support the significance of the relics, the story of the stolen hosts was expanded with many additional details. In new versions of the story the Jews were given proper names and associated with particular places, so 'historicizing' the story—a phenomenon on which we will say more in Chapter 5. Even though legal records show that it was quite different people who had originally been executed, two men called Jonathas from Edingen and Jan from Leuven were now named as the main culprits. It was alleged that the hosts had miraculously started to bleed after the thieves pierced them with knives on Good Friday. Scared by this sign of Christian power, the Jews were said to have ordered the convert 'Katharina' to take the hosts to Cologne; instead, she was so impressed by the miracle that she took them to the parish priest of Brussels's chapel church. But new miracles also came to be associated with the miraculous hosts; not least, they helped to see off a major epidemic. Texts in Latin and Dutch, as well as songs, did much to spread the tale further, and throughout the sixteenth and seventeenth centuries it became a subject for plays and other performances by so-called chambers of rhetoric, literary societies for middle-class males. The annual procession, in the meantime, became ever more elaborate.

[14] Edward Muir, *Civic ritual in Renaissance Venice* (Princeton, 1981), 133–45.

[15] Catherine Chédeau, 'Le Siège des Suisses à Dijon en 1513', in *Prendre une ville au XVIe siècle. Histoire, arts, lettres*, ed. Gabriel Audisio (Aix en Provence, 2004), 17–32. See also Benedict, 'Divided memories?', 391.

[16] This and the following paragraphs are based on Luc Dequeker, *Het Sacrament van Mirakel. Jodenhaat in de Middeleeuwen* (Leuven, 2000); see also Van der Steen, *Memory wars*, 85–6, 121–2, 268–70, 295.

The growing popularity of the legend of the bleeding hosts or 'sacrament of miracle' owed much to the appearance of new stakeholders. When Philip the Good, Duke of Burgundy, succeeded to the independent duchy of Brabant in 1430, it was crucial for him to secure his control over Brussels, the main town of the duchy. One of his ways of doing so was to show his devotion to what was now the city's main relic, the Sacrament of Miracle. He dedicated his son Charles to the Sacrament, commissioned a window for a brand new chapel dedicated to the miracle that was being erected in St Gudula church, and arranged for a meeting of the noble Order of the Golden Fleece in the church in 1435, so bringing the cream of the Burgundian elite together to share in the sacred power of the hosts.

The attractions of the devotion did not end here; the ducal devotion to this Eucharistic miracle was also a good way of ingratiating the dynasty with the papacy, which was at that time fighting off challenges to the doctrine of 'transubstantiation' by the heretical followers of John Wyclif in England and Jan Hus in Bohemia. That hosts could bleed was seen as evidence that during the ritual of the mass they were truly transformed into the body of Christ, a process known as their 'transubstantiation'. When Protestant challenges to this doctrine re-emerged in the sixteenth century, the Dukes of Burgundy and their successors of the House of Habsburg renewed their support for the devotion, also by suggesting that its Protestant critics were no better than Jews. As their main seat of government in the Netherlands, Brussels was a good place to assert this point of view, and new stained-glass windows portraying members of their dynasty in the enlarged Sacrament chapel in the sixteenth century expressed this commitment.

During the Revolt of the Netherlands against the Habsburgs, a Calvinist regime in Brussels briefly interrupted the devotion, which the Reformed rebels condemned and ridiculed in 1581, but this made it all the more suitable a focus for public memory once Habsburg power was restored in 1585. Not only was it now used as evidence of the errors of the Protestant enemy, a new version of the legend from the late sixteenth century also declared that the Duke of Brabant had, in 1370, decided to banish the Jews forever from his territories. This precedent was invoked throughout the seventeenth century by those who wanted to prevent Jews from once more settling in the duchy.

By now, the Sacrament of Miracle, the city of Brussels, and the House of Habsburg had become inseparable. Brussels commemorated that fact over and over again in new windows, a set of twenty paintings and huge tapestries for St Gudula, as well as public displays during annual processions and the 'jubilees' of the Miracle in 1620, 1670, and 1720. Displays during the centenary of the restoration of the dynasty and Catholicism in 1685, and many printed texts, constantly reminded the people in Brussels, Brabant, and the Habsburg Netherlands that the Habsburgs protected them against unbelievers. When the Sacrament of Miracle took on a similar sort of role as a 'national' symbol of the new state of Belgium in the nineteenth century, this tradition could thus simply assume the Habsburg mantle. Yet as the devotion gained a dynastic and even national significance, it did not lose its local importance. Throughout the early modern and modern age, the Sacrament of Miracle remained a source of Brussels and Brabantine as much as of dynastic pride; the cult ended only in the 1960s.[17]

If in Brussels it was princes who sought to deploy local memories for their own gain, in other instances it was towns that deployed local memories to associate themselves with their rulers. Hilary Bernstein has shown how the magistrate of the French city of Poitiers exerted itself to promote the memory of the 'Miracle of the Keys', with which the Virgin Mary herself had prevented an instance of treason. At Easter 1200 a man from Poitiers, who had been bribed to hand the keys of the city to the English enemy, broke into the mayor's office but did not find the keys in their usual place. When he went to the English camp to bring the bad news, everyone there was suddenly faced with a vision of a great queen, who was accompanied by a bishop and many armed men. The vision scared the English so badly that they began to fight each other, in the process making enough noise to wake the population of Poitiers, who raised a hue and cry in the city. The mayor went to look for the city keys, and having discovered that these were missing, instituted a search that ended at the Virgin's Altar at the cathedral; it was found that she had taken the keys into safe keeping. So, at any rate ran the version of the story that the town council had recorded in Poitiers's statute book in 1463.[18]

There was more to this story than veneration for the Virgin Mary or even anti-Englishness. Bernstein argues that it was part of a conscious campaign by Poitiers, which had received its original city rights from English overlords, to try and rewrite its history into one of loyalty to the kings of France. When recording its privileges in the mid-fifteenth century, the city council ignored the fact that both its walls and its rights to dispense justice were actually held by virtue of grants from their previous English rulers, but instead commemorated their long-standing tradition of mutual love for the kings of France. At the time the council had the story recorded, in 1463, this was especially relevant since it was hoping that Poitiers might become a seat of *parlement*, a royal law court, instead of their southern neighbour Bordeaux, which had been implicated in a revolt. To help the king make up his mind about this issue, the council of Poitiers not only emphasized its own loyalty, but also helpfully reminded him of Bordeaux's long track record as a supporter of English might and as an enemy of the kings of France. Although they never got their *parlement*, Bernstein shows that Poitiers's campaign to rewrite its own history was so effective that the kings of France, in the course of the sixteenth century, began to integrate the city's long-standing tradition of loyalty into their own rhetoric when communicating with the city. This, in turn, gave Poitiers a sense of entitlement, which it exploited in its relations with the kings of France, whom they warned not to 'fail' their loyal city of Poitiers during the Wars of Religion in the sixteenth century.

---

[17] Luc Duerloo, 'Pietas albertina. Dynastieke vroomheid en herbouw van het vorstelijk gezag', *Bijdragen en Mededelingen Betreffende de Geschiedenis der Nederlanden-Low Countries Historical Review* 112 (1997): 1–18; Pollmann, *Catholic identity*, 159–75. Very similar strategies were deployed by the Austrian Habsburgs, on which see Louthan, *Converting Bohemia*.

[18] Hilary J. Bernstein, *Between crown and community. Politics and civic culture in sixteenth-century Poitiers* (Ithaca NY, 2004), 164–85.

In Poitiers the magistrates were not the only proponents of the story of the miracle; it also suited the cathedral chapter, where the keys had been found and which also owned the bones of St Hilaire. New images of the Virgin with her keys and St Hilaire were commissioned for the church portal, and from the early fifteenth century an annual procession was held on Easter Monday to commemorate the miracle. As religious tensions rose in the course of the sixteenth century, the tale gained new significance as the symbol of the city's long-standing relationship with the Virgin and its loyalty to the Catholic Church. Inevitably it became the focus of Protestant aggression. When attacking Poitiers in 1562, Reformed troops searched for the hidden image of the Virgin of the Keys, paraded it through the city, and burned it in public. After the 'miraculous' lifting of a Protestant siege in 1569, the city's Catholics retaliated by instituting another commemorative procession modelled on that for the Key Miracle on Easter Monday.[19] In the course of two centuries, memories of the Miracle of the Keys had thus become deeply politicized and had proven highly relevant for a range of political purposes; they were used at various points to define and redefine the relationship of the city to its overlords, its neighbours, and the Church. The tale had been spread through a variety of media, of which the annual procession and accompanying sermons, as well as the church imagery, must have done most to keep it alive among the population at large.

The tales of the Sacrament of Miracle and the Miracle of the Keys give us a good sense of how the local religious past could be used to position a city in the larger world of the dynasty, and even the nation, without a loss of local dignity or identity. In doing so, the cities of Brussels and Poitiers, of course, deployed typically Catholic mnemonic tools: relics and processions, saints and miracles. Other parties could also benefit by association with such memory practices. Rachel Greenblatt has shown how the Jewish community of Prague, for instance, instituted an annual day of commemoration in tandem with the Catholic feasts that commemorated the entry of the Emperor Frederick II in the city in 1620. At that time, the Jewish community already held an annual celebration of their safe deliverance in 1611, when groups of Protestants had been raiding the city's religious houses, and Jews had feared their synagogues might become the next target.[20]

Protestants were ostentatiously to break with some Catholic ways of commemorating the past, rejecting the veneration of saints and relics, and no longer using processions, but they rapidly developed alternatives. In Lutheran lands there emerged something of a memory cult around the Reformers themselves. Luther, like his collaborator Philip Melanchthon, was frequently depicted on Lutheran altarpieces. Such commemorative acts echoed traditions that could be both personal and more local in character. Images of Luther, such as those on display in many sixteenth- and seventeenth-century homes, were reported to be incombustible.[21] Private people also collected items associated with the Reformer. Thus, the Sastrow family in Stralsund, whom we met in Chapter 1, was extremely proud of its possession of an autograph

[19] Bernstein, *Between crown and community*, 164–85.
[20] Greenblatt, *To tell their children*, 118–19.   [21] Scribner, 'Incombustible Luther'.

letter by Martin Luther.[22] Long before 'Reformation day' became a public holiday in Lutheran Germany, cities like Regensburg decided to have an annual celebration on 31 October to commemorate the day in 1517 when Martin Luther had fixed his theses on the church door of Wittenberg. In 1667, the feast was placed on the annual calendar of the Lutheran duchy of Saxony, and it spread from there to become one of the major feasts in the Lutheran calendar. No one knows when the special 'Reformation buns' were first produced to accompany the feast, but these became a fixture of the celebrations in Saxony. Everywhere in Protestant Europe, favourite forms of Protestant commemoration were annual services of thanksgiving, prayer, or penance to commemorate important major events, not least the Reformation of the churches themselves. The centenaries of the publication of Luther's theses in 1617 and 1717 were celebrated throughout Protestant Europe and accompanied by a flurry of commemorative medals, prints, and sermons. Protestant rulers, such as Elizabeth I and James I of England, instituted national days of commemoration to replace the old feasts of the Church that had now been abandoned. The accession day of Elizabeth became a fixture in the English calendar, as was Guy Fawkes Day, when the English commemorated the failed attempt by Catholic plotters in 1605 to blow up Parliament. Localities invented their own ways of participating in such national forms of commemoration. By the 1580s most communities in England had developed a ritual to celebrate the 'crownation' of Elizabeth on 17 November 1558, which was also seen as the start of the Reformation. This usually involved bell-ringing, a commemorative sermon, and illuminations, but some places added plays and pageants, gunshots, and drumming. The celebrations of Guy Fawkes Day became the occasions for highly politicized and rowdy displays of anti-popery, with huge bonfires for burning the pope in effigy, as well as celebrations of 'liberty'.[23]

MEDIATING LOCAL MEMORY

Although religion was thus probably the oldest and most common vehicle to shape community memories, it was by no means the only one. There were also secular traditions to draw on, many of them very visible. Images, inscriptions on city gates and other public places, but also place names, were already widely used to serve as reminders of past events. Banners and flags of defeated enemies were routinely kept as trophies and memory objects, and sometimes displayed in churches. The Italian city republic of Florence commissioned famous frescoes of its military victories for the Palazzo della Signoria, now the Palazzo Vecchio, one of the city's main public buildings; many other city halls across Europe had similar imagery, albeit not always of such superb quality. The Holland city of Haarlem revered the memory of the city's crusading heroes, whose ships had allegedly broken the chain that was meant to protect the port of Damietta in

---

[22] Sastrow, *Social Germany*. Ulinka Rublack, 'Grapho-Relics. Lutheranism and the Materialization of the Word', *Past and Present*, supplement 5 (2010), 144–66.
[23] Cressy, *Bonfires and bells*, 50–9, 171–87. In Lewes, East Sussex, this continues to this day.

1218–19; it donated stained-glass representations of the episode to other cities, and in the sixteenth and seventeenth centuries Haarlem children annually paraded through town with miniature ships.[24]

Some forms of secular commemoration were thus also highly ritualized. At the end of decades of conflict that had, reputedly, started with the butchering of virtually all guildmasters by one of the burgomasters, from the mid-fourteenth century, on the day that later came to be known as *Schwörmontag*, the burgomaster of the imperial city of Ulm swore an annual public oath to serve the commonwealth and the interests of rich and poor. The original idea was to affirm the power-sharing arrangements between the city's patrician families and its guildmasters that had been agreed at the end of the conflict. By the mid-fifteenth century this had developed into a major feast, as well as a rite of passage for young men, so that after the emperor Charles V broke the power of the guilds in 1548, the city lobbied hard to gain permission to restore the ritual, even if that did nothing to restore the actual power of the guilds.[25] Commemoration could also be a form of communal punishment. From 1528, when they were defeated by neighbouring Holland, the city of Utrecht was obliged annually to send a pig to The Hague, the seat of Holland's provincial government, as a sign of submission; to keep the memory of Utrecht's humiliation alive, the pig was first exposed to the mockery of the crowds in The Hague before being slaughtered.[26]

Secular memory traditions could become very elaborate. The Calvinist city republic of Geneva, for instance, developed a lively memory culture to celebrate its repulsing of an attack by Catholic Savoyards that is known as the *Escalade*. On 12 December 1602 the Savoyards tried to take the city by scaling Geneva's walls in the darkness of the night; they did not manage to do so unnoticed, however, and the citizens, male and female, rushed from their homes to keep the enemy off the walls. Having defeated the Savoyard soldiers, the Genevans were keen to share this feat with the world. Pamphlets and newsprints about their victory were sent abroad, and new versions of the tale continued to appear in print throughout the seventeenth century. But there were also plays and images and dozens of songs on the subject, annual sermons and ritual meetings were organized, and there were particular dishes associated with the feast. Some of these forms of commemoration were apparently sponsored by the authorities. It was probably an institution of some sort that in 1620 commissioned a large painting of the attack, while a stained-glass depiction of it may also have been an institutional commission. Yet tales and legends about individuals also gained a place in the rituals. Thus, the rice soup served at a banquet for the wounded was said to be inspired by the kettle of rice soup that local heroine 'Mother Royaume' was believed to have emptied on the

[24] Willem Frijhoff, 'Damiette appropriée. La mémoire de croisade, instrument de concorde civique (Haarlem, XVIe–XVIIIe siècle)', *Revue du Nord* 88 (2006): 7–42; Joke Spaans, *Haarlem na de Reformatie. Stedelijke cultuur en kerkelijk leven (1577–1620)* (The Hague, 1989), 128–30.

[25] Wolf-Henning Petershagen, *Schwörpflicht und Volksvergnügen. Ein Beitrag zur Verfassungswirklichkeit unde städtische Festkultur in Ulm* (Ulm, 1999); Wolf-Henning Petershagen. *Schwörmontag. Ein Ulmer Phänomen* (Ulm, 1996).

[26] J.J. Dodt van Flensburg, *Archief voor kerkelijke en wereldsche geschiedenissen, inzonderheid van Utrecht*, 7 vols (Utrecht, 1838–48), vol. VI, p. 79.

heads of the Savoyard attackers, while a baby whose birth had woken the women who had first raised the alarm about the Savoyards was honoured in a poem as the saviour of the city.[27]

Although the commemorative tradition did, from the start, include a religious service at which psalms were sung and special sermons were preached, the records of the *Compagnie des pasteurs* in Geneva show that the Calvinist ministers were concerned about some aspects of the elaborate memory practices that developed in Geneva. Being opposed to prayers for the dead, they had their doubts about the monument that was erected in honour of the seventeen citizens who had died in the defence of the city, and they were also sceptical about the banquet that was given annually in honour of the thirty wounded, whose injuries testified to 'the holy union for the good of the fatherland'.[28] Yet things got much more worrying than that. In 1605 and 1606, the consistory already had to call a number of members to account for 'playing farces and eating cheese soup', loudly singing profane songs, drinking, and dancing on Escalade Day.[29] Some of the songs about the Escalade were considered unsuitable by the pastors, and they were also unhappy about the play-acting that had quickly become an Escalade Day tradition.

Especially once the commemoration became a local holiday, the festivities developed carnivalesque traits, which the pastors deplored, yet masquerading and banqueting were very much part of the Escalade festivities, and fundamentally the festival proved too popular, among all ranks of society, to abolish it. Genevans in eighteenth-century Paris even formed a special society to celebrate it. Meanwhile, the pastors made the best of it by harping on the confessional significance of the Escalade. In the tense 1660s, when the peace with the Savoyards again seemed under pressure, the secular authorities had to urge the Genevan ministers to tone down on the rhetoric and told them 'that if their [scripture] texts really require them to discuss the Antichrist, not to identify him as the pope at this time, and not to use any invective'.[30]

Various proposals to abolish the festivities were discussed in the course of the eighteenth century, but the festival proved indestructible; all the authorities did was occasionally to intervene when printed invective against the Savoyards got too offensive. Only in the 1780s, when the Genevans actually needed Savoyard political and military support against a coalition of the French, Bernese, and Sardinians, was the festival abolished; yet soon after the revolutionaries of the 1790s took charge of Geneva they revived it and recast it as a 'national' and revolutionary festival and a celebration of liberty, equality, and fraternity. It survived the restoration and continues to be celebrated as a local festival.[31] What had begun as a classic instance of community commemoration was spiced up by confessional and regional rivalry, became a revolutionary and 'national' memory practice, and eventually morphed into a local feast for Genevans of all religions.

---

[27] Jean Paul Ferrier, 'Histoire de la fête de l'escalade', in *L'escalade de Genève, 1602. Histoire et tradition*, ed. Paul F. Geisendorf et al. (Geneva, 1952), 489–530, esp. 498.

[28] Ferrier, 'Histoire de la fête', 493.   [29] Ferrier, 'Histoire de la fête', 493–5.

[30] Ferrier, 'Histoire de la fête', 500.   [31] Ferrier, 'Histoire de la fête', 501–20.

THE DUTCH REPUBLIC: FROM LOCAL TO NATIONAL MEMORY

If Geneva's festival was mainly a celebration of the military bravery of its citizens, the memory culture of the Dutch city of Leiden centred mostly on the heroics of suffering. In previous chapters we have already seen something of the extensive memory culture that the city of Leiden developed around the relief of the rebel city on 3 October 1574, after a long siege by a Spanish Habsburg army. There was little military action during the siege, but the citizens were cut off from the outside world, and soon food became scarce and disease rampant; between May and October, about 6,000 of the city's 15,000 inhabitants perished. Leiden's ordeal was ended by a spectacular rescue operation, which involved the flooding of large parts of the province of Holland to enable a rebel fleet of 400 flat barges and 8,000 soldiers to come to the rescue. Much was at stake; Leiden's fall would have given the Spanish Habsburg armies easy access to the remaining rebel strongholds in South Holland and would probably have spelled the end of the Dutch Revolt. Its liberation, on the other hand, so demoralized the underpaid Habsburg troops that these began to mutiny, enabling the rebels to secure their control over the province.[32]

No wonder then that, on the very day of their liberation, Leiden's authorities decided to institute an annual sermon to give thanks for the relief of the city. This was soon complemented by an annual fair, a parade by the city militia, and public dramatic performances. The city commissioned commemorative medals for all major participants in the defence of the city (Figure 4.1), while inscriptions were also placed at various strategic points in the town—the one on the town hall was carved into an altar stone which the Reformed rebels had removed from the parish church of St Peter (Figure 4.2). The city also commissioned a large tapestry depicting its deliverance, which was put on display in the town hall and so could be seen by all—in the early modern period, town halls were very public places. Soon, paintings and stained-glass church windows followed.[33]

The annual celebration of the relief of Leiden became the central feast on the city's calendar, and one with a surprising staying power—like Escalade Day in Geneva, it was interrupted only for a decade or two around 1800 and continues to exist. This is all the more remarkable since by 1600 most of the city's inhabitants were newcomers who had no personal memories of the siege. By 1620 the city's depleted population had grown to 25,000, mostly because of mass immigration by Flemish and Brabantine textile workers, who left their homes after the Habsburgs reconquered the Southern Netherlands. Perhaps because many of these shared bad memories of Habsburg rule, they were quick to identify with, and appropriate,

[32] Robert Fruin, *Het beleg en ontzet der stad Leiden* (The Hague, 1874); Henk den Heijer, *Holland onder water. De logistiek achter het ontzet van Leiden* (Leiden, 2010).
[33] R.C.J. van Maanen, *Hutspot, haring en wittebrood. Tien eeuwen Leiden, Leienaars en hun feesten* (Leiden, 1981) and Moerman and Van Maanen, eds, *Leiden, eeuwig feest*.

Figure 4.1. Anonymous after a design by Dirk Jacobsz, *Etching of a medal commemorating the relief of Leiden in 1574*, eighteenth century, Rijksmuseum, Amsterdam. The front, here represented at the top, shows the siege of Jerusalem by the king of the Assyrians, in 2 Kings 19, whose soldiers are fleeing from an angel; the reverse, here at the bottom of the image, shows the spectacular operation by which Leiden was relieved.

the war memories of their new home town, and in 1620 it was reported that the immigrants, too, were flocking to the commemorative services held on 3 October.[34]

Yet this identification was probably helped along also because in Leiden siege memories were clearly an asset. As we have seen in Chapter 2, Burgomaster Adriaen van der Werf of Leiden and his descendants successfully promoted the tale of his

---

[34] Bernard Dwinglo. *Aenspraecke van Bernardus Dvinglo, aen de Remonstrans-gesinde ghemeynte ende borgherije der stadt Leyden, over het ontset der selfder stede gedaen op den 3. octobris 1620* (n.p., 1620), Aiir.

Figure 4.2. Inscription commemorating the famine during the 1574 siege on Leiden's town hall, 1577. The chronogram in the middle reads: 'After black famine left almost six thousand dead, God took pity and gave us bread, as much as we could wish for'. Photo by the author.

pivotal significance for the last weeks of the siege, when he had allegedly shamed citizens who wanted to surrender rather than to suffer more famine, by offering them his own body to eat. The story is today considered apocryphal, and it probably originated in a campaign by Van der Werf himself to increase his political credit. Yet it became immensely popular among the urban ruling classes of the Dutch Republic, who came to see Van der Werf as an exemplary local leader.[35] The burgomaster was not the only hero to emerge in Leiden. There were special rewards for some citizens who had distinguished themselves, like two men whose pigeons had been used to communicate with William of Orange and the rebel camp. They were given the right to use a coat of arms and to carry the name 'Van Duivenbode' (pigeoncarrier) (Figure 4.3). The men immediately enshrined their new privileges

Figure 4.3. Gablestone of the Van Duivenbode family home on Rapenburg 94, Leiden, late sixteenth century, restored 1818. Photo by the author.

in a gable stone on their house, thus creating yet another marker of the siege in the urban landscape, and when the pigeons died, they stuffed them with hay and presented them to the city government, which put them on display in the town hall. The story lived on. In 1748, when a descendant of the Duivenbode family travelled to The Hague to present a petition to the Prince of Orange, he told him all about the role the family's pigeons had played in the relief of the city.[36] The funerary monument with which the family commemorated this ancestral feat in one of the city's churches was one of the few to be spared when revolutionary activists in the late eighteenth century purged the city churches of aristocratic monuments.

Women, too, attained heroic status in Leiden. Admittedly Leiden lacked a heroic female combatant, of the type of Geneva's Mother Royaume. But from the

---

[36] Erfgoed Leiden en Omstreken, Bibliotheek LB 784-1, *Verhaal van het voorgevallene te Leiden, 1748–22 October 1751*. I am most grateful to Frank de Hoog for alerting me to this passage and providing a transcription. He has identified the author as Joost van Leeuwen.

Figure 4.4. Cornelis Visscher II, *Magdalena Moons*, 1649. Rijksmuseum, Amsterdam. After Famiano Strada, a well-informed Italian historian of the Revolt, had suggested in the 1630s that an anonymous woman had persuaded the Habsburg commander Valdéz to postpone his attack on Leiden, so creating a window of opportunity for the rebels, the playwright Bontius included such a character, named 'Amalia', in his popular play on the siege. When Leiden locals began to speculate about the historical identity of this woman, and her lack of virtue, Moons's nephew decided to publish her story and assert her respectability as the fiancée of Valdéz. He had this portrait made in 1649. It was published in a series of Leiden Revolt heroes; in the background we see a view of the city.

mid-seventeenth century there emerged tales about a local heroine, Magdalena Moons, who had allegedly talked the Spanish commander Valdéz into postponing his attempts to attack the city of Leiden, and so gained enough time for it to be relieved (Figure 4.4). She was included in plays as a latter-day Queen Esther, by the eighteenth century even figuring as the 'best friend' of the daughter of Burgomaster Van der Werf.[37] Even without a heroine in the family, however, there were many people who carefully transmitted their memories of Leiden's siege. Many people cherished objects that had been found in the deserted army camps: a cooking pot, a flask of wine, a set of playing cards were taken home and kept as secular relics of the siege. Other people kept cannon balls, banners, and flags.[38] The paper emergency coins that had been minted during the siege became collectors' items and were popular enough by 1600 for forgeries to appear.[39] They all made excellent triggers for telling and retelling the story of 3 October.

In 2006 historian Thera Wijsenbeek concluded that most of the six thousand casualties of Leiden's siege had died of a range of epidemic diseases that contemporaries identified as 'plague'. Although there were serious food shortages, famine was not the primary cause of death. The city government had actually been efficient in sharing out the available rations, and right until the end of the siege there was a ration of horse meat available for all citizens.[40] Yet no one would have guessed this from the memory culture in the city. Perhaps because 'plague' was widely seen as a form of divine punishment, it was not deemed as suitable for commemoration as famine. In local memory it was hunger that had given the people of Leiden and their rulers the chance to show their mettle. Almost immediately the memory culture in the city began to focus on the hunger that the people of Leiden had endured in their struggle for liberty. One reason for this may also have been that the famine had been followed by a miraculous feeding of the multitudes, which in the mind of contemporaries clearly evoked Christ's multiplication of bread and fishes at the Sea of Galilee. Although the rebel armies had also brought cheese with them, it was their handing out of herring and white bread to the starving citizenry that became iconic for the relief of the city. Paintings and prints showed how the Leiden population wolfed down the food (Figure 4.5).[41] And as time went on, the stories of the famine got ever more harrowing. In his history of the Revolt of the Netherlands, Amsterdam poet and historian Pieter Cornelisz Hooft in 1642 evoked what hunger had done to Leiden's citizens:

> shabby women, crouching on the dung hills, with their gowns pulled over their heads [so as not to be recognized] were picking over the bones which might still contain something edible. Other bones, chewed first by the dogs, were sucked dry by boys, and when a piece

[37] Robert Fruin, 'Magdalena Moons en haar verhouding tot Valdes', *Jaarboek van de Maatschappij der Nederlandse Letterkunde* (1879): 161–75; Els Kloek, 'Moons, Magdalena', in *Digitaal vrouwenlexicon van Nederland*, accessed 28 February 2008, http://www.inghist.nl/Onderzoek/Projecten/DVN/lemmata/data/moons.

[38] De Graaf, 'De Leidsche hutspot'; E. Pelinck, 'Overlevering, legende en relieken van het beleg en ontzet van Leiden', *Leids Jaarboekje* 46 (1954): 100–10; Marianne Eekhout, 'Herinnering in beeld. Relieken van Leids ontzet', *Leids Jaarboekje* 103 (2011): 33–47.

[39] Arent Pol and Bouke Jan van der Veen, *Het noodgeld van Leiden. Waarheid en verdichting* (The Hague, 2007).

[40] Thera Wijsenbeek-Olthuis, *Honger*, 3 Oktoberlezing (Leiden, 2006).

[41] Pollmann, *Herdenken, herinneren, vergeten*. See also Figure 2.6.

Figure 4.5. Detail of Willem de Haen, *Annonae Importatio/The entry of the beggar armies after the siege on 3 October 1574* (1614), UB Leiden. Illustrating Jan Orlers's successful history of Leiden, the figures on the left demonstrate the iconic status which bread and fish had attained in the commemoration of this episode.

of meat fell on the floor at the place where they handed out the meat, they leaped at it and wolfed it down raw. The blood was scooped out of the gutters and slurped down.[42]

In a play about the siege from 1680, a citizen describes his wife's death from hunger:

Her body, skeleton like, no longer human, her hands blackened, her bosom desiccated, her innards shrunk. In short, she seemed a shadow of wrinkle, skin and bone. My seven children filled the house with tears and weeping. My suckling lamb lay in its mother's lap and cried, then drawing on his mother's breast, dry and barren, then again let go and with his tears moistened the breast from which he had been sucking blood for milk. 'Oh dearest', said I, 'how is't?' My voice reached her ears, she opened her pale mouth and faintly spoke these words: 'I die, that you may live in remembrance of our troth', and shut her mouth and died...A woman like a pearl.[43]

As we will see in Chapter 6, consciously or unconsciously the focus on collective victimhood was also a move to try and heal the rifts in the city's population. The Dutch Revolt was a civil war, and Leiden's population had been deeply divided about both its support for the rebel cause and the ensuing reformation of the city. The hunger narrative was a way to emphasize that all had suffered, rebels and loyalists, rich and poor, Catholics and Protestants, and so to create a version of the past on which all

---

[42] P.C. Hooft, *Nederlandsche Historien*, in *Pieter Corneliszoon Hooft, Alle de gedrukte werken, 1611–1738*, ed. W. Hellinga and P. Tuynman, 9 vols (Amsterdam, 1972), IV, p. 345.
[43] Hendrik Brouwer, *Het belegh van Leyden. Treurspel* (n.p., 1683), 50–6.

might agree.[44] These were certainly not just memories of the ruling classes. Family tales about the famine were shared among the poor as well as among the wealthy in the city. A greengrocer who had wanted to sacrifice his horse and a peasant father who had hidden in a hole in the ground rather than serve the Spanish passed on these stories to their grandchildren. One of the local chambers of rhetoric included bread and fish in its emblem. Sixty years after the relief of the city, a survivor donated money to give bread to the inhabitants of the Stevenshof on 3 October. The Schaeck family, who were the happy owners of a cooking pot that had been abandoned by the Spanish, gathered for an annual meal on the eve of the feast (Figure 4.6), as did the family who are the main protagonists in a '3 October banquet' described by pamphleteer and second-generation immigrant Passchier de Fijne.[45]

Figure 4.6. Cooking pot, believed to have been found in one of the Spanish sconces after the siege, Museum De Lakenhal, Leiden. The pot was owned by the Leiden Schaeck family, who had it inscribed. It achieved national fame once seventeenth-century poet Joost van den Vondel immortalized it in one of his works. He reported that the Schaeck family celebrated the annual anniversary of the relief with a commemorative meal.

[44] Brouwer, *Het belegh van Leyden*, 50–6.
[45] Pollmann, *Herdenken, herinneren, vergeten*; Brouwer, *Het belegh van Leyden*, 50–6; Passchier de Fijne, *Den ouden Leytschen patroon ofte derden octobers bancket: waer in kortelijck en waerachtelijck wort voorgeset de stercke belegeringhe der stad, de groote benautheyt der borgeren, ende de wonderbare wercken Godes betoont in 't ontsetten vande stad Leyden: geschiet inden jaere onses Heeren 1574, op den 3. october, wesende sondagh 's morgens* (Leiden, 1630).

In the course of the seventeenth century, the tale of Leiden's suffering and its virtuous civic resistance became very well known throughout the Dutch Republic. An important role in this process was played by the alumni of Leiden University, who all experienced the 3 October celebrations and took memories of these with them when they served throughout the Republic as Reformed pastors. We know of several alumni who preached and published sermons about the siege and relief of Leiden in towns and villages elsewhere. Books about the subject were given as prizes to schoolboys in other Holland cities, and Bontius's play based on the events was not only staged in Amsterdam for a week every year, but travelling troupes also took it to stages throughout the province of Holland.[46] The story of Leiden's suffering lent itself well to reimagining the past, especially in a prosperous Republic where few people died of hunger, and Leiden's local memories thus became part of a larger Holland, and even Netherlandish, narrative. That the population of Leiden had held out in such circumstances implied a type of heroism ideally suited to a bourgeois Republic where most power was devolved to urban level.

But more generally, too, victimhood had come to play a central role in the public memory culture of the Dutch Republic. The Republic had come into being in 1579 as a union of seven sovereign provinces, which agreed to join forces to fight the Habsburgs, to collectively finance this war effort, and not to contract a peace separately from the others. In a judicial and religious sense, the provinces remained autonomous and the only joint institutions they had were initially the States General, in which all the provinces met, and the army. The States General did little to develop national memory practices around the Revolt, and there was no annual commemoration of its important dates. It took until 1612 before they commissioned a fitting funerary monument for the *pater patriae*, William of Orange, for instance (Figure 4.7). That a national memory culture came into being at all was mainly owing to the state's critics. From around 1600, there was growing talk of peace with the one-time enemy, the king of Spain. There was much opposition to such proposals, especially among exiles from the Southern Netherlands who feared that a peace would mean an end to efforts to reconquer the homelands from which they had been exiled. In an effort to show that Spanish proposals could not be trusted, these opponents of peace consciously began to invoke memories of the early days of the Revolt and especially memories of Spanish 'cruelty'. In prints, plays, and pamphlets they tried to remind their compatriots of what had happened thirty years earlier, especially during the regime of the notorious Habsburg commander, the Duke of Alba, who had presided over the punitive sackings and massacres of a series of Netherlandish cities in the 1570s. In an obvious attempt to evoke translocal solidarity, these exiles focused their memories on the whole of the Netherlands, rather than just single towns and provinces. They used highly effective methods— focusing on iconic forms of cruelty, for instance, and constantly stressing the need

[46] Pollmann, 'Een "blij-eindend" treurspel'; Petrus Molinaeus, *Predikatie over Psalm 124: toegepast op het streng en benaeuwt beleg en wonderbaer ontzet der stadt Leyden* (Rotterdam, 1694); Johannes Alderkerk, *De wonderdaden des Allerhoogsten Godts, doorlugtig gezien in de grontlegginge en voortzettinge van Nederlants vryheyt, in zonderheit kragtdadig gebleken in het vermaarde beleg ende ontzet der stadt Leyden* (Leiden, 1734).

Figure 4.7. Isaac Junius, decorative faience tile with a view of the funerary monument for William of Orange in the Nieuwe Kerk, Delft, produced for an anonymous Delft pottery, *c.*1655–65, Rijksmuseum, Amsterdam. The funerary monument for *pater patriae* William of Orange was commissioned by the States General of the Dutch Republic more than twenty-five years after his assassination. The allegorical figure with the hat on the left is the figure of liberty. The monument was the subject of many paintings as well as this tile, and may have had symbolic political significance for the Orangist party in the Dutch Republic during the period of 'True Freedom' after 1650.

to tell younger generations about the outrages of the past.[47] An influential children's book, a dialogue between father and son, explained that 'no one deserves to be called a Netherlander, who commits these memories to oblivion', while the French translation of this popular text was described as a 'catechism of the state'.[48] Although the opponents of peace did not succeed in preventing a truce, their commemorative agenda soon proved exceptionally successful, especially once it gained the support of the sons of William of Orange and the Reformed Church,

Figure 4.8. Anonymous, *Allegory on the miserable state of the Netherlands.* Painting after an anonymous 1568 print that is known as *Alva's throne.* On the left we see the Duke enthroned, and being advised by the Devil through the mouth of Habsburg adviser Cardinal Granvelle. Allegories of the Netherlandish provinces, in chains, are at his feet; on the right, local politicians stand muted and immobile. After the resumption of the war between the Republic and the kings of Spain in 1621, paintings of this subject were commissioned all over the Dutch Republic. Museum Prinsenhof, Delft.

[47] Judith Pollmann, 'No man's land. Reinventing Netherlandish identities, 1585–1621', in *Networks, regions and nations. Shaping identities in the Low Countries, 1300–1650*, ed. Robert Stein and Judith Pollmann, Studies in medieval and Reformation traditions (Leiden, 2010), 241–62.

[48] *Spieghel der ievcht, ofte corte Cronijcke der Nederlantsche geschiedenissen.: In de welcke... verhaelt... worden, de voornaaemste Tyrannien ende... wreedtheden, die door het beleydt der Coningen van Hispaengien... in Nederlandt bedreven zijn...* (Amsterdam, 1614); *Le miroir de la jevnesse,: représentant en l'abrégé des choses arrivées au Pays Bas. La tyrannie d' Espagne, l'innocente patience des Provinces Vnies, et la main puissante de Dieu. Au commencement progres & affermissement de leur liberté. Pour l'instruction de la jeunesse & memoire a la posterité* (Middelburg, 1616).

who began to use it to fight their political enemies inside as well as beyond the Netherlands.[49] In the 1620s and 1630s there was a flurry of images, books, and monuments centred on what had by now evolved into a canonical history of the Revolt (Figure 4.8).

The appearance of such national versions of the past did not mean the end of local histories, however. Quite the opposite. The creation of a 'national' version of the history of the Revolt helped to amplify local tales and assign them a place in a larger whole. As we have seen, this was certainly true of Leiden. But the canon conversely also worked to legitimize memories of violence that would not normally have been sanctioned. Erika Kuijpers has shown how the existence of a larger canon about the Revolt offered local storytellers in the countryside of the Waterland region of Holland a socially acceptable frame for the bloodcurdling memories they had to relate about their guerrilla tactics against Spanish soldiers, 'papists', and other enemies. Through the canon, what had once been a cruel civil war in which Netherlanders had fought each other had become a story of 'Netherlandish' resistance to a 'Spanish enemy'. In that context it was acceptable not only for Waterland peasants to brag about murder and plunder, and have a good laugh over the 'enemy' ears they had once pinned to their hats. It also became acceptable to publish these memories.[50]

While most of its first proponents were orthodox Calvinists, the national canon of the Dutch Revolt was remarkably unconfessional in nature. This is understandable if we consider that Calvinist church members there were a religious minority living in a pluralist society. Anyone wanting to gain political influence had to do so with arguments that would appeal to a wider audience than that of their own denomination. As Jasper van der Steen has noted, the consequence of this was that the local and national memory cultures of the Dutch Republic were very religiously generic. Even if authors would pay frequent tribute to God's active hand in the outcome of the Revolt, neither in Leiden nor more generally was this an exclusively 'Reformed' memory.[51] *Within* the various churches, the commemoration of the Revolt was deeply confessional, but the public sphere had to do with secular memory culture as a second best alternative to the sort of united, religious-tinged memory culture that the Habsburg authorities in Brussels could solicit as a matter of course.[52]

Yet, however second best, the national canon became deeply embedded into popular culture. Cheap songbooks, plays, and images kept the stories alive and passed them on to new generations, as did schoolbooks and sermons. Even an Amsterdam fairground had a display entitled 'the Tyranny of Alba', and when, in 1672, an anxious working-class wife sent a letter about the recent French invasion of the Dutch Republic to her husband, who was a trumpeter working abroad, she told

[49] Pollmann, *Het oorlogsverleden*; Jasper van der Steen, 'Goed en Fout in de Nederlandse Opstand', *Historisch Tijdschrift Holland* 43/2 (2011): 82–97; Van der Steen, *Memory wars*.

[50] Kuijpers, 'Between storytelling and patriotic scripture'.

[51] Van der Steen, 'Goed en fout'.

[52] Judith Pollmann, 'Met grootvaders bloed bezegeld. Het religieuze verleden in de zeventiende eeuw', *De Zeventiende Eeuw* 29/2 (2013): 154–75.

him that the French armies were behaving 'worse than those of the Duke of Alba'. A century after the duke had been active, this woman knew her national history.[53]

CONCLUSION

In his 1994 book *Commemorations. The politics of national identity*, editor John Gillis suggested a tripartite division of the history of memory into pre-national, national, and post-national phases. The pre-national phase, Gillis believed, characterized all Western societies up until the end of the eighteenth century; the post-national began in the 1960s.

The post-national phase in which people were living their lives in 1994 was, according to Gillis, characterized by 'an anarchy of memory'. 'The nation is no longer the site or frame of memory for most people,' and national history is 'no longer a proper measure of what people really know about their pasts'. History has become both 'more global and more local', while memory has become more democratic but also more individual. It is no longer bound to a time and space, and 'we cannot rely on the support of collective memory in the same way people in earlier periods could... Grandparents are no longer doing the memory work they once performed.' It is 'wives and mothers who pick up the slack'. At the same time we are under 'a constant compulsion' to remember because 'we are swimming in a flood of change'.[54]

Although Gillis acknowledged that some of these phenomena might have their roots before the late 1960s, he emphasized that this state of affairs was fundamentally new and unprecedented. Not only was it quite different from the national memory that came before; he also believed that it differed dramatically from the pre-national memory practices of the early modern West, the world before the age of revolutions. Yet Gillis also noted that actual knowledge of early modern memory practices was quite limited, and in 1994, that was, indeed, the case. Two decades later, however, we have come to a much better understanding of pre-modern community memory practices. When we take a longer-term view of collective memories, we can see that rather than regarding these as 'stages' in a linear history of memory, as Gillis did, it is more useful to picture them as very interrelated modes of thinking about the collective past. Exploring the lively traffic between different forms of community memory in early modern Europe, this chapter has argued that it is in this traffic that we find the key to understanding how notions of the national could spread and be used as a rhetorical tool in early modern society, without destroying alternative ways of thinking about the past, like the local. We have seen that at a local level there was a range of oral and visual media available, which could be used to publicly commemorate important events, and that

---

[53] Pollmann, *Het oorlogsverleden*.
[54] Gillis, 'Memory and identity', 11–17, 6–7, 14–15. An earlier version of these comments was published in Judith Pollmann, 'Memory before and after nationalism. A revision', in *Conflicted pasts and national identities. Narratives of war and conflict*, ed. Michael Böss (Aarhus, 2014), 31–42.

literacy was no prerequisite for sharing in such public memories. As important as the availability of cheap print, certainly, was the support of the clergy. Although we know very little of most sermons that were preached in early modern Europe, there is enough evidence to show that priests and pastors were crucial mediators of the significance of public memories, even when these concerned what we would consider to be secular events. Annual rituals, visual markers and places in the landscape also helped to keep memories alive and to connect local people to narratives of supra-local significance. Thus late seventeenth- and eighteenth-century Ireland was littered with spots that were associated with the exploits of Oliver Cromwell, while in England any destroyed castle or abbey was likely to be associated with his name, which had converged with that of his distant relative Thomas Cromwell, who in the dissolution of the monasteries of the sixteenth century was also responsible for the desacralization of space and objects.[55]

An implicit assumption in the debate about national consciousness and memory has sometimes been that we can speak of national memory only if it is the *primary* frame of public historical reference for most people.[56] Yet even in the heyday of nationalism that has rarely been the case. In Europe, the nineteenth century was the great age of not only national history, but also of the institutionalization of regional and local history. In everyday life, then as now, many people identify as strongly with the past of their villages and cities and regions as they do with that of the nation at large.[57] This was certainly also true in early modern Europe. Yet as we will see in Chapter 7, people might equally identify with the memory culture of a transnational ethnic or religious group, without that necessarily causing problems. In fact, such transnational memories could be used to bolster both local and national objectives as much as to incite transnational solidarities. That is not really so different from how they are used today. Very evident in the dynamics of public memory is the importance of stakeholders—in all the examples discussed above there were many people, groups, and institutions involved in the imagining of mnemonic communities, and in shaping, appropriating, and perpetuating collective memories. In this way, local memories could not only find their way to the national stage, but national memories could also be harnessed to serve local interests. And as we will see in Chapter 7, they could also travel much further, as global and 'cosmopolitan' memories emerged.

---

[55] Covington, 'The odious demon'; Fox, *Oral and literate culture*, 255–8.

[56] Hastings, *The construction of nationhood*, 31–2, highlighted this issue but did little to flesh it out.

[57] Cf. E.J. Hobsbawm, *Nations and nationalism since 1780. Programme, myth, reality* (1990; 2nd edn Cambridge, 1992), 155–92.

5

Living Legends: Myth, Memory, and Authenticity

In the German city of Hamelin, there is no getting away from it.[1] Everywhere in the old town there are reminders of the story of the Pied Piper, who, on a fateful day in June 1284, played tunes so sweet that 130 enchanted children followed him out of the city gates to disappear into a mountain never to be seen again. Yet if modern Hamelin trades heavily on its reputation as the Pied Piper's city, this is not such a recent phenomenon as we might imagine. Travellers' accounts tell us that, as early as the sixteenth century, references to the children and the piper could be found everywhere in Hamelin. People had sculpted and stained-glass images of the Pied Piper in their homes, inscriptions on houses and public buildings referred to the tale, and local people were reported to obey the ban on drumming and piping in the street through which the children were believed to have left. The event had been so momentous, travellers and chroniclers recounted, that the people in Hamelin even dated events using their own calendar, which started in the year of the children's disappearance.[2]

As we have seen in the previous chapters, a fair number of local memories in early modern Europe were related to events that we now consider fictional or that had fictional elements—and the tale of the Pied Piper also falls into that category. Some scholars have argued that it survived precisely because it was a good story; it had the sort of mythical characteristics that tend to stand the test of time and that also made it interesting beyond its local context.[3] Yet while this is undoubtedly important, not all pre-modern myths and legends have had as successful and lasting a career as the Pied Piper story. What did it take for a pre-modern memory to live on and be remembered generation after generation? In this chapter we will see that for such a tale to have persisted and to have made it beyond its local world, it needed not only mythical characteristics but also the flavour of authenticity provided by the practice of memory.

---

[1] This chapter was first published as Judith Pollmann, 'Of living legends and authentic tales. How to get remembered in early modern Europe', *Transactions of the Royal Historical Society* 6th series 23 (2013): 103–25. I am grateful to the Royal Historical Society and Cambridge University Press for the permission to republish it here.
[2] An indispensable survey and extracts of available source material to 1860 in the *Quellensammlung zur Hamelner Rattenfängersage*, ed. Hans Dobertin (Göttingen, 1970).
[3] Radu Florescu, *In search of the Pied Piper* (London, 2005), 205.

Students of myth and legend have taught us that cultures develop recurring narrative and explanatory patterns that crop up again and again when people mentally and culturally try to structure their world. The archetypes or 'motifs' that twentieth-century folklorists and mythologists identified appear everywhere. Familiar tales of origin and deliverance, of failure and success, of gender and generations, and of the relationships between humans and the divine appear in new settings. Such cultural patterns structure the way we tell stories and thus also how we remember.[4]

But myth is not history, and until quite recently, scholars have treated the two not only as very different, but also as mutually exclusive habits of thought.[5] Historians used to think of myths as deplorable things that other people believe in and wrongs they need to right. History in its modern incarnation is a way of engaging with the past that distinguishes between past and present, deploys a time-frame, follows clear habits of reasoning, and is based on a critical assessment of available evidence. Myth, on the other hand, is usually hazy about timeframes, more often than not depends on a suspension of disbelief, and approaches evidence as something that is explained by a story, rather than used to test that story's reliability. That is true not just for the supernatural stories that scholars used to insist were 'real' myths, but also for what we call 'legends', popular but unlikely tales about humans that are located in time and space.[6]

Once upon a time, scholars believed that in the *longue durée* of human development, history had replaced myth. Myth, they argued, was something that belonged to a primitive, pre-literate and pre-scientific way of life, not to the modern world. Today, scholarship has abandoned the 'myth of mythlessness', the notion that a world ruled once by myth has had to give way to a world ruled by reason.[7] Scholars from Roland Barthes to Marina Warner have pointed out that today's world actually continues to be pervaded by myth.[8] Even so, few myths today can hold an 'epistemological monopoly'; they coexist with other ways of thinking about the world, and some of those ways are historical.

Of course, distinctions between myth and history are not always clean and clear. Myths and legends can take on shapes that look, and indeed are, quite historical,

---

[4] Brockmeier, *Beyond the archive*, believes this is a modern development, but there is a similarity, of course, to Bartlett's schemes.

[5] See e.g. Jack Goody and Ian Watt, 'The consequences of literacy', *Comparative Studies in Society and History* 5 (1963): 304–45; M.I. Finley, 'Myth, memory and history', *History and Theory* 4 (1965): 281–302; and C.A. Tamse, 'The political myth', in *Britain and the Netherlands V. Some political mythologies. Papers delivered to the fifth Anglo-Dutch historical conference*, ed. J.S. Bromley and E.H. Kossmann (The Hague, 1975), 1–18. Changing views of the relationship between history and myth are helpfully discussed in Laura Cruz and Willem Frijhoff, 'Introduction. Myth in history, history in myth', in *Myth in history, history in myth. Proceedings of the third international conference of the Society for Netherlandic History (New York: June 5–6, 2006)*, ed. Laura Cruz and Willem Frijhoff (Leiden, 2009), 1–16.

[6] Although some scholars insist that the term myth should in fact only be used to describe tales about the realm of the supernatural, modern theorists take a broader approach, see Robert A. Segal, *Myth. A very short introduction* (Oxford, 2004).

[7] E.g. Segal, *Myth*; Laurence Coupe, *Myth*, 2nd edn (London, 2009), 9–15.

[8] Roland Barthes, *Mythologies suivi de Le Mythe, aujourd'hui* (Paris, 1957); Marina Warner, *Managing monsters. Six myths of our time*, The Reith Lectures (London, 1994).

while histories often acquire mythical features. In some instances, we can follow this process fairly closely. Surveying the transmission of eyewitness tales about the Dutch Revolt, my research team found that diarists who were writing contemporaneously often expressed their fear, anger, and frustration about the pointlessness of events as they unfolded. At best they referred to them quite generically as God's punishment for a decadent society.[9] Yet as will see in Chapter 7, a few decades *after* the events few of the tales that people told each other about their own war experiences were 'pointless'. Rather, war experiences had been framed in narrative formats that either helped to give some sort of providential or moral significance to the tales or that suggested some form of control. Such stories told how villagers and townspeople had outwitted their military opponents with cunning and deceit, escapes were miraculous, sacrifices rewarded. In the process, many of these historical experiences had therefore become the stuff of legend and had acquired mythical characteristics. Individual experiences that could not be framed in such a mythical way, such as those relating to defeat, loss, and shame, were much less likely to be remembered.[10] Mythmaking, then, was an essential stage in the development of social memories of the Dutch Revolt; such myths were not the product of fading and failing memories, as some have thought, but intrinsic to the production of social memory itself.[11]

Yet we also noted something else: for such myths and legends to catch on and survive, a good story alone was not enough. These stories *continued* to thrive only when they were framed historically and/or supported by material evidence. Stories apparently need an association with a place or a date, an object or a person, to be believed, and to be transmitted, even if such stories can also be transplanted to another context when that suits the needs of the storyteller. In early modern Europe such evidence did not necessarily need to be that precise; the ability to point to a place in the landscape could be adduced as 'proof' that an event had taken place there. Sarah Covington has shown, for instance, how the Irish constantly evoked memories of Oliver Cromwell's campaigns with reference to the landscape. In nineteenth-century Lorraine, certain caves were associated with memories of Swedish cruelties during the Thirty Years War, while Philippe Joutard has shown how memories of resistance in the Cevennes from the sixteenth century onwards were passed on through a combination of Old Testament associations and spatial markers.[12] Objects were also very important as carriers of memory and support for tales. Thus, Marianne Eekhout has shown how cannonballs served as vehicles for memory practices and storytelling in the early modern Netherlands.[13] Myths without such a supporting framework of time,

---

[9] Examples cited for instance in Pollmann, *Catholic identity*, 57–9, 94–100, 113–24, 131–5, 153–8.

[10] Erika Kuijpers, 'The creation and development of social memories of traumatic events. The Oudewater massacre of 1575', in *Hurting memories and beneficial forgetting. Posttraumatic stress disorders, biographical developments, and social conflicts*, ed. Michael Linden and Krzysztof Rutkowski (London and Waltham MA, 2013), 191–201; and Kuijpers, 'Between storytelling and patriotic scripture'. On the mythologizing of the siege of Leiden, Pollmann, *Herdenken, herinneren, vergeten*.

[11] On mythmaking as the result of failing memories see e.g. Fox, *Oral and literate culture*, 225.

[12] Covington, 'The odious demon'; David Hopkin, *Soldier and peasant in French popular culture, 1766–1870* (Suffolk, 2003); Joutard, *La Légende des Camisards*.

[13] Marianne Eekhout, 'De kogel in de kerk. Herinneringen aan het beleg van Haarlem, 1573–1630', *Holland. Historisch Tijdschrift* 43 (2011): 108–19.

space, and evidence might easily be dismissed as 'fables' and old wives' tales—although that did not necessarily stop early modern antiquarians from repeating them.[14] Yet if and when a decent frame was in place, mythical tales and legends had a better chance than most of 'catching on' and of capturing the historical imagination.

Students of legends and folktales are familiar with this effect. 'Legends', as Timothy R. Tangherlini has put it,

> are best characterized as historicized narrative. The process of historicization may be likened to diachronic ecotypification [the way in which cultural practices, including narratives, will adapt to suit a new environment (JP)]. The believability of the narrative is underscored by the historicization of the account.[15]

This chapter explores how such a historicization of narrative operated in early modern Europe. As we have already seen in Chapters 2 and 3, the practice of history changed considerably in this period. There was growing scepticism about some myths, as we will see in the Hamelin case. Moreover, standards of evidence changed, and techniques for assessing its value and authenticity were refined and improved. But we will see that this did not necessarily endanger the survival and spread of myths and legends; quite the opposite, often it was actually new historical and antiquarian methods and techniques that were used to strengthen, embellish, and support them.

We will see that in the dynamic between myth and history an important mediating role was played by memory practices.[16] In sixteenth-century Hamelin people practised memory not only by storytelling, but also in observing the taboo on dancing in one of the streets, in the commissioning and exhibiting of memorial inscriptions and images, and even, allegedly, by a new form of timekeeping. By doing so, they maintained a powerful presence for the story in the urban landscape; this in turn persuaded visitors and historians that there had to be 'something in it'. In that way memory practices like those in Hamelin helped to authenticate myth and so functioned as a mediator between mythical and historical ways of thinking about the past. In this chapter, we will explore this dynamic further by analysing the development of two Dutch tales, both of which also happen to involve children, before returning to the children of Hamelin.

BABY, CAT, AND CRADLE

On the night of 18–19 November 1421 the so-called St Elizabeth flood swallowed the better part of the South Holland area known as the Grote Waard. Much of the land was lost for good; part of the area was to remain marshland and is today

---

[14] Woolf, *The social circulation*, 352–91.

[15] Timothy R. Tangherlini, '"It happened not too far from here…". A survey of legend theory and characterization', *Western Folklore* 49 (1990): 371–90, at 379. On the concept of ecotype see David Hopkin, 'The ecotype, or a modest proposal to reconnect cultural and social history', in *Exploring cultural history. Essays in honour of Peter Burke*, ed. Joan-Paul Rubiés, Melissa Calaresu, and Filippo de Vivo (Farnham, 2010), 31–54.

[16] E.g. Connerton, *How societies remember*; Olick and Robbins, 'Social memory studies'.

called the Biesbosch. A number of villages were never rebuilt, and the city of Dordrecht became an island, as it still is today. Two thousand people may have died in the flood, and the event made a big enough impression for people to remember it well into the sixteenth century. In 1560, a seventy-two-year-old man named Theeus Aspersoon, for instance, recalled that his father and a great-uncle who had lived to the age of ninety had told him about the drowning of the village of Wieldrecht.[17] Such memories were supported by material remains. An early sixteenth-century witness claimed that when sailing through the area, he had seen the vestiges of the towers of the drowned village churches sticking out over the waters.[18] We also possess a remarkable pictorial representation of the flood; some-time around 1490 people from the drowned village of Wieldrecht and their des-cendants in Dordrecht commissioned an altarpiece for the Grote Kerk's altar of St Elizabeth, whose feast at that time fell on 19 November. For the outer panels they ordered two images commemorating the event. These showed not only the drowning of their village and the villagers' flight to the safety of Dordrecht, but also included a remarkable detail. In the top middle of the picture on the left we see a small cradle afloat, containing a baby and a cat (Figures 5.1a and 5.1b).[19] A historical account from 1514 gives us the background story: on the waters raised by the flood, a cradle had drifted into Dordrecht, which contained a male baby who had a cat for company.[20] Floating infants are a well-known narrative motif in European folktales; in the motif-index, in which scholars have listed and analysed such narrative motifs, there is a special category reserved for 'future hero found in boat'; the most famous example of such a hero is the Old Testament prophet Moses. Sometime between 1421 and 1490 a tale with a similar motif had appar-ently been born in Dordrecht.[21]

This was by no means the only mythical tale to originate from the flood. By 1500, for instance, it was said that as many as seventy-two villages had been lost in the event.[22] The actual number had been much lower, yet seventy-two is a number associated in the Bible with the number of peoples at the Tower of Babel, and the number of disciples sent out by Christ among the nations in Luke 10:1. This may be the reason why the number took hold of the imagination; it was probably no accident that witness Theeus Aspersoon was reported to be seventy-two years of age.

---

[17] Elizabeth Gottschalk, *Stormvloeden en rivieroverstromingen in Nederland/Storm surges and river floods in the Netherlands. 2. De periode 1400–1600* (Assen, 1975), 74. Gottschalk discusses all sources relating to the flood, including the transmission of tales about it.

[18] 'Chrysostomus Neapolitanus to Count Nugarola, c. 1514', in Hadrianus Junius, *Batavia* (Leiden, 1588), 182–7. The letter was first published in Martinus Dorpius, *Dialogus: in quo Venus et Cupido omnes adhibent versutias: ut Herculem animi ancipitem in suam militiam invita Virtuta perpel-lant. Eiusdem Thomus Aululariæ Plautinæ adiectus cum prologis…Chrysostomi Neapolitani epistola de situ Hollandiæ viuendique Hollandorum institutis. Gerardi Nouiomagi de Zelandia epistola consimilis* ([Louvain, 1514]).

[19] Liesbeth Helmus, 'Het altaarstuk met de Sint Elisabethsvloed uit de Grote Kerk van Dordrecht. De oorspronkelijke plaats en de opdrachtgevers', *Oud-Holland* 105 (1991): 127–39.

[20] 'Chrysostomus Neapolitanus to Count Nugarola', 182–3.

[21] Van de Waal, *Drie eeuwen*, I, 255 and II, 121.

[22] Gottschalk, *Stormvloeden*, 73 suggests it first made an appearance in the *Magnum Chronicon Belgicum* of *c.*1500.

Figure 5.1a. Master of the St Elizabeth panels, *Elizabeth's flood of 1421*, outer left wing panel of an altarpiece *c*.1490–5. The altarpiece was commissioned by descendants of the inhabitants of the village of Wieldrecht, which had been lost in the flood, who had found a safe haven in the city of Dordrecht. At the front, villagers are trying to bring their possessions to safety. Rijksmuseum, Amsterdam. The circle indicates the baby, cat, and cradle.

The figure was also repeated on commemorative inscriptions, like the one that appeared above a city gate in Dordrecht in 1609:

> On the land and water seen here
> 72 parishes, as the chronicle says,
> Were inundated by the force of the water
> In the year 1421[23]

---

[23] See for this and a discussion of the meaning of the number Jan van Herwaarden et al., *Geschiedenis van Dordrecht tot 1572* (Dordrecht and Hilversum, 1996), 162. The inscription is cited in Matthijs

Figure 5.1b. Detail of 5.1a: baby, cat, and cradle.

By the time that gate was built, there were actually already many doubts about this figure. Yet while scholars debated how many villages had actually disappeared, the inscription resolved this problem by invoking the authority of a 'chronicle' to support its claim. The figure of seventy-two continued to recur until well into the twentieth century.[24]

Other mythical elements disappeared much faster. In 1588 humanist Hadrianus Junius claimed that the flood had been the result of human intervention. A man had been so angry with his neighbours that he had made a breach in the sea dyke that protected their land, thus provoking the flooding of de Grote Waard. The man was said to have suffered great remorse about the unexpected consequences of this act of spite.[25] Yet this tale did not catch on and disappeared from view. The same happened with an earlier sixteenth-century tale, which explained the flood as the punishment for the penny-pinching of the owners of the land, who had failed to pay their labourers their dues.[26] A late-seventeenth-century author, who produced one of the most emotive descriptions of the flood, saw it as a providential punishment for the decadence of the area's prosperous inhabitants.[27] Even this tale, which fitted in very well with contemporary beliefs, made one appearance only.

However, the tale of the infant who survived the flood turned out to have remarkable staying power. It has been suggested that it may have been someone

Balen, *Beschryvinge der stad Dordrecht, vervatende haar begin, opkomst, toeneming, en verdere stant...* (Dordrecht, 1677), 769.

[24] Ruben Koman, *Bèèh...!. Groot Dordts volksverhalenboek. Een speurtocht naar volksverhalen, bijnamen, volksgeloof, mondelinge overlevering en vertelcultuur in Dordrecht* (Bedum, 2005).

[25] Junius, *Batavia*, 249.

[26] Gottschalk, *Stormvloeden*, 73–4 discusses e.g. the version of Reinier Snoy (1477–1537), whose *De Rebus Batavicis* was published in Frankfurt in 1620.

[27] Gerrit Spaan, *Beschrijvinge der stad Rotterdam, en eenige omleggende dorpen, verdeeld in III. Boeken* (Rotterdam, 1698), 13–16.

who was associated with the tale of the cradle and the cat who insisted on the inclusion of the cradle in the altar panels in 1490; perhaps descendants of a survivor. This idea is supported by the fact that other early paintings of the flood did not include the cradle.[28] But however that may be, it seems that the tale was initially limited to a smallish circle. That the tale of the cradle survived at all, and that all accounts of the flood after 1600 were to include it, had everything to do with the intervention of a learned author. In a book that Erasmus's humanist friend Martin Dorpius published in 1514, he included a description of the County of Holland, allegedly written by an author called Chrysostomos Neapolitanus and recounting the tale of a baby boy who had floated to safety with a cat in his cradle during the 1421 flood. There are indications that the author may have been using a pseudonym and that the true author, probably the humanist Cornelis Aurelius, had meant it as a bit of a joke; nevertheless, its humanist setting lent it a veracity that greatly helped to authenticate the story in subsequent historiography and pictorial representations.[29]

One sign of this is that the account appears to have influenced local memory culture. In 1635 an eighty-year-old Haarlem widow called Lysbeth Pieters signed an affidavit to the effect that she had often heard her grandmother tell how the latter's grandfather, Pieter van Nederveen, had miraculously floated to safety during the great flood of 1421. There was no mention of a cat in her account, but she said that the baby had worn a coral 'paternoster' necklace, with a pendant displaying a coat of arms and his name. Because of this, the boy had been recognized as a nobleman and brought up accordingly.

Lysbeth made her statement at the request of a distant cousin, named Moses Jans van Nederveen, who lived in Dordrecht and who made gunpowder for a living. Moses was quite an unusual name in the seventeenth-century Republic, so the choice of this name itself suggests that his family may have associated itself with the tale of the floating infant. They and Moses may have been interested in the story because it would support claims to a higher social status, but that Moses now also wanted some written evidence for this may have been because there were other claimants around in Dordrecht.[30] By the seventeenth century, the Dordrecht family of Roerom had apparently also started to claim a connection with the baby in the cradle. Local historian Matthijs Balen in the 1670s was the first to mention this connection and name the child in print. He included a reference to the cat, but in his version of the tale, the baby had undergone a sex change. Balen claimed that the child had been a girl and identified her as a woman named Baete, who

[28] Helmus, 'Het altaarstuk'.

[29] As has been argued by Jan van Herwaarden, *Between Saint James and Erasmus. Studies in late-medieval religious life. Devotion and pilgrimage in the Netherlands*, trans. Wendie Shaffer and Donald Gardner, Studies in Medieval and Reformation Traditions 97 (Leiden, 2003), 571–8; Van de Waal, *Drie eeuwen*, 255–6 was dismissive of the influence of the story, but he missed Junius's inclusion of the Colonna letter in his *Batavia*. This was republished again in Petrus Scriverius, *Batavia illustrata* (Leiden, 1609), 129 ff., and so fairly well known.

[30] Noordhollands archief, Inv. 164 Notary archives Jacob van Bosvelt, 7 July 1635, fo. 172r–172v. It was published in *De genealogieën van Nederveen*, ed. F.B.M. Nederveen and C.J. Nederveen (Geertruidenberg, 2006), 44–5. I am most grateful to Marten Jan Bok for bringing the existence of this document to my attention.

had eventually married a man called Jakob Roerom. Baete had been nicknamed Beatrix, 'felicitous', and it was under this name that she was from now on to be known. Through the offspring of her marriage with Jakob Roerom, Beatrix had become the great-great-grandmother of a series of elite families. Balen listed them carefully and demonstrated the connection a second time in the genealogical tables that he included in his book. Balen allowed for other survivors. He also mentioned a family who had survived the flood by clinging to a wooden beam yet he did not mention the Nederveen family.[31] Apparently, he knew nothing about the alternative claims of the descendants of Pieter van Nederveen. However that may be, it is evident that by the seventeenth century the tale of the baby in the cradle had become a tale of origin for at least two Dordrecht families.

Since then, there has been a steady stream of reports about individual people who claimed they descended from the infant who had been rescued. Mostly they mentioned Beatrix, but some also continued to maintain that the baby had been a boy. In 1885 an 'old' painting of cradle, baby, and cat was sold at auction, which had been kept as evidence of a family association with Beatrix, together with a coral necklace with a gold locket that was said to have been found together with the baby.[32] It may have been an echo of the claims about the coral paternoster made by the Nederveen family, which in another version of the family history before 1800 had added details about the jewellery and at last also claimed that the baby had been accompanied by a cat.[33] In a 1698 version of the tale there was also mention of jewels that were associated with the baby.[34] Descendants of survivors continue to live to this very day. In 2007, a woman came forward in Dordrecht to tell the tale of her descent from Beatrix. Meanwhile, the Nederveen family has also been active in reappropriating the story for their family, through a local history journal, a published family genealogy, and a strategic gift of a copy of their ancestor's affidavit to Dordrecht's local archive.[35]

Yet it was not just individual stakeholders who spread the tale. From the eighteenth century there was a trend towards broader appropriation of the story. The myth proved capable of moving in time and space. Scholars have found references to at least three other medieval and early modern Netherlandish floods in which the tale of the cradle, cat, and baby reappears; all of the early modern stories appear to have been inspired by a version of the tale from Dordrecht.[36] The tale was included in a print of the flood made by Romeyn de Hooghe in 1675, and in an influential print that Jan Luyken made of such a tale in Groningen the baby even took centre stage (Figure 5.2).[37] Even in the twenty-

---

[31] Balen, *Beschryvinge*, 770, 1205.

[32] J.R.W. Sinninghe, *Hollandsch sagenboek. Legenden en sagen uit Noord- en Zuid-Holland* (The Hague, 1943), 270–1.

[33] First published in the nineteenth century without much detail on provenance and date, this was republished in *De genealogieën van Nederveen*, 42–3. It appears to have been written before 1800.

[34] Spaan, *Beschrijvinge*, 13–16.

[35] Van de Waal, *Drie eeuwen*, 258; Koman, *Groot Dordts volksverhalenboek*, 109, note 327; *De genealogieën van Nederveen*; C. Nederveen, 'Pieter, opgevist, met een kat legghende bij sigh', *Oud-Dordrecht* 25 (2007): 26–8. This also refers to the recent tale of the descendant of Beatrix.

[36] Koman, *Groot Dordts volksverhalenboek*, 106–7; Van de Waal, *Drie eeuwen*, 255.

[37] Romeyn de Hooghe, *Sint Elisabethsvloed* (1675), Rijksmuseum, Amsterdam, RP-P-OB-76.843

Figure 5.2. Jan Luyken, *Flood in Groningen of 1686,* 1698, Rijksmuseum, Amsterdam.

first century the appeal of the tale has not waned; the tale of a floating baby is central to the plot of a Dutch film *De storm* from 2009, which is set during the great floods of 1953.

The story of the baby, cat, and cradle was in itself modelled on an archetypal mythical tale of delivery, which is most familiar through the biblical story of Moses. This may well explain its appearance and its attraction in fifteenth-century Dordrecht. A story like this was undoubtedly shaped by the existence of an archetype about the providential rescue of floating babies, and their special mission; and that was also the reason why it stuck and survived. It had more potential than other rescue tales, in that it concerned a baby, suggested miraculous delivery and special divine favour; and this in turn also made it attractive to be associated with it. At the same time it was essential for the long-term survival and career of the myth that it was coupled with an identifiable event and that there was supporting evidence to authenticate that event and its enormity. The flood of 1421 was only the first of a series, and at the time of their happening, later floods undoubtedly generated tales of their own. Yet in the longer term all flood stories came to be associated with the flood of 1421. This telescoping effect is quite well

and Jan Luyken, *Watersnood in Groningen in 1686* (1698), Rijksmuseum, Amsterdam, RP-P-1896-A-19368-1562.RP-P-1896-A-193-O. An eighteenth-century house in Alblasserdam has a gable stone representing baby, cat, and cradle.

known among students of memory.[38] It is significant in that it helped to reinforce an appearance of precision, which was necessary to support the absorption of memories into learned and popular historical tales. In this process, memory practices were an important catalyst; the painting and the inscription, the family tales, the jewels have fired the interplay between myth and history, personal and public versions of the story. Oral, written, and material evidence served to mutually support and reinforce one another.

In all this, the role of the cat in the story remains something of an enigma. The cat seems to have become more important for the tale when, from the late seventeenth century onwards, it was not just said to have been present, but also to have been instrumental in the rescue of the baby, by making sure that the cradle remained well balanced.[39] In tales about floating babies in other Dutch floods, the cat was also included. The cat was first dismissed in 1808 by the poet Reyer van Someren, who explained that in his lengthy poetic account of the tale, he had 'left out the cat because it is an unpoetic being'.[40] Much more than earlier observers, Van Someren seemed to think that one might divorce the myth from the historical evidence. He did this without wanting to diminish the importance of either because, in an appendix to his poem, he explained and documented exactly how he had handled the historical facts. This points to a division of labour between myth and history in nineteenth-century culture, in which the role of myth was not necessarily to be historically true, but rather to testify to the antiquity of a tale and so, sometimes implicitly, lend support to its spiritual or psychological significance. As we will see, this had also been happening in Hamelin. Even so, its historical dimensions also remained important. In the nineteenth century, the tale of baby, cat, and cradle was adopted as a toponomical explanation for the Kinderdijk (or children's dyke) which people claimed owed its name to the finding of Beatrix's cradle there. Subject of fierce debate and competition, and eventually disproven with considerable solemnity, the tale of this association was to become especially popular and is still used today to enhance Kinderdijk's status as a quintessentially Dutch tourist attraction.[41]

MYTHOLOGIZING HISTORY

Yet if memory practices can help to perpetuate and authenticate myths, early modern myth also helped to perpetuate historical memories, as we can see in another tale of deliverance. In 1685, an unknown editor was completing work on the second, extended edition of a very influential book, known in English as the *Martyrs' mirror*. This scholarly Mennonite martyrology had first been published by Thieleman van Bracht two decades earlier and was now being updated. Just as he

---

[38] Simon Kemp, 'Association as a cause of dating bias', *Memory* 4 (1996): 131–43.
[39] Spaan, *Beschrijvinghe*, 13–16.
[40] Reyer van Someren, *De St. Elisabethsnacht, Anno 1421. Dichtstuk in drie zangen* (Utrecht, 1841), 90; see also Van de Waal, *Drie eeuwen*, 258.
[41] Koman, *Groot Dordts volksverhalenboek*, 105–6.

was ready to go to press, the editor was contacted by a man who said he was a great-grandson of a woman called Anneke Jans, one of the sixteenth-century martyrs who was celebrated in this book.[42] Anneke had been executed in Rotterdam on 24 January 1539. Her crime was that she was an Anabaptist; she rejected infant baptism and had herself been rebaptized as an adult. Like many martyred heretics Anneke had left a 'testament', in which she testified to her resolve to die for the faith. It was addressed to her son Esaiah and commenced: 'Hear my son, the teachings of your mother, and open your ears to hear the speech of my mouth. Behold, today I am going the way of the prophets, apostles and martyrs, to drink the cup that they have drunk.' Soon after her death, it appeared in print as a song.[43] A prose version of the testament had been printed for the first time in 1562 in a famous collection of martyrs' testimonies called *Het offer des Heeren* or *The sacrifice of the Lord*. It had also been included in the first edition of the *Martyrs' mirror*.

The existence of Anneke's son was thus already well known. But Anneke's great-grandson now produced new material: an extract from the court records detailing the verdict, a letter by Anneke to her son, copied in the hand of his grandfather Esaiah, and a great deal of information regarding Esaiah's life. The great-grandson explained that Esaiah had been a baby of fifteen months when his mother received her death sentence. On her way to be executed, she had called upon the bystanders and asked if one of them would be prepared to look after her son. She had had a purse with some money ready for his support, which she would give to anyone who would promise to raise him as their own son. A poor baker, who already had six children to support, had stepped forward to take on this charge and promised that he would do as she asked. She handed the child over to him 'in the name of the father, son and holy spirit', and proceeded to her martyr's death by drowning.

When the baker came home with the child, his wife was at first very angry, yet soon it emerged that God's 'blessing which he had hoped for by accepting this child' started to flow freely. The baker's business thrived, and he eventually bought himself a brewery (a big social step up for a baker) and left his children much wealth. His foster child Esaiah also became a brewer and eventually even made it to be burgomaster of Rotterdam. So prominent did Esaiah become that he had acted as godfather to a daughter of the city's pensionary and later states-man Johan van Oldenbarnevelt, while Oldenbarnevelt had done the same for his son. The man who had denounced Anneke, by contrast, had come to a terrible end. As he left the place where she had been drowned, a bridge he was crossing

---

[42] Tieleman van Braght, *Het bloedig tooneel of martelaers spiegel der doops-gesinde of weerelose Christenen, die, om 't getuygenis van Jesus haren salighmaker, geleden hebben, ende gedood zijn, van Christi tijd af, tot desen*, 2nd edn (Amsterdam, 1685), 48–9, 143–4. Van Braght had died in the 1660s. We do not know who re-edited the text.

[43] Werner O. Packull, 'Anna Jansz of Rotterdam. A historical investigation of an early Anabaptist heroine', *Archiv für Reformationsgeschichte* 78 (1987): 147–73; Els Kloek, 'Anneke Esaiasdr', in *Digitaal Vrouwenlexicon van Nederland*, accessed 3 May 2016, http://www.historici.nl/Onderzoek/Projecten/DVN/lemmata/data/Esaiasdr.

collapsed, and he himself died, too, by drowning. All of his family ended up in utter destitution.[44]

The tale as it was told here had a number of very satisfactory mythical elements: the baker had to overcome resistance from his wife but did the right thing and was rewarded; Anneke's son was clearly divinely favoured. The traitor, on the other hand, had not only been punished, but deservedly died the same death that she had had to endure so unjustly. These were familiar narrative schemes, such as we also see at work in the other chapters in this book. The beautiful symmetry was maintained in the transmission of the tale, by carefully leaving out all the bad news that was also there to report. Thus, Esaiah's grandson apparently failed to mention that Esaiah had had to leave Rotterdam in 1602 because his brewery had gone bankrupt; one of his sons had already been bankrupted in 1598.[45] Moreover, neither he nor the martyrologist wanted to spell out that, in a religious sense, the story did not quite work. No Anabaptist or Mennonite could have become burgomaster of Rotterdam, both because Mennonites rejected office-holding and because, increasingly, only Reformed men could hold political office. Moreover, if the Reformed city pensionary and later statesman Oldenbarnevelt was involved in the baptism of Esaiah de Lint's children, these cannot have been adults at the time, but would have been baptized as infants and in accordance with the Reformed rite, rather than that of the Mennonite successors to the Anabaptists.

In a confessional, denominational sense, then, the tale was not as satisfactory as it might have been. Nevertheless, to have a martyr among one's ancestors conferred enormous prestige in the Dutch Republic, so much so, apparently, that it hardly mattered anymore if he or she had died for what was the 'wrong' faith.[46] Moreover, Esaiah's grandson had taken a great deal of trouble in offering precise information to enhance the authenticity of his tale. The story was supported by details about Anneke's arrest, the age of her child, the names of the breweries of the baker and Esaiah, and the precise location of the collapsing bridge. And as a morality tale it was apparently so irresistible that the editor of the Mennonite *Martyr's mirror* not only thought he should include it, but also chose to have it illustrated. As in the case of the floating cradle, it was an image by Jan Luyken that greatly enhanced the profile of the story (Figure 5.3).[47]

As a consequence, the tale of Anneke Jans became one of the most famous Mennonite martyrs' tales, even beyond the Netherlands; she inspired poems and a popular historical novel. She was, moreover, also appropriated both as a Rotterdam

---

[44] Van Braght, *Het bloedig tooneel*, 143–4.

[45] E.A. Engelbrecht, *De vroedschap van Rotterdam, 1572–1795*, Bronnen voor de geschiedenis van Rotterdam (Rotterdam, 1973), 41–2. Esaiah was *vroedschap* (town councillor) from 1575 to 1602 and held office many times in the 1590s.

[46] Pollmann, 'Met grootvaders bloed bezegeld', 156–61.

[47] Jan Luyken, *Anneke Jans, condemned to death, hands her son, the later Esaias de Lind, over to a baker, 1539* (1698), Rijksmuseum, Amsterdam, RP-P-OB-44.272. Sarah Covington, 'Jan Luyken, the Martyrs mirror and the iconography of suffering', *The Mennonite Quarterly Review* 85 (2011): 441–76 has argued that we should see the emotive nature of Luyken's work as an expression of a Mennonite sensibility, but I do not think this is necessary.

Figure 5.3. Jan Luyken, *Anneken Jans hands over her son to a baker, 1539,* illustration for the second edition of Tieleman van Braght, *Het bloedig tooneel of martelaers spiegel der doops-gesinde of weerelose Christenen* (Amsterdam, 1685), Rijksmuseum, Amsterdam.

and as a Reformed heroine.[48] The De Lint family, in the meantime, continued to support their links to the story with a silver tazza, which has a later inscription suggesting that it was given to the family by Johan van Oldenbarnevelt as a *pillegift*, a gift for his godchild at the occasion of his baptism. When it came to Rotterdam's Museum Boymans van Beuningen in 1996, a press release underlined its importance with reference to its links with Oldenbarnevelt and Anneke Jans, as well as its long transmission in the De Lint family.[49] Again, we see how important it is for a

---

[48] See Kloek, 'Anneke Esaiasdr'; Adrien Bogaers, 'Het pleegkind', in Adrien Bogaers, *Balladen en romancen* ([Amsterdam], 1846), 1–18 interestingly presented Anneke's child as a little girl, who later married the baker's son. The novel by M. van der Staal, *Anneke Jansz. Historisch verhaal uit den eersten tijd der hervorming* (Rotterdam, 1914), was last reprinted in Middelburg in 2006. 'Anneke Jans. Op 24 januari in de Schie verdronken', *Nieuwe Rotterdamsche Courant*, 22 January 1939.

[49] Geeraert de Rasier, *Tazza* (before 1587), currently on loan to Museum Boymans van Beuningen, Rotterdam, Inv. No. MBZ 489. I am most grateful to Esaiah's descendant Jan de Lint, who first told me about the existence of the tazza and gave me copies of some documentation, and to Alexandra van Dongen, curator of Museum Boymans van Beuningen, Rotterdam, who arranged a viewing of the tazza and made some of the information in the museum's files available to me. This included the press release announcing the transfer of the tazza to the museum on 2 November 1996. That the museum

memory career that the mythical and the historical claims mutually support each other, and how essential memory practices are for the transmission, sometimes even the creation, of evidence; oral traditions, written tales, and material culture intermingle to create a tale that benefits both from a transcendent message and from a semblance of historical plausibility.

SCHOLARS AS MYTHMAKERS

In this process, an interesting role was and is being played by learned authors, who have a crucial role not only in the authentication of myths, but also in their amplification. This may come as something of a surprise because historians of historiography have usually seen the rejection of mythical tales of origin, for instance, as the hallmark of new, and modern, scholarly standards that arose in the course of the early modern period. Conversely, they have so far shown less interest in the supporting role that modern historical techniques could come to play in the reframing and perpetuation of legends. Yet by collecting and listing both direct and circumstantial evidence, and by deciding which parts of a tale they choose to believe and which ones to dismiss, scholars did and do not only enable stories to grow and expand, but also fix these new versions. We can find an excellent example of this process in the tale of the Pied Piper of Hamelin.

In 1654 the pastor Samuel Erich wrote a book entitled the *Exodus hamelensis*, in which he surveyed the arguments in favour of the story of the Pied Piper.[50] He quoted at length from a whole series of chronicles that recounted versions of the tale, pointed to the abundant existing material evidence in the city, and concluded that even though there was no written evidence at all for the story for the years between the thirteenth and the sixteenth centuries, both the popularity and the continuity of the tale suggested that it had to be genuine. Moreover, even though he personally had not had the opportunity to see the council's records, other authors suggested that these also confirmed the story.

The fact that Erich wanted to write this book at all, of course, points to the existence of scepticism. A year earlier, Hamelin Burgomaster Gerhard Reiche had already reported that he considered the story a 'fable'; there was no mention of it in the archives, it was telling that a fourteenth-century chronicler from the city had not considered it worth mentioning, and there was contradictory evidence on the location, the year in which it had happened, and so on.[51] Erich's attempt to rescue that story did not have the desired effect. In 1655 Hamelin senator Sebastian

did not seize the opportunity to buy the tazza in 2002 was partly because of uncertainty about the date of the inscription.

[50] Samuel Erich, *Exodus hamelensis, das ist der Hämelischer Kinder Außgang* (Hannover, 1654). I used the Dutch translation, *De uytgang der Hamelsche kinderen of de verbaasde geschiedenis van 130 burgerskinderen, dewelke in 't jaar 1282 te Hamelen, aan de Weser, in Neder-Saxen, door een gewaanden speelman uyt de stadt verleydt, en...in de Koppelberg verdweenen zijn.: Aan de toetsteen der waarheit beproeft*, trans. Isaac Le Long (Amsterdam, 1729).

[51] The report from Burgomaster Gerhard Reiche in *Quellensammlung*, doc. 69, 77–8.

Spilker listed a range of objections to Erich's book, and in 1659 the Dutch scholar Martin Schoock published a lengthy tract entitled *Fabula hamelensis*, in which he demolished Erich's arguments in favour of the tale, which he dismissed as 'pathetic'. He cited a range of late-medieval chronicles that had reported many similar stories, but which had been silent about the piper. While Schoock conceded that there might be reason to believe tales that had been transmitted from one century to the next, as long as these were in accordance with reason, this was simply not true for the story of the piper, which could boast only about 150 years of transmission and was unbelievable to boot.[52]

The dispute between Erich and Schoock turned the issue into something of an academic cause célèbre—it became a popular topic for university disputations.[53] And the sceptics seemed to have a good point. There was no evidence for the antiquity of the tale. All there was, but that was in itself remarkable, was material evidence and a whole range of sixteenth- and early seventeenth-century sources, both published and unpublished, that reported the tale. Among those reporting were some reputable intellectuals, notably Johan Weyer, best known today for his scepticism about the witch hunts, and the Jesuit scholar Athanasius Kircher, as well as the prolific Catholic propagandist Richard Verstegan. Visitors to the city itself were all told about the tale and reported about its many representations as well as the existence of the 'Drummerfree' street. They were told that the people of Hamelin used their own calendar, which started with the year in which the children disappeared, and found evidence for that on a 1556 inscription on the New Gate, which did indeed state that the gate had been built 272 years after the disappearance of the children.[54]

It is clear that up to around 1650, the people of Hamelin were quite proud of their tale and did not consider it in any way problematic. That they could be so was apparently because they did not attach the same moral to the story as modern readers tend to do; in the sixteenth century, this was not a salutary tale about the fate of those who refused to pay the Pied Piper his due for the destruction of the city's rats and who had thus triggered the rat catcher's terrible revenge. Rather the piper was identified with the Devil and the tale presented as a warning to keep a close watch on one's children.[55] In that sense it fitted well with the vogue for demonology and social disciplining that came with the Reformation era, when Hamelin had turned into a Lutheran city.[56] That a text about the children was inscribed on

---

[52] *Quellensammlung*, doc. 72, 80–4; Martinus Schoock, *Fabula hamelensis sive disquisitio historica* (Groningen, 1659), 151–5.

[53] Discussed in Heinrich Spanuth, *Der Rattenfänger von Hameln. Vom Werden und Sinn einer alten Sage* (Hamelin, 1951), 56.

[54] On the inscription, *Quellensammlung*, doc. 10, 22–3.

[55] As such, he was described in the first printed accounts in Jobus Fincelius, *Wunderzeichen* (Jena, 1555); Caspar Goltwurm Athesinus, *Wunderwerck und Wunderzeichen Buch* (Frankfurt, 1557); and Andreas Hondorff, *Promptuarium exemplorum. Historienn- und Exempelbuch aus heiliger Schrifft und vielen andern... Historien* (Leipzig, 1573), on which see *Quellensammlung*, doc. 9, 21–2; doc. 11, 23–4; and doc. 17, 29. Also in a local inscription from the mid-1550s, *Quellensammlung*, doc. 10, 22–3.

[56] R. Po-Chia Hsia, *Social discipline in the Reformation. Central Europe, 1550–1750* (London and New York, 1989).

a city gate and that it was Burgomaster Popperdieck who paid for a stained-glass image of it to be put up in the local church in 1572 also suggest that in the sixteenth century the tale suited the local elite agenda.[57] New elements frequently appeared in the story. From the mid-sixteenth century, the sources started to mention a connection with rats; the piper had now become a rat catcher; in modern versions of the tale, the abduction of the children is the rat catcher's revenge for the city's failure to pay him for his services.[58] Speculation about the fate of the children similarly evolved. From around 1600 several sources suggested that the children had resurfaced in Transylvania; a century later, the New World was also mentioned.[59]

Yet in the course of the seventeenth century, as demonology went out of fashion among the educated, the tale seems to have become unpopular with the authorities. As we have seen, Burgomaster Reiche and Senator Spilker found the story an embarrassment, and in 1660 the church window was removed. That might have been that. Yet what the sceptics had not really been able to explain, of course, is how the story could have become so popular in the first place. Moreover, since the tale continued to circulate in scholarly texts, some of them demonological, others relating to natural history, visitors to Hamelin and other curious scholars continued to ask after the tale. As a consequence, the rationalists of the early Enlightenment did not forget about the children of Hamelin, quite the opposite. Soon, they came to see it as their challenge to explain the existence of the tale by looking for its 'historical roots'.[60] People who wanted to dismiss the role of the Devil turned to the evidence to try and come up with a better alternative. Philosopher Gottfried Wilhelm Leibniz believed the tale related to a children's crusade.[61] Other eighteenth-century scholars explained it with reference to a battle in which many Hamelin youngsters could have died or sought links with St Vitus's dance and with natural disasters in the area.

Bits of evidence, some of them new, materialized and continued to be scrutinized. A copy of the council book had a version of the tale on the cover that was long considered credible evidence, but no one can say when that originated. The archives of Hamelin yielded two letters in which Jews were given permission to settle in the town and that were dated, like the new gate, with reference to the children's disappearance. By the late nineteenth century they were proven to be forgeries.[62]

---

[57] Werner Ueffing, 'Die Hamelner Rattenfängersage und ihr historischer Hintergrund', in *Geschichten und Geschichte. Erzählforschertagung in Hameln, Oktober 1984*, ed. Norbert Humburg (Hildesheim, 1985), 186.

[58] Spanuth, *Der Rattenfänger*, 100–1.

[59] The Transylvanian link was first mentioned in print by Richard Verstegan, *A restitution of decayed intelligence* (Antwerp, 1605), cited in *Quellensammlung*, doc. 45, 58–9. Later authors cited the evidence of a chronicle from Transylvania (Siebenbürgen) that referred to local German-speakers with accents that resembled that of the Hamelin area; a New World connection was first mooted in 1701, see *Quellensammlung*, doc. 105, 103.

[60] The ongoing interest can be traced through the *Quellensammlung*. On the Enlightenment interest see also Spanuth, *Der Rattenfänger*, 58–69.

[61] *Quellensammlung*, doc. 96a–b, 96–9.

[62] *Quellensammlung*, doc. 5a and 5b, 18–19. I am not persuaded by Dobbertin's arguments for believing them genuine. See also Ueffing, 'Die Hamelner Rattenfängersage', 187.

In 1936, two historians struck gold. In a fourteenth-century manuscript kept in the city of Lüneburg, they found an addition in a later hand, written sometime between 1430 and 1450, which not only included a version of the tale, and a reference to the use of a new calendar, but also mentioned the name of an eyewitness, the daughter of one of the burgomasters, who in 1284 had apparently 'seen the children go'. Since that name could be matched with existing evidence, this may just be proof that this version of the tale, without rats, goes back to the fourteenth century.[63]

This does not in itself do anything to answer the question of what, if anything, happened to the children from Hamelin and why. Still, for a new generation of scholars it was the impetus to go on searching, and indeed to continue using evidence that was produced centuries after the 'event' was said to have taken place. While early modern scholars connected the tale to the migration of young Germans to Transylvania or even the New World, modern ones have suggested that the children were *Ostsiedler*, migrants who had left for Bohemia or Pomerania, for instance.[64] Polish phonebooks were traced for the presence of Hamelin names in Pomerania, and in recent decades Hamelin historian Hans Dobbertin has argued that the tale originated in the move by a thirteenth-century nobleman by name of Nicholas von Spielenberg to recruit young Hamelers to settle on his family lands in Pomerania; they themselves wanted to flee their rat-infested city.[65] As evidence for his theory about the noble piper, Hans Dobbertin refers to the stags on an image of the Pied Paper produced in 1592, which he believes refer to the coat of arms of this noble family (Figure 5.4). He has not yet persuaded all his colleagues.[66]

Hamelin's case is not exceptional. There are interesting parallels, for instance, in the evolution of the myths surrounding William Tell and other tales relating to the foundation of the Swiss *Eidgenossenschaft*. Already supported by memory places like the 'Tell chapel' we encountered at the start of Chapter 3, and popularized in plays, by the late sixteenth century the tale of William Tell's opposition was widespread, and his figure even took on sacred significance. Yet the tales of Tell's exploits and their relationship with the foundation of the *Eidgenossenschaft* were given their coherence and stability by scholar Aegidius Tschudis, who around 1550 first produced an account which integrated various tales, dated them, and offered a historical context. In the Enlightenment, the discovery of tales similar to that of Tell in Scandinavian lore briefly led to dismissal of the tale of his shooting of the apple as a 'Danish fairy-tale', yet that did not stop the enormous popularity of the tale. Very much as in the case of Hamelin there has, until very recently, been incessant and extensive learned study of the 'historical kernel' behind the complex of myths surrounding the origins of Swiss cooperation, which were deemed all the

---

[63] Spanuth, *De Rattenfänger*, 91–100; *Quellensammlung*, doc. 4, 15–18.

[64] Spanuth, *Der Rattenfänger*; Bernd Ulrich Hucker, 'Die Auszug der Hämelschen Kinder aus quellenkritischer Sicht', in *Geschichten und Geschichte. Erzählforschertagung in Hameln, Oktober 1984*, ed. Norbert Humburg (Hildesheim, 1985), 96–8.

[65] Florescu, *In search of the Pied Piper*, 155–70; see for a critique of Dobertin's argument, Ueffing, 'Die Hamelner Rattenfängersage'.

[66] Florescu, *In search of the Pied Piper*, 166–7; Ueffing, 'Die Hamelner Rattenfängersage', 186.

Figure 5.4. Traveller Augustin von Mörsperg included this drawing in his *Reisechronik*, a travel account of *c.*1592, fo. 193f, which is now at the Schlossmuseum, Sondershausen. The caption reads: Image of a piper who appeared once upon a time, in the year 1284, in Hamelen on the Weser, found in Braunschweig.

more necessary because they served as counterweight to the chronic divisions and instability in the federation.[67]

CONCLUSION

For the defender of the Hamelin story, pastor Samuel Erich, it was self-evident that fables could not survive for long. For a story to be believable it needed supporting detail. As he explained, a statement such as 'it is said that a certain woman has been elected pope somewhere' could easily be dismissed as a fantasy. Yet if one were to say

in the year of our Lord 853, during the reign of emperor Lotharius the Pious, a certain woman named Joan was exercising the dignity of pope in Rome, it is immediately evident that this tale is not a fantasy but rather a truthful history, especially when witnesses agree on it.[68]

---

[67] Peter Kaiser, 'Befreiungstradition', in *Historisches Lexikon der Schweiz* (Bern, 2009), accessed 11 June 2015, http://www.hls-dss.ch/textes/d/D17474.php; Olaf Mörke, 'Städtemythen als Element politischer Sinnstiftung in der Schweizer Eidgenossenschaft und in der Niederländischen Republik', in *Städtische mythen*, ed. Bernhard Kirchgässner and Hans-Peter Becht, Stadt in der Geschichte 28 (Ostfildern, 2003), 91–118; Lerner, 'Cultural memories of a Swiss revolt'.

[68] Erich, *De uytgang der Hamelsche kinderen*, 26.

Mundane as Erich's reasoning was, he was quite right, of course, that stories are much more likely to be believed if they are firmly anchored in supporting detail. They need to be set in a time and a place, they need a 'friend of a friend' who has heard it himself, and they are helped along by the existence of spatial and material markers; this is how a narrative is 'historicized'. This chapter has shown how in early modern Europe, such a historicization of narrative could come about. The agents of this process of historicization could be manifold. Much depended on the presence of stakeholders, people like the Nederveen and Roerom families in Dordrecht, the descendants of Anneke Jans, or the elite and the local historians of Hamelin. Yet the process also depended on the interplay of myth, memory, and history, and the interaction of stakeholders with authoritative mediators, many of whom were scholars.

In his 2003 book on *Mythistory* Joseph Mali argued that myth plays a larger role in the historical discipline than is usually acknowledged. Writing in an intellectual history tradition, Mali sees the eighteenth-century historian and philosopher Giambattista Vico as the godfather of the realization that myth is fundamental to the writing of history. The cases I have discussed suggest that underlying such theoretical reflections on the relationship between myth and history, there may have been a historical practice in which historians already knew how to make myth productive.[69] Myth and history have often been presented as subsequent phases in a linear development, but much as we saw when discussing analogous historical reasoning in Chapter 2, it seems that for most of Western history myths and mythical patterns of explanation have had to coexist with other ways of structuring knowledge about the past, and thus with history. The spread of literacy has undoubtedly affected the nature of that coexistence. As Carrie Benes and Adam Fox have shown for medieval Italy and early modern England respectively, in pre-modern literate societies there was much interaction between written and oral culture; written texts did as much to spread and perpetuate myths as did villagers spinning their tales.[70] But there is more at stake here than the traffic of ideas and motifs between literate and oral cultures. We have seen that when it comes to the transmission of collective memories, myth and history actually feed off one another in an even more fundamental sense. Rather than to think of myth and history as each other's opposites, as different paradigmatic *ideal types* of engaging with the past, or as successive *phases* in the history of historical consciousness, this chapter has suggested it is more helpful to explore them as two forms of engagement with that past that are in fact closely interrelated and indeed interdependent.

Some scholars have seen this coexistence, and the blurring of history and myth that it entails, as a typically contemporary and postmodern phenomenon.[71] I think this is unnecessary. The three tales I have explored suggest that the blurring of history and myth is not some sort of postmodern phenomenon only; in fact,

---

[69] Joseph Mali, *Mythistory. The making of a modern historiography* (Chicago and London, 2003).

[70] Carrie Benes, *Urban legends. Civic identity and the classical past in Northern Italy, 1250–1350* (University Park PA, 2011); Fox, *Oral and literate culture*, 213–58.

[71] Coupe, *Myth*, 15.

it has been common practice for at least five centuries. Does that mean, then, that this blurring is typical for the 'early modernity' of the period under discussion? Where early modernists have seen myth and history coexist, they have sometimes read this as a sign that myth was 'already' beginning to lose its sway and increasingly needed the backup of historical evidence if it was to be taken seriously.[72] Yet the cases I have discussed here do not really support such assumptions about a linear development away from myth and towards the use of evidence. Folklore studies suggest that to be successful, mythical tales about the past have always needed the support of things in the here and now; they need references to names of places and people, to objects in the material world, to features in the landscape or days in the calendar, or testimony that is passed on orally or in writing. The study of early modern memory practices helps us to understand how such references could come into existence, how they achieved authority, and how they changed over time. In early modern Europe the transmission of tales was definitely affected by the appearance of new media, new figures of authority, and new notions about evidence. Yet the application of new criteria for historical evidence from the seventeenth century did not necessarily result in the decline of myths. Quite the opposite, by declaring such stories mythical and by using the existence of memory practices as evidence of their long-standing mythical significance as well as their historical kernel, scholars soon found reasons to go on taking them seriously as an object of study and of historical enquiry.

---

[72] E.g. Woolf, *The social circulation*, 390–1.

6

Acts of Oblivion

On 19 September 1946 Winston Churchill gave a speech in Zurich in which he called for the foundation of 'the United States of Europe', starting with the setting up of a Council of Europe. He defended the need for this action as follows:

> The guilty must be punished. Germany must be deprived of the power to rearm and make another aggressive war. But when all this has been done, as it will be done, as it is being done, there must be an end to retribution. There must be what Mr Gladstone many years ago called 'a blessed act of oblivion'.

> We must all turn our backs upon the horrors of the past. We must look to the future. We cannot afford to drag forward across the years that are to come the hatreds and revenges which have sprung from the injuries of the past.

> If Europe is to be saved from infinite misery, and indeed from final doom, there must be an act of faith in the European family and an act of oblivion against all the crimes and follies of the past.[1]

Although Europe did indeed get its Council, and the creation of a 'United States of Europe' has remained on the agenda of at least some people until this day, the European family has not seen fit to subscribe to an act of oblivion. Churchill thought that oblivion would mean that 'the wrongs and injuries which have been inflicted will have been washed away on all sides by the miseries which have been endured', but we have concluded that it is not as simple as that. There can be no trade-off between memories of the Shoah, the London Blitz, and the slave labourers on the Burma railway line, on the one hand, and the firebombing of Dresden, the victims of Hiroshima, and the rapes of women in Berlin, on the other. We believe that all of these horrors need to be remembered.

Whereas Churchill believed that it was only through oblivion that peace might be attained and protected, many societies have, in the last half century or so, drawn completely different lessons from the horrors of World War II. Inspired by the insights of psychologists, most policy- and opinion makers today think that it is more dangerous for societies to forget than to remember. Oblivion is undesirable and indeed impossible because ignoring the long-term impact of traumatic memories on individuals and groups prevents the healing of the wounds of conflict. Moreover, crimes against humanity are too serious to be the subject of amnesties, and oblivion might not even be so successful in bringing peace. There is thus no point to acts of oblivion. Instead, there is now a powerful new paradigm, that of the

---

[1] Winston Churchill, 'United States of Europe speech, 19 September 1946', accessed 25 May 2015, http://www.winstonchurchill.org/resources/speeches/1946-1963-elder-statesman/united-states-of-europe.

need for 'Truth and Reconciliation', so named after the South African Commission that used this method after the end of the apartheid regime in 1994.[2]

Yet this was not always so. From the Middle Ages until the nineteenth century, acts of oblivion were a favourite instrument in any peacemaker's toolkit. Churchill already reminded his audience that he was not the first to moot the idea that an act of oblivion could be an effective way of coping with a legacy of violent conflict. He referred to the 'blessed act of oblivion' for which William Gladstone had pleaded in order to give Home Rule to Ireland in 1886. With even more justification Churchill could have mentioned the French Constitutional Charter of 1814, which had restored the Bourbon monarchy in France after the rule of Napoleon Bonaparte.[3] Had he wanted to go further back in time, he could have invoked the Act of Indemnity and Oblivion that the English Parliament had agreed to in 1660 when it accepted the restoration of the monarchy. He could have mentioned the oblivion clauses in the Peace of Westphalia of 1648, which ended the Thirty Years War, or the Edict of Nantes of 1598, which put a temporary end to the religious civil wars in France. And while the *Kappeler Landfriede* of 1529, which put a temporary end to the religious wars in Switzerland, was perhaps the first instance in which oblivion was agreed to in an attempt to overcome the divisions of the Reformation, there were also many such clauses in medieval peace treaties.[4] For centuries, the acts and peace treaties that ended civil wars and revolutionary upheaval in Europe routinely contained clauses in which former enemies or their victors declared that all that had happened in the past would be 'forgotten'. But what did peacemakers mean by that? And did such a policy for amnesia ever work? Exploring the aims and practice of oblivion in early modern Europe, this chapter will examine whether oblivion could function as a viable strategy for peacekeeping and ask why, as a political solution, it was eventually superseded.

As we have seen, memories are subject to constant change. They transform under the influence of retelling and of memories shared by others. In this way individual memories and group memories can start to converge and reinforce one another, so that collective memories emerge that can become powerful agents of conflict; to end conflicts we may need to 'forget' in able to forgive and move on.[5] This solution, at least, was tried in three major European conflicts in this period, which will be discussed in this chapter.

[2] But see for critical notes on the genesis and alleged universality of this paradigm Rosalind Shaw, 'Memory frictions. Localizing the Truth and Reconciliation Commission in Sierra Leone', *The International Journal of Transitional Justice* I (2007): 183–207; David Rieff, *In praise of forgetting: Historical memory and its ironies* (New Haven, 2016).

[3] In fact Gladstone had called for 'blessed oblivion', see below note 62. *French Constitutional Charter of 4 June 1814*, accessed 21 October 2013, http://www.napoleon-series.org/research/government/legislation/c_charter.html. See on this Sheryl Kroen, *Politics and theater. The crisis of legitimacy in Restoration France, 1815–1830* (Berkeley CA, 2000).

[4] Claire Gantet, 'Mémoires du conflit, mémoires conflictuelles au lendemain de la guerre de Trente Ans', in *Vergeben und vergessen? Vergangenheisdiskurse nach Besatzung, Bürgerkrieg und Revolution/ Pardonner ou oublier? Les Discours sur le passé après l'occupation, la guerre civile et la revolution*, ed. Reiner Marcowicz and Werner Paravicini, Pariser historische Studien 94 (Munich, 2009).

[5] On processes of forgetting, see e.g. Willem A. Wagenaar and Hans Crombag, *The popular policeman and other cases. Psychological perspectives on legal evidence* (Amsterdam, 2005), ch. 8.

The first of these are the French Wars of Religion, which broke out in 1562 when the young French king Charles IX and his mother tried to resolve the growing tension between Catholic and Calvinist 'Huguenot' nobles in the kingdom by promulgating an edict of toleration, which tried to create a form of coexistence between Catholics and Calvinists. What had been intended as a measure to keep the peace unfortunately triggered the first of a series of civil wars, in which Catholics and Calvinists took up arms both against each other and against a series of weak kings. Each of these wars was ended with an 'edict of pacification'; from 1563 these always include references to amnesties and oblivion. Yet because the edicts did not succeed in creating working arrangements for Catholic–Protestant disarmament and coexistence, they were not a success.

In 1584, when it became clear that King Henri III would die without an heir, the stakes in the conflict rose even higher; claims of the heir apparent, the Calvinist Henri of Navarre, were disputed by a Catholic League, which instead promoted first a cardinal and then a female successor whose mother was French, but whose father was the king of Spain. War again ensued. Only after Henri of Navarre had abandoned his Protestant faith in order to gain the throne and had fought a long war against the League and the Spanish father of his rival claimant could he in 1598 at last promulgate a peace that seemed as if it might last, the Edict of Nantes. Again, that promised oblivion; this time there was a chance to implement it.[6]

We have already briefly encountered memory practices relating to the second conflict that will be discussed in this chapter: the Revolt of the Netherlands, which began as an uprising of the Low Countries against their overlords, the Habsburg kings of Spain, and developed into a war that lasted eight decades. The rebellion was triggered in 1566 both by growing dissatisfaction about the highhanded way in which the Habsburgs tried to combat heresy and by a sense that the crown encroached on local and noble privileges. After a short period of open Calvinist preaching in the summer of 1566 had descended into a wave of iconoclasm, the king sent an enforcer, the Duke of Alba, with an army to suppress religious dissidence and all those who had seemed to encourage and tolerate it, including the nobility. One of the Netherlandish magnates, William of Orange, went into exile in his native county of Nassau in the Holy Roman Empire and then became the leader of a campaign of armed resistance, which in 1572 first gained solid ground in the provinces of Holland and Zeeland. Although Alba soon left, his successors were unable to suppress the rebellion, not least because of endemic mutinies by Habsburg soldiers. By 1576, these became such a problem that all other Netherlandish provinces joined the rebellion and demanded the departure of Spanish troops. In the so-called Pacification of Ghent they solemnly agreed that all that had happened since 1566 would be considered 'forgotten and be regarded as not having occurred'. Soon, however, the rebel camp began to split; Catholics resented the rapidly growing power of aggressive Calvinist minorities, especially in

---

[6] See for an introduction to the wars e.g. Mack P. Holt, *The French Wars of Religion, 1562–1629* (Cambridge, 1995); Denis Crouzet, *Les Guerriers de Dieu. La Violence au temps des troubles de religion, vers 1525–vers 1610*, 2 vols (Seyssel, 1990).

the Southern provinces of Brabant, Flanders, and Hainaut. Moreover, a new Habsburg commander, Alessandro Farnese, Duke of Parma, began an effective campaign to reconquer the South. By 1585 Farnese had 'reconciled' all the cities of the Southern Netherlands and concluded a series of agreements that all included an oblivion cause. These established what would prove to be a definitive split between a rebellious Dutch Republic and a Catholic Habsburg state in the Southern Netherlands. The war between the two states would continue until 1648.[7]

The third and final conflict to be explored here are the Civil Wars and Interregnum that rocked the kingdoms of England, Scotland, and Ireland from 1639 to 1660. The conflict started in Scotland as a protest against the unpopular ecclesiastical policies that King Charles I tried to impose on his Scottish subjects. When the king called a parliament in England in order to ask for support against the Scots, MPs took the opportunity not only to demand redress of their own grievances against the religious policies promoted by Charles and his archbishop Laud, but also to raise a number of other long-standing fiscal and political issues. A Catholic revolt against Protestant planters in Ireland in 1641 raised parliamentary suspicions that the king's earlier attempts to ask for Catholic support there pointed to a hidden agenda to recatholize England. In 1642 a majority in the House of Commons came out in open resistance against the king and called the nation to arms. Charles's handling of the opposition was so dismal that from 1642 he found himself at war with subjects in all three of his kingdoms, which now plunged into a civil war that became all the more intractable for the lack of agreement among the parliamentarians and their army on the alternatives to Charles's religious policies. Having imprisoned the king in 1647, a small section of Parliament, the so-called Rump, brought the king to trial and had him executed on 30 January 1649. A new godly regime, now under the direction of former army commander Oliver Cromwell, spent the next ten years subduing the Irish and Scots, and fighting the Dutch, but failed to come to a religious settlement that satisfied the myriad of radical and less radical Protestant groups that had emerged during the turmoil of the Civil Wars, especially within the armies and London. After Cromwell's death, with his son as a brief but unlikely successor, the Interregnum regime lost all momentum; by 1660, its main general and Parliament started negotiations with the exiled son of King Charles, Charles II, about a restoration. This included an Act of Indemnity and Oblivion, which offered a limited amnesty, as well as 'oblivion' of things past.

What was the point of the oblivion clauses in the edicts and peace agreements drawn up by such warring parties? Their first aim was evidently to offer a legal amnesty for past acts of violence and rebellion. This made sense when fear of retribution for such acts had, or could, become a motive for prolonging a violent conflict.

[7] See on the Dutch Revolt the classic account by Geoffrey Parker, *The Dutch Revolt* (Harmondsworth, 1977); or for a more recent survey Anton van der Lem, *De Opstand in de Nederlanden, 1568–1648. De Tachtigjarige oorlog in woord en beeld* (Nijmegen, 2014). In 2007 Henk van Nierop explored the political thinking behind act of oblivion clauses in the Revolt in an unpublished conference paper, 'The politics of oblivion. The Dutch civil war and the quest for stability, 1566–1609', Leiden University (2007). I am grateful to him for making a copy available to me.

It was 'to take away the causes of mistrust and dissidence', for instance, that Habsburg commander Farnese in the 1580s made a point of offering exceptionally generous terms to the surrendering rebellious Calvinists in the Southern Netherlands; no one was to be punished for rebellion or heresy, and not even for lese-majesty, and all Protestants were given time to sell their goods and leave the country. Anyone who wanted to do so could reconcile with the Catholic Church, with no further questions being asked.[8] For the Habsburgs this was a new strategy, devised especially with a view to avoid the mistakes that had been made in earlier stages of the Revolt of the Netherlands, when cities had been so afraid of the acts of retribution by the Duke of Alba that they had decided to fight on rather than surrender. In France, too, many realized that the culture of retribution had to end if the kingdom was ever to be freed from the paralysis of conflict and division.[9] The 1598 Edict of Nantes offered an amnesty that was slightly less generous than that in the Netherlands: it exempted from the amnesty 'execrable cases': instances of rape, arson, and theft that had occurred 'to exercise private vengeance, contrary to the duties of war', lack of respect for passports and safeguards, and murders and pillaging that had occurred 'without orders having been given'.[10] In England, the Act of Indemnity and Oblivion was intended as a guarantee to the Presbyterians in the English Parliament who had supported Cromwell that they would not be penalized for this by the new king. Only a small number of named people, mainly those responsible for the regicide of Charles I, were exempted from the amnesty in the Act.[11]

Secondly, oblivion clauses aimed to put a stop to disputes about property that had changed hands as a direct or indirect result of revolts and civil conflict. Acts of oblivion tried to establish the rules by which these issues would be settled and defined cut-off points. In this way they helped new regimes to sort out what were often several decades' worth of transactions, claims and counterclaims, in an attempt to contain these disputes as a source of further conflict. Yet it is significant that oblivion clauses usually did not limit themselves to outlining the two quite specific issues of legal amnesties and property claims. Instead they were framed in a much more general way, stipulating that people should 'forget', 'ignore', 'keep silent about', 'bury' the injuries and the differences of the past.[12] Thus, the Edict of Nantes of

[8] *Articvlen, ende conditien vanden tractate, aengegaen ende ghesloten tusschen...den prince van Parma,...ter eenre, ende de stadt van Antvverpen ter ander syden: Den XVII Augusti, m.d.LXXXV* (Antwerp, 1585).

[9] Mark Greengrass, 'Amnestie et "oubliance". Un discours politique autour des édits de pacification pendant les guerres de religion', in *Paix des armes, paix des âmes. Actes du colloque international tenu au Musée national du château de Pau et à l'Université de Pau et des Pays de l'Adour 1998*, ed. Paul Mironneau and Isabelle Péblay-Clottes (Paris, 2000), 113–23; Olivier Christin, 'Mémoire inscrite, oubli prescrit. La Fin des troubles de religion en France', in *Vergeben und vergessen? Vergangenheisdiskurse nach Besatzung, Bürgerkrieg und Revolution/Pardonner ou oublier? Les Discours sur le passé après l'occupation, la guerre civile et la revolution*, ed. Reiner Marcowicz and Werner Paravicini, Pariser historische Studien 94 (Munich, 2009), 81–8, at 88.

[10] Cited in Greengrass, 'Amnistie et "oubliance"', 114.

[11] Neufeld, *The Civil Wars*.

[12] Ross Poole, 'Enacting oblivion', *International Journal of Politics, Culture, and Society* 22 (2009): 149–57; Paul Connerton, 'Seven types of forgetting', *Memory Studies* 1 (2008): 59–71; Michael Woolf, 'Amnesty and *oubliance* at the end of the French Wars of Religion', in *Clémence, oubliance et*

1598 stipulated that 'the memory of everything which occurred on one side or the other since the beginning of March 1585...and the preceding troubles, and because of them, will remain extinguished and suppressed as things that did not happen'. The very same phrase can be found in most of the treaties concluded during the Dutch Revolt: the events of the past would be treated 'as if they had not occurred'.[13] In England, there was not only an agreement not to discuss the wars at all for three years; the Act stipulated financial penalties for anyone who:

> within the space of three yeares next ensueing shall presume malitiously to call or alledge of, or object against any other person or persons any name or names, or other words of reproach any way tending to revive the memory of the late Differences or the occasions thereof.[14]

The start of the king's reign was officially declared to be 1649, as if there had been no Interregnum.

Why was it so important to pretend that things had not happened at all? One reason for this was undoubtedly that memory was far too politically potent for it to be left to chance. As we have seen in Chapter 5, there were long established traditions for the commemoration of public events. It was thus unsurprising that public memorialization had begun as soon as the troubles in France, the Netherlands, and the British Isles unfolded and had become part and parcel of the conflict. Throughout France, for instance, Catholic city governments had set up annual processions during the wars to commemorate victories over the Calvinist heretics; cities like Toulouse, Besançon, Rouen, Orléans, and Poitiers, for instance, all developed such a tradition. There had also been monuments erected that could be considered offensive. In Paris, the house where Jean Chastel had attempted to assassinate Henri of Navarre in 1594 was destroyed by an order of the *parlement* of Paris, together with a commemorative pyramid placed on the spot to remind all passers-by of this evil deed and of the Jesuit involvement in this assassination plot.[15] It should have gone after the Edict of 1598, but remained standing until 1605, when it was finally destroyed because of its anti-Jesuit associations. In a similar move, when the Duke of Alba ordered in 1568 that the Brussels palace of the Count of Culemborg be torn down in retribution for Culemborg's role in inciting rebellion in the Low Countries, he decreed that a column be placed on the spot, to remind people of the punishment for such behaviour.[16] Just as had happened in

---

pardon en Europe, 1520–1650, ed. Michel De Waele, special issue of *Cahiers d'Histoire* 16 (1996): 46–68.

[13] See e.g. *Traicté de la Paix, faicte conclue et arrestée entre les Estatz de ces pays bas, assemblez en...Bruxelles, et le Sr. Prince d'Orenges, Estatz de Hollande et Zelande, avecq leurs associez et publiée le VIIIe iour de Novembre, 1576, avecq l'agreation et confirmation du Roy...nostre Sire surce ensuyuie* (Brussels, 1576).

[14] 'Charles II, 1660: An Act of Free and Generall Pardon Indempnity and Oblivion', *Statutes of the Realm* V, 1628–80. Great Britain Record Commission (n.p., 1819), 226–34, clause xxiv, accessed 28 May 2015, http://www.british-history.ac.uk/statutes-realm/vol5/pp226-234#h3-0024.

[15] Christin, 'Mémoire inscrite, oubli prescrit', 83–4.

[16] Van der Steen, *Memory wars*.

Paris, this column was itself destroyed after the Pacification of Ghent decreed oblivion in the Netherlands.

In the British Isles, commemoration had taken on a variety of forms. The massacre of Protestants in Ireland in 1641 was commemorated annually on 23 October throughout the Isles, while, as we will see in Chapter 7, heavily edited extracts from the depositions of the victims were widely published and were thus etched into Protestant memory.[17] Royalists came to venerate Charles I as a martyr, avidly reading his spiritual autobiography, the *Eikon Basilike. The Pourtrature of His Sacred Majestie in His Solitudes and Sufferings*, which was reprinted thirty times in 1649 alone. Cromwell's Commonwealth regime, in the meantime, also developed memory policies. Thus, it named its battleships after major victories the parliamentarians had won during the conflict; after 1660 these were given the names of members of the royal family.[18] It was a continuation of a practice that, as we saw in Chapter 4, had first commenced in the reign of Queen Elizabeth I, who had replaced Catholic religious holidays with days to celebrate her own reign and political achievements.[19]

Moves to publicize the eradication of the memory of one's enemies, known in ancient Roman times as *damnatio memoriae*, were a clear act of aggression and interpreted as such. A related form of obliterating memories was to pointedly recycle goods or materials for purposes contrary to those for which they had been used before. As we have seen, in the 1570s Calvinist rebels in Leiden redeployed the Catholic altar stone that they had taken out of the main parish church as a commemorative plaque on the town hall, inscribing it with a text rejoicing in their deliverance from Catholic Habsburg rule. In the village of Doorn, saints' images that the Calvinists had broken were buried face down in the parish church, as was customary with the bodies of criminals, under the route that the Reformed walked towards their communion table.[20] When Calvinist temples were demolished in the Southern Netherlands in 1567, the wood was reused for the gibbets and pyres on which Protestants were being executed.[21] To commemorate his victory over the rebels, the Duke of Alba in 1571 commissioned a statue of himself that had been cast from the bronze cannon he had captured from rebel leader William of Orange.[22]

It is no wonder, then, that early modern peacemakers were well aware that they not only needed to encourage warring parties to put down their arms, or to prevent

---

[17] Jane Ohlmeyer and Micheál Ó Siochrú, 'Introduction. 1641, fresh contexts and perspectives', in *Ireland 1641. Contexts and reactions*, ed. Jane Ohlmeyer and Micheál Ó Siochrú (Manchester, 2013), 1–16; and Nicholas Canny, '1641 in a colonial context', in *Ireland 1641. Contexts and reactions*, ed. Jane Ohlmeyer and Micheál Ó Siochrú (Manchester, 2013), 52–70.

[18] Stoyle, 'Remembering the English Civil Wars', 23.   [19] Cressy, *Bonfires and bells*.

[20] Moerman and Van Maanen, *Leiden, eeuwig feest*, 21.

[21] Pasquier de le Barre and Nicolas Soldoyer, *Mémoires de Pasquier de le Barre et de Nicolas Soldoyer pour servir à l'histoire de Tournai, 1565–1640*, ed. Alex Pinchart, 2 vols, Collection de mémoires rélatifs à l'histoire de Belgique 8–9 (Brussels, 1859–65), II, 221–365, at 283.

[22] The statue was taken down in 1575 and later generations believed that the bronze was again recycled into a cross. Judith Pollmann and Monica Stensland, 'Alba's reputation in the early modern Low Countries', in *Alba. General and servant to the crown*, ed. M.E. Ebben, M. Lacy-Bruijn, and R. van Hövell tot Westerflier (Rotterdam, 2013), 309–25, at 314–18.

litigation, but that the public memorialization of rebellion and conflict would also need to be managed if it was not to become a source of contention. Yet if it thus made sense for peacemakers to attempt to manage memorialization, it is not so self-evident why they thought acts of oblivion were the best way of doing so. As the political scientist Ross Poole has pointed out, there is not only the practical problem of how one can police such injunctions to forget; even in its legal application there seems to be a paradox. After all, to assess whether something can or cannot fall within the meaning of the Act, a legal system has to have knowledge of the things that it is supposed to forget.[23] In the Southern Netherlands, people who wanted to claim rewards for loyalty during the Revolt had no option other than to discuss its existence.[24] In France, commissioners were instructed to let Huguenots meet at places where they had also met at particular times during the wars, but that, of course, necessitated knowledge of the same events that had supposedly been forgotten.[25] The awkward situations that this produced are evident from the account that the militant Catholic bourgeois Jean Burel left of the attempts to implement oblivion in the city of Le Puy-en-Velay in the Auvergne. In September 1598 he reported how a Parisian official had arrived in town with a message that, to Burel, at least, was quite unwelcome:

> I am here on the king's behalf and to show you what the king wants and that all that has happened should be forgotten as if it had not come to pass, and he also wants that you will elect consuls from both camps, without reproaching each other but all living in peace.[26]

The good people of Le Puy were thus simultaneously asked to identify people 'from both camps' to serve as consuls and to forget that such camps existed. If this was oblivion, it was clearly not total. Twelve years later, when news reached Le Puy that King Henri had been assassinated by a Catholic, Catholics in Le Puy immediately set out to seize the castle of a Calvinist, assuming that the Edict had died with the king. Only explicit orders by the queen-mother, now regent of their new ruler, eight-year-old Louis XIII, persuaded them to desist.[27]

It is perhaps no wonder, then, that historians of early modern Europe have not been at all convinced that acts of oblivion actually worked. Recent work on Germany, England, France, and the Habsburg Netherlands has found that in places where such an act was in force, this did not stop people from commemorating the conflicts that oblivion clauses had taught them to forget. In a German context, Claire Gantet has shown that in a bi-confessional German town like Augsburg, for instance, the annual feast to celebrate the Peace of Westphalia was actually an occasion during which Lutheran Augsburgers aggressively asserted the

---

[23] Poole, 'Enacting oblivion'.   [24] Van der Steen, *Memory wars*, 116–19.
[25] Philip Benedict, 'Shaping the memory of the French Wars of Religion. The first centuries', in *Memory before modernity. Practices of memory in early modern Europe*, ed. Erika Kuijpers et al. (Leiden and Boston, 2013), 111–25, at 113.
[26] Jean Burel, *Mémoires de Jean Burel. Journal d'un bourgeois du Puy à l'époque des guerres de religion*, ed. A. Chassaing (Le Puy-en-Velay, 1898), 467.
[27] Burel, *Mémoires de Jean Burel*, 501–3.

gains they had made.[28] The Civil Wars and regicide also cast a long shadow over Restoration England. Not only did King Charles II feel he had to take very public revenge on the memory of Oliver Cromwell, whose body was disinterred and displayed on the gallows in 1661.[29] A recent study by Matthew Neufeld on England concluded that the Act of Indemnity and Oblivion was soon superseded by new legislation, which aimed above all to minimize the influence of dissenting Protestants. The need for such legislation was demonstrated in government-sanctioned histories and other accounts of the wars. In these histories, there was a selective oblivion of sorts, for instance of the events during the 'Commonwealth', when England had a republican regime, but there were also many forces at work to publicize a government-sanctioned version of events that pointed to the 'ambitions' (rather than the religious views) of dissident Protestants as the root cause of the war and the regicide, that highlighted the sacrifices of royalist 'martyrs' during the wars, and vilified Oliver Cromwell as a tyrant. Edward Legon has argued that there were, in fact, many who continued to cherish memories of the Commonwealth and at times even ventured to express these in public.[30]

In France there were many visual reminders of war episodes. Inscription and captions on damaged images in France pointed out that the heretics had been to blame for the mutilation.[31] One of the most popular images of the early seventeenth century was a procession of armed Leaguers among whom Catholic clergy figured prominently (Figure 6.1).[32] Calvinists in France, for their part, also kept the memories of the wars alive, even if historians often shied away from mentioning events like the St Bartholomew's massacre of 1572. Philip Benedict has shown that many Calvinist psalm books contained lists of memorable dates, with a heavy focus on the events of the wars of the sixteenth century. Some Catholics took offence—in 1645 the royal commissioner at the national synod of the Huguenots in Charenton informed them that the entry in a Genevan Reformed psalm book that spoke of the 'detestable council of Trent' was offensive to Catholics and contravened the oblivion clauses.[33] Olivier Christin has suggested that the main effect of *oubli* in France was that it made it possible for the king to superimpose his own version of the events of the past.[34]

Of course, there were always individuals who were pleased with the opportunity to wipe the slate clean of embarrassing memories. Thus the memoirs of merchant Pieter Seeghers in Antwerp carefully omitted all references to the time when he had been a Calvinist. Once reconciled to the Catholic Church, he did not particularly want his descendants to be aware of this part of his history.[35] In the Dutch Republic the Calvinist lawyer Arnoud van Buchel crossed out all the angry poems against

---

[28] Gantet, 'Mémoires du conflit'.   [29] Stoyle, 'Remembering the English Civil Wars', 23.

[30] Neufeld, *The Civil Wars*, 17–54; Edward James Legon, 'Remembering revolution. Seditious memories in England and Wales, 1660–1685', doctoral dissertation, University College London (2015), accessed 27 June 2016, http://discovery.ucl.ac.uk/1470038/1/Thesis%20%5BCorrected%5D.pdf.

[31] Christin, 'Mémoire inscrite, oubli prescrit', 85.

[32] Tom Hamilton, 'The procession of the League. Remembering the Wars of Religion in visual and literary satire', *French History* 30/1 (2016): 1–30.

[33] Benedict, 'Divided memories'.   [34] Christin, 'Mémoire inscrite, oubli prescrit', 80.

[35] Pieter Seghers, *Pieter Seghers. Een koopmansleven in troebele tijden*, ed. Karel Degryse (Antwerp and Baarn, 1990).

Figure 6.1. Anonymous, *The procession of the Holy League in Paris,* *c.*1600, Musée Carnavalet, Paris. One of many early seventeenth-century versions of this satirical image mocking the armed clerical support for the Holy League in the French Wars of Religion. Historian Tom Hamilton has recently demonstrated that it originally referred to a particular incident on 14 May 1590, when a Carthusian, of course not used to carrying a firearm, accidentally killed a bystander. It was used and reused for a variety of polemical purposes in the course of the seventeenth century.

William of Orange that he had written when he was still a young Catholic who hoped for a Habsburg victory.[36] The Dutch widow Magdalena Moons, whom we met in Chapter 4 as the wife of a Habsburg commander, inked out a reference to his name from a legal document. In the Dutch Republic this was no longer a connection to be proud of.[37] Yet what happened when people did not want to forget? There was no way such a policy could be enforced. Someone like chronicler Jean Burel, for instance, who had been an avid supporter of the defeated Holy Catholic League in Le Puy, was certainly sceptical about the policy of oblivion and had no intention of forgetting that his king had at one time been a heretic. As he remarked sarcastically:

> We have all been injured by one another, but the king wants and intends all this to be put to rest and without any memory. May God put to rest all heresies, and may he lose all memory of them.[38]

The Flemish lawyer Guillaume Bulteel from Ypres, a Catholic who had been in exile during the period in the 1580s when the city had been ruled by Calvinists, was outraged that Calvinist turncoats could insinuate themselves back into the town council of Ypres as if nothing had happened.[39] The city of Valenciennes, at that time part of the Netherlands, had accepted an oblivion clause when the city

---

[36] Pollmann, *Religious choice.*   [37] Kloek, 'Magdalena Moons'.
[38] Burel, *Mémoires de Jean Burel,* 465.   [39] Pollmann, *Catholic identity,* 139.

returned to Habsburg rule, but that apparently did not stop locals from knowing exactly which families had at one time or another supported the Calvinist cause.[40]

Governments themselves were often ambiguous about what they did and did not want to be forgotten. As we have seen, the Habsburg authorities in the Southern Netherlands were prepared to forget the support of their subjects for the Revolt. Yet because they simultaneously needed to justify the ongoing war with the Dutch Republic, they could not afford to let memories of the past disappear completely. The Habsburg archdukes Albert and Isabella therefore not only encouraged memories of their dynasty's commitment to the Low Countries, but also reminded their subjects how dangerous the rebel heresy had shown itself to be. The authorities thus did not always act consistently when implementing oblivion clauses; early seventeenth-century attempts to commission a national history of the Revolt for Southern Netherlandish schoolbooks never came to fruition, but it is interesting that the thought of commissioning it had arisen in the first place.[41] In France, oblivion was also not at all complete. Olivier Christin has argued that it was above all an 'expression of [royal] authority', showing that it was the king alone who had the right to decide what was and what was not to be forgotten. Indeed, Henri IV's own 'miraculous' entry into Paris in 1594 was commemorated with an annual procession, which in 1617 was merged with an existing procession that celebrated the liberation of Paris from the English in 1436. In England, the crown's ambiguity about its own policy of oblivion was also palpable. Vengeance did not end with the exposure of Cromwell's corpse on the gallows, because the execution date of Charles I also became a solemn day of remembrance in the Church of England's calendar and an occasion for sermons that both honoured the king's memory and denounced the sin of rebellion.[42]

It was not just rulers who found it difficult to let bygones be bygones. Both people and communities who wanted to use their war record as a source of prestige were prone to pointing the finger at others who had not been as loyal as they themselves.[43] In Catholic towns in which oblivion was in force, stories also abounded about Virgins and saints whose intervention had fended off attacks by iconoclastic heretics or whose images had proven indestructible. Both the cities of Halle and Chartres, for instance, made relics of heretical cannonballs from which they had been protected by the Virgin. Various studies have shown how French Catholic towns that were near Protestant enclaves continued to use annual processions on the feast days of local saints and the Virgin to remind their citizens how miraculously attacks by Protestants had been averted and heretical plots had been foiled; the Edict of Nantes did not put a stop to this practice.[44]

[40] Yves Junot, 'L'Impossible Survie. La Clandestinité protestante à Valenciennes au début du XVIIe siècle', *Mémoires du Cercle Archéologique et Historique de Valenciennes* 11 (2010): 175–83; Yves Junot, *Les Bourgeois de Valenciennes. Anatomie d'une élite dans la ville (1500–1630)* (Villeneuve d'Ascq, 2009), 90–100. See also the discussion in Eekhout, 'Material memories'.

[41] Van der Steen, *Memory wars*, 81–2.

[42] Stoyle, 'Remembering the English Civil Wars', 23.

[43] Van der Steen, *Memory wars*, 179–90; Eekhout, 'Material memories', 173–206.

[44] Jean-Baptiste-Pierre Bacon, *Panégyrique de Henri Le Grand ou éloge historique de Henri IV, Roi de France* (London, 1769), 166; Benedict, 'Divided memories?', 391.

People found creative ways of circumventing oblivion clauses, for instance by appropriating older episodes for new commemorative purposes. Calvinists pointedly included in their calendar dates like the expulsion of the Knights Templar from the kingdom of France or that of the murder of Emperor Henry VII, who had been poisoned by a Dominican monk, so as to point to the pre-Reformation history of clerical rebellion and disloyalty.[45] Catholics did likewise. As we have seen, Catholics in the city of Antwerp, which for some time had been a bulwark of Protestantism, after 1585 revived their devotion to the twelfth-century saint Norbert, whose local claim to fame was that he had defied the heretic Tanchelm.[46] In Brussels, we saw that the bleeding hosts that had originally been framed as the victims of wicked Jews were reframed as the miraculous survivors of attacks by Calvinist iconoclasts. In Orléans, there had long been a procession to commemorate Jeanne d'Arc's relief of the city in 1429, but in the Wars of Religion Jeanne also became the emblem for the city's commitment to Catholicism. Her image that had been destroyed by Huguenots was among the first to be restored; it was depicted on medals and lauded in print.[47]

Yet if we want to conclude that acts of oblivion did not work, it seems unlikely they could have survived as such a popular policy instrument for so long and throughout Europe. Before we declare them unworkable, then, we probably need to examine more closely what contemporaries tried to achieve when they asked for 'perpetual silence' on events of the past. Here, the work of Ross Poole is again very helpful. The point of Acts of Oblivion, he says, is not really to prevent people from knowing about the past, but to demand that they do not *act* upon that knowledge. The purpose of memory, he argues, is that it is knowledge that has implications for the present and offers an agenda, even an imperative, to act. What acts of oblivion do, by contrast, is to say that past events are *not* acknowledged as a legitimate reason for action in the present; they are *of the past*.[48]

This may also explain why acts of oblivion were especially apposite for use in early modern Europe. As we have seen in Chapter 2, early modern Europeans preferred to legitimize the present by drawing analogies with the past, if necessary by reimagining that past to their liking. Laws were considered right and just if they were customary, and customs were therefore by implication also good. Under normal circumstances early modern people were therefore not so quick to declare events to be *of the past*; that may be why it took an act of oblivion to make them do so. Secondly, early modern Europeans were still living in a judicial environment in which it was not automatically the responsibility of the state to take action against crime; although it would increasingly do so, there was still considerable scope for action by individual victims. This, too, made it relevant to formally 'deactivate' the past.

When we look at early modern commemorative practices from this perspective, we see that perhaps the acts worked rather better than we have given them credit for, in the sense that they successfully redirected imperatives to act. Historian Dianne Margolf, for instance, has explored the legal consequences of the exception

[45] Benedict, 'Divided memories?', 381. [46] Pollmann, *Catholic identity*, 175–8.
[47] Spicer, '(Re)building the sacred landscape'. [48] Poole, 'Enacting oblivion'.

which the amnesty in the Edict of Nantes had made for 'execrable crimes'. It was possible for people to be prosecuted for things that had happened *during* the Wars of Religion but not for things that had happened *because* of them. Whether they liked it or not, litigants had to exert themselves to show that the violence inflicted on their families had been motivated by other, often also older, personal conflicts and grievances; they had to prove that even if the violence looked religious it had not actually been so. In the process, Margolf says, the past was thus 'reinterpreted rather than obliterated'.[49] It was possible to acknowledge that terrible things had happened and even to punish people for them, but by forcing litigants to reconsider and reinterpret the motives for that violence, it was legally and perhaps even socially possible to separate these events from the religious issues at stake.

Defendants, on their part, were permitted by the Edict to frame the violence that had been perpetrated in the name of religion as regrettable and inevitable, but in the process had to admit that it was therefore also non-memorable and should not be repeated. In time, this strategy made it possible to reframe collective memories of violence. Philip Benedict has discussed an example of how this was done: in the course of the seventeenth century, French historians of both confessions came to agree that motives of extremists in the French Wars of Religion had not *really* been religious, but had been the 'pretext' under which ambitious nobles fought for power. It was the adherents of the defeated Catholic Holy League who were scapegoated as the prime examples of such noble ambition, and they had been supported by foreigners and unruly clerics to boot.[50] In the long run this had some unforeseen and deplorable side-effects; it was arguably the success of this line of argument that enabled Louis XIV to reframe the remaining Calvinist Huguenots as disobedient subjects and to revoke the Edict of Nantes in 1685. Yet earlier in the century, this alternative view of events had helped to defuse the tensions between the former foes; the gruesome interconfessional street violence that had characterized the wars of the sixteenth century was not repeated.

In a similar way, Southern Netherlandish preachers and historians around 1600 began to emphasize that what had happened during the Revolt had not been a struggle between citizens of different religions, but one between loyal citizens and foreign heretics who had tried to lure them into the snares of the Devil. Although some of the citizens had been a bit misguided by ambitious nobles, scholars admitted, they had soon come to their senses.[51] Individuals appropriated such versions of events. In 1634–5, for instance, the Southern Netherlandish nobleman Jan van Marnix tried to ingratiate himself with the new Habsburg governor by presenting him with a potted history of the Revolt, from which he not only excised the role that two of his uncles had played in the rebellion but also explained how the 'ignorant' people of the South had been misled by ambitious 'Hollanders'.[52] Such an appropriation could also take place lower down the social ladder. Neufeld has

---

[49] Dianne Margolf, 'Adjudicating memory. Law and religious difference in early seventeenth-century France', *The Sixteenth Century Journal* 27 (1996): 399–418.
[50] Benedict, 'Shaping the memory'.   [51] Pollmann, *Catholic identity*, 170–5.
[52] Van der Steen, *Memory wars*, 187–8.

shown how English veteran soldiers, when justifying their claim to county pensions after the 1660 Restoration, framed their requests so as to match the official version of events, with their supporting witnesses echoing the same story. Neufeld concludes:

> Maimed royalist veterans demonstrated what histories officially sanctioned by the Restoration regime taught: that the true outcome of the civil wars was not in fact Parliament's military victory in 1646 (and again in 1648 and 1651) but rather God's mysterious intervention in the affairs of England, leading to the monarchy's and the church's victory in 1660.

Although veterans could benefit from this official version, this was not so true for others. The effect of the English way of handling the past was to exclude dissenting Protestants and bar them from a legitimate place in the divine plan. Rather than defusing the conflict, the sanctioned histories served to demonstrate that they remained a clear and present danger.[53]

Yet, even in England there seems to have been a level of success; Mark Stoyle found that the petitions from royalist veterans after 1660 mostly refrained from specifying who their enemy had been, rarely using the word 'rebel' to describe them or 'civil war' to describe the conflict.[54] From elsewhere, there are more evident success stories to report. In the Dutch Republic, memories transformed, and the terrible divisions between the citizens disappeared from public memory. Once the Pacification of Ghent in 1576 decreed oblivion of all that had happened in the civil war phase of the conflict, both cities and publicists in Holland and Zeeland tended to emphasize shared experiences of suffering rather than to emphasize divisions; by designating the enemy primarily as 'Spanish', it was possible to reimagine the Revolt as a struggle between locals and foreigners. This was what had enabled the city of Leiden to start celebrating the memories of the city's relief in 1574 in the ways discussed in Chapter 4.

That Leiden's siege would be celebrated at all was not self-evident; nearly half the city's population had died in the siege, and thus for a rebel cause that by no means everyone supported. During the siege, there had been riots and bitter divisions over the rebel magistrate's refusal to surrender while scores of citizens were dying every day. Catholic exiles, who had rejected the city's handover to the rebels in the first place, had left the town in 1572–3, only to see their possessions sequestered and passed on to rebel leaders, who had once themselves been exiled and had been the victim of confiscations by the Duke of Alba. Even many of those in favour of rebellion had been shocked when rebel armies had attacked churches and convents, terrorized priests and banished Catholic worship. If the end of the siege thus brought joy, there were also many issues unresolved and a legacy of great bitterness. When one of the Catholic refugees, a Beguine, ventured back into Leiden after the siege was over, she was quickly apprehended, her clothes were ripped off her body,

---

[53] Neufeld, *The Civil Wars*, 80.
[54] Mark Stoyle, 'Memories of the maimed. The testimony of Charles I's former soldiers, 1660–1730', *History* 88 (2003): 204–26.

youngsters taunted her as a 'traitress', and she was escorted out of the city without permission to see her family or her fellow Beguines.[55] The oblivion clauses that came into force through the Pacification of Ghent in 1576 forced the city to put an end to such recriminations. The exiles could return home, their properties were returned, and the rebel exiles could be compensated.[56]

As we have seen in Chapter 4, the city of Leiden accelerated the process of healing by 'overwriting' the terrible conflicts and civic violence that had wrecked the city between 1572 and 1574, with a new narrative that focused on the collective experiences of famine and celebrated the sacrificial bravery of the suffering citizens of all religions. Not all Catholics were equally impressed by this; in his memoirs the angry jurist and later Catholic priest Franciscus Dusseldorpius continued to deplore the loss of his ancestral Leiden to the Revolt and blamed the evil advisers of the Duke of Alba for having encouraged Catholics to leave their cities to their rebel fate.[57] Yet it seems that other Catholic exiles bought into it; Pieter van Veen, son of a Catholic magistrate who had fled the city during the rebellion, in 1615 presented the city with a painting of a by now famous scene, in which the rebel armies handed out herring and white bread to the starving Leiden population (Figure 6.2).

What acts of oblivion effectively helped to produce, then, was a narrative that, by bracketing off and 'forgetting' one part of the past, encouraged people to reinvent a new form of continuity between past and present. In England's case that did not work very well because the Stuarts were ambiguous about it and because their former royalist supporters in the elite were keen to demand their pound of flesh. Nevertheless, even in England, there was no resumption of military conflict. In the Dutch city of Leiden oblivion created a version of events in which citizens past, present, and future were all united in their patriotism and commitment to local freedom; what had been a civil war was rewritten as a conflict between alien, Spanish soldiers and Leiden or even 'Dutch' patriots.[58] The success of an act of oblivion should thus perhaps not be measured by an absence of aggressive rhetoric about the past. Rather, we should assess what it did to the memory about former enemies. The purpose of the commemorative processions in French and Southern Netherlandish Catholic cities, for instance, was to establish a historical link between local and religious identity. Implicitly this was, of course, an act of aggression: it excluded dissenters from that narrative. Yet the processions framed the dissenters not as locals; rather, they helped to reframe them as outsiders who had tried but failed to subdue cities whose citizens had 'always' been united in their commitment to Catholicism. It was precisely this virtue of denial and the promise

---

[55] Wouter Jacobsz, *Dagboek van broeder Wouter Jacobsz (Gualtherus Jacobi Masius), Amsterdam 1572–1578 en Montfoort 1578–1579*, ed. I.H. van Eeghen, 2 vols (Groningen, 1959), I, 370–1.

[56] Louis Sicking, *Geuzen en glippers. Goud en fout tijdens het beleg van Leiden*, 3 Oktoberlezing (Leiden, 2003), accessed 3 May 2016, https://openaccess.leidenuniv.nl/handle/1887/14308; Pollmann, 'Herdenken, herinneren, vergeten'.

[57] Franciscus Dusseldorpius, *Uittreksel uit Francisci Dusseldorpii Annales, 1566–1616*, ed. R. Fruin (The Hague, 1893), 113–14, 131. I thank Carolina Lenarduzzi for his reference.

[58] Pollmann, 'Herdenken, herinneren, vergeten'.

Figure 6.2. Pieter van Veen, *The relief of Leiden* (1615) (after a painting by his brother Otto, now in the Rijksmuseum). Museum De Lakenhal, Leiden.

of renewed continuity which royal advocate Antoine de Loisel presented in a discourse on oblivion he held in the city of Agen in 1582. As Mark Greengrass has noted, Loisel presented oblivion in an organic, almost medical sense:

> Let us efface the troubles from our memory and commit them to perpetual and eternal oblivion and we shall all be reunited. Let us recognize that we are all subjects of the same King, who to set us an example of such oblivion, has himself and, as the first to do so, forgotten the offenses he has suffered during the wars.[59]

Just over two centuries later the French king expressed something quite similar in the Constitutional charter in 1814:

> In thus attempting to renew the chain of the times, which disastrous errors have broken, we have banished from our recollection, as we might wish it were possible to blot out from history, all the evils which have afflicted the fatherland during our absence.[60]

[59] Cited in Greengrass, 'Amnestie et "oubliance"', 117.
[60] *Charte constitutionnelle française du 4 juin 1814*, accessed 3 May 2016, http://fr.wikisource.org/ wiki/Charte_constitutionnelle_du_4_juin_1814. See for a discussion of the (lack of) impact of this Act of Oblivion e.g. Kroen, *Politics and theater*; and M.M. Lok, '"Un oubli total du passé". The political and social construction of silence in Restoration Europe (1813–1830)', *History and Memory* 26/2 (2014): 40–75.

By declaring some part of the past over and done with, it was possible to re-establish a narrative of continuity, and of unity, that might be new but had the virtue of looking old.

Having established that acts of oblivion were particularly suitable for societies that set a high stake on continuity between past and present, it may also become easier to understand why they became obsolete. As we have seen, in the course of the eighteenth and nineteenth centuries, the old and customary began to lose some of its cultural prestige. Side by side with the old love of continuity, there emerged a new way to think about the relationship between past and present, which argued that progress and civilization might demand the abandoning of custom. When William Gladstone proposed 'blessed oblivion' to the House of Commons in 1886, he probably did not use the term accidentally; he deployed it to remind his audience that it was such an act of oblivion that in 1660 had enabled England to restore its monarchy.[61] Yet at the same time he was turning the concept on its head. Gladstone wanted to end the long and dismal history of English rule in Ireland by giving the Irish the right to rule themselves. Opponents argued against this, on the grounds that English rule was a tradition that needed to be defended. Yet, as Gladstone pointed out, the Irish thought of English rule only as a tradition of oppression:

> My right honourable Friend the Member for East Edinburgh asks us to-night to abide by the traditions of which we are the heirs. What traditions? By the Irish traditions?...find, if you can, a single voice, a single book, find, I would almost say, as much as a single newspaper article...in which the conduct of England towards Ireland is anywhere treated except with profound and bitter condemnation. Are these the traditions by which we are exhorted to stand?...what we want to do is to stand by the traditions of which we are the heirs in all matters except our relations with Ireland, and to make our relations with Ireland to conform to the other traditions of our country. So we treat our traditions—so we hail the demand of Ireland for what I call a blessed oblivion of the past.[62]

Gladstone urged the MPs to grant the Irish a 'blessed oblivion' and permit them to forget about a tradition of hatred. Whereas early modern peacekeepers had counselled oblivion in order to re-establish continuity, 'to renew the chain of the times', Gladstone thought of oblivion as a method to forge discontinuity. If only the Irish were given home rule, they would forget about the past and focus on 'other traditions' instead.

Having said that, it is no easier for modern people to put the past behind them than it was for those who lived in early modern Europe. Many modern societies have come to believe that there can be no reconciliation without truth—but we cannot always guarantee that truth will result in justice being done. Experts on

---

[61] The connection was certainly made by Churchill when, in his Zurich speech, he said that Gladstone had called for 'a blessed act of oblivion'.

[62] William Ewart Gladstone, 'Speech of William Ewart Gladstone MP, British Prime Minister, to the House of Commons on Home Rule for Ireland, 7 June 1886', accessed 28 April 2016, http://hansard.millbanksystems.com/commons/1886/jun/07/second-reading-adjourned-debate.

what we now call 'transitional justice' are wrestling with the very dilemmas that faced peacemakers in early modern Europe; amnesties leave many people dissatisfied and justice undone, but they are sometimes also the only way in which to stop cycles of violence and retribution, and create enough stability for the rule of law to return.[63] The Spanish high court has recently ruled that even if the acts of violence committed during the Spanish Civil War of 1936–9 should be classified as crimes against humanity, the Amnesty agreed in 1977, after the fall of the Franco regime, had emerged out of a 'consensus of social forces at the time and was an integral part of national reconciliation and transition to democracy'.[64] In Sierra Leone, the appalling violence was still on everyone's mind when negotiations in 1999 brought about an amnesty for the perpetrators of war crimes. Yet without an amnesty there would probably have been no chance for peace at all. It was only once hostilities had ceased that there was room for a war crimes tribunal and for a start to a process of truth and reconciliation.[65]

Many people come to believe that the pursuit of truth is essential if we are to achieve reconciliation, and such a pursuit of truth seems to fly right in the face of a desire for oblivion. Interestingly enough, however, recent research suggests that many people in Sierra Leone found truth and reconciliation counterproductive. They argued that 'these things repeat if you talk about them so much' or said that 'if they want to heal the wounds, let them send jobs'. Rosalind Shaw has argued that perhaps the paradigm of truth and reconciliation does not work in every environment. For many Sierra Leoneans 'forgiving and forgetting' was as good a way of dealing with past pain as rehearsing the sorrows of the past—what they felt they needed were the jobs and means to repair their lives.[66] Political analyst David Rieff, too, has recently been highlighting the risks of commemoration and argued that we should not overlook the virtues of oblivion.[67]

Critics of the Truth and Reconciliation Commission in South Africa have said that it achieved more truth than reconciliation, yet its effects have, paradoxically, been much like those that acts of oblivion aspired to; theoretically there was amnesty only for those who owned up to their parts in the violent history of apartheid, but in practice, those who did not tell the truth were not prosecuted. Most people in South Africa now say that they want to forget about the past, and in some ways they are succeeding: a young scholar researching the topic in 2012 found that many students in South Africa had never heard of the Truth and

---

[63] Charles Villa-Vicencio, 'Learning to live together with bad memories', in *Truth in politics. Rhetorical approaches to democratic deliberation and beyond*, ed. Philippe Joseph Salazar, Sanya Osha, and Wim van Binsbergen, special issue of *Quest. An African Journal of Philosophy* 16 (2002): 37–49; Franklin Oduro, 'The challenge of reconciliation in postconflict African states', *International Journal of Transitional Justice* 6 (2012): 558–69.

[64] Naomi Roht Arriaza, 'The Spanish Civil War, amnesty and the trials of Judge Garzón', *ASIL Insights* 16/24 (2 July 2012), accessed 10 June 2015, http://www.asil.org/insights/volume/16/issue/24/spanish-civil-war-amnesty-and-trials-judge-garz%C3%B3n.

[65] Priscilla Hayner, 'Negotiating justice. The challenge of addressing past human rights violations', in *Contemporary peacemaking. Conflict, peace processes and post-war reconstruction*, ed. John Darby and Roger MacGinty, 2nd edn (Basingstoke, 2008), 328–38.

[66] Shaw, 'Memory frictions'.   [67] David Rieff, *In praise of forgetting* (New Haven, 2016).

Reconciliation Commission.[68] We might call that evidence of success. South Africans have 'forgotten' the situation that, in 1994, made everyone fear for the outbreak of civil war in their country, precisely because the commission helped to defuse the tension. Since then, they have achieved a consensus on the evils of the apartheid system and have thus adopted a shared frame of thinking about the past—even if many people still refuse to admit to their own role in that past, some wounds remain open, and there is hot debate on what this should mean for the present.[69] In many ways, then, truth and reconciliation have achieved the same effect that policymakers in early modern Europe had in mind. For them oblivion was never an end in itself. Like Truth and Reconciliation commissions they aspired to a form of closure that relegated the past to the past and enabled both societies and the people in them to reinvent themselves along new lines. They did not always succeed. But they saw few alternative strategies that might secure peace in societies torn by civil conflict.

---

[68] Stefanie Schütten, 'South Africa reconciled? To what extent can the South African society be regarded as reconciled, eighteen years after the first democratic elections?', ResMA dissertation, Universiteit Utrecht (2012), 27, 29.

[69] Oduro, 'Challenge of reconciliation'; Villa-Vicencio, 'Learning to live together'.

7

Remembering Violence: Trauma, Atrocities, and Cosmopolitan Memories

On 2 November 1576 middle-aged Christina de Bitter, her elderly mother, and some other relatives barricaded the door of the cellar of their house in the city of Antwerp, hoping that this would spare them a confrontation with the Spanish troops who were putting this prosperous city to the sack. After the death of their Habsburg governor in the spring, a dangerous power vacuum had emerged in the Low Countries. In 1575 their overlord, King Philip II of Spain, had gone bankrupt, and the Spanish troops who were fighting the rebels in the Low Countries had not been paid for over a year. As they were wont to do in such situations, the soldiers organized a mutiny and went to take what they were owed by themselves.[1] Having sacked the cities of Maastricht and Aalst, they had made their way to Antwerp, where, having rejoined regular Habsburg forces, they defeated an army of citizens and local troops that had tried to defend the city. The city's wealth was now theirs for the taking. Going from house to house in small groups, the soldiers carried off everything of value that they could find and demanded money, either cash in hand or in the form of 'ransoms'—a promise of payment in return for the safety of the householders. Being in competition with other groups of soldiers, the soldiers were keen to maximize their gains from any one house, and to do so quickly, so that they could get to the next house before any of their peers did. The best way to speed things up, or so they judged, was to use violence, first to intimidate the householders by kicking in doors, screaming, shouting, and vandalizing the house, then to grab what was of value, and to terrorize the residents into saying where they had hidden any other goods or money. As the soldiers were well aware, Antwerpers had suspected what was coming to them. Many of them had hidden their money, or themselves, and so had Christina de Bitter.

Yet Christina was unlucky. The soldiers found the cellar, blew up the door, and grabbed Christina, demanding to know the whereabouts of her husband and of the family's valuables. Christina had anticipated such a request by making sure she had some money on her person, which she now gave to them. Yet they were not satisfied and demanded she disclose the location of the rest, meanwhile torturing her by stringing her up with a piece of fuse rope. Letting her down, they found she still

[1] Geoffrey Parker, 'Mutiny and discontent in the Spanish army of Flanders 1572–1607', *Past & Present* 58 (1973): 38–52.

refused to speak, so they strung her up once more, and once again. Three times she refused to speak; in the end,

> the ruffians, finding themselves unable to break her steadfastness, and not wanting to waste any more time, ran out of the house with all they could carry, and left her in the noose. One of the family, hearing the noise die down, ventured out and found her hanging from a ladder, nearly strangled... She regained consciousness... but never her previous cheerfulness, after the strangulation which weakened her sagacity, and of which her mind forever bore the scar.[2]

Throughout the sixteenth and seventeenth centuries, unfortunate men and women in Europe suffered experiences like those of Christina. Sacks like that of Antwerp were a recurring feature in the Italian wars of the first half of the sixteenth century, the wars of religion in France and the Low Countries in the second half of the century, and the Thirty Years War that tore apart the Holy Roman Empire between 1618 and 1648. Not only mutineers would plunder; if a city, according to the laws of war at the time, was too slow to surrender, commanders might also give regular troops permission to put a city to the sack.[3] More often than not, early modern soldiers were underpaid; they had to feed themselves and were badly supported, so opportunities to plunder were very welcome. Yet they were almost always under pressure to do so as quickly as possible, both because their commanders usually gave them only a limited timeslot in which to do the job and because they were in competition with each other. It was this pressure, perhaps more than bloodthirstiness, that explains the extreme violence that was often used. Frequently, fires would break out while terrified residents were trying to escape, sometimes jumping into rivers where many drowned; this happened for instance in the Netherlandish cities of Zutphen in 1572 and in Maastricht in 1579. After the sack of Antwerp, chronicler and eyewitness Bernardino de Mendoza noted that while about 2,500 bodies had been buried, another 5,000 people had drowned or had perished in the fires.[4] The material losses were also enormous and the scars terrible.

Even so, city-dwellers were usually much better off in wartime than people in the countryside, who were likely to find their harvests taken from them and their livestock stolen whenever armies were passing through; women were not safe, and anyone who resisted might find him- or herself injured or dead. As armies were approaching, peasants would try to hide in caves or hollows, or flee to nearby cities, if there were any, sleeping in churches and barns until it was safe to return. Yet the poorest among them might be refused entry or be expelled as urban supplies began to run out. Others might try to protect themselves from soldiers in the area by paying protection money, but such arrangements would by no means

---

[2] Hooft, *Nederlandsche Historien*, 472–63.

[3] Lauro Martines, *Furies. War in Europe, 1450–1700* (New York, 2013), 55–81.

[4] Bernardino de Mendoza, *Commentaires memorables de Don Bernardin de Mendoce, chevallier ambassadeur en France pour le Roy Catholique, des guerres de Flandres & Pays Bas depuis l'an 1567 jusques a l'an mil cinq cens soixante & dixsept...* (Paris, 1591), cited in *La Furie espagnole. Documents pour servir à l'histoire du sac d'Anvers*, ed. P. Génard (Antwerp, 1876), 222.

always work. Villages were routinely torched, and peasants who resisted killed on the spot.[5]

In this sense, then, the tale of Christina was, sadly, unexceptional. What makes the account very special, however, is that it tells us something of the effect these events had on Christina's later life. According to historian Pieter Hooft, who married Christina's granddaughter and so heard of and transmitted her tale, Christina had lost her 'sagacity', perhaps the result of brain damage, and never regained her 'previous cheerfulness' after this horrific experience. In short, Christina suffered what people today call a 'war trauma'. Possibly she developed what is now known as post traumatic stress disorder (PTSD), a syndrome that is found among a small minority of the survivors of episodes of violence or other forms of sudden loss of control over one's own life.[6] This is not in itself surprising—scholars have traced PTSD among people in many different cultures, and there is every reason to believe it was also present in pre-modern societies. Research also suggests, however, that its symptoms may differ among cultures. Scholars have become aware that the ways in which people in different societies experience and express emotional memories are extremely varied; we should expect early modern ways of coping with such memories to have been different from what they are today.[7]

When early modernists seek evidence of memories of violent experiences, they therefore must look beyond the very rare evidence of early modern memories of violence that is immediately recognizable as related to 'war trauma'. The first aim of this chapter is to explore the way we can access early modern memories of violence.[8] The second theme of this chapter is to show how memories of violence were deployed in politics, religion, and polemics. While victims themselves were often quiet about their experiences, other contemporaries proved quite willing to recall

---

[5] J.A. Lynn, 'How war fed war. The tax of violence and contributions during the *Grand Siècle*', *Journal of Modern History* 65 (1993): 286–310; Ronald Asch, '"Wo der soldat hinkömbt, da ist alles sein". Military violence and atrocities in the Thirty Years War re-examined', *German History* 18 (2000): 291–309; Marjolein 't Hart, *The Dutch Wars of Independence. Warfare and commerce in the Netherlands, 1570–1680* (London and New York, 2014), 101–25.

[6] Rolf J. Kleber and D. Brom, 'Incidentie van posttraumatische stress-stoornissen na front-ervaringen, geweldsmisdrijven, ongevallen en rampen', *Tijdschrift voor Psychiatrie* 31 (1989): 675–91.

[7] Kuijpers, 'The creation', 191. Psychiatrist Mario Braakman argues that what psychiatrists call the 'somatization' of feelings is actually a much more common way of expressing emotions than to talk about them in emotional terms, see for his views e.g. Rolf J. Kleber, 'Weg van het Trauma', Inaugural lecture and summaries of the accompanying symposium 'Trauma. Dilemma's in kennis en toepassing', Radboud Universiteit Nijmegen (9 February 2007), accessed 3 May 2016, https://www.yumpu.com/nl/document/view/20414850/weg-van-het-trauma-oratie-van-profdr-rolf-j-kleber, at 28.

[8] In doing so, I am making grateful use of the work of historian and former colleague Erika Kuijpers, who is currently completing a book entitled *Trauma, memories and emotions in early modern Europe*. Some of her work in progress is discussed in Kuijpers, 'The creation'; Erika Kuijpers, 'Fear, indignation, grief and relief. Emotional narratives in war chronicles from the Netherlands (1568–1648)', in *Disaster, death and the emotions in the shadow of the apocalypse, 1400–1700*, ed. Jennifer Spinks and Charles Zika (London 2016), 93–111; Erika Kuijpers, '"O, Lord, save us from shame". Narratives of emotions in convent chronicles by female authors during the Dutch Revolt, 1566–1635', in *Destroying order, structuring disorder. Gender and emotions in medieval and early modern Europe*, ed. Susan Broomhall (Farnham, 2015), 127–46. I am also drawing on the articles we wrote together: Judith Pollmann and Erika Kuijpers, 'Why remember terror? Memories of violence in the Dutch Revolt', in *Ireland 1641. Contexts and reactions*, ed. Jane Ohlmeyer and Micheál Ó Siochrú (Manchester, 2013), 176–96; and Pollmann and Kuijpers, 'Introduction'.

them. Indeed, early modern Europe witnessed the blossoming of a genre known as the 'atrocity narrative'—harrowing, sometimes almost pornographic, descriptions of violent experiences. As we will see, historians have long been aware that such stories were exploited for their propaganda value, but it is only recently that they have discovered that early modern atrocity stories came to form a corpus that could be used to pre- and remediate memories of conflict; memories of one atrocity could come to shape the narrating, memory, and perhaps even the experience of another. Finally, the chapter will explore the way in which atrocity stories travelled between and beyond polities. It will argue that in their spread, use, and reuse, early modern atrocity stories turned into transnational, and even 'cosmopolitan', memories, connecting the memory cultures of different parts of Europe and even of different parts of the globe.

SCARS

Over the past decades much research has been done to explore how experiences of extreme violence are remembered and how individuals and communities handle such memories.[9] It is not self-evident for such memories to emerge. Twentieth-century victims of war have often had to wait decades before their tales were heard. Political regimes and communities often consciously try to conceal or eradicate the past. In Chapter 6, we explored the Acts of Oblivion that early modern peace-makers deployed for this purpose.[10] Yet victims themselves are often also reluctant to tell their tales. One important condition for the collective commemoration of violence is the existence of what Aleida Assmann has called a *Solidargemeinschaft*—a community of solidarity.[11] Victims share their experiences with their peers, their community, and finally with the world at large only if these are prepared to listen and acknowledge their experiences. This does not always happen in post-war situations, let alone in a situation where war continues and there is a threat of further violence, where people have gone adrift, or are completely preoccupied with survival. As a result, the development of collective memory practices can be much delayed.[12]

The first and natural impulse of victims of violence themselves is often to remain silent. Violent experiences do not just incite indignation among the victims but can also be experienced as the result of failure, sin, or weakness, and thus create feelings of shame and guilt that are not so easy to integrate in a positive image of oneself or one's community.[13] To revive them means to revive pain, and many people prefer to avoid this. As one survivor of the horrific sack of Rome in 1527

---

[9] See for overviews e.g. LaCapra, *Representing the Holocaust*; Cubitt, *History and memory*, 208–14; Erll, *Kollektives Gedächtnis*, 46–8, 86–90; Assmann, *Der lange Schatten*; Winter, *Remembering war*, 2–69.

[10] Connerton, 'Seven types of forgetting'.   [11] Assmann, *Der lange Schatten*, 75.

[12] Henri Rousso, *The Vichy syndrome. History and memory in France since 1945* (Cambridge MA, 1991).

[13] Assmann, *Der lange Schatten*, 74–5; Winter, *Remembering war*, 52–76.

put it twenty years after the event: 'What more can I say than that our suffering was such, that to recount it would revive the torture, the damage and the shame.'[14] In 1610 Michael Heberer, too, found it difficult to recall the massacre of Protestants he had witnessed in 1585 Marseille. 'The bloodbath, strangling and raging heard and seen in the city was such, that it pains me to remember it, and I will refrain from telling about it at length.'[15] Peasant farmer Kasper Preis in Fulda found it impossible to describe his experiences in the Thirty Years War, in part because he was afraid he would not be believed:

> To tell of all the miseries and misfortune is not within my power, not even what I know and have seen myself...and if I did report everything which I have seen and so painfully experienced no-one living in a better age would believe it, but *in summa* the times were awful beyond all measure.[16]

It is therefore perhaps not so surprising that we possess few accounts by survivors themselves that articulate memories of pain and sorrow in the emotional terms that modern observers in the West have come to expect from survivors of episodes of extreme violence. Only some evidence, like that about Christina Bitter, points to experiences that we recognize from the modern world. In England, Mark Stoyle notes, some civil war veterans got 'disabled in their senses' or had 'fallen lunatick' as a consequence of their experiences. One servant girl who had been forced to witness the killing of fellow-servants was said to be 'ever after distracted from the fright'.[17] In Ireland, Mrs Reanall was unable to eat salmon from the river Barrow, after she had seen the corpses of infants and other victims of the 1641 massacres taken out of the weir.[18] A seventeenth-century historian of the 1575 massacre at Oudewater in Holland reported that a soldier who had taken part in the sack was forever haunted by the memory of his cruel deeds and had recurring visions of the little children he had murdered: 'God struck his soul in a terrible manner.'[19] Yet it is significant that it was never the victims themselves who tell us about these long-term effects of their experiences.

Survivors of sacks and massacres themselves tended to be much more quiet and restrained about what had happened to them, at least initially. Having read dozens of German war diaries and memoirs from the Thirty Years War, Geoff Mortimer found that 'personally attested records of more extreme suffering are rare in these accounts'.[20] Male French Calvinists who recounted their experiences

---

[14] Marcello Alberini, *Il sacco di Roma. L'edizione Orano de I ricordi di Marcello Alberini*, ed. P. Farenga (Rome, 1997), 278, cited in Thérèse Peeters, 'Van Caput Mundi tot "Coda Mundi". Over de beleving van de plundering van Rome in 1527', BA dissertation, Leiden University (2012), 22.

[15] Claudia Ulbrich, '"Hat man also bald ein solches Bluthbad, Würgen und Wüten in der Stadt gehört und gesehen, dass mich solches jammert wider zu gedenken". Religion und Gewalt in Michael Heberer von Brettens "Aegyptica Servitus" (1610)', in *Religion und Gewalt. Konflikte, rituale, deutungen (1500–1800)*, ed. Kaspar von Greyerz and Kim Siebenhüner (Göttingen, 2006), 85–108, at 87.

[16] Cited in Geoff Mortimer, *Eyewitness accounts of the Thirty Years War, 1618–1648* (Basingstoke, 2002), 176.

[17] Stoyle, 'Remembering the English Civil Wars', 21.

[18] Ohlmeyer and Ó Siochrú, 'Introduction', 3.

[19] Arnoldus van Duin, *Oudewaters moord. Of waerachtig verhael van d'oudheid, belegering, innemen en verwoesten der geseide stad* (Oudewater, 1669), A3v.

[20] Mortimer, *Eyewitness accounts*, 171.

in the St Bartholomew's Day massacre did so in the third person, and 'emphasised the need to repress and control the emotions they felt at the time', notes historian Sue Broomhall; a female survivor, Charlotte Arbaleste, mainly described the emotions of those around her.[21] Of course, many of the victims of such episodes could not write at all. Yet even in areas with very high literacy, such as the Low Countries, very few people who survived the great sacks of the Netherlands in the 1570s left an account of what had happened to them. From Naarden, where the Habsburg armies killed virtually the whole male population on 1 December 1572, we know of two accounts that were produced more or less contemporaneously, but in both cases the authors also had another, apologetic, aim for their text.[22] Two contemporary accounts of Antwerp's Spanish Fury, four years later, were both propaganda pieces directed at foreign audiences.[23]

To be sure, early modern people definitely thought that episodes of many deaths, great violence, and political turmoil were worth remembering and memorializing. In Ham-en-Artois in 1303, thirteen witnesses were asked to recall all criminal prosecutions they knew of. Hannah Skoda reconstructed their evidence; each of the ten cases that had occurred in the area since 1260 'was remembered by an average of six witnesses, and each witness remembered an average of seven crimes'. The tales differed in the details, but had clearly also been discussed and transmitted collectively. As Skoda concludes: 'violence may have been a frequent method of contesting social relations, but it was still shocking and impressive'.[24] Jewish communities had a long tradition of commemorating both medieval and more recent pogroms and massacres, of which there were many in a Europe where anti-Semitism was a matter of course and anti-Jewish violence endemic.[25] Plague epidemics had always elicited record-keeping, and throughout the early modern period so did civil wars and political crises. Very often, it was at such moments of crisis that private chroniclers, throughout Europe, decided to pick up their pens.[26] Thus, in 1566 Ghent merchant Cornelis van Campene thought it was urgent that someone record the evil deeds of the Calvinists, those 'satellites of Satan', who had been breaking images throughout the Netherlands; many people were to feel the need to record events during the Dutch Revolt. Sometimes, they did so primarily to put on record who was to blame for the conflict, but often also presented the evils of their own time as a divine punishment for the sins of all in their community.[27] In late-sixteenth-century

---

[21] Sue Broomhall, 'Disturbing memories. Narrating experiences and emotions of distressing events in the French Wars of Religion', in *Memory before modernity. Practices of memory in early modern Europe*, ed. Erika Kuijpers et al. (Leiden and Boston, 2013), 253–67, at 258–61.

[22] Kuijpers, 'Fear, indignation, grief and relief'.

[23] Pollmann and Kuijpers, 'Why remember terror?'.

[24] Hannah Skoda, *Medieval violence. Physical brutality in Northern France, 1270–1330* (Oxford, 2013), 83.

[25] Greenblatt, *To tell their children*, 14–18.

[26] See on plague chronicles Miquel Parets, *A journal of the plague year. The diary of the Barcelona tannerMiquel Parets*, ed. and trans. James S. Amelang (Oxford, 1991). On chronicling in times of crisis Pollmann, 'Archiving the present'.

[27] Cornelis van Campene and Philip van Campene, *Dagboek van Cornelis en Philip van Campene. Behelzende het verhaal der merkwaardigste gebeurtenissen, voorgevallen te Gent sedert het begin der*

Le Puy-en Velay, in Auvergne, Jean Burel thought that he should keep a chronicle so that the young would learn to recognize the wrath of God, as he had done, in the string of 'great wars, famine, plague and discord' that he had witnessed in his town, which was being torn apart by the Wars of Religion.[28]

Burel's point was echoed by German chroniclers in the seventeenth century: 'Hunger and sorrow, poverty and misery were the fruits of war and the punishment for our sins. Pray God that we do not forget our sufferings and grief. If only our descendants know what we have experienced they will be pious.'[29] Some of them wanted to structure events. *Hofrat* Volkmar Happe in Thuringia analysed the consequences of the comet of 1618:

> What from this comet followed by way of terrible upheaval, war, murder, price-rises, plague, alterations of princedoms and seigneuries, the evangelical religion persecuted, and driven out of many places and conversely the reintroduction of the papist horror, that can be learned from the following in the order in which it happened.[30]

Even so, these accounts tend to describe and order events, rather than reflect on them. Their authors may be very angry and keen to name the guilty, but it is only rarely that they dwell on the emotional impact events had on the author him- or, rarely, herself. The only early modern authors to systematically reflect on the emotive impact of violent events were monks and nuns, who were trained in the religious analysis and spiritual interpretation of emotions.[31]

There were early modern ways of recording memories of violence that we may not immediately recognize as emotive, for instance when people quantified and enumerated losses in people, properties, and goods. Anthropologists and historians have come to recognize the great emotional and social importance that material objects can have for memory and identity; we should therefore take the listing of losses and destruction very seriously.[32] To be sure, such forms of memorialization often came into being for practical reasons. Early modern communities recorded their war experiences and listed war damage when requesting tax reductions, for instance. A parliamentary committee recorded thousands of depositions by the victims of the 1641 massacre in Ireland; most of these focused on enumerating the material losses that they had suffered, in the clear and understandable hope of some compensation.[33] But scholars have come to think that enumeration itself was

---

godsdienstberoerten tot den 5en april 1571, ed. F. de Potter (Ghent, 1870); a number of these texts are discussed in Pollmann, *Catholic identity*.

[28] Burel, *Mémoires de Jean Burel*.   [29] Mortimer, *Eyewitness accounts*, 177.

[30] Andreas Bähr, 'Inhaltliche Erläuterungen zu Volkmar Happes Chronik aus dem Dreißigjährigen Krieg', in *Volkmar Happe (1587–1647/59). Chronicon Thuringiae*, ed. Hans Medick, Norbert Winnige, and Andreas Bähr, Mitteldeutsche Selbstzeugnisse aus der Zeit des Dreißigjährigen Krieges, accessed November 2008, http://www.mdsz.thulb.uni-jena.de/happe/erlaeuterungen.php.

[31] Mortimer, *Eyewitness accounts*, 171; Charlotte Woodford, *Nuns as historians in early modern Germany* (Oxford, 2002); Kuijpers, 'O, Lord, save us from shame'; Pollmann, *Catholic identity*, 133–5.

[32] Daniel Miller, *Stuff* (Cambridge, 2010); Auslander, 'Beyond words'; John Horne and Alan Kramer, *German atrocities in 1914. A history of denial* (New Haven and London, 2001), 189.

[33] Aidan Clarke, 'The 1641 massacres', in *Ireland 1641. Contexts and reactions*, ed. Jane Ohlmeyer and Micheál O'Siochrú (Manchester, 2013), 37–51, at 43.

also an important way of recalling memories of loss and expressing the enormity of what happened. This was evident in the Italian wars in the early sixteenth century, where war monuments on battlefields began to record the number of dead.[34] In the siege of the Holland city of Haarlem in 1572–3, several people recorded, and memoirists copied, daily lists of cannonball hits, and cannonballs were always to retain a central role in memories of the siege there.[35] An Italian observer in besieged Paris in 1590 expressed the horrors by listing 'numbers dead, resources used and alms distributed'.[36] At around the same time a Bruges merchant wrote a 'lamentation' on the fate of his unfortunate city; its trade in ruins, its churches destroyed, its population decimated, he expressed his grief in listing the names of buildings, religious orders, and prominent families who had been affected by the wars.[37]

Yet while it was thus quite common to write about war and crises out of a sense that it was important and necessary that such things should be remembered, it was not self-evident for early modern people to recall personal experiences of fear, loss, and shame for their own sake or to share these with a larger audience, unless, that is, they had a practical reason to narrate them or could give them some positive meaning. Psychologists have noted that the resilience of people who experience violence depends to some extent on their ability to reframe their memories of these experiences in a way that is meaningful, even positive. Since memories change every time they are recalled, it is possible to change the emotive charge of a memory. Today, there are forms of therapy, such as Eye Movement Desensitization and Reprocessing (EMRT), that stimulate the reprocessing of memories in the brain with the help of repetitive visual stimuli.[38] But it can also be done by giving the memory a spin that is less painful and storing it in a form that has more positive connotations.

The latter was a strategy for which early modern people were culturally well equipped.[39] Christian religious culture, especially, offered early modern believers ways of reframing their memories in such a way that they became evidence of special grace and a source of pride. Christians were taught that suffering in this world was unimportant because it was only in the afterlife that true happiness could exist or that suffering should be seen as a beneficial spiritual exercise to renounce ties with the world and prepare for death. Thus, the loss of children, spouses, and other loved ones could be routinely described as a form of liberation, a departure for a better life, and something to be thankful for. At the same time, and in our eyes perhaps rather paradoxically, this did not stop people from seeing their own survival, or even their own suffering, as a sign of special grace or as a reward.

---

[34] John Gagné, 'Counting the dead. Traditions of enumeration and the Italian wars', *Renaissance Quarterly* 67 (2014): 791–840.

[35] Eekhout, 'De kogel in de kerk'.   [36] Broomhall, 'Disturbing memories', 261–3.

[37] Zeghere van Male, *De lamentatie van Zeghere van Male. Brugge na de Opstand tegen Spanje, 1590*, ed. A. Dewitte and A. Viaene (Bruges, 1977).

[38] Jonathan I. Bisson et al., 'Psychological treatments for chronic post-traumatic stress disorder. Systematic review and meta-analysis', *The British Journal of Psychiatry* 190/2 (2007): 97–104.

[39] Kuijpers, 'Fear, indignation, grief and relief'.

Man's duty was above all to accept his fate and rejoice in the fact that God moved in mysterious ways.

A crucially important element in this way of thinking was providentialism, the belief that God Himself constantly intervened in the world and in people's lives. War, violence, and plague were widely seen as God's punishment for the sinfulness of the people He had created in His image.[40] Yet, for most people, this explanation did not conflict with the notion that they themselves had been singled out for survival, and that loved ones who had not, were nevertheless in a better place. This made it possible to give meaning to terrible experiences, although this way of thinking did not work for everyone. In 1581 Evangelista de Vintura confessed to the Inquisition in Venice that ever since his mother and siblings had died during the plague of 1556–66 and he had lost all his property, he had doubted the existence of divine providence. As a result, he said, 'I have been forgetful of my salvation and have lived far from the true and correct Christian way of life.'[41] Yet few people were willing to draw such a conclusion, or at least to do so publicly. To despair was traditionally seen as a form of sin; to trust and to try and identify the marks of God's interventions in one's life was everything, even when they had moments of doubt. Thus refugee friar Wouter Jacobsz in 1570s Amsterdam noted:

> The almighty God saw very well, in what heavy misery the good people sat here, and how mercilessly the wicked treated them at this time, yet He still looked on and behaved to us as if He were asleep, had we not known for sure that He always keeps us in His sight.[42]

This was certainly not just theory. Andreas Bähr has shown, for instance, how seventeenth-century people could reframe an experience of fear as an occasion where it had been possible to overcome one's fear by putting one's faith in God instead.[43] Hans Medick noted that in three accounts of the horrific sack of Magdeburg of 1631 survivors recounted their tales as evidence of God's special providence in sparing them. This providential point of departure did not stop people from also crediting themselves and their relatives with positive contributions to the outcome. One of the fascinating examples Medick discusses is that of David Friese, who recalled the role that he as a twelve-year-old, and his siblings, had played in the family's survival of the Magdeburg sack:

> Then he came at father with a pick-axe. Mother ran up to them straightaway screaming and we children stood around the soldier begging and crying that he should please

---

[40] Protestant approaches to providential thinking are analysed e.g. in Alexandra Walsham, *Providence in early modern England* (Oxford, 1999), yet this was by no means restricted to them. See e.g. Pollmann, *Catholic identity*, 57–67.

[41] Nicholas Davidson, 'Unbelief and atheism in Italy, 1500–1700', in *Atheism from the Reformation to the Enlightenment*, ed. Michael Hunter and David Wootton (Oxford and New York, 1992), 55–88, at 82–3.

[42] Pollmann, *Catholic identity*, 134.

[43] Andreas Bähr, 'Remembering violence. The fear of violence and the violence of fear in seventeenth-century war memories', in *Memory before modernity. Practices of memory in early modern Europe*, ed. Erika Kuijpers et al. (Leiden and Boston, 2013), 269–82.

let father live. Christian, my fourth brother, then a small child who could barely walk and stammer a few words, spoke in the greatest fear to the soldier: 'oh please let father live. I'll gladly give you the three pennies I get for Sundays'. This coming from an unformed and in those days simple child, touched the soldier's heart, perhaps by God's merciful providence, so that he immediately changed and turned to us in a friendly manner.[44]

The children had, 'perhaps' by God's providence, rescued the lives of their family, and this made the tale worth remembering not only as a source of pain, but also as a triumph. In a similar vein, a boy who survived the 1512 sack of Brescia with terrible wounds to his face and jaw seems to have told the story mainly as a way to celebrate his mother, who had prevented his wounds from festering by licking them clean herself.[45] In this context it is also interesting to note that the family tale of Christina de Bitter with which this chapter opened was not transmitted as evidence of the damage she had suffered, but as a story with a happy ending; through her steadfastness, Christina had saved the family fortune.

It is significant that it was stories like these, with a happy ending or an uplifting moral, that most easily emerged in the public sphere; memories of violence that lacked a positive frame eventually did emerge, but had to wait until much later. Historian Erika Kuijpers has been able to reconstruct this process for the small Dutch town of Oudewater, which had been sacked in 1575 by a Habsburg army; scores of its 3,000 inhabitants died, their possessions were carried off, and much of the city went up in smoke.[46] The first personal tales about the sack to be publicized were an account of a fortunate escape and a tale about the miraculous preservation of the body of a Protestant minister who had been hanged by the soldiers—both tales in which the positive prevailed. Yet after that there was public silence; collective commemoration took some decades to emerge, partly because the city had been destroyed and depopulated, but perhaps also because of recrimination and conflicts between survivors, some of whom claimed that the Catholic Habsburg troops had been provoked unnecessarily by a mock procession on the city's walls, in which a sacred host had been publicly fed to the dogs.[47] Yet as the town was strategically located, it was rebuilt and people returned, and as a memory culture about the early days of the Revolt began to emerge throughout Holland, an annual day of commemoration was also instituted in Oudewater; there is evidence for this from 1608 onwards. It may have been at around the same time that the authorities in the Dutch province of Holland took the remarkable and exceptional decision to award an annual pension to all remaining survivors of the sack; the first list of 321 pensioners dates from 1615.[48]

On the lists of beneficiaries there are some indications that the pensioners supported their claims with personal memories, although this was not a condition for receiving the money, since a baby who had been in her mother's womb was also

[44] Medick, 'Historical event and contemporary experience', at 40.
[45] Martines, *Furies*, 63–4.   [46] Kuijpers, 'The creation'.
[47] Pollmann and Kuijpers, 'Why remember terror?', 182.
[48] Unfortunately, we have been unable to find evidence about the reasons for this remarkable decision, which was unprecedented and unique for the Dutch Republic.

entitled to a pension. Of some victims on the list it was said that they had lost 'father and mother', and of a woman by the name of Japikje Pieters it said she 'lay under bodies'. Much later this woman's name and a full version of her tale recurred in the tales collected by local grocer Arnold Duin, who in 1666 published an account, 'Murder of Oudewater', which he claimed to base on eyewitness accounts.[49] The tales collected by Duin were classic examples of 'reframed' memories of trauma; the book is replete with lucky escapes, divine intervention, support from angels, innocence protected, and faith placed in God. Duin also included graphic descriptions of enemy cruelty, but those citizens who died were said to have done so bravely and with great resolve and patriotism.

It is unlikely that it was Duin himself who was responsible for the reframing because he also recorded some memories with a different flavour. The tales Duin collected from people who, like Japikje, had been children at the time, included some very vivid memories of their experiences of the sack. Japikje herself had survived by hiding under a pile of dead bodies. Having fled to neighbouring and royalist Utrecht, Japikje's mother had been shocked to find the clothes of her dead son for sale there because Utrechters had swiftly come to the soldiers' camps near Oudewater to buy their booty off them. Another survivor, Jan van Dam, recalled having burnt the soles of his feet as a soldier forced him to carry goods over the hot embers and stones in the burning town. Memories such as these were 'pointless'; they had no moral and did not necessarily serve as testimony to divine intervention, bravery, or happy endings, but it had apparently become possible to tell them, and they added to the authenticity of the story. This was perhaps not least because by the mid-seventeenth century there were very few surviving witnesses left, and the need was felt to hear what these had to say; 'communicative memory' was now turning into 'cultural memory', and contemporaries were well aware of it. The interest is also evident from the fact that twenty years before Duin published his book, some of the local tales had already been immortalized in a large painting of the sack that the town had commissioned, perhaps on the occasion of the Peace of Münster of 1648, that formally ended the Revolt and eighty years of war. From 1650 residents walked from the commemorative annual sermon to the town hall to view the painting together—they continue to do so to this day.[50] Perhaps helped along by the pension scheme, survivors in Oudewater had become willing to tell their stories, most of them reframed into positive tales, some of them now pointless; the emergence of a collective memory culture, as well as the passage of time, had given meaning to all memories of the sack.

ATROCITY TALES

Yet it was not only the personal memories of the sack that shaped the war memories of the people in Oudewater. At least some of these were also influenced by media representations, and it is to these we should now turn. Like many of the violent

---

[49] Van Duin, *Oudewaters moord.*   [50] Kuijpers, 'The creation'.

Figure 7.1. Frans Hogenberg, *The sack of Oudewater*, 1575, Rijksmuseum, Amsterdam.

episodes in the Dutch Revolt and the French Wars of Religion, Oudewater's fate had been turned into a print by Frans Hogenberg, a Protestant Antwerp artist who had settled in Cologne (Figure 7.1). There, he produced an immensely influential series of images of the wars, which were later complemented by additional material, so as to produce pictorial histories of the great religious wars in France and the Netherlands. Hogenberg was able to give his images a sense of veracity because he also published maps and images of cities throughout the Netherlands—the setting of his newsprints therefore usually looked authentic.[51] Some of the dead were named, and the captions to his prints also suggest precision and first-hand information on what had happened there during sacks and sieges. Thus, his caption to the Oudewater image reads:

> Here is to be seen in what form, great tyranny and gross violence have been perpetrated in Oudewater by ruffians without a sense of God or honour, who killed, plundered, and committed vice [*unzucht*], have violated many women and wives, one of whom

[51] Ramon Voges, 'Das Auge der Geschichte. Die Bildberichte Franz Hogenbergs zu den Französischen Religionskriegen und dem Aufstand der Niederlande (ca. 1560–1610)', doctoral thesis (Paderborn, 2016). On his representation of massacres, see Ramon Voges, 'Macht, Massaker und Repräsentationen. Darstellungen asymetrischer Gewalt in der Bildpublizistik Franz Hogenbergs', in *Gewalträume. Soziale Ordnungen im Ausnahmezustand*, ed. Jörg Baberowski and Gabriele Metzler (Frankfurt am Main and New York, 2012), 29–70.

they strung up naked, and miserably violated, and have pulled an infant from her body, and have thrown it away like dirt.

Hogenberg had begun his war prints project by plagiarizing some prints from the *Quarante tableaux*, a famous 1570 book of forty prints and engravings with scenes from the French Wars of Religion that is usually named after its main contributors, Jacques Tortorel and Jean Perrissin. Philip Benedict, who has studied this collection, emphasizes that these prints aimed to inform the viewers rather than to manipulate them with images of atrocity; Hogenberg's aims were probably more overtly political.[52] However that may be, it is clear that these collections stood at the beginning of a tradition of ever more graphic representations of violence, the purpose of which was clearly to shock the viewers as much as to inform them.

The mutilation of the pregnant woman in Oudewater was only a detail in Hogenberg's print, but it came to exemplify what had happened there. In 1598 a set of seventeen images on the 'Tyranny of the Spanish' was published, which included a print of the Oudewater massacre. This image now zoomed in on a scene that had been a detail in Hogenberg's print but would become the iconic representation of this gruesome episode. In 1620 it appeared in yet another and even more graphic version (Figure 7.2). This iconic status, in turn, seems to have prompted the recalling of memories. In 1624 someone took the trouble of testifying in front of a notary that the pregnant woman had been 'Anna van Danswijk', mother of two. In the 1650 pensions list, survivor Anna Pilgrums attested that the woman had been her aunt and pregnant with twins. In Duin's book, she was given yet another name and said to have been pregnant with triplets.[53]

Whether the woman had ever existed is not at all clear. We do not know how Hogenberg gathered his information or whether he just filled the picture and the caption with generic expectations about the nature of violence during sacks. Women were certainly frequent victims of soldierly violence. Yet it is also evident that Hogenberg's print mirrored a propaganda claim that was made in many early modern and modern wars: the enemy was showing his true nature and violating the laws of war by targeting the innocent: women, children, the sick, and the elderly, as well as priests and pastors.[54] The story of the pregnant woman whose body was being cut open was a stock character in such texts and in representations of cruelty.

---

[52] Philip Benedict, *Graphic history. The wars, massacres and troubles of Tortorel and Perrissin* (Geneva, 2007); Voges, 'Macht, Massaker und Repräsentationen'.

[53] Kuijpers, 'The creation'.

[54] J.C. Theibault, 'Landfrauen, Soldaten und Vergewaltigungen während des Dreißigjährigen Krieges', *Werkstatt Geschichte* 19 (1998): 25–39; John A. Lynn, *Giant of the Grand Siècle. The French army, 1610–1715* (Cambridge and New York, 1997), 191–3; as well as K. Jansson, 'Soldaten und Vergewaltigung im Schweden des 17. Jahrhunderts', in *Zwischen Alltag und Katastrophe*, ed. Benigna von Krusenstjern, Hans Medick, and Patrice Veit (Göttingen, 1999), 195–225, and U. Rublack, 'Wench and maiden. Women, war and the pictorial function of the feminine in German cities in the early modern period', *History Workshop* 44 (1997), 1–21.

GROUWELYCKHEYT TOT OUDEWATER

Oudewater ſachmen branden	Moorden dan die ionge ſpruyten
Alles wert gemaeckt ter ſchanden	Hingen Maechden aen haer tuyten
Niet en wert aldaer geſpaert	Staecken doot die nu al krom
T'ſy hoe Iongh of out beiaert	Waren door haer ouderdom
Moeders ſonder te ontfarmen	Vrouwen ſchenden en ſchoffieren
Hinghen ſy op aen haer armen	Was het doen van deſe gieren
Sneden uyt haer tere vrucht	Soo langh ſachmen haer ter weer
Met een boos en fel gerucht	Tot de Stadt gantſch lach ter neer

Figure 7.2. Anonymous, *Horrors at Oudewater*, 1575, illustration for *De Spaensche Tiranye gheschiet in Nederlant* (Amsterdam, 1620), Rijksmuseum, Amsterdam.

Quite regardless of whether or not such a woman had existed in 1575 Oudewater, it seems that under the influence of Hogenberg's print and its successors, after five decades people in the city had begun to 'remediate' the print so as to embellish their own memories of this iconic pregnant victim of Spanish cruelty.[55] That it is possible for such re- and pre-mediations of memory to happen is quite well attested for modern Europe. Historians of World War I, for instance, have reconstructed

---

[55] Marianne Eekhout, 'Furies in beeld. Herinneringen aan gewelddadige innames van steden tijdens de Nederlandse Opstand op zeventiende-eeuwse schilderijen', *De Zeventiende Eeuw* 30 (2014): 243–66.

the process by which previous war experiences influenced both the reality and representation of violence in 1914 Belgium, where German soldiers, recalling resistance by civilians in the Prussian wars of 1870, came to fear that *francs-tireurs* were hiding among the civilian population and responded with a terror campaign that resulted in thousands of Belgian civilian casualties. Belgian refugees, in turn, came to spread stories about their experiences that remediated memories of earlier atrocities; thus the widespread belief among them that German soldiers severed babies' hands has been retraced to the well-publicized atrocities that Belgian colonials had perpetrated in Congo.[56]

By 1914 the pre- and remediation of such stories was helped along, of course, by the mass media; cheaper newspapers, photography, schoolbooks, and the radio. Yet, the phenomenon was not conditional on the existence of such new forms of mass mediation. David Hopkin has shown that peasants in Lorraine modelled both their expectations and their memories of the Prussian invasion of 1870 on oral memory traditions, especially folktales about the Swedes who had invaded in the course of the seventeenth century.[57] Joan Redmond has noted that atrocity tales about the 1641 massacre in Ireland were premediated by reports about the violence in the Munster plantations in 1598, as well as by atrocity tales from the Thirty Years War, while historian Guy Beiner found that contemporary accounts of what occurred in Ireland during the French invasion of 1798 were shaped by earlier memories and tales from early Christian and Gaelic–Celtic traditions. He concludes: 'at some level, the social memory of Ninety-Eight began long before 1798!'[58]

Long before the age of cheap newspapers, moreover, early modern print media had already become very influential in shaping and even in pre-mediating memories of atrocity. The sixteenth and seventeenth centuries are known not only as a period of vicious warfare and religious conflict; there were also new media with which to spread news about this. Pamphlets, song sheets, and broadsheets were within reach of large sections of the reading public, and their impact amplified through the traditional means of copying, storytelling, singing, preaching, and reading aloud.[59] The authors of such texts claimed veracity and impartiality, but were, of course, often deeply partisan, and to make their point, they were often also highly selective about the types of violence they reported.

Authors tried to authenticate their texts by adding details. In England, extracts from the depositions that had been taken among the Protestant victims of the Irish massacre of 1641 were heavily reworked and turned into a pamphlet by John Temple, *Irish Rebellion; or an history of the beginning and first progress of the generall rebellion raised within the kingdom of Ireland upon the…23 Oct. 1641. Together with the barbarous cruelties and bloody massacres which ensued thereupon* (1646),

[56] Horne and Kramer, *German atrocities*, 140–74, 200–4, 223.

[57] Hopkin, *Soldier and peasant*, 240–51.

[58] Joan Redmond, 'Memories of violence and New English identities in early modern Ireland', *Historical Research* 89 (2016), 708–29; Beiner, *Remembering*, 318.

[59] Andrew Pettegree, *The invention of news. How the world came to know about itself* (New Haven and London, 2014), 116–38.

that gained enormous influence both in England and abroad. To increase impact and credibility, Huguenot leader Pierre Jurieu in 1681 also began to include eye-witness evidence in his accounts of the forced conversion of French Calvinists to Catholicism. He collected and published letters and other documents setting out the experiences of the unfortunate Calvinist families in the Poitou who had been exposed to 'dragonnades', that is, billeting of soldiers who were under order to harass their hosts into conversion to Catholicism.[60] Such attention to authenticating accounts had always been part and parcel of the martyrs' books, in which both Protestants and Catholics collected the experiences of their martyrs. Yet there the emphasis had always been placed on the ideas for which believers had died, rather than on the nature of the violence they had suffered. As we have seen in Chapter 1, it was not the violent death itself that made one a martyr, but the fact that martyrs died for their faith that mattered.

In atrocity literature, on the other hand, there was much attention to the details of the violence. Some deaths were considered much more unacceptable than others. While there were no Geneva conventions in force to regulate what was licit in war or to prescribe rules for treatment of prisoners and civilians, early modern Europeans had clear ideas on what was, and was not, permissible in times of war. Violence as such was not enough to shock the readership; then as now violence by and against soldiers was what was to be expected, although religious wars sometimes saw a lapse of the chivalric custom of 'giving quarter' to defeated enemies of noble extraction—that is, to let them surrender unharmed—because these were 'rebels' or 'traitors' against God.[61] In the Civil Wars in the British Isles, for instance, all sides accused the other of refusing to give quarter to defeated enemy soldiers.[62] Violence against able-bodied civilians, too, could be licit in certain circumstances, for instance when they were rebels. That such violence could include death penalties, mutilation, and torture was also accepted; these were part and parcel, after all, of judicial violence and not as such considered criminal. Violence against rustics could even be seen as entertaining. Around 1600, Netherlandish genre painters introduced the genre of the *boerenverdriet* (literally: peasants' sorrow), scenes of soldiers terrorizing peasants, which were often paired with scenes of *boerenvreugd* (peasants' joy), in which peasants were seen retaliating (Figure 7.3).[63]

Yet violence against priests and pastors, women and children, the sick and the old was formally out of bounds and considered as shocking as it is today.[64] Anyone who wanted to charge their enemies with cruelty therefore tended to focus on

---

[60] David van der Linden, *Experiencing exile. Huguenot refugees in the Dutch Republic, 1680–1700* (Farnham, 2015), 180–2.

[61] D.J.B. Trim '"Put all to the sword". The effects of Reformation on the ethics of war in sixteenth-century Germany and England', in *Sister Reformations* II—*Schwesterreformationen* II. *Reformation and ethics in Germany and in England—Reformation und Ethik in Deutschland und in England*, ed. Dorothea Wendebourg and Alec Ryrie (Tübingen, 2014), 271–98.

[62] Barbara Donagan, 'Atrocity, war crime, and treason in the English Civil War', *The American Historical Review* 99 (1994): 1137–66.

[63] Jane S. Fishman, *Boerenverdriet. Violence between peasants and soldiers in early modern Netherlandish art* (Ann Arbor MI, 1982).

[64] Geoffrey Parker, 'The etiquette of atrocity. The laws of war in early modern Europe', in *Empire, war and faith in early modern Europe*, ed. Geoffrey Parker (London, 2003), 143–68.

Figure 7.3. Boëtius Adamsz Bolswert after David Vinckboons, *Peasants' sorrow. Spanish soldiers force entry into a home*, 1610, Rijksmuseum, Amsterdam. The caption describes the exchange between the householder and the soldiers: 'Hey peasant, open up, you have visitors...', to which he replies, 'You are outside and will stay there...'.

these innocent victims, more than on any men who had also died. This had been so since antiquity. The Roman orator Quintilian, who was considered an authority on rhetoric in early modern Europe, recommended that any description of a captured town should be amplified by descriptions of the destruction of secular and religious buildings, the wailing of women and children, and violence perpetrated against the young and the elderly.[65] Violence against women had (and still has) a special role to play in such descriptions. The rape of women was often represented as a way of dishonouring their menfolk, as much as the women themselves. This makes rape, attacks on genitals, and nudity, a central theme in atrocity narratives.[66]

This was perhaps never more so than in the mediation of the sack or 'rape' of the German town of Magdeburg (literally: Virgin's fortress) in 1631. Hundreds of pamphlets and songs described how this Protestant city had fallen victim to Catholic armies, drawing comparisons with the Fall of Jerusalem and that of

[65] Katrin Hirt, 'Der Sacco di Roma in einer zeitgenössischen italienischen Versflugschrift. Das Massaker und die Einheit der Nation', in *Bilder des Schreckens. Die mediale Inszenierung von Massakern seit dem 16. Jahrhundert*, ed. Christine Vogel (Frankfurt am Main, 2006), 38–50, at 47.

[66] David Lederer, 'The myth of the all-destructive war. Afterthoughts on German suffering, 1618–1648', *German History* 29 (2011): 380–403.

Babylon. Hans Medick has analysed how the city's fall came to epitomize the miseries of the war, for both Protestants and Catholics. Generals threatened other cities with giving them the 'Magdeburg treatment', and preachers used it as an example. In Bremen, for instance, Pastor Zimmerman preached that the 'piteous misfortune' of this city was a 'mirror' of bloody persecution 'in which we can see quite plainly the great wrath of Satan towards us, which can also befall us should we pass into the hands of the enemies of the Gospel'.[67] Yet even when the name of a city did not invite such comparisons, rape and violence against children were central to atrocity accounts. They played a significant role, for instance, in James Cranford's influential *Teares of Ireland* (1642), which was illustrated by a print series that referred to the atrocity tales from the 1641 depositions (Figure 7.4). Catholics had their own atrocity tales to relate, of course. The martyrdom of priests, both in Protestant areas and in the New World, was often painted in lurid detail, but atrocities against laypeople were also exposed. The sack of the small town of Tienen by Dutch and French armies in 1635, for instance, was widely publicized and triggered outrage among the people of the Southern Netherlands.[68]

One consequence of the existence of atrocity narratives is that scholars struggle to separate fact from fiction in memories of atrocity. It is perhaps not hard to reject tales about Savoyard soldiers who baked the bodies of their Waldensian victims in an oven with the intention of eating them. Christine Vogel has argued that this tale remediated the biblical episode in which tyrant Nebuchadnezzar has his opponents thrown into the fiery furnace.[69] The story of the impaling and roasting on a spit of a Waldensian virgin may also be a little far-fetched. Geoff Mortimer has shown how tales about cannibalism, and particularly sadistic types of torture like the early modern variant of 'waterboarding' known as the 'Swedish draught', abounded in German egodocuments, but usually as something that people had heard about happening to others or had read about in printed media.[70]

It is hardest to know what to make of tales of rape. It is well known that rape was considered so shameful that many victims and their families preferred to cover up any memories of it, just as they still do today, or blamed the victims; considering this, many modern scholars have been inclined to fill in the silences in the sources, using atrocity narratives as evidence for the incidence of rape. Yet when Geoff Mortimer analysed mentions of rape in the German male eyewitness accounts he studied, he noted that while many of them reported on rape as something that routinely happened elsewhere, when describing what had been happening in their own communities they recorded that women escaped it: 'our Lord God protected the womenfolk so that they [the soldiers] did not get a single one'.[71]

---

[67] Medick, 'Historical event and contemporary experience', 37.

[68] Jean Marc de Pluvrez, *Tienen 1635. Geschiedenis van een Brabantse stad in de zeventiende eeuw* (Tienen, 1985).

[69] Christine Vogel, '"Piemontesische Ostern". Mediale inszenierungen des Waldenser-Massakers von 1655', in *Bilder des Schreckens. Die mediale Inszenierung von Massakern seit dem 16. Jahrhundert*, ed. Christine Vogel (Frankfurt am Main, 2006), 74–92.

[70] Mortimer, *Eyewitness accounts.*   [71] Mortimer, *Eyewitness accounts*, 170.

At one Mr. Atkins house 7 Papistes brake in
& beate out his braines, then riped upe his
wife with Childe, after they had rauished her,
& Nero like vewed natures bed of conception
then tooke they the Childe & sacrificed it
in the fire

English Protestantes striped naked & turned
into the mountaines, in the frost, & snowe, whe=
reof many hundreds are perished to death,
& many lyinge dead in diches & Sauages
upbraided them sayinge now are ye wilde
Irisch as well as wee,

Figure 7.4. James Cranford, *The teares of Ireland, plate* 4 (London, 1642), perhaps by Wenceslaus Hollar. Yet another pregnant woman's abdomen is being cut in the image at the top. The image below shows naked Protestant men and women being driven into the snow: 'now are ye wilde Irisch as well as wee', say the Catholic rebels. © British Library.

Figure 7.5. Jacques Callot, *Soldiers near a hospital*, from Jacques Callot, *Les Misères et les malheurs de la guerre* (1633), Rijksmuseum, Amsterdam. The caption highlights the 'hazards' to which the 'children of Mars' are exposed. Some end up so mutilated that they can only crawl, the lucky ones go off to war, and may end on the gallows, or in hospital.

One thing is certain; the media underrepresented adult male suffering in the early modern period, and so have modern historians. It is typical that scholars of the most famous representations of war in seventeenth-century Europe, Jacques Callot's series, *The miseries of war* of 1633, have long struggled to explain what these prints were trying to do (Figure 7.5). Only recently have they also come to be seen as a reflection on the fate of soldiers, underpaid, subject to harsh discipline, detested, and prey for angry peasants when these could lay their hands on them— rather than a straight condemnation of the 'horrors of war'.[72]

MIRRORING THE PAST: COSMOPOLITAN MEMORY

Early modern atrocity narratives invariably emphasized that the enemy could not be called Christian; to compare perpetrators to 'Turks' or 'Jews' was the order of the day, although they could also be described as 'barbaric', 'wild', or 'savage'. As we have seen in Chapter 3, this was an increasingly significant remark to make about one's opponents in early modern Europe because Europeans prided them-selves on being more 'advanced' and 'civilized' than people from other continents. Yet rather confusingly, non-Europeans did not appear only as 'savages' in European memory cultures, but also as victims. When people in the seventeenth-century Dutch Republic talked about the bad days of the Dutch Revolt, they often drew a parallel between their suffering ancestors and the fate of the American Indians who had fallen victim to 'Spanish cruelty' earlier in the sixteenth century. Building on the catalogue of complaints about *conquistador* cruelty in the New World which the Spanish missionary Bartolomé de las Casas had collected in 1552 and pub-lished in order to try and influence royal policies, the Dutch used the fate of the

---

[72] Katie Hornstein, ' Just violence. Jacques Callot's *Grandes misères et malheurs de la guerre*', *Bulletin of the University of Michigan Museums of Art and Archaeology* 16 (2005), 29–48.

indigenous peoples of Central and South America both to demonstrate that the true aim of the Habsburgs was to turn all their subjects into slaves and to point to a parallel between themselves and these fellow victims: like the Indians the Dutch were 'innocent'.[73]

The Dutch were not the only ones to be impressed by this account. De Las Casas's aim had, of course, not been to declare that all the Spanish were cruel, but this is definitely how it was read (and why the book was later banned by the kings of Spain). The text was first issued in Dutch in 1578, in French in 1579, in English in 1583, and in German in 1597, and it was frequently reissued in the seventeenth and eighteenth centuries. The interest in De Las Casas's report about the alleged twenty million American victims of Spanish atrocities was part of a European-wide phenomenon that is known as the 'Black Legend' about Spain, a complex of stereotypes and allegations about the 'nature' of the Spanish that was used by a range of critics to try and challenge Spanish claims that they were defending the true faith against all its enemies. In an ironic reversal of the early modern Spanish efforts to prevent contamination of old Christian blood by that of Jewish and 'Moorish' converts to Christianity, Spain's enemies liked to blame the exceptional cruelty, arrogance, and ambition of the Spanish and their princes on their Jewish and Muslim ancestry. Although it was Protestant enemies of the Spanish Habsburgs who were the greatest proponents of the Black Legend, the Legend originated in the Franco-Spanish wars fought in Italy in the first half of the sixteenth century, and this anti-Hispanism flourished among Catholic Frenchmen and Italians as much as among English and German Protestants.[74]

Even so, the Dutch and the English were certainly among its most avid proponents. The Dutch, especially, made explicit comparisons between themselves and innocent Indians. Wolfgang Cilleßen has shown how representations of atrocities in the Americas and those in the Low Countries fused to become a very powerful representation of Spanish tyranny.[75] Almost simultaneously with the print series that had foregrounded violence against women and children in the Revolt, for instance, there had appeared an illustrated version of the *Brevísima relación*. These plates both reflected earlier Dutch war propaganda and in turn shaped representations of the wars in the Low Countries and way beyond, as is evident from the representation of particular forms of cruelty in the Indies, that included hanging a woman in her

---

[73] Benjamin Schmidt, *Innocence abroad. The Dutch imagination and the New World, 1570–1670* (Cambridge, 2001); Wolfgang Cilleßen, 'Massaker in der niederländischen Erinnerungskultur. Die Bildwerdung des Schwarzen Legende', in *Bilder des Schreckens. Die mediale Inszenierung von Massakern seit dem 16. Jahrhundert*, ed. Christine Vogel (Frankfurt am Main, 2006), 93–135; Dagmar Freist, 'Lost in time and space? *Glocal* memoryscapes in the early modern world', in *Memory before modernity. Practices of memory in early modern Europe*, ed. Erika Kuijpers et al. (Leiden and Boston, 2013), 203–22.

[74] Schmidt, *Innocence abroad*; Sverker Arnoldsson, *La leyenda negra. Estudio sobre sus origines* (Göteborg, 1960); William S. Maltby, *The Black Legend in England. The development of anti-Spanish sentiment, 1558–1660* (Durham NC, 1971); Swart, 'The Black Legend'; Judith Pollmann, 'Eine natürliche Feindschaft. Ursprung und Funktion der schwarzen Legende über Spanien in den Niederlanden, 1560–1581', in *Feindbilder. Die Darstellung des Gegners in der politischen Publizistik des Mittelalters und der Neuzeit*, ed. F. Bosbach (Cologne, 1992), 73–94; Cilleßen, 'Massaker'.

[75] Cilleßen, 'Massaker'.

doorway and feeding her children to the dogs—the scene closely mirrored that from Oudewater. The series were, moreover, to be popularized together in 1620 in a set of books, the *Mirror of Spanish tyranny in the West Indies*, and the *Mirror of Spanish tyranny in the Netherlands*.[76] These were frequently reprinted and remediated; when the French armies of Louis XIV invaded the Dutch Republic in 1672, there appeared new editions of the 'Mirrors', in which the word 'Spanish' had been replaced systematically with the word 'French', and the same images were still being used, as if they considered events of 1672.[77] In England, De Las Casas's work also had a long career ahead of it; in the 1650s Lord Protector Oliver Cromwell and his supporters were using Black Legend arguments to justify the need for an attack on the Spanish West Indies, much as the Dutch had used it in the 1620s to argue for the urgency of their own forays into the New World. No wonder that De Las Casas's text was reissued in 1656 as the *Teares of the Indians*, evoking, in its turn, memories of Cranford's 1642 *Tears of Ireland*.[78]

In 2002 Daniel Levy and Nathan Sznaider introduced a new term in the field of memory studies, that of 'cosmopolitan memory':

> cosmopolitanism refers to a process of 'internal globalization' through which global concerns become part of local experiences of an increasing number of people. Global media representations, among others, create new cosmopolitan memories, providing new epistemological vantage points and emerging moral-political interdependencies.[79]

This plea to start thinking about collective memory beyond the confines of the nation state was extremely important and welcome. Yet the example of the Black Legend suggests that Levy and Sznaider's idea that the advent of the cosmopolitan memory of the Holocaust is the result of a 'decoupling of collective memory and the nation state', and thus a new phenomenon, may have been too hasty. When we broaden the chronological perspective, we can see that 'cosmopolitan memories' of the type they discussed with reference to the Holocaust actually emerged well before the advent of the nation state. The commemoration of the fate of the American Indians was certainly not the only example of a cosmopolitan memory, nor was it the first. In the Middle Ages, conflicts with Muslims, especially the Crusades, had produced a pan-European set of memories both of Crusader heroes

---

[76] Bartholomé de Las Casas, *Den spiegel der Spaensche tijrannije, gheschiet in West-Indien. Waer in te sien is de onmenschelycke wreede feyten der Spanjaerdē, met t'samen de beschryvinghe der selver landen, volckerēn aert ende natuere* (Amsterdam 1620).

[77] Donald Haks, 'De Franse tirannie. De verbeelding van een massamoord', in *Romeyn de Hooghe. De verbeelding van de late Gouden Eeuw*, ed. Henk van Nierop et al. (Zwolle and Amsterdam, 2008), 86–100.

[78] See on Cromwell's policy and the media campaign to support it Maltby, *The Black Legend*, 112–22; Bartholomé de Las Casas, *The tears of the Indians: being an historical… account of the cruel massacres and slaughters of above twenty millions of innocent people; committed by the Spaniards in the Islands of Hispaniola, Cuba, Jamaica, &c. as also, in the continent of Mexico, Peru, & other places of the West-Indies, to the total destruction of those countries. Written in Spanish by Casaus… and made English by J. P.* [i.e. John Phillips], ed. and trans. John Philips (London, 1656).

[79] David Levy and Nathan Sznaider, 'Memory unbound. The Holocaust and the formation of cosmopolitan memory', *European Journal of Social Theory* 5 (2002): 87–106, at 87.

and of their 'Saracen' foes, so that heroes like Roland, Richard the Lionheart, and Saladin entered the popular imagination.[80]

In their study of cosmopolitan memories, Levy and Sznaider do in fact note that religious solidarities have, of course, always created their own form of cosmopolitanism. Although they do not consider historical parallels before 1800 in any detail, we do not have to look far in early modern Europe to find them.[81] After the Reformation both Catholics and Protestants frequently commemorated the fate of co-religionists abroad. As we have seen in Chapter 1, Catholic, Calvinist, and Mennonite martyrologists all collected and published tales of religious persecution from across Europe and beyond, printing the suffering of martyrs from different countries side by side. Believers were invited to see themselves as part of a transnational religious community, and this included frequent references to a shared past of suffering, exile, and martyrdom, as well as shared victories.[82] Such references did not necessarily have to be spelled out. Nicholas Canny has shown that Temple's account of the Catholic plot against the Protestants in Ireland in 1641 was modelled on older discourses about attacks on English Protestants that derived from the colonial sphere. Without making explicit reference to the event, Temple actually remediated an existing account about a Native American attack on a settlement in Virginia in 1622.[83]

Yet quite often transnational examples were evoked explicitly. In Italy, Germany, Bohemia, France, and the Dutch Republic for instance, seventeenth-century Catholic poets and playwrights celebrated the memory of Mary Queen of Scots as a tragic victim of Protestant cruelty and a model of Catholic steadfastness and sacrifice, a martyr who had died for her faith.[84] And it was because Protestants throughout Europe already revered the memory of the medieval Waldensian communities of the Southern Alps as a type of proto-Protestants, that there was a particularly strong international outcry when the Dukes of Savoy renewed their persecutions of this minority group in the seventeenth century. The Waldensians continued to function as a *lieu de mémoire* for Protestant Europe throughout the eighteenth and nineteenth centuries; an English committee in aid of the Waldensian missions in fact remains active to this day.[85]

---

[80] Nicolas L. Paul and Suzanne Yeager, eds, *Remembering the Crusades. Myth, image and identity* (Baltimore, 2012); Nicholas L. Paul, *To follow in their footsteps. The Crusades and family memory in the high Middle Ages* (Ithaca NY and London, 2012).

[81] A point also made by Freist, 'Lost in time and space?'.

[82] Gregory, *Salvation at stake.*   [83] Canny, '1641 in a colonial context'.

[84] An overview of publications about Mary Stuart to 1700 in John Scott, *A bibliography of works relating to Mary, Queen of Scots, c. 1544–1700* (Edinburgh, 1896); Veronica Carta, 'Adattamenti e rielaborazioni nel passaggio di codice: dall'immagine ai versi. Il martirio di Maria Stuarda nel Poema heroico di Bassiano Gatti', *Between. Rivista dell' Associazione di Teoria e Storia Comparata dell Literatura* 2 (2012), accessed 3 May 2016, http://ojs.unica.it/index.php/between/article/view/680. For a nice example of how an ordinary Catholic grocer in Amsterdam appropriated such transnational imagery, see Herman Verbeeck, *Thoneel der Verandering deser Werelt* (1667), Stadsbibliotheek Haarlem, MS 187 A 4. Alexander Wilkinson, *Mary Queen of Scots and French public opinion, 1542–1600* (Basingstoke, 2004) shows how this all started, with hundreds of references to Mary in the polemics of the French Wars of Religion.

[85] Albert Lange, ed., *Dall' Europa alle valle valdesi. Atti del XXIX convegno storico internazionale. Il Glorioso rimpatrio (1689–1989). Contesto—significato—imagine*, Torre Pellice (To), 3–7 Settembre 1989 (Turin, 1990). See for the committee, http://www.waldensian.org.uk/.

Confessional memory also created its own canon of iconic events and people. For generations of Protestants in the Dutch Republic, the British Isles, and Central Europe, the French Massacre of St Bartholomew's Day in 1572 symbolized the iniquities of popish rulers. Early modern Protestant pamphleteers and preachers routinely invoked this massacre when listing the evils of Catholicism. Christopher Marlowe was probably the first to write a play about it in the 1590s; plays about this 'blood wedding' and its chief villains were also staged in the mid-seventeenth-century Netherlands and used to point to the dangers of trusting the Catholic monarchs of France. At the end of the seventeenth century, during the wars with the French king Louis XIV, new and popular prints of the Bartholomew's Day massacre were also being issued. By the eighteenth century, the massacre was still a popular topic in the German theatre.[86] In the longer run some of these transnational Protestant memories morphed into *lieux de mémoire* for the Enlightenment. In the eighteenth century, memories of the inquisitions, especially those of Spain and Portugal, outgrew the context of confessional solidarities to become the exemplars of obscurantism and the bugbear of all those striving for freedom of thought and speech, and they have remained so until today.[87]

The Catholic Church was by its nature a cosmopolitan institution, and this showed in its memory practices, not just of the ecclesiastical but also of the secular past. In Rome, for instance, the St Bartholomew's Day massacre was also memorialized, but this time in the papal *Sala regia* in a series of frescoes commissioned from Giorgio Vasari. Pope Gregory XIII also had a medal struck to commemorate this French victory over the heretics. The battle of Lepanto of 1571, in which a Holy League of Catholic rulers had defeated the Turks with the help of the Virgin Mary, also became a *lieu de mémoire* across the Catholic world. In Venice, it was associated with the feast of the martyr St Justina and commemorated with a major annual procession in which the standard of Alvise Mocenigo, the doge during whose regime the battle had been fought, was on display. Plays, verse, paintings, and medals kept the memory alive. Because Pope Gregory had also linked the victory with the popular devotion to the rosary, and through the efforts of the Dominican order for whom the rosary devotion was a key hallmark, the memories of Lepanto were further amplified (Figure 7.6).[88] To commemorate it, a feast for

---

[86] Robert Kingdon, *Myths about the St. Bartholomew's Day massacres 1572–1576* (Cambridge MA, 1988), 216–20; Barbara Diefendorf, 'Memories of the massacre. Saint Bartholomew's Day and Protestant identity in France', in *Voices for tolerance in an age of persecution*, ed. Vincent P. Carey, Ronald Bogdan, and Elizabeth A. Walsh (Seattle and London, 2004), 45–62. Barbara Diefendorf, 'Blood wedding. The Saint Bartholomew's Day massacre in history and memory', lecture, Boston (2006), accessed 3 May 2016, http://www.youtube.com/watch?v=5UIfXUoEKgo; Canny, '1641 in a colonial context', 59; H. Duits, *Van Bartholomeusnacht tot Bataafse Opstand. Studies over de relatie tussen politiek en toneel in het midden van de zeventiende eeuw* (Amsterdam, 1990), 36–93; David El Kenz, 'Le Massacre de la Saint-Barthélemy est-il un lieu de mémoire victimaire (fin XVIᵉ siècle–début 2009)?', in *Commémorer les victimes en Europe, XVIe–XXIe siècles*, ed. David El Kenz and François-Xavier Nérard (Seyssel, 2011), 217–36.

[87] Francesco Bethencourt, *The Inquisition. A global history, 1478–1834*, trans. Jean Birrell (Cambridge, 2009), 364–415, first published as *L'Inquisition à l'époque moderne* (Paris, 1995).

[88] Fenlon, *The ceremonial city*, 263–85.

Figure 7.6. Paolo Veronese, *Allegory on the battle of Lepanto*, *c.*1572, Galleria dell' Accademia, Venice.

Our Lady of Victory was also included in the church calendar; first celebrated mainly locally, in 1716 it was extended to all of the Roman Catholic Church.

Transnational memories like these could be appropriated and reapplied to local situations. When in 1629 the Augustinians in Paris built a church dedicated to Our Lady of Victory, for instance, they did so in celebration of the recent Catholic defeat of the Calvinists at La Rochelle and with financial support from the king of

France. By association, the victory at La Rochelle thus was made to equal that of Lepanto. When the Austrian Habsburgs reasserted Catholic power over the Spanish Netherlands and the rebel kingdom of Bohemia, they called upon a range of historical associations to reinforce the significance and meaning of their victory, including that of Lepanto and Our Lady of Victory.[89] In such ways cosmopolitan memories were widely used to invest local events with a deeper meaning and significance that was recognized both locally and abroad, much as we saw that local memories could take on a national significance.

CONCLUSION

In 1755 the French philosopher Voltaire wrote a famous poem about the earthquake that had just struck Lisbon, destroying 80 per cent of its buildings and killing tens of thousands of its inhabitants.[90] The objective of the poem was less to sympathize with the victims than to use their plight to attack the ideas of the German philosopher Gottfried Wilhelm Leibniz, who in a 1710 book had tried to account for the existence of evil by arguing that whatever God wanted had to be good. In response, Voltaire argued that the earthquake proved that this 'optimist' philosophy was ridiculous because there was no way a good God should have allowed this to happen. Two centuries earlier, as we have seen, the Venetian Inquisition had arrested Evangelista de Vintura for his loss of faith in God after a plague epidemic. Voltaire now publicly aired a conclusion very similar to the one Vintura had drawn; if such evil happened, this was because there was no providential God.

Although many of Voltaire's contemporaries did not agree with this conclusion, scholars have often seen Voltaire's poem as the beginning of a new quest for answers to the problem of evil and also as the beginning of a new problem that modern Europeans continue to struggle with: how to make sense of suffering. The providential answer was certainly no longer good enough for many in the post-Auschwitz generations. Some people have argued that it is the resulting gap in our consciousness that explains both the existence of trauma and the modern interest in victimhood.[91]

This chapter has shown that the way early modern Europeans dealt with memories of violence in some respects resembled those of the modern world. There was certainly as much pain in early modern Europe as there has been since. Early modern people, too, found it hard to articulate painful memories and needed a *Solidargemeinschaft* to do so. The twentieth century did not invent victimhood. The early modern world was as fascinated by the pain and sufferings of others as is our own; memories of atrocity were powerful, both in shaping transnational

---

[89] Luc Duerloo and Marc Wingens, *Scherpenheuvel. Het Jeruzalem van de Lage Landen* (Leuven, 2002).

[90] Voltaire, *Poème sur le désastre de Lisbonne* (n.p., 1755).

[91] See for a very helpful discussion of this problem Jeffrey K. Olick, *The politics of regret. On collective memory and historical responsibility* (New York, 2007), 153–73.

public opinion, and in the pre- and remediation of memories of individual victims of violence.

What the early modern world did not have was a psychological theory to account for the lasting damage such experiences can produce or to explain the re-emergence of painful memories later in life. That we find so little trace of post-traumatic stress disorder in early modern sources may be because early modern culture struggled to articulate such pain. On the other hand, there is also evidence to suggest that early modern people may have been more resilient because their belief in providence allowed them to turn evil into something that could somehow also be remembered as beneficial. There was much in early modern Christian culture to point people towards such an interpretation, and, as long as they could bring themselves to believe it, this could bring some solace for the suffering that was so often their share.

Conclusion

The aim of this book has been both to survey what we now know about the ways in which people practised memory in early modern Europe and to reconsider what this means for our understanding of the differences between modern and early modern memory. Seven chapters on, it is time to take stock and see where has this brought us.

Memory mattered to early modern Europeans as much as it does to those living in the twenty-first century, and partly for the same reasons. Then as now, memory practices supported the formation of both personal and communal identities, memories were used and manipulated in support of religious and political causes, and invoked to create and support personal status and family prestige. Memories could play an insidious role, in legitimizing and perpetuating conflict, and in supporting the definition and exclusion of outsiders. They could also help to maintain collective identity in the face of persecution and exclusion. But there were also some major differences between pre-modern and modern memory cultures, most importantly in the enormous and mostly unquestioned prestige that the past enjoyed among early modern Europeans as a source of moral, legal, social, and political authority.

Although the personal memories of early modern Europeans remain an intractable subject, we have seen that it was in everyone's interest to retain some knowledge both of one's personal past and of the past of one's ancestors, and to make sure one was remembered, at the very least in the prayers of one's descendants. Those who chose to write down their memories originally tended to do so in fact-oriented accounts that focused on the exemplary value of the author's own experiences and that privileged exemplary and providential tales. The rise of the novel led to the emergence of a new script for remembering one's life that used personal memories to explore the uniqueness of one's own personality and life trajectory. The eighteenth-century vogue for the exploration of 'sentiment', originally something associated with religious and devotional practices, offered a new language in which to do so. Unsurprisingly in a Christian culture that revolved around the passion and suffering of the Son of God, victimhood played a central role in many memory practices—the early martyrs of the Church were an important role model for religious dissidents of all confessions. Both Jews and Christians of many different varieties also interpreted their own situation through the lens of God's covenant with the biblical people of Israel, and believers used this to give meaning to their experiences, often those of exile or marginality. While memories of conversion, exile, and martyrdom were considered extremely edifying, it was unusual for victims of violence to reflect on the emotional impact of personal mental pain and suffering—such memories usually required a happy or edifying ending to be passed on.

In public memory, the medieval religious formats of commemoration that associated community memories with the feasts of saints and holy relics remained alive, but new variations appeared. Protestant societies developed alternatives for public commemoration, through annual sermons, fasts, and celebrations, and by creating alternative 'jubilees', of which the centenary of the Reformation, in 1617, was only the first. Building on ecclesiastical traditions, towns were well ahead in the development of and support for secular public memory practices, using a wide range of media. Princes, whose commemorative practices initially focused on dynastic memories and their own victories, were relatively late in the creation of secular public memory practices and only gradually began to associate themselves with the memories of their subjects. Where 'national' and 'cosmopolitan' memory cultures emerged this was often the work of non-state actors, who sought to mobilize support for political alternatives to state policies. Atrocity and martyrs' tales formed one important category of transnational or 'cosmopolitan' memory, which proved especially important for transnational religious communities. The importance of public memory was also evident in the agreements to 'forget' civil conflict; these were used as an instrument for deactivating memories and overwriting them with other, less contentious or uncomfortable, interpretations of the past.

Between 1500 and 1800 there was much that changed in the public memory practices of early modern Europe. First of all, there were changes in the mediation of memories. The authority of 'very old men' continued to be invoked on all sorts of occasions, but it was increasingly important to record memories on paper if they were to have legal or cultural status. This development did not completely disempower the illiterate, however; we saw that communities proved able to mobilize someone with some writing skills when necessary and could also use the existence of written evidence to their advantage. Moreover, the range of media used in memory practices became more elaborate than it had been around 1500. The liturgical and religious forms of commemoration that had been in use at that time, of course, remained very much in evidence; sermons continued to play a central role in the transmission and reinterpretation of the past, and annual feasts presented a rhythm for delivering them. We have also seen how religious imagery was remediated in secular memory practices. The number of media that were used in memory practices expanded continually and not only through the spread of print. Fireworks, plays, and the re-enactment of battles were added to the processions, songs, and sermons that had been in place around 1500. Statues and monuments commemorating non-religious and non-royal figures became much more common. Public buildings were more and more often adorned with tapestries, paintings, and stained glass relating to the past. Commemorative medals, once commissioned to reward those who had played a prominent role in events, became a must for all sorts of occasions. There was a growing commodification of secular memory-related objects; all sorts of people began to make money out of commemorative prints, medals, plates, snuffboxes, board games, and teacups.[1] Significantly, there were very few memory practices and media that disappeared as new ones emerged; many early modern memory practices are in fact still with us today. It is one sign among many that new ways of doing memory did not replace older ones, as is so often assumed in the memory studies field, but have come to exist side by side with them, in an ever growing repertoire of ways to do memory.

Long before the age of revolutions, then, memory practices were evolving. Not only were new media being used, the subject matter of memories also evolved; this constituted a second major area of change. The Reformation had a considerable impact on memory cultures. Not only were the religious debates to a large extent conducted through historical arguments. Even more fundamentally, the Reformers contested traditional ways of doing memory, such as praying for the dead, the value of saints' relics, and the veneration of saints, and so turned them into flash-points for conflict and confessional identifiers, while at the same time necessitating alternatives for those who rejected the death masses, patron saints, and annual processions of the past. Commemorative sermons remained a fixture, but they often celebrated new events. Within the new religious denominations, laypeople were invited to self-identify through recent memories of exile and martyrdom. Although religion remained important throughout the period, dealing with pain-ful memories may have become harder as old providential strategies to detect a spiritual benefit or other form of 'secondary gain' in suffering, lost traction. For those who sought to unite religiously divided communities, secular public mem-ory practices had to be developed further than they had been in the Middle Ages; this encouraged the proliferation of forms of political memory that focused on 'civic', 'patriotic', and even 'national' memories, many of which were to be reused and further developed in nineteenth-century Europe. But secular, patriotic, memories could also be closely tied to religious agendas, as we saw happen, for instance, in the commemoration of Guy Fawkes Day or of the battle of Lepanto.

In a third, and most fundamental change, towards the end of this period it became considerably easier to reject the authority of the past. In Chapter 3 I argued that the respect for custom and tradition came under pressure from a mixture of political, intellectual, and cultural developments. The codification of legal custom 'froze' it, and so made it steadily more obsolete, while a more intensive and sophis-ticated study of ancient canonical texts and historical evidence simultaneously destabilized ancient texts as a benchmark for 'truth'. As there was always someone who could pull an alternative historical or philological card, people grew sceptical and more wary of truth claims that were based on historical and philological evi-dence, however sophisticatedly presented. This, in turn, made it more attractive to explore the possibilities of using 'natural law' as a source of legitimacy, especially since this had already proven to be useful in thinking about situations for which

---

[1] See for examples e.g. Eekhout, 'Material memories'; Marian Füssel, 'Emotions in the making. The transformation of battlefield experiences during the Seven Years' War (1756–1763)', in *Battlefield emotions 1500–1800. Practices, experience, imagination*, ed. Erika Kuijpers and Cornelis van der Haven (London, 2016), 149–72, at 158–9; Walsham, 'Domesticating the Reformation'.

there was no precedent or where it was unclear which laws should apply, as in contacts with the peoples of the New World or in determining rights to trade.

Of key importance in this context was the hierarchical way of thinking about 'civility' that emerged as a consequence of extra-European commercial expansion; once Europeans imagined there to be a hierarchy of civilizations, it became possible to conceive of the *abandoning* of custom as a hallmark of civility and to imagine a virtuous position that involved, and even required, the rejection of at least some of the ways of the ancestors in matters moral, legal, and political for the sake of 'progress'. The first people to defend such a position did not necessarily recognize the radical use to which this might be put when driven to its logical conclusions; people who were quite keen to suggest that peasants lose their customary rights when 'rational' agriculture required it, for instance, hardly imagined that a similar argument might be used to attack their equally customary entitlement to social status. Yet, of course, this is exactly what was to happen in the age of revolutions, when the rejection of custom morphed into attempts at systemic change and innovation. Even then, as scholars have come to realize, revolutionary ideas on change were often a mix of quite traditional calls for the restoration of old rights and pleas for the adoption of completely new principles, such as the idea that people had a natural right to pursue happiness or that the equality of all men (or even women) before God should extend to them having equal rights.[2] What remains to be discussed here, then, is to what extent these changes reflected, or caused, a sea change in attitudes to the past and in the role of memory.

HISTORY AND MEMORY

In 1994 the medievalist Patrick Geary noted that Maurice Halbwachs's path-breaking book of 1925 on collective memory had included one major and unfortunate 'false dichotomy':

> Perhaps because he failed to see the political parameters of collective memory forma-
> tion, he assumed that collective memory was a natural, non-purposeful creation of a
> group while history was an intentional, political and manipulative process. He thus
> postulated a fundamental opposition between the two. The former creates a bond
> between present and past, the latter disrupts this continuity: the former is highly
> selective, retaining those aspects of collective identity, while the latter recovers and
> reorganizes this lost difference. Collective memory is made up of a multiplicity of
> group memories, while history unifies the past into one. Collective memory is oral,
> history written. History begins where collective memory ends.[3]

To Geary himself, the most serious problem with the distinction is that it 'ignores the social and cultural context of the historian' and thus the dynamic between

---

[2] See e.g. Brecht Deseure, *Onhoudbaar verleden. Geschiedenis als politiek instrument tijdens de Franse periode in België* (Louvain, 2014); Marc H. Lerner, *A laboratory of liberty. The transformation of political culture in republican Switzerland, 1750–1848* (Leiden, 2011).

[3] Patrick Geary, *Phantoms of remembrance. Memory and oblivion at the end of the first millennium* (Princeton, 1994), 10–11.

memory and the writing of history that we saw in evidence in Chapter 5, and that he himself highlighted for the Middle Ages. That Halbwachs had come up with this dichotomy is understandable. In 1925, when Halbwachs was writing, historians were convinced that modern methods for source criticism and causal explanation enabled them to produce objectively true knowledge about historical processes. Halbwachs apparently wanted to make clear that in emphasizing the instability of memory, he was not questioning the 'scientific' achievements of the historical discipline. Almost a century later, historians themselves are much more aware that their discipline is influenced by social, cultural, and political processes, and more likely to concede that their activities are basically one more way of 'doing memory', albeit a disciplined, critical, systematic, and carefully evidenced way of doing it. This means that the stark division between memory and history is no longer tenable, even though it continues to inspire discussions in some circles.

Nevertheless, Halbwachs's red herring has had momentous consequences for our approach to the history of memory. In the memory studies field, the dichotomy between memory and history has often taken on a temporal dimension, which has resulted in the assumption that, over time, history has *replaced* memory, rather than being a sophisticated variety of it. Inspired by Halbwachs, Nora placed such a temporal development at the core of his distinction between the *milieux de mémoire*, which had been 'swept away' by history, and the *lieux de mémoire* left behind. Others have argued that it is a function of 'post-modernity' that history is again on the decline and is being 'replaced' by memory.[4] The assumption that new ways of thinking *replace* older ones, rather than *coexist* with them, has a long history in Western thought. In a variation on the notion of progress that we saw emerge in the Enlightenment, historians and social scientists have long believed that traditional societies evolved into non-traditional, that is to say 'modern', societies by trading in old concepts and values (like those associated with memory) for new ones (like those associated with history). In Chapters 2 and 5, we saw scholars also make such assumptions about the demise of analogical ways of thinking about the past, and of myth. Although the idea that modern society is 'on its way to traditionlessness' is theoretically outdated among social scientists, it nevertheless hovers over the memory studies field and has amplified the linear approach to the history of memory.[5] As a result, the history of memory has come to be treated as an irreversible process and zero-sum game, in which the rise of one way of engaging with the past means the irrevocable decline of another.[6]

So far, studies about the history of memory have used long-term historiographical developments, that is to say, changes in the way in which historians write history, to gauge changes in memory and have extrapolated these to the rest of society without much further ado. This, for instance, is what gave rise to the idea that the discovery of a 'linear' notion of the past among philosophers of history should be identified as one of the key stages in the emergence of modern memory and indeed

---

[4] Olick and Robbins, 'Social memory studies', 120.

[5] Edward Shils, *Tradition* (Chicago, 1981) cited in Olick, *The politics of regret*, 178.

[6] Koselleck, *Vergangene Zukunft*; Denys Hay, *Annalists and historians. Western historiography from the eighth to the eighteenth centuries* (London, 1977); Burke, *Renaissance sense of the past*.

of modernity.[7] We have already discussed some of the consequences of this in the Introduction and in Chapter 2. In order to determine when such changes occurred and why, students of modernity and historians of memory have tried to establish at what point Europeans came to recognize and identify change when they saw it. Building on an idea first mooted by Eric Hobsbawm, they have tended to argue that it was the experience of change itself that undermined the authority of the past because far-reaching changes made reasoning by historical analogy simply untenable; the past was too different to be repeatable.[8] Some people have argued that such a sense of change was already emerging in late-seventeenth-century England. The Canadian scholar Daniel Woolf, for instance, thinks that the new attitude to novelty that he discerns in late-seventeenth-century England was the product of 'a heightened sense of change'. In *The social circulation of the past*, he argues that because change was palpable and visible, people learned to accept that it was not per se frightening. As a consequence, the past came to be seen as the result of a cumulative process—people no longer looked to the past for analogies, but were more inclined to think in terms of causes and consequences of change. Others have identified economic change as the driving force in this process.[9]

Yet it is especially the late eighteenth century that has frequently been presented as a period of change so breathtaking that it forever changed Europeans' and Americans' perceptions of the relationship between past, present, and future. Indeed the events of the Revolutionary and Napoleonic periods fundamentally disrupted Ancien Régime societies, while the Industrial Revolution led to economic changes that profoundly affected the way people worked and lived. Personal records of the period testify to a heightened awareness of change; a feeling of being cut off from one's past manifested itself, along with the feeling of acceleration of time. In this way, the past rapidly grew into a 'foreign country'.[10] As Richard Terdiman put it:

> In Europe in the period of the 1789–1815 Revolution, and particularly in France, the uncertainty of relation with the past became especially intense. In this period people experienced the insecurity of their culture's involvement with its past, the perturbation of the link to their own inheritance, as what I want to term a 'memory crisis': a sense that their past had somehow evaded memory, that recollection had ceased to integrate with consciousness.[11]

Terdiman is only one of many who argue for the long-term impact of this rupture. In his *Stranded in the present. Modern time and the melancholy of history* (2004), for instance, Peter Fritzsche has shown how both autobiographical and literary texts in

---

[7] Matt K. Matsuda, *The memory of the modern* (New York, 1996), 11–13.

[8] This section revisits some of the points made by Brecht Deseure and myself in our, 'The experience of rupture and the history of memory', in *Memory before modernity*, ed. Erika Kuijpers et al. (Leiden and Boston, 2013), 315–29. I am grateful to him for his permission to reuse some of the material.

[9] Woolf, *The social circulation*.

[10] Berman, *All that is solid*, 17; Peter Fritzsche, 'Specters of history. On nostalgia, exile and modernity', *American Historical Review* 105/5 (2001): 1587–618; Terdiman, *Present past*, 3–32.

[11] Terdiman. *Present past*, 3–4.

the nineteenth century were pervaded by a sense of a rift and ever faster change, and argued that nostalgia was one of its main results.[12] Philosopher Frank Ankersmit, too, has argued that the experience of the age of revolutions became a catalyst for the emergence of new conceptions of the past. His 2005 *Sublime historical experience* evokes how the French Revolution and the Industrial Revolution changed life 'in every conceivable aspect':

> Undoubtedly these dramatic transformations belong to the most decisive and profound changes that Western man has undergone in the course of history. In all these cases he entered a wholly new world and, above all, he could only do so on condition of forgetting a previous world and of shedding a former identity...In all these cases having had to abandon a traditional and familiar previous world has been extremely painful and it was always experienced as such.[13]

Ankersmit speaks of 'feelings of profound and irreparable loss, of cultural despair and of hopeless disorientation', for which he believes there was no solace because in cases such as these there is no possibility to reconcile one's present and one's former identity. People 'who experience such rupture adopt a new identity which necessarily revolves around the awareness of what they have lost; they can yearn for the past, they can aspire to knowledge of it, but they must accept that they can no longer be part of it. Hence, their need to "forget", and engage with the past in a new fashion.'[14]

Such dramatic invocations of the psychological impact of change are far removed from Koselleck's sober assessment of changes in the philosophy of history, but they build on his sense that the key to understanding modern attitudes to past, present, and future lies in capturing the moment that people became aware of the distance between themselves and people of the past. Yet I think that the relationship between the emergence of historical consciousness and the history of memory is much less significant than historians of memory have so far been arguing. In the remainder of this conclusion I should like to reassess the idea that a heightened sense of change created a lasting transformation in the meaning and practice of memory.

NOTHING IN THE WORLD REMAINS THE SAME?

In this book I have argued that throughout the early modern period, and before, people had been well aware of change and of the differences between past and present.

---

[12] Fritzsche, *Stranded in the present*. Arianne Baggerman, 'Lost time. Temporal discipline and historical awareness in nineteenth-century Dutch egodocuments', in *Controlling time and shaping the self. Developments in autobiographical writing since the sixteenth century*, ed. Arianne Baggerman, Rudolf Dekker, and Michael Mascuch (Leiden and Boston, 2011), 455–535; Arianne Baggerman, '"Zo een vrijheid begeer ik nimmer meer te beleven". Het witwassen van het verleden in Nederlandse ego-documenten (1800–1850)', *De Negentiende Eeuw. Documentatieblad Werkgroep 19e Eeuw* 33 (2009): 74–95, in a Dutch context, found little evidence for nostalgia but nevertheless a great sense of change and novelty pervading the diaries and life-writings from the first half of the nineteenth century.

[13] Ankersmit, *Sublime historical experience*, 321–4.

[14] Ankersmit, *Sublime historical experience*, 321–4.

Even when people maintained cyclical notions of history, believing that history was repeatable, or when they thought of history in terms of eschatology, as a stage on the way to the end of time, this did not stop them from being aware that societies change. Wars, social change, disease, new technologies did not go unnoticed, and in Chapter 2 we have seen that there is plenty of testimony that early modern people identified real and imagined changes.[15] On the whole, pre-modern people were more impressed by the analogies between past and present than by the differences, but, as such, a 'sense of change' had long existed and had quite happily coexisted with the analogical forms of thinking about the past we discussed in Chapters 2 and 3. This also suggests, however, that a sense of change was a less important catalyst for transformation in memory cultures than theorists of memory, and theorists of modernity, have been alleging. While it is undeniable that Europe experienced enormous change around 1800 and that many contemporaries commented on this, it is wrong to assume that this dislocation therefore led to a *lasting* shift in the way people thought about the past.

In this book we have seen that early modern Europe made use of three distinct ways of thinking about change. The first, which we encountered in Chapter 2, approached change as a fact of life, related especially to technical innovation, economics, and material change, and was often positive about these developments. This attitude long predated the early modern era. One can see a Bavarian monk cheerfully declare around 1030:

> Not only is it proper for new things to change the old ones, but even, if the old ones are disordered they should be entirely thrown away, or if, however, they conform to the proper order of things but are of little use, they should be buried with reverence.[16]

I would argue that the enthusiasm about change that Woolf and others have noted in seventeenth-century England was also of this type; as Paul Slack has shown, this could be developed into a discourse about the blessings of 'improvement'.[17] Much less positively received, also in England, were alleged 'innovations' in the moral, legal, social, or political order, the second type of change we can discern in early modern Europe. We have seen in Chapters 2 and 3 that people who wanted to introduce changes of this type almost always claimed they were 'restoring' an old right or order that had either fallen into oblivion or had been 'corrupted' by people who had sought to 'innovate'; everyone knew that 'a lust for novelties' was a deplorable human trait. Third, there was also the model of conversion that we encountered in Chapter 1, a change that involves the rejection of the past, in order to become a 'new man', just as Christ's bringing of the 'new law' had put an end to the validity

---

[15] Geary, *Phantoms of remembrance*; Ralf-Peter Fuchs, *Geschichtsbewusstsein und Geschichtsschreibung zwischen Reformation und Aufklärung. Städtechroniken, Kirchenbücher und historische Befragungen in Hessen, 1500 bis 1800* (Marburg, 2000); Ralf-Peter Fuchs, 'Erinnerungsschichten. Zur Bedeutung der Vergangenheit für den "gemeinen Mann" der Frühen Neuzeit', in *Wahrheit, Wissen, Erinnerung. Zeugenverhörprotokolle als Quellen für soziale Wissensbestände in der frühen Neuzeit*, ed. Ralf-Peter Fuchs and W. Schulze (Münster, 2002), 89–154; Stoyle, 'Remembering the English Civil Wars'.

[16] Cited in Geary, *Phantoms of remembrance*, 8.

[17] Slack, *From Reformation to improvement*; Slack, *The invention of improvement*.

of the 'old law'. It was the latter attitude that most closely resembled the way the revolutionaries in France approached the task of changing their society from 1789, a conscious form of rupture that enabled people to turn their backs, not only on their own past, but also on all those who did not join them. In this secular form, this was indeed truly new. It created a powerful rhetoric that allowed people to see themselves as 'modern' and dismiss others as 'old-fashioned' and 'behind the times', which has been tremendously influential.

For those who were less keen on the revolutions, however, the second, much more traditional, way of responding to change was equally customary and has also remained common. Change indeed caused feelings of dislocation in revolutionary Europe, but the way it did so was hardly unique.[18] The changes brought about by the Reformations of the sixteenth century, for instance, were equally momentous, not only because they were accompanied by political shifts and religious wars or because they divided families, but also because they called into question fundamental relationships between the living and the dead, the sacred and the profane, the material and the spiritual, and past and present. As we saw in Chapter 2, this sense of sudden change and of dramatic loss proved important incentives for many in sixteenth-century Europe to reflect on their loss. Indeed, in a path-breaking lecture of 1985 entitled 'The perception of the past in early modern England', Keith Thomas credited the Reformation with a transformation in historical consciousness in terms that are very similar to the ones used by scholars like Terdiman, Fritzsche, and Ankersmit to describe the impact of the age of revolutions:

> The dramatic rupture with the medieval past occasioned by the Reformation created a sense of separateness and of an unbridgeable divide. This made it possible to perceive the recent past, not just as a collection of founding myths and precedents but as the embodiment of an alternative way of life and set of values.[19]

Unlike Thomas, I think this is important *not* because I should like to propose the Reformation as the alternative 'critical juncture' or paradigm shift in the history of memory. Quite the opposite. I can think of a range of other examples of experiences of dislocation that have made people painfully aware of the differences between past and present and that led to a nostalgic interest in the world of the past. In Europe, the Black Death of the mid-fourteenth century is a good example.[20] In China, the collapse of the Ming dynasty in the mid-seventeenth century evoked dislocation and nostalgia of a type that is fascinatingly similar to some of what we see in Europe.[21] What the example of the Reformation shows, above all, is that the

---

[18] Students of modernity have been aware of earlier upheaval but assert that its psychological impact was of necessity more limited because at those times change was not associated with continuous change or progress. See e.g. Hobsbawm, 'The social function of the past'; Fritzsche, *Stranded in the present*, 17. Yes, as we saw in Chapter 2 and will see below, this is exactly how the proponents of the Reformation presented the changes that had been forged.

[19] Thomas, *The perception of the past*, 9.

[20] See e.g. *The chronicle of Jean de Venette*, ed. Richard A. Newhall, trans. Jean Birdsall (New York, 1953), 48–51, cited http://www.u.arizona.edu/~afutrell/w%20civ%2002/plaguereadings.html, with a range of other examples.

[21] Lynn A. Struve, *Voices from the Ming-Qing cataclysm. China in tigers' jaws* (New Haven, 1993).

heightened experience of change may be a *temporary* and in fact also *reversible* cultural feature, which can die out with the generation that experienced the dislocation of radical change, or even before.

Rupture is not necessarily of lasting significance, precisely because memories can be, and often are, readjusted. As we saw in Chapter 6, Acts of Oblivion were predicated on this ability to create new forms of continuity so as to arrive at closure on uncomfortable parts of the past. Historian John Pocock observed in 1962:

> If a traditional relationship with the past has been ruptured, the first instinct of society's intellectuals may be to restore it, and this may be attempted by reshaping myth, by historisation or by the construction of a new image of the past in terms of some new continuity of which society has become aware in the present.[22]

This is precisely what we can see intellectuals, and others, do after the Reformations. It took Calvinists in England and the Dutch Republic only a generation to start defending what they now considered to be their 'old' religion against the challenges of 'novelties' imposed by dissidents in their respective Reformed churches.[23] In Bohemia, seventeenth-century Catholic antiquarians exerted themselves to hide their history of dissent, reformation, and rebellion under a new powerful narrative cloak that foregrounded the age-long love between Bohemians, the Catholic Church, and their Habsburg rulers. It was very similar to what happened in Flanders and Brabant, also rocked by reformation, civil war, economic devastation, and depopulation in the sixteenth century, where seventeenth-century engagement with the past came to be focused on continuity with a past of medieval glory, everlasting Catholic piety, and loyalty to the ruling house.[24] Thomas noted something similar for England: people who welcomed the English Reformation could nevertheless come to long for the days of 'Merry England', when food had been cheap, and people had cared for one another. In the seventeenth century, the days of Merry England were associated with the sixteenth-century reign of the Tudors, while in the late eighteenth century people looked back with nostalgia on the days of Queen Anne, and by 1820 to mid-eighteenth-century England.[25]

We can even see it happen in individuals. Arnoud van Buchel's nostalgia about the Catholic past that we highlighted in Chapter 2, for instance, did not last; he soon began to appropriate the notion that the changes which his society had witnessed had in fact been for the good. He became a Reformed Protestant, first reluctantly so, but later developing into a real hardliner, and, as we have seen in Chapter 6, at some point in his life he literally crossed out the angry poems about the Revolt and Reformation that he had written as a youngster. Van Buchel always remained a deeply conservative man, and he continued to document the past,

---

[22] J.G.A. Pocock, 'The origins of the study of the past. A comparative approach', *Comparative Studies in Society and History* 4/2 (1962): 209–46, at 217, also cited in Louthan, *Converting Bohemia*, 128.

[23] Charles H. Parker, 'To the attentive, nonpartisan reader. The appeal to history and national identity in the religious disputes of the seventeenth-century Netherlands', *The Sixteenth Century Journal* 28 (1997): 57–78.

[24] Louthan, *Converting Bohemia*, 127–45; Pollmann, *Catholic identity*, 161–79; Van der Steen, *Memory wars*, 217–28.

[25] Thomas, *The perception of the past*.

yet his notion of what deserved preservation underwent a transformation; in the 1580s he had bemoaned the Reformation, but in the 1620s he was idealizing the early phases of Revolt and Reformation. 'Oh poor Republic', he exclaimed about the new state whose founding he had once deplored, 'that once flourished, but now lies trampled under the feet of the same men who disregard the benefits they have reaped, and with shameless prevarication try their hardest to suppress the hereditary liberty.'[26] His nostalgia thus remained, but it associated itself with a new, idealized picture of the recent past, in which 'hereditary liberty' had flourished, which enabled him to reconcile it with his identity in the present. If this sort of transformation can happen *within* a generation, it is no wonder that the children and grandchildren born to those traumatized by dislocation end up integrating many of the 'new' developments into their picture of the 'old' order. This invention of tradition was as central a feature of the memory cultures of early modern Europe, as it was to be after 1800, when 'national' history was widely used to forge such continuities. People have found ways to experience their histories as a continuum, not by ignoring them, but by reimagining them to suit their present needs.

All in all, the idea that it was experiences of momentous change that should be held responsible for permanent shifts in European ways of thinking about the past, and by extension for modernity, thus underestimates both the resilience of people who experience change and the role of memory in enabling this resilience. Rather than explain how people came to be aware of differences between past and present, I have argued, it is more important to ask, first, why and how the past lost some of its unquestionable moral authority and, second, why people could come to think of systemic political, moral, and social change as desirable. Interestingly, this was very much how the question was put by Eric Hobsbawm when he published his essay 'The social function of the past. Some questions' in 1972. He noted then that 'we know very little about the process which turned the words "new" and "revolutionary" (as used in the language of advertising) into synonyms for "better" and "more desirable", and research is badly needed here'.[27]

Building on the work of early modernists over the last few decades, this book has offered a new answer to this question. I have argued that the changing authority of the past was an unintended side effect of other cultural developments, two of which, humanism and the Reformation, paradoxically had originally been predicated on the notion that there was a better, pre-medieval, past that should be restored. It was the intellectual stalemate caused by the inconsistencies in an ever-growing body of knowledge about the past, coupled with the third development, European expansion, that made it convenient to start believing that there could be such a thing as moral, political, and social progress as well as material and economic improvement. Together, this made it possible to propose new and more positive ways of thinking about the moral properties of change.

Yet the new ways did not obliterate older ones. These continue to be with us and have in fact been highlighted by students of modern memory, who have discovered

[26] Pollmann, *Religious choice*, 151–2, 162.
[27] Hobsbawm, 'The social function of the past', 10.

that the memory cultures of our own day use pre-modern memory practices like anachronism and the historicization of myth, and who have noted that our society, too, is replete with anxieties about the pace of change. 'Glocal', hybrid, diasporic, and cosmopolitan memories have been identified as the products of very recent changes, greater mobility, democracy, globalization, and the Internet, but we have seen that there are much older precedents for them. Students of memory are habitually assuming that where new ways of doing memory appear, old ones must be collapsing. This book has offered a plea, not only to try to take a longer view, but to make that a less linear and binary one. The history of memory is not to be imagined as a series of paradigm shifts, forged through critical junctures, memory crises, and cultural revolutions, but is actually much more cumulative. Pre-modern and modern ways of practising memory can exist side by side and in the same individuals, individuals who in the twenty-first century seem set to remain just as creative, inconsistent, and pragmatic in their appeals to the past as humans have always been.

Bibliography

ARCHIVAL SOURCES

Erfgoed Leiden en Omstreken. Bibliotheek LB 784-1. Joost van Leeuwen. *Verhaal van het voorgevallene te Leiden, 1748–22 October 1751.*

Gemeente Archief Alkmaar, Collectie Handschriften, Eikelenberg, Volume E A 20, 1409.

Stadsbibliotheek Haarlem. MS 187 A 4. Herman Verbeeck. *Thoneel der Verandering deser Werelt* (1667).

Utrecht University Library. MS 1053 160v–163v. 'Arnoldus Buchelius to Matthaeus Vossius, 10 June 1637'.

PRINTED PRIMARY SOURCES

Alderkerk, Johannes. *De wonderdaden des Allerhoogsten Godts, doorlugtig gezien in de grontlegginge en voortzettinge van Nederlants vryheyt, in zonderheit kragtdadig gebleken in het vermaarde beleg ende ontzet der stadt Leyden* (Leiden, 1734).

Anonymous. 'Anneke Jans. Op 24 januari in de Schie verdronken'. *Nieuwe Rotterdamsche Courant*, 22 January 1939.

Anonymous. 'Discurs zweyer vom Adel auss der freyen Reichs-Ritterschafft. Wie man die Unterhane tractiren und recht nützlich gebrauchen solle' (1670). In *Bäuerlicher Widerstand und feudale Herrschaft in der frühen Neuzeit*, ed. Winfried Schulze (Stuttgart, 1980), 233–47.

Articvlen, ende conditien vanden tractate, aengegaen ende ghesloten tusschen...den prince van Parma,... ter eenre, ende de stadt van Antvverpen ter ander syden: Den XVII Augusti, m.d.LXXXV (Antwerp, 1585).

Artyckelen ende besluiten der Inquisitie van Spaegnien om die van de Nederlanden te overvallen of verhinderen (n.p., [1568]).

Aubrey, John. *Aubrey's natural history of Wiltshire. A reprint of The natural history of Wiltshire* (Newton-Abbot, 1969).

Aubrey, John. *Three prose works. Miscellanies, Remaines of gentilisme and judaisme, Observations*, ed. John Buchanan-Brown (Carbondale IL, 1972).

Aubrey, John. *Brief lives*, ed. Richard W. Barber (Woodbridge, 1982).

Augustine of Hippo. *De baptismo libri VII*, introduction and notes by G. Bavaud, trans. Guy Finaert, ed. Y. Congar, Traités anti-donatistes 2 (Bruges, 1964).

Bacon, Jean-Baptiste-Pierre. *Panégyrique de Henri Le Grand ou éloge historique de Henri IV, Roi de France* (London, 1769).

Balen, Matthijs. *Beschryvinge der stad Dordrecht, vervatende haar begin, opkomst, toeneming, en verdere stant...* (Dordrecht, 1677).

Baudartius, Willem. 'Autobiographie van Wilhelmus Baudartius'. In O.C.B.R. Roelofs, *Wilhemus Baudartius*, (Kampen, 1947), 201–23.

Bogaers, Adrien. 'Het pleegkind'. In Adrien Bogaers, *Balladen en romancen* ([Amsterdam], 1846), 1–18.

Bontius, Reynerius. *Belegering ende het ontset der Stadt Leyden* (Leiden, 1645), ed. A.J.E. Harmsen. Accessed 28 April 2016. http://www.let.leidenuniv.nl/Dutch/Ceneton/Bontius/Bontius1645.html.

Bontius, Reynerius. *Belegering en ontsetting der stadt Leyden [...]. Treur-bly-eynde-spel.* (Amsterdam, 1736).

Brouwer, Hendrik. *Het belegh van Leyden. Treurspel* (n.p., 1683).

Bunyan, John. *Grace abounding to the chief of sinners* (London, 1904). http://www.gutenberg. org/files/654/654-h/654-h.htm. Accessed 12 April 2013.

Burel, Jean. *Mémoires de Jean Burel. Journal d'un bourgeois du Puy à l'époque des guerres de religion*, ed. A. Chassaing (Le Puy-en-Velay, 1898).

Butzbach, Johannes. *Des Johannes Butzbach Wanderbüchlein. Chronika eines fahrenden Schülers*, ed. and trans. D.J. Becker (Leipzig, 1906).

Cardano, Girolamo. *The book of my life (De vita propria liber)*, trans. Jean Stoner (London, 1931).

Charles II. '1660: An Act of Free and Generall Pardon Indempnity and Oblivion'. In *Statutes of the Realm* V, 1628–80. Great Britain Record Commission (n.p., 1819), 226–34. Accessed 28 May 2015. http://www.british-history.ac.uk/statutes-realm/vol5/ pp226-234#h3-0024.

Charte constitutionnelle française du 4 juin 1814. Accessed 3 May 2016. http://fr.wikisource. org/wiki/Charte_constitutionnelle_du_4_juin_1814.

Chavatte, Pierre-Ignace. *Chronique mémorial des choses mémorables par moy Pierre-Ignace Chavatte 1657–1693. Le mémorial d'un humble tisserand lillois au Grand Siècle*, ed. Alain Lottin (Brussels, 2010).

Churchill, Winston. 'United States of Europe speech' (Zurich, 19 September 1946). Accessed 25 May 2015. http://www.winstonchurchill.org/resources/speeches/1946-1963-elder-statesman/ 2970-united-states-of-europe.

Cluverius, Philip. *De Germania antiqua* (n.p., 1616).

Constitutional Charter of France of June 4, 1814. Accessed 21 October 2013. http://www. napoleon-series.org/research/government/legislation/c_charter.html.

De Acosta, José. *De procuranda Indorum salute* (Seville, 1588).

De Fijne, Passchier. *Den ouden Leytschen patroon ofte derden octobers bancket: waer in kortelijck en waerachtelijck wort voorgeset de stercke belegeringhe der stad, de groote benautheyt der borgeren, ende de wonderbare wercken Godes betoont in 't ontsetten vande stad Leyden: geschiet inden jaere onses Heeren 1574, op den 3. october, wesende sondagh 's morgens* (Leiden, 1630).

De Las Casas, Bartholomé. *Den spiegel der Spaensche tijrannije, gheschiet in West-Indien. Waer in te sien is de onmenschelycke wreede feyten der Spanjaerdē, met t'samen de beschry-vinghe der selver landēn, volckerēn aert ende natuere* (Amsterdam, 1620).

De Las Casas, Bartholomé. *The tears of the Indians: being an historical...account of the cruel massacres and slaughters of above twenty millions of innocent people; committed by the Spaniards in the Islands of Hispaniola, Cuba, Jamaica, &c. as also, in the continent of Mexico, Peru, & other places of the West-Indies, to the total destruction of those countries. Written in Spanish by Casaus...and made English by J. P.*, ed. and trans. John Philips (London, 1656).

De le Barre, Pasquier and Nicolas Soldoyer. *Mémoires de Pasquier de le Barre et de Nicolas Soldoyer pour servir à l'histoire de Tournai, 1565–1640*, ed. Alex Pinchart, 2 vols, Collection de mémoires rélatifs à l'histoire de Belgique 8–9 (Brussels, 1859–65).

De Mesmes, Henri. *Mémoires inédits de Henri de Mesmes, seigneur de Roissy et de Malassise*, ed. Édouard Fremy (Paris, 1886; repr. Geneva, 1970).

De Venette, Jean. *The chronicle of Jean de Venette*, ed. Richard A. Newhall, trans. Jean Birdsall (New York, 1953). Accessed 29 June 2016. http://www.u.arizona. edu/~afutrell/w%20civ%2002/plaguereadings.html.

Degryse, Karel, ed. *Pieter Seghers. Een koopmansleven in troebele tijden* (Antwerp and Baarn, 1990).

Díaz, Bernal. *The conquest of New Spain*, trans. J.M. Cohen (Harmondsworth, 1963).

Dobertin, Hans, ed. *Quellensammlung zur Hamelner Rattenfängersage* (Göttingen, 1970).

Dodt van Flensburg, J.J. *Archief voor kerkelijke en wereldsche geschiedenissen, inzonderheid van Utrecht*, 7 vols (Utrecht, 1838–48), vol. VI.

Dorpius, Martinus. *Dialogus: in quo Venus et Cupido omnes adhibent versutias: ut Herculem animi ancipitem in suam militiam invita Virtuta perpellant. Eiusdem Thomus Aululariæ Plautinæ adiectus cum prologis…Chrysostomi Neapolitani epistola de situ Hollandiæ viuendique Hollandorum institutis. Gerardi Nouiomagi de Zelandia epistola consimilis* ([Louvain], 1514).

Dusseldorpius, Franciscus. *Uittreksel uit Francisci Dusseldorpii Annales, 1566–1616* ed. Robert Fruin (The Hague, 1893).

Dwinglo, Bernardus. *Aenspraecke van Bernardus Dvinglo, aen de Remonstrans-gesinde ghemeynte ende borgherije der stadt Leyden, over het ontset der selfder stede gedaen op den 3. octobris 1620* (n.p., 1620).

Engelbrecht, E.A. *De vroedschap van Rotterdam, 1572–1795*, Bronnen voor de geschiedenis van Rotterdam (Rotterdam, 1973).

Erich, Samuel. *Exodus hamelensis, das ist der Hämelischer Kinder Außgang* (Hannover, 1654).

Erich, Samuel. *De uytgang der Hamelsche kinderen of de verbaasde geschiedenis van 130 burgerskinderen, dewelke in 't jaar 1282 te Hamelen, aan de Weser, in Neder-Saxen, door een gewaanden speelman uyt de stadt verleydt, en…in de Koppelberg verdweenen zijn.: Aan de toetsteen der waarheit beproeft*, trans. Isaac Le Long (Amsterdam, 1729).

Fink, August, ed. *Die Schwarzschen Trachtenbücher* (Berlin, 1963).

Geisendorf, Paul F. et al., eds. *L'Escalade de Genève, 1602. Histoire et tradition* (Geneva, 1952),

Génard, P., ed. *La Furie espagnole. Documents pour servir à l'histoire du sac d'Anvers* (Antwerp, 1876).

Geuse liet-boeck, waer in begrepen is den oorsprongh vande troubelen der Nederlandsche oorlogen (Amsterdam, 1661).

Gladstone, William Ewart. 'Speech of William Ewart Gladstone MP, British Prime Minister, to the House of Commons on Home Rule for Ireland' (7 June 1886). http://hansard.millbanksystems.com/commons/1886/jun/07/second-reading-adjourned-debate. Accessed 28 April 2016.

Gottschalk, Elizabeth. *Stormvloeden en rivieroverstromingen in Nederland. Storm surges and river floods in the Netherlands. 2. De periode 1400–1600* (Assen, 1975).

Gregory, Brad S., ed. *The forgotten writings of the Mennonite martyrs*, Documenta Anabaptistica Neerlandica VIII (Leiden and Boston, 2002).

Guicciardini, Francesco. *Ricordi. Diari. Memorie*, ed. Mario Spinella (Rome, 1981).

[Hagendorf, Peter]. *Ein Söldnerleben im Dreissigjährigen Krieg. Eine Quelle zur Sozialgeschichte*, ed. Jan Peters (Berlin, 1993).

Happe, Volkmar. *Volkmar Happe (1587–1647/59): Chronicon Thuringiae*, ed. Hans Medick, Norbert Winnige, and Andreas Bähr. http://www.mdsz.thulb.uni-jena.de/happe/erlaeuterungen.php. Accessed November 2008.

Hooft, P.C. *Nederlandsche Historien*. In Pieter Corneliszoon Hooft, *Alle de gedrukte werken, 1611–1738*, ed. W. Hellinga and P. Tuynman, 9 vols (Amsterdam, 1972), vols 4 and 5.

Ignatius of Loyola. *The autobiography of St. Ignatius of Loyola. With related documents*, ed. John C. Olin and trans. Joseph F. O'Callaghan (New York, 1974).

Jacobsz, Wouter. *Dagboek van broeder Wouter Jacobsz (Gualtherus Jacobi Masius), Amsterdam 1572–1578 en Montfoort 1578–1579*, ed. I.H. van Eeghen, 2 vols (Groningen, 1959).

Jamerey-Duval, Valentin. *Mémoires. Enfance et education d'un paysan au XVIIIe siècle*, ed. Jean Marie Goulemot (Paris, 1981).

Junius, Hadrianus. *Batavia* (Leiden, 1588).

Le miroir de la jevnesse,: représentant en l'abrégé des choses arrivées au Pays Bas. La tyrannie d' Espagne, l'innocente patience des Provinces Vnies, et la main puissante de Dieu. Au commencement progres & affermissement de leur liberté. Pour l'instruction de la jeunesse & memoire a la posterité (Middelburg, 1616).

Le Roy, Louis. *De la vicissitude ou variété des choses en l'univers* (1575), ed. Philippe Desan (Paris, 1988).

Luther, Martin. 'Vorrede zu Band I der Opera Latina der Wittenberger Ausgabe. 1545'. In *Luthers Werke in Auswahl*, trans. Andrew Thorton and ed. Otto Clemen, 6th edn (Berlin, 1967), vol. IV, 421–8. http://www.iclnet.org/pub/resources/text/wittenberg/luther/preflat-eng.txt. Accessed 22 June 2016.

Machiavelli, Niccolò. *Discourses*, ed. Bernard Crick, trans. Leslie J. Walker and Brian Richardson (London, 1970).

Mallet, Edme-François. 'Coutume'. In *Encyclopédie ou dictionnaire raisonné des sciences, des arts et des métiers*, ed. Denis Diderot and Jean Baptiste le Rond d'Alembert (1751–2). http://xn--encyclopdie-ibb.eu/index.php/non-classifie/712614146-COUTUME. Accessed 2 June 2016.

Manteau, Jacques. 'Memorie'. In *Tweehonderd-jarig jubelfeest ter gedagtenisse der verlossinge van de stad Zierikzee uit de Spaensche dwingelandij plegtig geviert op den zevenden november 1776 in eene kerkelijke leerreden over psalm LXVI vs. 12*, ed. Joannes van de Velde (Zierikzee, 1777).

Molinaeus, Petrus. *Predikatie over Psalm 124: toegepast op het streng en benaeuwt beleg en wonderbaer ontzet der stadt Leyden* (Rotterdam, 1694).

Monballyu, J., ed. *Costumen van de stad en van de kasselrij Kortrijk*, vol. 2, *Turben afgenomen door de Kortrijkse schepenbank, 1485–1581. Costumen van het graafschap Vlaanderen, kwartier Gent XII* (Brussels, 1989).

Nederveen, F.B.M. and C.J. Nederveen, eds. *De genealogieën van Nederveen* (Geertruidenberg, 2006).

Opstelten, I.W. *Antwoorden kamervragen over heffing dertiende penning Kamerik* (The Hague, 2012). http://www.rijksoverheid.nl/documenten-en-publicaties/kamerstukken/2012/09/22/antwoorden-kamervragen-over-heffing-dertiende-penning-kamerik.html. Accessed 2 August 2013.

Origen. *The Philocalia of Origen*, ed. J Armitage Robinson (Edinburgh, 1911), chapter XIII. http://www.tertullian.org/fathers/origen_philocalia_02_text.htm#C13. Accessed 23 June 2016.

Parets, Miquel. *A journal of the plague year. The diary of the Barcelona tanner Miquel Parets*, ed. and trans. James S. Amelang (Oxford, 1991).

Platter, Felix. *Tagebuch (Lebensbeschreibung), 1536–1567*, ed. Valentin Lötscher (Basel and Stuttgart, 1976).

Platter, Thomas and Felix Platter. *Thomas und Felix Platter, zur Sittengeschichte des XVI. Jahrhunderts*, ed. Heinrich Boos (Leipzig, 1878).

Prion, Pierre. *Pierre Prion, scribe*, ed. Emmanuel le Roy Ladurie and Orest Ranum (Paris, 1985).

Rem, Lucas. *Tagebuch des Lucas Rem aus den Jahren 1494–1541. Ein Beitrag der Handelsgeschichte der Stadt Augsburg*, ed. B. Greiff (Augsburg, 1861).

Rousseau, Jean-Jacques. *Les Confessions* 1782 (livres I–VI) and 1789 (livres VII–XII) (Paris, 1889). http://athena.unige.ch/athena/rousseau/confessions/rousseau_confessions.html. Accessed 22 January 2016.

Sastrow, Bartholomäus. *Social Germany in Luther's time. Being the memoirs of Bartholomew Sastrow*, ed. H.A.L. Fisher and trans. Albert D. Vandam (Westminster, 1902).

Schoock, Martinus. *Fabula hamelensis sive disquisitio historica* (Groningen, 1659).

Schwarz, Matthäus and Veit Konrad Schwarz. *The first book of fashion. The book of clothes of Matthaeus and Veit Konrad Schwarz of Augsburg*, ed. Ulinka Rublack, Maria Hayward, and Jenny Tiramani (London and New York, 2015).

Scriverius, Petrus. *Batavia illustrata* (Leiden, 1609).

Sinnighe, J.R.W. *Hollandsch sagenboek. Legenden en sagen uit Noord- en Zuid-Holland* (The Hague, 1943).

Snoy, Reinier. *De Rebus Batavicis* (Frankfurt, 1620).

Spaan, Gerrit. *Beschrijvinge der stad Rotterdam, en eenige omleggende dorpen, verdeeld in III. Boeken* (Rotterdam, 1698).

Spieghel der ievcht, ofte corte Cronijcke der Nederlantsche geschiedenissen.: In de welcke…verhaelt…worden, de voornaaemste Tyrannien ende…wreedtheden, die door het beleydt der Coningen van Hispaengien…in Nederlandt bedreven zijn… (Amsterdam, 1614).

Spieghel der Spaensche Tyrannye. Gheschiet in Nederlandt. Waer in te sien is de ommenschen-licke ende wreede handelinghen der Spaengiaerden, die sy in dese ende andere omleggende plaetsen bedreven hebben (Amsterdam, 1620).

Teresa of Ávila. *The life of Saint Teresa of Ávila by herself*, ed. and trans. J.M. Cohen (Hardmondsworth, 1957).

Traicté de la Paix, faicte conclue et arrestée entre les Estatz de ces pays bas, assemblez en…Bruxelles, et le Sr. Prince d'Orenges, Estatz de Hollande et Zelande, avecq leurs associez et publiée le VIIIe iour de Novembre, 1576, avecq l'agreation et confirmation du Roy…nostre Sire surce ensuyuie (Brussels, 1576).

Van Braght, Tieleman. *Het bloedig tooneel of martelaers spiegel der Doops-gesinde of weerelose Christenen, die, om 't getuygenis van Jesus haren Salighmaker, geleden hebben, ende gedood zijn, van Christi tijd af, tot desen*, 2nd edn (Amsterdam, 1685).

Van Campene, Cornelis and Philip van Campene. *Dagboek van Cornelis en Philip van Campene. Behelzende het verhaal der merkwaardigste gebeurtenissen, voorgevallen te Gent sedert het begin der godsdienstberoerten tot den 5en april 1571*, ed. F. de Potter (Ghent, 1870).

Van de Waal, H. *Drie eeuwen vaderlandsche geschied-uitbeelding, 1500–1800. Een iconologi-sche studie*, 2 vols (The Hague, 1952).

Van der Staal, M. *Anneke Jansz. Historisch verhaal uit den eersten tijd der hervorming* (Rotterdam, 1914).

Van der Sterre, Johannes Chrysostomus. *Het leven vanden H. Norbertus, sticht-vader der ordre van Praemonstreyt ende apostel van Antwerpen* (Antwerp, 1623).

Van Duin, Arnoldus. *Oudewaters moord. Of waerachtig verhael van d'oudheid, belegering, innemen en verwoesten der geseide stad* (Oudewater, 1669).

Van Male, Zeghere. *De lamentatie van Zeghere van Male. Brugge na de Opstand tegen Spanje, 1590*, ed. A. Dewitte and A. Viaene (Bruges, 1977).

Van Someren, Reyer. *De St. Elisabethsnacht, anno 1421. Dichtstuk in drie zangen* (Utrecht, 1841).

Van Veen, Otto. *Batavorum cum Romanis Bellum* (Antwerp, 1612).

Voltaire. *Poème sur le désastre de Lisbonne* (n.p., 1755).

Von Hutten, Ulrich. *Arminius Dialogus Huttenicus. Quo homo patriae amantissimus, Germanorum laudem celebrauit* (Haguenau, 1529).

Von Schweinichen, Hans. *Denkwürdigkeiten*, ed. Herman Oesterley (Breslau, 1878).

Weinsberg, Hermann. 'Liber decrepitudinis'. In *Digitale Erfassung sowie historische und sprachgeschichtliche Auswertung der Aufzeichnungen des Kölner Bürgers Hermann Weinsberg (1518–1597)*, ed. Manfred Groten et al., diplomatic edition (2002). http://www.weinsberg.uni-bonn.de/Edition/Liber_Decrepitudinis/Liber_Decrepitudinis.htm. Accessed 28 April 2016.

Weinsberg, Hermann. 'Liber iuventutis'. In *Digitale Erfassung sowie historische und sprachgeschichtliche Auswertung der Aufzeichnungen des Kölner Bürgers Hermann Weinsberg (1518–1597)*, ed. Manfred Groten et al., diplomatic edition (2002). http://www.weinsberg.uni-bonn.de/Edition/Liber_Iuventutis/Liber_Iuventutis.htm. Accessed 28 April 2016.

Weinsberg, Hermann. 'Liber senectutis'. In *Digitale Erfassung sowie historische und sprachgeschichtliche Auswertung der Aufzeichnungen des Kölner Bürgers Hermann Weinsberg (1518–1597)*, ed. Manfred Groten et al., diplomatic edition (2002). http://www.weinsberg.uni-bonn.de/Edition/Liber_Senectutis/Liber_Senectutis.htm. Accessed 28 April 2016.

Whytehorne, Thomas. *The autobiography of Thomas Whytehorne*, ed. James M. Osborn (Oxford, 1961).

SECONDARY STUDIES

Algazi, Gadi. 'Lords ask, peasants answer. Making traditions in late medieval German village assemblies'. In *Between history and histories. The making of silences and commemorations*, ed. Gerald Sider and Gavin Smith (Toronto, 1997), 199–229.

Amelang, James S. *The flight of Icarus. Artisan autobiography in early modern Europe* (Stanford, 1998).

Anderson, Benedict. *Imagined communities. Reflections on the origin and spread of nationalism* (1983; 2nd rev. edn London, 1991).

Andries, Lisa. *La Bibliothèque bleue au dix-huitième siècle. Une tradition éditoriale* (Oxford, 1989).

Ankersmit, Frank. *Sublime historical experience* (Stanford, 2005).

Appudarai, Arjun. 'The past as a scarce resource'. *Man*, new series 16 (1981): 201–19.

Armogathe, Jean Robert. 'Postface'. In *La Querelle des anciens et des modernes*, ed. Anne-Marie Lecoq (Paris, 2001), 801–49.

Arnoldsson, Sverker. *La leyenda negra. Estudios sobre sus orígines* (Göteborg, 1960).

Asch, Ronald. '"Wo der soldat hinkömbt, da ist alles sein". Military violence and atrocities in the Thirty Years War re-examined'. *German History* 18 (2000): 291–309.

Assmann, Aleida. *Erinnerungsräume. Formen und Wandlungen des kulturellen Gedächtnisses* (Munich, 1999).

Assmann, Aleida. *Der lange Schatten der Vergangenheit. Erinnerungskultur und Geschichtspolitik* (Munich, 2006).

Assmann, Jan. *Das kulturelle Gedächtnis. Schrift, Erinnerung und politische Identität in frühen Hochkulturen* (Munich, 1992).

Assmann, Jan. 'Communicative and cultural memory'. In *Cultural memory studies. An international and interdisciplinary handbook*, ed. Astrid Erll and Ansgar Nünning (Berlin and New York, 2008), 109–18.

Aston, Margaret. 'English ruins and English history. The Dissolution and the sense of the past'. *Journal of the Warburg and Courtauld Institutes* 36 (1973): 231–55.

Auslander, Leora. 'Beyond words'. *The American Historical Review* 110 (2005): 1015–45.

Baggerman, Arianne. '"Zo een vrijheid begeer ik nimmer meer te beleven". Het witwassen van het verleden in Nederlandse ego-documenten (1800–1850)'. *De Negentiende Eeuw. Documentatieblad Werkgroep 19e Eeuw* 33 (2009): 74–95.

Baggerman, Arianne. 'Lost time. Temporal discipline and historical awareness in nineteenth-century Dutch egodocuments'. In *Controlling time and shaping the self. Developments in autobiographical writing since the sixteenth century*, ed. Arianne Baggerman, Rudolf Dekker, and Michael Mascuch (Leiden and Boston, 2011), 455–535.

Bähr, Andreas. 'Inhaltliche Erläuterungen zu Volkmar Happes Chronik aus dem Dreißigjährigen Krieg'. In *Volkmar Happe (1587–1647/59). Chronicon Thuringiae*, ed. Hans Medick, Norbert Winnige, and Andreas Bähr, Mitteldeutsche Selbstzeugnisse aus der Zeit des Dreißigjährigen Krieges. http://www.mdsz.thulb.uni-jena.de/happe/erlaeuterungen.php. Accessed November 2008.

Bähr, Andreas. 'Remembering violence. The fear of violence and the violence of fear in seventeenth-century war memories'. In *Memory before modernity. Practices of memory in early modern Europe*, ed. Erika Kuijpers et al. (Leiden and Boston, 2013), 269–82.

Baker, Keith M. 'Enlightenment and the institution of society. Notes for a conceptual history'. In *Main trends in cultural history. Ten essays*, ed. Willem Melching and Wyger Velema (Amsterdam and Atlanta, 1994), 95–120.

Barthes, Roland. *Mythologies suivi de Le Mythe, aujourd'hui* (Paris, 1957).

Bartholomeus, Annemieke. 'De iconografie van Cornelis de Vos. De burgers van Antwerpen brengen de monstrans en gewijde vaten terug naar de heilige Norbertus'. *Rubensbulletin* 2 (2008): 131–5.

Bartlett, Frederic C. *Remembering. A study in experimental and social psychology* (Cambridge, 1932).

Bayly, Christopher. *The birth of the modern world, 1780–1914* (Malden and Oxford, 2004).

Beaune, Colette. *Naissance de la nation France* (Paris, 1985).

Beiner, Guy. *Remembering the year of the French. Irish folk history and social memory* (Madison, 2007).

Benedict, Philip. *Graphic history. The wars, massacres and troubles of Tortorel and Perrissin* (Geneva, 2007).

Benedict, Philip. 'Divided memories? Historical calendars, commemorative processions and the recollection of the Wars of Religion during the Ancien Régime'. *French History* 22/4 (2008): 381–405.

Benedict, Philip. 'Shaping the memory of the French Wars of Religion. The first centuries'. In *Memory before modernity. Practices of memory in early modern Europe*, ed. Erika Kuijpers et al. (Leiden and Boston, 2013), 111–25.

Benedict, Philip, Hugues Faussy, and Pierre-Olivie Léchot, eds. *L'Identité huguenote. Faire Mémoire et écrire l'histoire (XVIe–XXIe siècle)* (Geneva, 2014).

Benes, Carrie. *Urban legends. Civic identity and the classical past in Northern Italy, 1250–1350* (University Park PA, 2011).

Benton, Lauren. *Law and colonial cultures. Legal regimes in world history, 1400–1900* (Cambridge, 2002).

Bercé, Yves-Marie. *Croquants et nu-pieds. Les Soulèvements paysans en France du XVIe au XIXe siècle* (Paris, 1974).

Bercé, Yves-Marie. *Révoltes et revolutions dans l'Europe moderne, XVIe–XVIIIe siècles* (Paris, 1980).

Berchtold, Jacques and Marie-Madeleine Fragonard, eds. *La Mémoire des guerres de religion. La Concurrence des genres historiques (XVIe–XVIIIe siècles)* (Geneva, 2007).

Bergier, Jean-François. *Guillaume Tell. Légende et réalité dans les Alpes au Moyen Age* (Paris, 1984).

Berman, Marshall. *All that is solid melts into air. The experience of modernity* (1st edn, 1982; London, 1988).

Bernstein, Hilary J. *Between crown and community. Politics and civic culture in sixteenth-century Poitiers* (Ithaca NY, 2004).

Bethencourt, Francesco. *The Inquisition. A global history, 1478–1834*, trans. Jean Birrell (Cambridge, 2009).

Bisson, Jonathan I. et al. 'Psychological treatments for chronic post-traumatic stress disorder. Systematic review and meta-analysis'. *The British Journal of Psychiatry* 190/2 (2007): 97–104.

Blickle, Peter. *From the communal reformation to the revolution of the common man*, trans. Beat Kümin (Leiden, 1998).

Bolter, David J. and Richard Grusin. *Remediation. Understanding new media* (Cambridge MA, 1999).

Borchardt, Frank L. *German antiquity in Renaissance myth* (Baltimore and Londen, 1971).

Bourdieu, Pierre. *Esquisse d'une théorie de la pratique, précédé de trois études d'ethologie kabyle* (Geneva, 1972).

Bowden, Brett. *The empires of civilization. The evolution of an imperial idea* (Chicago, 2009).

Bright, Janette and Gillian Clark. *An introduction to the tokens at the Foundling Museum* (London, 2011).

Brockmeier, Jens. *Beyond the archive. Memory, narrative and the autobiographical process* (Oxford, 2015).

Broomhall, Sue. 'Disturbing memories. Narrating experiences and emotions of distressing events in the French Wars of Religion'. In *Memory before modernity. Practices of memory in early modern Europe*, ed. Erika Kuijpers et al. (Leiden and Boston, 2013), 253–67.

Broomhall, Susan. 'Reasons and identities to remember. Composing personal accounts of religious violence in sixteenth-century France'. *French History* 27/1 (2013): 1–20.

Brown, Patricia. *Venice and antiquity. The Venetian sense of the past* (New Haven, 1996).

Bugge Amundsen, Arne. 'Churches and the culture of memory. A study of Lutheran church interiors in Østfold, 1537–1700'. In *Arv. Nordic Yearbook of Folklore 2010* (Uppsala, 2010), 117–42.

Burke, Peter. *The Renaissance sense of the past* (London, 1969).

Burke, Peter. 'The virgin of the Carmine and the Revolt of Masaniello'. *Past & Present* 99 (1983): 3–21.

Burke, Peter. 'History as social memory'. In *Memory. History, culture and the mind*, ed. Thomas I. Butler (Oxford, 1989), 97–113.

Burke, Peter. *What is cultural history?* (Cambridge, 2004).

Butler, W.E. 'Grotius and the law of the sea'. In *Hugo Grotius and international relations*, ed. Adam Roberts, Benedict Kingsbury, and Hedley Bull (Oxford, 1990), 209–20.

Bynum, Caroline Walker. 'Did the twelfth century discover the individual?' *Journal of Ecclesiastical History* 31 (1980): 1–17.

Canny, Nicholas. '1641 in a colonial context'. In *Ireland 1641. Contexts and reactions*, ed. Micheál O'Siochrú and Jane Ohlmeyer (Manchester, 2013), 52–70.

Carrosso, Marinella. 'La Généalogie muette. Un cheminement de recherche sarde'. *Annales. Économies, Sociétés, Civilisations* 46 (1991): 761–9.

Carta, Veronica. 'Adattamenti e rielaborazioni nel passaggio di codice: dall'immagine ai versi. Il martirio di Maria Stuarda nel Poema heroico di Bassiano Gatti'. *Between. Rivista dell' Associazione di Teoria e Storia Comparata dell Literatura* 2 (2012). Accessed 3 May 2016. http://ojs.unica.it/index.php/between/article/view/680.

Chakrabarty, Dipesh. 'Minority histories, subaltern pasts'. *Postcolonial Studies* 1 (1998): 15–29.

Chakrabarty, Dipesh. *Provincializing Europe. Postcolonial thought and historical difference* (Princeton, 2000).

Chew, Elizabeth V. '"Repaired by me to my exceeding great cost and charges": Anne Clifford and the uses of architecture', in *Architecture and the politics of gender in early modern Europe*, ed. Helen Hills (Aldershot 2003), 99–114.

Chiao, Joan Y., ed. 'Cultural neuroscience', special issue of *Social Cognition and Affective Euroscience* 5/2–3 (2010): 109–10.

Christin, Olivier. 'Mémoire inscrite, oubli prescrit. La Fin des troubles de religion en France'. In *Vergeben und vergessen? Vergangenheisdiskurse nach Besatzung, Bürgerkrieg und Revolution/Pardonner ou oublier? Les Discours sur le passé après l'occupation, la guerre civile et la revolution*, ed. Reiner Marcowicz and Werner Paravicini, Pariser historische Studien 94 (Munich, 2009), 81–8.

Church, William F. *Constitutional thought in sixteenth-century France. A study in the evolution of ideas* (Cambridge MA, 1941).

Ciappelli, Giovanni. 'Family memory. Functions, evolutions, recurrences'. In *Art, memory and family in Renaissance Florence*, ed. Giovanni Ciappelli and Patricia Lee Rubin (Cambridge, 2000), 26–38.

Cilleßen, Wolfgang. 'Massaker in der niederländischen Erinnergungskultur. Die Bildwerdung der Schwarzen Legende'. In *Bilder des Schreckens. Die mediale Inszenierung von Massakern seit dem 16. Jahrhundert*, ed. Christine Vogel (Frankfurt am Main, 2006), 93–135.

Clarke, Aidan. 'The 1641 massacres'. In *Ireland 1641. Contexts and reactions*, ed. Jane Ohlmeyer and Micheál O'Siochrú (Manchester, 2013), 37–51.

Connerton, Paul. *How societies remember* (Cambridge, 1989).

Connerton, Paul. 'Seven types of forgetting'. *Memory Studies* 1 (2008): 59–71.

Coupe, Laurence. *Myth*, 2nd edn (London, 2009).

Covington, Sarah. 'Jan Luyken, the Martyrs mirror and the iconography of suffering'. *The Mennonite Quarterly Review* 85 (2011): 441–76.

Covington, Sarah. '"The odious demon from across the sea". Oliver Cromwell, memory and the dislocations of Ireland'. In *Memory before modernity. Practices of memory in early modern Europe*, ed. Erika Kuijpers et al. (Leiden and Boston, 2013), 149–64.

Cressy, David. *Bonfires and bells. National memory and the Protestant calendar in Elizabethan and Stuart England* (London, 1989).

Crick, Julia and Alexandra Walsham, eds. *The uses of script and print, 1300–1700* (Cambridge, 2004).

Crouzet, Denis. *Les Guerriers de Dieu. La Violence au temps des troubles de religion, vers 1525–vers 1610*, 2 vols (Seyssel, 1990).

Cruz, Laura and Willem Frijhoff. 'Introduction. Myth in history, history in myth'. In *Myth in history, history in myth. Proceedings of the third international conference of the Society for Netherlandic History(New York: June 5–6, 2006)*, ed. Laura Cruz and Willem Frijhoff (Leiden, 2009), 1–16.

Cubitt, Geoffrey. *History and memory* (Manchester, 2007).

Davidson, Nicholas. 'Unbelief and atheism in Italy, 1500–1700'. In *Atheism from the Reformation to the Enlightenment*, ed. Michael Hunter and David Wootton (Oxford and New York, 1992), 55–88.

Davis, Natalie Zemon. 'Fame and secrecy. Leon of Modena's *Life* as an early modern autobiography'. *History and Theory* 27, supplement 27 (1988): 103–18.

De Graaf, H.J. 'De Leidsche hutspot'. *Leids jaarboekje* 21 (1927–8): 65–75.

De Grazia, Margreta. 'The modern divide. From either side'. *Journal of Medieval and Early Modern Studies* 37 (2007): 453–68.

De Grazia, Margreta. 'Anachronism'. In *Cultural reformations. Medieval and Renaissance in literary history*, ed. Brian Cummings and James Simpson (Oxford, 2010), 13–32.

De Haan, Ido. *Na de ondergang. De herinnering aan de Jodenvervolging in Nederland, 1945–1995* (The Hague, 1997).

De Pluvrez, Jean Marc. *Tienen 1635. Geschiedenis van een Brabantse stad in de zeventiende eeuw* (Tienen, 1985).

Dekker, Rudolf. *Holland in beroering. Oproeren in de 17de en 18de eeuw* (Baarn, 1982).

Den Heijer, Henk. *Holland onder water. De logistiek achter het ontzet van Leiden* (Leiden, 2010).

Dequeker, Luc. *Het Sacrament van Mirakel. Jodenhaat in de Middeleeuwen* (Leuven, 2000).

Deseure, Brecht. *Onhoudbaar verleden. Geschiedenis als politiek instrument tijdens de Franse periode in België* (Louvain, 2014).

Deseure, Brecht and Judith Pollmann. 'The experience of rupture and the history of memory'. In *Memory before modernity. Practices of memory in early modern Europe*, ed. Erika Kuijpers et al. (Leiden and Boston, 2013), 315–29.

Diefendorf, Barbara. 'Memories of the massacre. Saint Bartholomew's Day and Protestant identity in France'. In *Voices for tolerance in an age of persecution*, ed. Vincent P. Carey, Ronald Bogdan, and Elizabeth A. Walsh (Seattle and London, 2004), 45–62.

Diefendorf, Barbara. 'Blood wedding. The Saint Bartholomew's Day massacre in history and memory'. Lecture, Boston (2006). Accessed 3 May 2016. http://www.youtube.com/watch?v=5UIfXUoEKgo.

Donagan, Barbara. 'Atrocity, war crime, and treason in the English Civil War'. *The American Historical Review* 99 (1994): 1137–66.

Douglas, Mary. *Leviticus as literature* (Oxford, 1999).

Draaisma, Douwe. *De heimweefabriek. Geheugen, tijd en ouderdom* (Groningen, 2008).

Draaisma, Douwe. *Vergeetboek* (Groningen, 2010).

Duchhardt, Heinz. 'Münster und der Westfälische Friede. Kollektives gedächtnis und Erinnerungskultur im Wandel der Zeiten'. Supplement of *Historische Zeitschrift*, new series 26 (1998): 853–63.

Duerloo, Luc. 'Pietas albertina. Dynastieke vroomheid en herbouw van het vorstelijk gezag'. *Bijdragen en mededelingen betreffende de geschiedenis der Nederlanden-Low Countries Historical Review* 112 (1997): 1–18.

Duerloo, Luc and Marc Wingens. *Scherpenheuvel. Het Jeruzalem van de Lage Landen* (Leuven, 2002).

Duits, H. *Van Bartholomeusnacht tot Bataafse Opstand. Studies over de relatie tussen politiek en toneel in het midden van de zeventiend eeuw* (Amsterdam, 1990).

Duke, Alastair. 'The search for religious identity in a confessional age. The conversions of Jean Haren'. In *Dissident identities in the early modern Low Countries*, ed. Judith Pollmann and Andrew Spicer (Farnham, 2009), 223–50.

Dunthorne, Hugh. *Britain and the Dutch Revolt* (Cambridge, 2013).

Edelstein, Dan. *The Enlightenment. A genealogy* (Chicago, 2010).

Eekhout, Marianne. 'De kogel in de kerk. Herinneringen aan het beleg van Haarlem, 1573–1630'. *Holland. Historisch Tijdschrift* 43 (2011): 108–19.

Eekhout, Marianne. 'Herinnering in beeld. Relieken van Leids ontzet', *Leids Jaarboekje* 103 (2011): 33–47.

Eekhout, Marianne. 'Furies in beeld. Herinneringen aan gewelddadige innames van steden tijdens de Nederlandse Opstand op zeventiende-eeuwse schilderijen', *De Zeventiende Eeuw* 30 (2014); 243–66.

Eekhout, Marianne. 'Material memories of the Dutch Revolt. The urban memory landscape in the Low Countries, 1566–1700', doctoral thesis, Leiden University (2014).

Eibach, Joachim and Marcus Sandl, eds. *Protestantische Identität und Erinnerung. Von der Reformation bis zur Bürgerrechtsbewegung in der DDR*, Formen der Erinnerung 16 (Göttingen, 2003).

El Kenz, David. 'Le Massacre de la Saint-Barthélemy est-il un lieu de mémoire victimaire (fin XVIe siècle–début 2009)?' In *Commémorer les victimes en Europe, XVIe–XXIe siècles*, ed. David El Kenz and François-Xavier Nérard (Seyssel, 2011), 217–36.

Elliott, J.H. 'Revolution and continuity in early modern Europe'. *Past & Present* 42 (1969): 35–56.

Elliott, J.H. 'The mental world of Hernan Cortes'. In *Spain and its world, 1500–1700. Selected essays*, ed. J.H. Elliott (New Haven and London, 1989), 27–41.

Erll, Astrid. *Kollektives Gedächtnis und Erinnerungskulturen. Eine Einführung* (Stuttgart, 2005).

Erll, Astrid. *Memory in culture*, trans. Sara B. Young (Basingstoke, 2011).

Erll, Astrid and Ansgar Nünning, eds. *Cultural memory studies. An international and interdisciplinary handbook* (Berlin, 2008).

Erll, Astrid and Ann Rigney, eds. *Mediation, remediation and the dynamics of cultural memory* (Berlin and New York, 2009).

Fenlon, Iain. *The ceremonial city. History, memory and myth in Renaissance Venice* (New Haven, 2007).

Fentress, James and Chris Wickham. *Social memory* (Oxford and Cambridge MA, 1992).

Ferguson, Arthur B. *Clio unbound. Perception of the social and cultural past in Renaissance England* (Durham NC, 1979).

Ferrier, Jean Paul. 'Histoire de la fête de l'escalade'. In *L'Escalade de Genève, 1602. Histoire et tradition*, ed. Paul F. Geisendorf et al. (Geneva, 1952), 489–530.

Filhol, René. 'La Rédaction des coutumes en France aux XVe et XVIe siècles'. In *La Rédaction des coutumes dans le passé et dans le present. Colloque organisé les 16 et 17 mai 1960 par le Centre d'histoire et d'ethnologie juridiques*, ed. John Gilissen (Brussels, 1962), 63–85.

Finley, M.I. 'Myth, memory and history'. *History and Theory* 4 (1965): 281–302.

Fishman, Jane S. *Boerenverdriet. Violence between peasants and soldiers in early modern Netherlandish art* (Ann Arbor MI, 1982).

Florescu, Radu. *In search of the Pied Piper* (London, 2005).

Forster, Robert and Jack P. Greene, eds. *Preconditions of revolution in early modern Europe* (Baltimore and London, 1970).

Fox, Adam. 'Remembering the past in early modern England. Oral and written tradition'. *Transactions of the Royal Historical Society* 6th series 9 (1999): 233–56.

Fox, Adam. *Oral and literate culture in England, 1500–1700* (Oxford, 2000).

Fox, Adam and Daniel Woolf, eds. *The spoken word. Oral culture in Britain, 1500–1850* (Manchester, 2002).

Fox, Robin. *The tribal imagination. Civilization and the savage mind* (Cambridge MA, 2011).

Fredriksen, Paula. 'Paul and Augustine. Conversion narratives, orthodox traditions and the retrospective self'. *Journal of Theological Studies* new series 37 (1986): 3–34.

Freedman, Paul H. and Monique Bourin, eds. *Forms of servitude in Northern and Central Europe*, Medieval texts and cultures of Northern Europe 9 (Louvain, 2005).

Freist, Dagmar. 'Lost in time and space? *Glocal* memoryscapes in the early modern world'. In *Memory before modernity. Practices of memory in early modern Europe*, ed. Erika Kuijpers et al. (Leiden and Boston, 2013), 203–22.

Frevert, Ute et al., eds. *Emotional lexicons. Continuity and change in the vocabulary of feeling, 1700–2000* (Oxford, 2014).

Friedrichs, Christopher E. 'Politics or pogrom? The Fettmilch uprising in German and Jewish history'. *Central European History* 19 (1986): 188–228.

Frijhoff, Willem. 'Damiette appropriée. La mémoire de croisade, instrument de concorde civique (Haarlem, XVIe–XVIIIe siècle)'. *Revue du Nord* 88 (2006): 7–42.

Frijhoff, Willem. 'Johan (van) Waalen'. In *Dordts biografisch woordenboek*, ed. Willem Frijhoff et al. Accessed 12 August 2013. http://www.regionaalarchiefdordrecht.nl/biografisch-woordenboek.

Fritzsche, Peter. 'Specters of history. On nostalgia, exile and modernity'. *American Historical Review* 105/5 (2001): 1587–618.

Fritzsche, Peter. *Stranded in the present. Modern time and the melancholy of history* (Cambridge MA, 2004).

Fruin, Robert. *Het beleg en ontzet der stad Leiden* (The Hague, 1874).

Fruin, Robert. 'Magdalena Moons en haar verhouding tot Valdes'. *Jaarboek van de Maatschappij der Nederlandse Letterkunde* (1879): 161–76.

Fuchs, Ralf-Peter. *Geschichtsbewusstsein und Geschichtsschreibung zwischen Reformation und Aufklärung. Städtechroniken, Kirchenbücher und historische Befragungen in Hessen, 1500 bis 1800* (Marburg, 2000).

Fuchs, Ralf-Peter. 'Erinnerungsschichten. Zur Bedeutung der Vergangenheit für den "gemeinen Mann" der Frühen Neuzeit'. In *Wahrheit, Wissen, Erinnerung. Zeugenverhörprotokolle als Quellen für soziale Wissensbestände in der frühen Neuzeit*, ed. Ralf-Peter Fuchs and W. Schulze (Münster, 2002), 89–154.

Füssel, Marian. 'Emotions in the making. The transformation of battlefield experiences during the Seven Years' War (1756–1763)'. In *Battlefield emotions 1500–1800. Practices, experience, imagination*, ed. Erika Kuijpers and Cornelis van der Haven (London, 2016), 149–72.

Fussell, Paul. *The Great War and modern memory* (New York, 1975).

Gagné, John. 'Counting the dead. Traditions of enumeration and the Italian wars'. *Renaissance Quarterly* 67 (2014): 791–840.

Gantet, Claire. 'Mémoires du conflit, mémoires conflictuelles au lendemain de la guerre de Trente Ans'. In *Vergeben und vergessen? Vergangenheisdiskurse nach Besatzung, Bürgerkrieg und Revolution/Pardonner ou oublier? Les Discours sur le passé après l'occupation, la guerre civile et la revolution*, ed. Reiner Marcowicz and Werner Paravicini, Pariser historische Studien 94 (Munich, 2009), 57–72.

Gaskill, Malcolm. *Between two worlds. How the English became Americans* (Oxford, 2014).

Geary, Patrick. *Phantoms of remembrance. Memory and oblivion at the end of the first millennium* (Princeton, 1994).

Gellner, Ernest. *Nations and nationalism* (Ithaca NY, 1983).

Gilbert, Felix. *Machiavelli and Guicciardini. Politics and history in sixteenth-century Florence* (Princeton, 1973).

Gilissen, J. *Historische inleiding tot het recht*, vol. 1, *Ontstaan en evolutie van de belangrijkste rechtsstelsels*, ed. F. Gorlé, 3rd rev. edn (Antwerp, 1991).

Gillis, John E. 'Memory and identity. The history of a relationship'. In *Commemorations. The politics of national identity*, ed. John R. Gillis (Princeton, 1994), 3–24.

Gombrich, E.H. 'Eastern inventions and Western response'. In *Science in culture*, ed. Peter L. Galison, Stephen R. Graubard, and Everett Mendelsohn (New Brunswick and London, 2001), 193–206.

Goody, Jack and Ian Watt. 'The consequences of literacy'. *Comparative Studies in Society and History* 5 (1963): 304–45.

Gordon, Bruce, ed. *Protestant history and identity in sixteenth-century Europe*, 2 vols (Aldershot, 1996).

Gordon, Bruce and Peter Marshall. 'Introduction'. In *The place of the dead. Death and remembrance in late medieval and early modern Europe*, ed. Bruce Gordon and Peter Marshall (Cambridge, 2000), 1–16.

Goulemot, Jean-Marie. 'Temps et autobiographie dans les *Confessions*. Une tentative de reinscription culturelle'. In *Lectures de Jean-Jacques Rousseau. Les Confessions I–IV*, ed. Jacques Berchtold, Elisabeth Lavezzi, and Christophe Martin (Rennes, 2012), 27–47.

Grafton, Anthony. *New worlds, ancient texts. The power of tradition and the shock of discovery* (Cambridge MA, 1992).

Graubard, Stephen R. ed. 'Multiple modernities'. Theme issue of *Daedalus* 129/1 (2000).

Greenblatt, Rachel L. *To tell their children. Jewish communal memory in early modern Prague* (Stanford, 2015).

Greene, Thomas M. *The light in Troy. Imitation and discovery in Renaissance poetry* (New Haven CT, 1982).

Greengrass, Mark. 'Amnestie et "oubliance". Un discours politique autour des édits de pacification pendant les guerres de religion'. In *Paix des armes, paix des âmes. Actes du colloque international tenu au Musée national du château de Pau et à l'Université de Pau et des Pays de l'Adour 1998*, ed. Paul Mironneau and Isabelle Péblay-Clottes (Paris, 2000), 113–23.

Greengrass, Mark, Michael Leslie, and Timothy Raylor, eds. *Samuel Hartlib and universal reformation. Studies in intellectual communication* (Oxford, 2002).

Gregory, Brad S. *Salvation at stake. Christian martyrdom in early modern Europe* (Cambridge MA, 1999).

Gregory, Brad S. 'Introduction'. In *The forgotten writings of the Mennonite martyrs*, ed. Brad S. Gregory, Documenta Anabaptistica Neerlandica VIII (Leiden and Boston, 2002), xiii–xlii.

Griffin, Emma. *Liberty's dawn. A people's history of the Industrial Revolution* (New Haven and London, 2013).

Grijp, Louis. 'Van geuzenlied tot Gedenck-clanck. Eerste deel: het geuzenliedboek in de Gouden Eeuw'. *De Zeventiende Eeuw* 10 (1994): 118–32.

Grosby, Steven, Joep Leerssen, and Caspar Hirschi. 'Continuities and shifting paradigms. A debate on Caspar Hirschi's *The origins of nationalism*'. *Studies on National Movements* 2 (2014): 1–48.

Gundersheimer, Werner L. *The life and works of Louis le Roy* (Geneva, 1966).

Haemers, Jelle. 'Social memory and rebellion in fifteenth-century Ghent'. *Social History* 36 (2011): 443–63.

Haks, Donald. 'De Franse tirannie. De verbeelding van een massamoord'. In *Romeyn de Hooghe. De verbeelding van de late Gouden Eeuw*, ed. Henk van Nierop et al. (Zwolle and Amsterdam, 2008), 86–100.

Halbwachs, Maurice. *Les Cadres sociaux de la mémoire* (Paris, 1925).

Hale, John. *The civilization of Europe in the Renaissance* (London, 1993).

Hall, Stuart. 'Introduction'. In *Formations of modernity*, ed. Stuart Hall and Bram Gieben (Cambridge, 1992), 1–16.

Hamilton, Tom. 'The procession of the League. Remembering the Wars of Religion in visual and literary satire'. *French History* 30/1 (2016): 1–30.

Harari, Yuval. *Renaissance military memoirs. War, history, and identity, 1450–1600* (Woodbridge, 2004).

Harari, Yuval. *The ultimate experience. Battlefield revelations and the making of modern war culture, 1450–2000* (Basingstoke, 2008).

Harrington, Joel F. *The faithful executioner. Life and death, honor and shame in the turbulent sixteenth century* (New York, 2013).

Hastings, Adrian. *The construction of nationhood. Ethnicity, religion, and nationalism* (Cambridge, 1996).

Hay, Denys. *Annalists and historians. Western historiography from the eighth to the eighteenth centuries* (London, 1977).

Hayner, Priscilla. 'Negotiating justice. The challenge of addressing past human rights violations'. In *Contemporary peacemaking. Conflict, peace processes and post-war reconstruction*, ed. John Darby and Roger MacGinty, 2nd edn (Basingstoke, 2008), 328–38.

Helmus, Liesbeth. 'Het altaarstuk met de Sint Elisabethsvloed uit de Grote Kerk van Dordrecht. De oorspronkelijke plaats en de opdrachtgevers'. *Oud-Holland* 105 (1991): 127–39.

Hirschi, Caspar. *Wettkampf der Nationen. Konstruktionen einer deutschen Ehrgemeinschaft an der Wende vom Mittelalter zur Neuzeit* (Göttingen, 2005).

Hirschi, Caspar. *The origins of nationalism. An alternative history from ancient Rome to early modern Germany* (Cambridge, 2012).

Hirt, Katrin. 'Der Sacco di Roma in einer zeitgenössischen italienischen Versflugschrift. Das Massaker und die Einheit der Nation'. In *Bilder des Schreckens. Die mediale Inszenierung von Massakern seit dem 16. Jahrhundert*, ed. Christine Vogel (Frankfurt am Main, 2006), 38–50.

Hiscock, Andrew. *Reading memory in early modern literature* (Cambridge, 2011).

Hobsbawm, Eric. 'The social function of the past. Some questions'. *Past & Present* 55 (1972): 3–17.

Hobsbawm, E.J. *Nations and nationalism since 1780. Programme, myth, reality* (1990; 2nd edn Cambridge, 1992).

Hobsbawm, Eric and Terence Ranger, eds. *The invention of tradition* (Cambridge, 1983).

Hodgkin, Katharine. 'Women, memory and family history in seventeenth-century England'. In *Memory before modernity. Practices of memory in early modern Europe*, ed. Erika Kuijpers et al. (Leiden and Boston, 2013), 297–313.

Holt, Mack P. *The French Wars of Religion, 1562–1629* (Cambridge, 1995).

Hopkin, David. *Soldier and peasant in French popular culture, 1766–1870* (Suffolk, 2003).

Hopkin, David. 'Legends of the allied invasions and occupations of eastern France, 1792-1815'. In *The bee and the eagle. Napoleonic France and the end of the Holy Roman Empire, 1806*, ed. Alan Forrest and Peter Wilson (Basingstoke, 2009), 214–33.

Hopkin, David. 'The ecotype, or a modest proposal to reconnect cultural and social history'. In *Exploring cultural history. Essays in honour of Peter Burke*, ed. Joan-Paul Rubiés, Melissa Calaresu, and Filippo de Vivo (Farnham, 2010), 31–54.

Hoppenbrouwers, Peter. 'The dynamics of national identity in the later Middle Ages'. In *Networks, regions and nations. Shaping identities in the Low Countries, 1300–1650*, ed. Robert Stein and Judith Pollmann (Leiden, 2010), 19–41.

Horne, John and Alan Kramer. *German atrocities in 1914. A history of denial* (New Haven and London, 2001).

Hornstein, Katie. 'Just violence. Jacques Callot's *Grandes misères et malheurs de la guerre*'. *Bulletin of the University of Michigan Museums of Art and Archaeology* 16 (2005): 29–48.

Houston, R.A. 'People, space, and law in late medieval and early modern Britain and Ireland', *Past & Present* 230 (2016): 47–89.

Hsia, R. Po-Chia. *Social discipline in the Reformation. Central Europe, 1550–1750* (London and New York, 1989).

Hucker, Bernd Ulrich. 'Die Auszug der Hämelschen Kinder aus quellenkritischer Sicht'. In *Geschichten und Geschichte. Erzählforschertagung in Hameln, Oktober 1984*, ed. Norbert Humburg (Hildesheim, 1985), 96–8.

Hunt, Lynn, Margaret C. Jacob, and Wijnand Mijnhardt. *The book that changed Europe. Picart and Bernard's 'Religious ceremonies of the world'* (Cambridge MA, 2010).

James, Henry. *The sense of the past* (London and Glasgow, 1917).

Jansson, K. 'Soldaten und Vergewaltigung im Schweden des 17. Jahrhunderts'. In *Zwischen Alltag und Katastrophe*, ed. Benigna von Krusenstjern, Hans Medick, and Patrice Veit (Göttingen, 1999), 195–225.

Joutard, Philippe. *La légende des Camisards. Une sensibilité au passé* (Paris, 1977).

Junot, Yves. *Les Bourgeois de Valenciennes. Anatomie d'une élite dans la ville (1500–1630)* (Villeneuve d'Ascq, 2009).

Junot, Yves. 'L'Impossible Survie. La Clandestinité protestante à Valenciennes au début du XVIIe siècle'. *Mémoires du Cercle Archéologique et Historique de Valenciennes* 11 (2010): 175–83.

Jütte, Robert. 'Die Frankfurter Fettmilch-Aufstand und die Judenverfolgung von 1614 in der kommunalen Erinneringskultur'. In *Memoria. Wege jüdischen Erinnerns. Festschrift für Michael Brocke zum 65. Geburtstag*, ed. Birgit E. Klein and Christiane E. Müller (Berlin, 2005), 163–76.

Jütte, Robert. 'Krankheit unter Gesundheit im Spiegel von Hermann Weinsbergs Aufzeichnungen'. In *Hermann Weinsberg, 1518–1597, Kölner Burger und Ratsherr. Studien zu Leben und Werk*, ed. Manfred Groten (Cologne, 2005), 231–51.

Kagan, Richard. *Lawsuits and litigants in Castile, 1500–1700* (Chapel Hill NC, 1981).

Kagan, Richard. *Clio and the crown. The politics of history in medieval and early modern Spain* (Baltimore, 2009).

Kaiser, Peter. 'Befreiungstradition'. In *Historisches Lexikon der Schweiz* (Bern, 2009). Accessed 11 June 2015. http://www.hls-dhs-dss.ch/textes/d/D17474.php.

Kansteiner, Wulf. 'Genealogy of a category mistake. A critical intellectual history of the cultural trauma metaphor'. *Rethinking History* 8 (2004): 193–221.

Kemp, Anthony. *The estrangement of the past. A study in the origins of modern historical consciousness* (New York, 1991).

Kemp, Simon. 'Association as a cause of dating bias'. *Memory* 4 (1996): 131–43.

Ketelaar, Eric. 'The genealogical gaze. Family identities and family archives in the fourteenth to seventeenth centuries'. *Libraries & the Cultural Record* 44 (2008): 9–28.

Kidd, Colin. *British identities before nationalism. Ethnicity and nationhood in the Atlantic world* (Cambridge, 1999).

Kilburn-Toppin, Jasmine. 'Material memories of the guildsmen. Crafting identities in early modern London'. In *Memory before modernity. Practices of memory in early modern Europe*, ed. Erika Kuijpers et al. (Leiden and Boston, 2013), 165–81.

King, John. 'Fiction and fact in Foxe's Book of Martyrs'. In *John Foxe and the English Reformation*, ed. John Loades (Aldershot, 1997), 12–35.

Kingdon, Robert. *Myths about the St. Bartholomew's Day massacres 1572–1576* (Cambridge MA, 1988).

Kleber, Rolf J. 'Weg van het Trauma'. Inaugural lecture and summaries of the accompanying symposium 'Trauma. Dilemma's in kennis en toepassing'. Radboud Universiteit Nijmegen (9 February 2007). Accessed 3 May 2016. https://www.yumpu.com/nl/document/view/20414850/weg-van-het-trauma-oratie-van-profdr-rolf-j-kleber.

Kleber, Rolf J. and D. Brom. 'Incidentie van posttraumatische stress-stoornissen na front-ervaringen, geweldsmisdrijven, ongevallen en rampen'. *Tijdschrift voor Psychiatrie* 31 (1989): 675–91.

Klein, Kerwin Lee. 'On the emergence of "memory" in historical discourse'. *Representations* 69 (2000): 127–50.

Kloek, Els. 'Magdalena Moons'. In *Digitaal vrouwenlexicon van Nederland*. http://www.inghist.nl/Onderzoek/Projecten/DVN/lemmata/data/moons. Accessed 28 February 2008.

Kloek, Els. 'Anneke Esaiasdr'. In *Digitaal Vrouwenlexicon van Nederland*. http://www.historici.nl/Onderzoek/Projecten/DVN/lemmata/data/Esaiasdr. Accessed 3 May 2016.

Knecht, Robert J. 'Military autobiographies in sixteenth-century France'. In *War, literature, and the arts in sixteenth-century Europe*, ed. J.R. Mulryne and Margaret Shewring (London, 1989), 3–21.

Koldeweij, A.M. *Der gude Sente Servas* (Assen and Maastricht, 1985).

Kolfin, Elmer. 'Past imperfect. Political ideals in the unfinished Batavian series for the town hall of Amsterdam'. In *Opstand als opdracht. Flinck, Ovens, Lievens, Jordaens, De Groot, Bol, Rembrandt/The Batavian commissions*, ed. Renske Cohen Tervaert (Amsterdam, 2011), 10–19.

Koman, Ruben. *Bèèh...! Groot Dordts volksverhalenboek. Een speurtocht naar volksverhalen, bijnamen, volksgeloof, mondelinge overlevering en vertelcultuur in Dordrecht* (Bedum, 2005).

Koselleck, Reinhart. *Vergangene Zukunft. Zur Semantik geschichtlicher Zeiten* (1979; Frankfurt am Main, 1989).

Kraye, Jill, ed. *The Cambridge companion to Renaissance humanism* (Cambridge, 1996).

Kroen, Sheryl. *Politics and theater. The crisis of legitimacy in Restoration France, 1815–1830* (Berkeley CA, 2000).

Krusenstjern, Benigna and Hans Medick, eds. *Zwischen Alltag und Katastrophe. Der Dreissigjährige Krieg aus der Nähe* (Göttingen, 1999).

Kuijpers, Erika. 'Between storytelling and patriotic scripture. The memory brokers of the Dutch Revolt'. In *Memory before modernity. Practices of memory in early modern Europe*, ed. Erika Kuijpers et al. (Leiden and Boston, 2013), 183–202.

Kuijpers, Erika. 'The creation and development of social memories of traumatic events. The Oudewater massacre of 1575'. In *Hurting memories and beneficial forgetting. Posttraumatic stress disorders, biographical developments, and social conflicts*, ed. Michael Linden and Krzysztof Rutkowski (London and Waltham MA, 2013), 191–201.

Kuijpers, Erika. '"O, Lord, save us from shame". Narratives of emotions in convent chronicles by female authors during the Dutch Revolt, 1566–1635'. In *Destroying order, structuring disorder. Gender and emotions in medieval and early modern Europe*, ed. Susan Broomhall (Farnham, 2015), 127–46.

Kuijpers, Erika. 'Fear, indignation, grief and relief. Emotional narratives in war chronicles from the Netherlands (1568–1648)'. In *Disaster, death and the emotions in the shadow of the apocalypse, 1400–1700*, ed. Jennifer Spinks and Charles Zika (London, 2016), 93–111.

Kuijpers, Erika. *Trauma, memories and emotions in early modern Europe* (forthcoming).

Kuijpers, Erika et al., eds. *Memory before modernity. Practices of memory in early modern Europe* (Leiden and Boston, 2013).

Kumar, Krishan. *The making of English national identity* (Cambridge MA, 2003).

LaCapra, Dominick. *Representing the Holocaust. History, theory, trauma* (Ithaca NY, 1994).

Landolt, Niklaus. *Untertanenrevolten und Widerstand auf der Basler Landschaft im 16. und 17. Jahrhundert* (Basel, 1996).

Lange, Albert, ed. *Dall' Europa alle valle valdesi. Atti del XXIX convegno storico internazionale. 'Il Glorioso rimpatrio (1689–1989). Contesto—significato—imagine' Torre Pellice (To), 3–7 Settembre 1989* (Turin, 1990).

Langford, Paul. *A polite and commercial people. England 1727–1783* (Oxford and New York, 1989).

Le Goff, Jacques. *Histoire et mémoire* (1st edn, 1977; Paris, 1988).

Lederer, David. 'The myth of the all-destructive war. Afterthoughts on German suffering, 1618–1648', *German History* 29 (2011): 380–403.

Legon, Edward James. 'Remembering revolution. Seditious memories in England and Wales, 1660–1685', doctoral dissertation, University College London (2015). http://discovery.ucl.ac.uk/1470038/1/Thesis%20%5BCorrected%5D.pdf. Accessed 27 June 2016.

Lerner, Marc H. *A laboratory of liberty. The transformation of political culture in republican Switzerland, 1750–1848* (Leiden, 2011).

Lerner, Marc H. 'Cultural memories of a Swiss revolt. The prism of the William Tell legend'. In *Rhythms of revolt. European traditions and memories of social conflict in oral culture*, ed. Éva Guillorel, David Hopkin, and Will Pooley (Abingdon, forthcoming).

Levitin, Dmitri. 'From sacred history to the history of religion. Paganism, Judaism, and Christianity in European historiography from Reformation to Enlightenment'. *The Historical Journal* 55 (2012): 1117–60.

Levy, David and Nathan Sznaider. 'Memory unbound. The Holocaust and the formation of cosmopolitan memory'. *European Journal of Social Theory* 5 (2002): 87–106.

Loades, David, ed. *John Foxe and the English Reformation* (Aldershot, 1997).

Lok, M.M. '"Un oubli total du passé". The political and social construction of silence in Restoration Europe (1813–1830)'. *History and Memory* 26/2 (2014): 40–75.

Louthan, Howard. *Converting Bohemia. Force and persuasion in the Catholic Reformation* (Cambridge, 2009).

Lowenthal, David. *The past is a foreign country* (Cambridge, 1985).

Lundin, Matthew. *Paper memory, A sixteenth-century townsman writes his world* (Cambridge MA, 2012).

Luria, Keith. 'The politics of Protestant conversion to Protestantism in seventeenth-century France'. In *Conversion to modernities. The globalization of Christianity*, ed. Peter van der Veer (New York and London, 1996), 23–66.

Lynn, J.A. 'How war fed war. The tax of violence and contributions during the *Grand Siècle*'. *Journal of Modern History* 65 (1993): 286–310.

Lynn, John A. *Giant of the Grand Siècle. The French army, 1610–1715* (Cambridge and New York, 1997).

Macdonald, Scot. *Rolling the iron dice. Historical analogies, regional contingencies, and Anglo-American decisions to use military force* (Westport CT, 2000).

McNally, R.J. and E. Geraerts. 'A new solution to the recovered memory debate'. *Perspectives on Psychological Science* 4/2 (2009): 126–34.

Mali, Joseph. *Mythistory. The making of a modern historiography* (Chicago and London, 2003).

Maltby, William S. *The Black Legend in England. The development of anti-Spanish sentiment, 1558–1660* (Durham NC, 1971).

Margolf, Dianne. 'Adjudicating memory. Law and religious difference in early seventeenth-century France'. *The Sixteenth Century Journal* 27 (1996): 399–418.

Marnef, Guido. 'Resistance and the celebration of privileges in sixteenth-century Brabant'. In *Public opinion and changing identities in the early modern Netherlands. Essays in honour of Alastair Duke*, ed. Judith Pollmann and Andrew Spicer (Leiden, 2007), 125–39.

Martines, Lauro. *Furies. War in Europe, 1450–1700* (New York, 2013).

Martínez, María Elena. *Genealogical fictions. Limpieza de sangre, religion and gender in colonial Mexico* (Stanford, 2008).

Matsuda, Matt K. *The memory of the modern* (New York, 1996).

Medick, Hans. 'Historical event and contemporary experience. The capture and destruction of Magdeburg in 1631', trans. Pamela Selwyn. *History Workshop Journal* 52 (2001): 23–48.

Meijer Drees, Marijke. 'Burgemeester van der Werf als vaderlandse toneelheld. Een politieke autoriteit in belegeringsdrama's'. *De Zeventiende Eeuw* 8 (1992): 167–76.

Miller, Daniel. *The comfort of things* (Cambridge, 2008).

Miller, Daniel. *Stuff* (Cambridge, 2010).

Moerman, Ingrid L. and R.C.J. van Maanen, eds. *Leiden, eeuwig feest* (Leiden, 1986).

Mörke, Olaf. 'Städtemythen als Element politischer Sinnstiftung in der Schweizer Eidgenossenschaft und in der Niederländischen Republik'. In *Städtische mythen*, ed. Bernhard Kirchgässner and Hans-Peter Becht, Stadt in der Geschichte 28 (Ostfildern, 2003), 91–118.

Mortimer, Geoff. *Eyewitness accounts of the Thirty Years War, 1618–1648* (Basingstoke, 2002).

Mout, M.E.H.N. 'Het Bataafse oor'. De lotgevallen van Erasmus' adagium 'Auris Batava' in de Nederlandse geschiedschrijving, *Mededelingen der Koninklijke Nederlandsche Akademie van Wetenschappen Afdeling Letterkunde*, new series 56 (1994).

Muir, Edward. *Civic ritual in Renaissance Venice* (Princeton, 1981).

Müller, Jan Dirk. *Gedechtnus. Literatur und Hofgesellschaft um Maximilian I* (Munich, 1982).

Müller, Johannes. *Exile memories and the Dutch Revolt. The narrated diaspora, 1550–1750* (Leiden, 2016).

Mumford, Jeremy Ravi. 'Litigation as ethnography in sixteenth-century Peru. Polo de Ondegardo and the Mitimaes'. *Hispanic American Historical Review* 88 (2008): 5–40.

Nagel, Alexander and Christopher S. Wood. *Anachronic Renaissance* (New York, 2010).

Nauert, Charles. *Humanism and the culture of Renaissance Europe* (Cambridge, 1995).

Nederveen, C. 'Pieter, opgevist, met een kat legghende bij sigh'. *Oud-Dordrecht* 25 (2007): 26–8.

Neisser, U. and Lisa K. Libby. 'Remembering life experiences'. In *The Oxford handbook of memory*, ed. Endel Tulving and Fergus I.M. Craik (Oxford, 2005), 315–32.

Neufeld, Matthew. *The Civil Wars after 1660. Public remembering in late Stuart England* (Woodbridge, 2013).

Newton, Hannah. *The sick child in early modern England, 1580–1720* (Oxford, 2012).

Nicholas, Paul. *To follow in their footsteps. The Crusades and family memory in the high Middle Ages* (Ithaca NY, 1999).

Nisbet, Robert. *History of the idea of progress* (London, 1980).

Nora, Pierre. 'Between memory and history. *Les Lieux de mémoire*'. Special issue of *Representations* 26/1 (1989): 7–24.

Nora, Pierre et al. *Les Lieux de mémoire*, 3 vols (Paris, 1984–92).

Nutton, Vivian. 'Humoralism'. In *Companion encyclopedia of the history of medicine*, ed. W.F. Bynum and Roy Porter, 2 vols (1993; repr. paperback edn, London, 1997).

O'Brien, Karen. *Narratives of Enlightenment. Cosmopolitan history from Voltaire to Gibbon* (Cambridge, 1997).

Oduro, Franklin. 'The challenge of reconciliation in postconflict African states'. *International Journal of Transitional Justice* 6 (2012): 558–69.

Ohlmeyer, Jane and Micheál Ó Siochrú. 'Introduction. 1641, fresh context and perspectives'. In *Ireland 1641. Contexts and reactions*, ed. Jane Ohlmeyer and Micheál Ó Siochrú (Manchester, 2013), 1–16.

Olick, Jeffrey K. *The politics of regret. On collective memory and historical responsibility* (New York, 2007).

Olick, Jeffrey K. and Joyce Robbins. 'Social memory studies. From "collective memory" to the historical sociology of mnemonic practices'. *Annual Review of Sociology* 24 (1998): 105–40.

Ozouf, Mona. 'Le Calendrier'. In *Dictionnaire critique de la Révolution française*, ed. François Furet and Mona Ozouf (Paris, 1988), 482–91.

Packull, Werner O. 'Anna Jansz of Rotterdam. A historical investigation of an early Anabaptist heroine'. *Archiv für Reformationsgeschichte* 78 (1987): 147–73.

Pagden, Anthony. *The fall of natural man. The American Indian and the origins of comparative ethnology* (Cambridge, 1982).

Pagden, Anthony. 'Dispossessing the barbarian. The language of Spanish Thomism and the debate over the property rights of the American Indians'. In *The languages of political theory in early-modern Europe*, ed. Anthony Pagden (Cambridge, 1987), 79–98.

Parker, Charles H. 'To the attentive, nonpartisan reader. The appeal to history and national identity in the religious disputes of the seventeenth-century Netherlands'. *The Sixteenth Century Journal* 28 (1997): 57–78.

Parker, Geoffrey. 'Mutiny and discontent in the Spanish army of Flanders 1572–1607'. *Past & Present* 58 (1973): 38–52.

Parker, Geoffrey. *The Dutch Revolt* (Harmondsworth, 1977).

Parker, Geoffrey. 'The etiquette of atrocity. The laws of war in early modern Europe'. In Geoffrey Parker, *Empire, war and faith in early modern Europe* (London, 2003), 143–68.

Passerini, Luisa. 'Memory'. *History Workshop* 15/1 (1983): 195–6.

Paul, Nicholas L. *To follow in their footsteps. The Crusades and family memory in the high Middle Ages* (Ithaca NY and London, 2012).

Paul, Nicholas L. and Suzanne Yeager, eds. *Remembering the Crusades. Myth, image and identity* (Baltimore, 2012).

Peeters, Thérèse. 'Van Caput Mundi tot "Coda Mundi". Over de beleving van de plundering van Rome in 1527', BA dissertation, Leiden University (2012).

Pelinck, E. 'Overlevering, legende en relieken van het beleg en ontzet van Leiden'. *Leids Jaarboekje* 46 (1954): 100–10.

Petershagen, Wolf-Henning. *Schwörmontag. Ein Ulmer Phänomen* (Ulm, 1996).

Petershagen, Wolf-Henning. *Schwörpflicht und Volksvergnügen. Ein Beitrag zur Verfassungswirklichkeit und städtische Festkultur in Ulm* (Ulm, 1999).

Pettegree, Andrew. 'Haemstede and Foxe'. In *John Foxe and the English Reformation*, ed. John Loades (Aldershot, 1997), 278–94.

Pettegree, Andrew. *The invention of news. How the world came to know about itself* (New Haven and London, 2014).

Piaget, Jean. *La Formation du symbole chez l'enfant. Imitation, jeu et rêve. Image et représentation* (Neuchatel, 1945).

Piggott, Stuart. *Ancient Britons and the antiquarian imagination. Ideas from the Renaissance to the Regency* (London, 1989).

Pocock, J.G.A. 'The origins of the study of the past. A comparative approach', *Comparative Studies in Society and History* 4/2 (1962): 209–46.

Pocock, J.G.A. *The ancient constitution and the feudal law. A study of English historical thought in the seventeenth century* (1957; rev. edn Cambridge, 1987).

Pol, Arent and Bouke Jan van der Veen. *Het noodgeld van Leiden. Waarheid en verdichting* (The Hague, 2007).

Pollmann, Judith. 'Eine natürliche Feindschaft. Ursprung und Funktion der schwarzen Legende über Spanien in den Niederlanden, 1560–1581'. In *Feindbilder. Die Darstellung des Gegners in der politischen Publizistik des Mittelalters und der Neuzeit*, ed. F. Bosbach (Cologne, 1992), 73–94.

Pollmann, Judith. '"A different road to God". The Protestant experience of conversion in the sixteenth century'. In *Conversion to modernities. The globalization of Christianity*, ed. Peter van der Veer (Routledge, New York, and London, 1996), 47–64.

Pollmann, Judith. *Religious choice in the Dutch Republic. The Reformation of Arnoldus Buchelius, 1565–1641* (Manchester, 1999).

Pollmann, Judith. 'Herdenken, herinneren, vergeten. Het beleg en ontzet van Leiden in de Gouden Eeuw'. 3 Oktoberlezing (Leiden, 2008). Accessed 3 May 2016. https://openaccess.leidenuniv.nl/handle/1887/16331.

Pollmann, Judith. *Het oorlogsverleden van de Gouden Eeuw* (Leiden, 2008).

Pollmann, Judith. 'No man's land. Reinventing Netherlandish identities, 1585–1621'. In *Networks, regions and nations. Shaping identities in the Low Countries, 1300–1650*, ed. Robert Stein and Judith Pollmann, Studies in medieval and Reformation traditions (Leiden, 2010), 241–62.

Pollmann, Judith. *Catholic identity and the Revolt of the Netherlands, 1520–1635* (Oxford, 2011).

Pollmann, Judith. 'Een "blij-eindend" treurspel. Herinneringen aan het beleg van Leiden, 1574–2011'. In *Belaagd en belegerd*, ed. H. van Amersfoort et al. (Amsterdam, 2011), 118–45.

Pollmann, Judith. 'Vondel's religion', in *Joost van den Vondel (1587–1679). Dutch playwright in the Golden Age*, ed. Jan Bloemendal and Frans-Willem Korsten (Leiden and Boston, 2012), 85–100.

Pollmann, Judith. 'Met grootvaders bloed bezegeld. Het religieuze verleden in de zeventiende eeuw'. *De Zeventiende Eeuw* 29/2 (2013): 154–75.

Pollmann, Judith. 'Of living legends and authentic tales. How to get remembered in early modern Europe'. *Transactions of the Royal Historical Society* 6th series 23 (2013): 103–25.

Pollmann, Judith. 'Memory before and after nationalism. A revision', in *Conflicted pasts and national identities. Narratives of war and conflict*, ed. Michael Böss (Aarhus, 2014), 31–42.

Pollmann, Judith. 'Archiving the present and chronicling for the future in early modern Europe'. In *The social history of the archive. Record keeping in early modern Europe*, ed. Liesbeth Corens, Kate Peters, and Alexandra Walsham, *Past & Present* 230 (2016): Supplement 11, 231–52.

Pollmann, Judith and Erika Kuijpers, 'Introduction. On the early modernity of modern memory'. In *Memory before modernity. Practices of memory in early modern Europe*, ed. Erika Kuijpers et al. (Leiden and Boston, 2013), 1–23.

Pollmann, Judith and Erika Kuijpers. 'Why remember terror? Memories of violence in the Dutch Revolt'. In *Ireland 1641. Contexts and reactions*, ed. Jane Ohlmeyer and Micheál Ó Siochrú (Manchester, 2013), 176–96.

Pollmann, Judith and Monica Stensland. 'Alba's reputation in the early modern Low Countries'. In *Alba. General and servant to the crown*, ed. M.E. Ebben, M. Lacy-Bruijn, and R. van Hövell tot Westerflier (Rotterdam, 2013), 309–25.

Pollmer, Almut. 'Kirchenbilder. Der Kirchenraum in der holländischen Malerei um 1650', doctoral dissertation, Leiden University (2011).

Poole, Ross. 'Enacting oblivion'. *International Journal of Politics, Culture, and Society* 22 (2009): 149–57.

Porter, Roy, ed. *Rewriting the self. Histories from the Renaissance to the present* (London, 1997).

Rau, Susanne. *Geschichte und Konfession. Städtische Geschichtsschreibung und Erinnerungskultur im Zeitalter von Reformation und Konfessionalisierung in Bremen, Breslau, Hamburg und Köln* (Hamburg and Munich, 2002).

Redmond, Joan. 'Memories of violence and New English identities in early modern Ireland'. *Historical Research* 89 (2016): 708–29.

Rieff, David. *In praise of forgetting: Historical memory and its ironies* (New Haven, 2016).

Rietveld, Marry. 'Hoe schrijf je je levensverhaal'. http://www.coachy.nl/zelfcoaching/hoe-schrijf-je-je-levensverhaal/. Accessed 14 January 2016.

Roht Arriaza, Naomi. 'The Spanish Civil War, amnesty and the trials of judge Garzón'. *ASIL Insights* 16/24 (2 July 2012). https://www.asil.org/insights/volume/16/issue/24/spanish-civil-war-amnesty-and-trials-judge-garz%C3%B3n. Accessed 10 June 2015.

Rösener, Werner. *Adelige und bürgerliche Erinnerungskulturen des Spätmittelalters und der Frühen Neuzeit*, Formen der Erinnerung 8 (Göttingen, 2000).

Rothberg, Michael. *Multidirectional memory. Remembering the Holocaust in the age of decolonization* (Stanford, 2009).

Rousso, Henri. *The Vichy syndrome. History and memory in France since 1945* (Cambridge MA, 1991).

Rublack, U. 'Wench and maiden. Women, war and the pictorial function of the feminine in German cities in the early modern period'. *History Workshop* 44 (1997): 1–21.

Rublack, Ulinka. *Dressing up. Cultural identity in Renaissance Europe* (Oxford, 2010).

Rublack, Ulinka. 'Grapho-Relics. Lutheranism and the Materialization of the Word', *Past and Present*, supplement 5 (2010), 144–66.

Sampson, R.V. *Progress in the age of reason. The seventeenth century to the present day* (London, 1956).

Schama, Simon. *The embarrassment of riches. An interpretation of Dutch culture in the Golden Age* (London, 1987).

Schiffman, Zachary Sayre. *The birth of the past* (Baltimore, 2011).

Schmidt, Benjamin. *Innocence abroad. The Dutch imagination and the New World, 1570–1670* (Cambridge, 2001).

Schöffer, Ivo. 'The Batavian myth during the sixteenth and seventeenth centuries'. In *Britain and the Netherlands V. Some political mythologies. Papers delivered to the fifth Anglo-Dutch historical conference*, ed. J.S. Bromley and E.H. Kossmann (The Hague, 1975), 78–101.

Schutte, O. 'De familiekroniek van der Moelen'. In *Uit diverse bronnen gelicht. Opstellen aangeboden aan Hans Smit ter gelegenheid van zijn vijfenzestigste verjaardag*, ed. E. Dijkhof and M. van Gent (The Hague, 2007), 293–307.

Schütten, Stefanie. 'South Africa reconciled? To what extent can the South African society be regarded as reconciled, eighteen years after the first democratic elections?', ResMA dissertation, Universiteit Utrecht (2012).

Schwyzer, Philip. *Literature, nationalism and memory in early modern England and Wales* (Cambridge, 2004).

Scott, John. *A bibliography of works relating to Mary, Queen of Scots, c. 1544–1700* (Edinburgh, 1896).

Scribner, Robert W. 'Incombustible Luther. The image of the Reformer in early modern Germany', *Past & Present* 110 (1986): 38–68.

Seaver, Paul. *Wallington's world. A puritan artisan in seventeenth-century London* (London, 1985).

Segal, Robert A. *Myth. A very short introduction* (Oxford, 2004).

Shaw, Rosalind. 'Memory frictions. Localizing the Truth and Reconciliation Commission in Sierra Leone'. *The International Journal of Transitional Justice* I (2007): 183–207.

Shell, Alison. *Oral culture and Catholicism in early modern England* (Cambridge, 2007).

Sherlock, Peter. *Monuments and memory in early modern England* (Aldershot, 2008).

Shils, Edward. *Tradition* (Chicago, 1981).

Sicking, Louis. *Geuzen en glippers. Goud en fout tijdens het beleg van Leiden*. 3 Oktoberlezing (Leiden, 2003). https://openaccess.leidenuniv.nl/handle/1887/14308.

Skinner, Quentin. *The foundations of modern political thought*, 2 vols (Cambridge, 1978).

Skoda, Hannah. *Medieval violence. Physical brutality in Northern France, 1270–1330* (Oxford, 2013).

Slack, Paul. *From Reformation to improvement. Public welfare in early modern England* (Oxford, 1999).

Slack, Paul. *The invention of improvement. Information and material progress in seventeenth-century England* (Oxford, 2015).

Smith, Anthony D. *Nationalism and modernism* (New York, 1998).

Smith, Anthony D. *Nationalism* (2001; 2nd edn Cambridge, 2010).

Spaans, Joke. *Haarlem na de Reformatie. Stedelijke cultuur en kerkelijk leven (1577–1620)* (The Hague, 1989).

Spaans, Joke. *De levens der Maechden. Het verhaal van een religieuze vrouwengemeenschap in de eerste helft van de zeventiende eeuw* (Hilversum, 2012).

Spanuth, Heinrich. *Der Rattenfänger von Hameln. Vom Werden und Sinn einer alten Sage* (Hamelin, 1951).

Spicer, Andrew. '(Re)building the sacred landscape. Orleans, 1560–1610'. *French History* 21/3 (2007): 247–68.

Stapelbroek, Koen and Jari Marjanen, eds. *The rise of economic societies in the eighteenth century. Patriotic reform in Europe and North America* (Basingstoke, 2012).

Starobinski, Jean. *Jean-Jacques Rousseau. La Transparence et l'obstacle, suivi de Sept essais sur Rousseau* (Paris, 1971).

Stein, Robert. 'Brabant en de Karolingische dynastie. Over het ontstaan van een historio-grafische traditie'. *Bijdragen en Mededelingen betreffende de Geschiedenis der Nederlanden— Low Countries Historical Review* 110 (1995): 329–51.

Stein, Robert. 'An urban network in the medieval Low Countries. A cultural approach'. In *Networks, regions and nations. Shaping identities in the Low Countries, 1300–1650*, ed. Robert Stein and Judith Pollmann (Leiden and Boston, 2010), 43–71.

Stevens, Paul. 'Bunyan, the Great War, and the political ways of grace'. *Review of English Studies* 59 (2008): 701–21.

Stewart, Charles. *Dreaming and historical consciousness in island Greece* (Cambridge MA, 2012).

Stoyle, Mark. 'Memories of the maimed. The testimony of Charles I's former soldiers, 1660–1730'. *History* 88 (2003): 204–26.

Stoyle, Mark. 'Remembering the English Civil Wars'. In *The memory of catastrophe*, ed. Peter Gray and Kendrick Oliver (Manchester, 2004), 19–30.

Strauss, Gerald. *Law, resistance and the state. The opposition to Roman law in Reformation Germany* (Princeton, 1986).

Struve, Lynn A. *Voices from the Ming-Qing cataclysm. China in tigers' jaws* (New Haven, 1993).

Stryer, Steven E. 'The past/present topos in eighteenth-century English literature. A pattern of historical thought and its stylistic implications in historiography, poetry, and polemic', DPhil dissertation, Oxford University (2007).

Swart, K.W. 'The Black Legend during the Eighty Years War'. In *Britain and the Netherlands V. Some political mythologies. Papers delivered to the fifth Anglo-Dutch historical conference*, ed. J.S. Bromley and E.H. Kossmann (The Hague, 1975), 36–57.

Sweet, Rosemary. *The writing of urban histories in eighteenth-century England* (Oxford, 1997).

'T Hart, Marjolein. *The Dutch Wars of Independence. Warfare and commerce in the Netherlands, 1570–1680* (London and New York, 2014).

Tallon, Alain. *Conscience nationale et sentiment religieux en France au XVIe siècle* (Paris, 2002).

Tallon, Alain, ed. *Le Sentiment national dans l'Europe méridionale aux XVIe et XVIIe siècles (France, Espagne, Italie)* (Madrid, 2007).

Tamse, C.A. 'The political myth'. In *Britain and the Netherlands V. Some political mythologies. Papers delivered to the fifth Anglo-Dutch historical conference*, ed. J.S. Bromley and E.H. Kossmann (The Hague, 1975), 1–18.

Tangherlini, Timothy R. '"It happened not too far from here …". A survey of legend theory and characterization'. *Western Folklore* 49 (1990): 371–90.

Taylor, Charles. *Sources of the self. The making of the modern identity* (Cambridge MA, 1989).

Terdiman, Richard. *Present past. Modernity and the memory crisis* (Ithaca NY and London, 1993).

Teuscher, Simon. *Lords' rights and peasant stories. Writing and the formation of tradition in the later Middle Ages* (Philadelphia, 2012).

Theibault, J.C. 'Landfrauen, Soldaten und Vergewaltigungen während des Dreißigjährigen Krieges'. *Werkstatt Geschichte* 19 (1998): 25–39.

Thomas, Keith. *The perception of the past in early modern England*, The Creighton Trust Lecture 1983 (London, 1983).

Thompson, E.P. *Customs in common* (New York, 1991).

Till, Karen E. 'Memory studies'. *History Workshop Journal* 62 (2006): 325–41.

Tonkin, Elizabeth. *Narrating our pasts. The social construction of oral history*, Cambridge studies in oral and literate culture 22 (Cambridge, 1992).

Tricard, Jean. 'Les Livres de raison français au miroir des livres de famille italiens. Pour relancer une enquête'. *Revue Historique* 304 (2002): 993–1011.

Trim, D.J.B. '"Put all to the sword". The effects of Reformation on the ethics of war in sixteenth-century Germany and England'. In *Sister reformations II—Schwesterreformationen I. Reformation and ethics in Germany and in England—Reformation und Ethik in Deutschland und in England*, ed. Dorothea Wendebourg and Alec Ryrie (Tübingen, 2014), 271–98.

Ueffing, Werner. 'Die Hamelner Rattenfängersage und ihr historischer Hintergrund'. In *Geschichten und Geschichte. Erzählforschertagung in Hameln, Oktober 1984*, ed. Norbert Humburg (Hildesheim, 1985), 184–91.

Ulbrich, Claudia. ' "Hat man also bald ein solches Blutbad, Würgen und Wüten in der Stadt gehört und gesehen, dass mich solches jammert wider zu gedenken". Religion und Gewalt in Michael Heberer von Brettens "Aegyptica Servitus" (1610)'. In *Religion und Gewalt. Konflikte, rituale, deutungen (1500–1800)*, ed. Kaspar von Greyerz and Kim Siebenhüner (Göttingen, 2006), 85–108.

Van der Coelen, Peter. 'De Bataven in de beeldende kunst'. In *De Bataven. Verhalen van een verdwenen volk*, ed. L.J.F. Swinkels (Amsterdam and Nijmegen, 2004), 144–87.

Van der Lem, Anton. *De Opstand in de Nederlanden, 1568–1648. De Tachtigjarige oorlog in woord en beeld* (Nijmegen, 2014).

Van der Linden, David. *Experiencing exile. Huguenot refugees in the Dutch Republic, 1680–1700* (Farnham, 2015).

Van der Steen, Jasper. 'Goed en fout in de Nederlandse Opstand'. *Historisch Tijdschrift Holland* 43/2 (2011): 82–97.

Van der Steen, Jasper. *Memory wars in the Low Countries, 1566–1700* (Leiden, 2015).

Van Es, T. 'Dertiende penning nieuw leven ingeblazen in Kamerik'. *Heemtijdinghen. Orgaan van de Stichts-Hollandse Historische Vereniging* 30 (1994): 12–26.

Van Herwaarden, Jan. *Between Saint James and Erasmus. Studies in late-medieval religious life. Devotion and pilgrimage in the Netherlands*, trans. Wendie Shaffer and Donald Gardner, Studies in medieval and Reformation traditions 97 (Leiden, 2003).

Van Herwaarden, Jan et al. *Geschiedenis van Dordrecht tot 1572* (Dordrecht and Hilversum, 1996).

Van Lieburg, F.A. *Levens van vromen. Gereformeerd piëtisme in de achttiende eeuw* (Kampen, 1991).

Van Liere, Katherine, Simon Ditchfield, and Howard Louthan. *Sacred history. Uses of the Christian past in the Renaissance world* (Oxford, 2012).

Van Maanen, R.C.J. *Hutspot, haring en wittebrood. Tien eeuwen Leiden, Leienaars en hun feesten* (Leiden, 1981).

Van Nierop, Henk. 'The politics of oblivion. The Dutch civil war and the quest for stability, 1566–1609'. Unpublished paper, Leiden University (2007).

Velten, Hans Rudolf. *Das selbst geschriebene Leben. Eine Studie zur deutschen Autobiographie im 16. Jahrhundert* (Heidelberg, 1995).

Verberckmoes, Johan. 'The imaginative recreation of overseas cultures in Western European pageants in the sixteenth to seventeenth centuries'. In *Forging European identities, 1400–1700*, ed. Herman Roodenburg, Cultural exchange in early modern Europe IV (Cambridge, 2007), 361–80.

Villa-Vicencio, Charles. 'Learning to live together with bad memories'. In *Truth in politics. Rhetorical approaches to democratic deliberation and beyond*, ed. Philippe Joseph Salazar, Sanya Osha, and Wim van Binsbergen, special issue of *Quest. An African Journal of Philosophy* 16 (2002): 37–49.

Vogel, Christine. ' "Piemontesische Ostern". Mediale inszenierungen des Waldenser-Massakers von 1655'. In *Bilder des Schreckens. Die mediale Inszenierung von Massakern seit dem 16. Jahrhundert*, ed. Christine Vogel (Frankfurt am Main, 2006), 74–92.

Voges, Ramon. 'Das Auge der Geschichte. Die Bildberichte Franz Hogenbergs zu den Französischen Religionskriegen und dem Aufstand der Niederlande (ca. 1560-1610)', doctoral thesis (Paderborn, 2016).

Voges, Ramon. 'Macht, Massaker und Repräsentationen. Darstellungen asymetrischer Gewalt in der Bildpublizistik Franz Hogenbergs'. In *Gewalträume. Soziale Ordnungen im Ausnahmezustand*, ed. Jörg Baberowski and Gabriele Metzler (Frankfurt am Main and New York, 2012), 29–70.

Von Greyerz, Kaspar et al., eds. *Religion und Gewalt. Konflikte, rituale, deutungen (1500–1800)* (Göttingen, 2006).

Vroom, Wim. *Het wonderlid van Jan de Wit en andere vaderlandse relieken* (Amsterdam, 1997).

Wagenaar, Willem A. *Identifying Ivan. A case study in legal psychology* (Cambridge MA, 1988).

Wagenaar, Willem A. and Hans Crombag. *The popular policeman and other cases. Psychological perspectives on legal evidence* (Amsterdam, 2005).

Walsham, Alexandra. *Providence in early modern England* (Oxford, 1999).

Walsham, Alexandra, ed. *Relics and remains*. Past & Present supplement 5 (2010).

Walsham, Alexandra. *The Reformation of the landscape. Religion, identity, and memory in early modern Britain and Ireland* (Oxford, 2011).

Walsham, Alexandra. 'Domesticating the Reformation. Material culture, memory, and confessional identity in early modern England'. *Renaissance Quarterly* 69/2 (2016): 566–616.

Warburg, Aby. *Der Bildatlas Mnemosyne*, ed. Martin Warnke and Claudia Brink, Aby Warburg Gesammelte Schriften vol. II.1 (Berlin, 2003).

Warner, Marina. *Managing monsters. Six myths of our time*, The Reith Lectures (London, 1994).

Watson, David. 'Jean Crespin and the writing of history in the French Reformation'. In *Protestant history and identity in sixteenth-century Europe* II. *The later Reformation* (Aldershot, 1996), 39–58.

Watt, Ian. *The rise of the novel. Studies in Defoe, Richardson and Fielding* (Berkeley CA, 1957).

Waxler, Jerry. 'Ten reasons why anyone should write a memoir'. http://memorywritersnetwork.com/blog/ten-reasons-boomers-should-write-their-memoir/. Accessed 14 January 2016.

Weiss, Roberto. *The Renaissance discovery of classical antiquity* (London, 1969).

Wijsenbeek-Olthuis, Thera. *Honger*, 3 Oktoberlezing (Leiden, 2006).

Wilkinson, Alexander. *Mary Queen of Scots and French public opinion, 1542–1600* (Basingstoke, 2004).

Wille, J. 'Het houten boek. Democratische woelingen te Dordrecht, 1647–1651'. *Stemmen des tijds. Maandschrift voor Christendom en cultuur* 1/2 (1912): 1154–79, 1263–84.

Winter, Jay. *Remembering war. The Great War between memory and history in the twentieth century* (New Haven, 2006).

Withuis, Jolanda. *Erkenning. Van oorlogstrauma naar klaagcultuur* (Amsterdam, 2002).

Wittrock, Björn. 'Early modernities. Varieties and transitions'. In 'Early modernities' theme issue of *Daedalus* 127/3 (1998): 19–40.

Wolf, Eric R. *Europe and the people without history* (Berkeley, 1982).

Woltjer, Juliaan. 'Dutch privileges, real and imaginary'. In *Britain and the Netherlands V, Some political mythologies. Papers delivered to the fifth Anglo-Dutch historical conference*, ed. J.S. Bromley and E.H. Kossmann (The Hague, 1975), 19–35.

Wood, Andy. 'The place of custom in plebeian political culture. England, 1550–1800'. *Social History* 22 (1997): 46–60.

Wood, Andy. 'Custom and the social organisation of writing in early modern England'. *Transactions of the Royal Historical Society* 6th series 9 (1999): 257–69.

Wood, Andy. *The politics of social conflict. The Peak Country, 1520–1770* (Cambridge and New York, 1999).

Wood, Andy. *The memory of the people. Custom and popular senses of the past in early modern England* (Cambridge, 2013).

Woodford, Charlotte. *Nuns as historians in early modern Germany* (Oxford, 2002).

Woolf, Daniel. *The social circulation of the past. English historical culture, 1500–1730* (Oxford, 2003).

Woolf, Michael. 'Amnesty and *oubliance* at the end of the French Wars of Religion'. In *Clémence, oubliance et pardon en Europe, 1520–1650*, ed. Michel De Waele, special issue of *Cahiers d'Histoire* 16 (1996): 46–68.

Worden, Blair. *Roundhead reputations. The English Civil Wars and the passions of posterity* (London, 2001).

Yardeni, Miriam. *La Conscience nationale en France pendant les guerres de religion (1559–1598)* (Louvain, 1971).

Yates, Frances. *The art of memory* (Chicago, 1966).

Yerushalmi, Y.H. *Zakhor. Jewish history and Jewish memory* (Seattle, 1982).

Zijlmans, Jori. 'Pieter Adriaensz van der Werf. Held van Leiden'. In *Heiligen of helden. Opstellen voor Willem Frijhoff*, ed. Joris van Eijnatten, Fred van Lieburg, and Hans de Waardt (Amsterdam, 2007), 130–43.

Index